SWANS OF THE KREMLIN

PITT SERIES IN RUSSIAN AND
EAST EUROPEAN STUDIES
Jonathan Harris, Editor

Swans of the & Kremlin

BALLET AND POWER
IN SOVIET RUSSIA

Christina Ezrahi

UNIVERSITY OF PITTSBURGH PRESS

DANCE BOOKS

Published by the University of Pittsburgh Press, Pittsburgh, Pa., 15260
Copyright © 2012, University of Pittsburgh Press
Manufactured in the United States of America
Printed on acid-free paper
10 9 8 7 6 5 4 3 2

Published in Great Britain in 2012 by Dance Books Ltd., Southwold House, Isington
Road, Binsted, Hampshire. GU34 4 PH

Library of Congress Cataloging-in-Publication Data

Ezrahi, Christina.
    Swans of the Kremlin : ballet and power in Soviet Russia / Christina Ezrahi.
        p.   cm. — (Pitt russian east european)
    ISBN 978-0-8229-6214-4 (pbk.)
    1. Ballet—Soviet Union—History. 2. Dance—Soviet Union—History. 3. Dance—
Political aspects—Soviet Union. I. Title.
    GV1663.E97 2012
    792.80947—dc23   2012030694

CIP catalog record is available from the British Library
ISBN 978-1-85273158-8

To Ariel, Lina, and Yariv

Contents

Acknowledgments

The sublime dancers of the Mariinsky-Kirov and the Bolshoi, who elevated the art of ballet throughout the tumultuous twentieth century, inspired this research. I would like to thank the staff at the Central State Archive of Literature and the Arts in St. Petersburg and of the Russian State Archive of Literature and the Arts in Moscow. Ballet is a visual art, and this book would not have been the same without the help of Natalia Metelitsa, Tatiana Vlasova, and Sergei Laletin from the St. Petersburg State Museum of Theater and Music, Elena Lollo, Alisa Meves, Elena Mochalova, and Olga Ovechkina from the Mariinsky Theater, and of Gwyneth Campling and Victoria Relph from the Royal Opera House, Covent Garden, who helped me obtain photographs for this book. I am grateful to the dancers of the Kirov and Bolshoi Ballet companies who have shared their thoughts with me over the years, above all Makharbek Vaziev, Olga Chenchikova, and Evgeny Goremykin.

I thank my editor, Peter Kracht, for his guidance and his enthusiasm about this project, which began at University College London's School of Slavonic and East European Studies. I am indebted to Alena Ledeneva and Geoffrey Hosking for their inspiring guidance and to Nancy Condee for her support. I would like to thank the Arts and Humanities Research Council and University College London for funding my work.

I am deeply grateful to my mother for sharing my love for Russian ballet and to my father for putting up with our enthusiasm. I am obliged to my parents-in-law, especially Sidra DeKoven Ezrahi and Ruth HaCohen, for nurturing me intellectually and gastronomically, but notably to Yaron Ezrahi, who has provided invaluable guidance at different stages. Above all, I would like to thank my husband, Ariel, who has become an expert on Russian ballet, my daughter, Lina, whose first words included Mariinsky and Bolshoi, and my son, Yariv, who chivalrously accompanied me to St. Petersburg even before he was born.

A Note on Transliteration
and Translation

In my transliteration from Russian to English, I have used a modified version of the Library of Congress (LOC) system in the text. I have made the following changes for the endings of names:

-ii in the LOC system becomes -y (Lunacharsky, not Lunacharskii)

-aia in the LOC system becomes -aya (Plisetskaya, not Plisetskaia)

For Russian names frequently used in English, I use the most common English transliteration instead of the LOC system (for example: Bolshoi Theater, not Bol'shoi Theater; Tchaikovsky, not Chaikovskii).

I have used strict LOC transliteration for Russian words other than names that appear in the text, in source notes, and in the bibliography.

Unless noted, all translations are my own.

There is no precise English equivalent to the Russian *uchilishche*. I translate the term as "institute."

SWANS OF THE KREMLIN

Introduction

ON 26 FEBRUARY 1917, Mathilda Kschessinskaya received an urgent call from General Halle, the chief of police of the fashionable Petrograd district where she lived. Kschessinskaya was not only prima ballerina assoluta of the Mariinsky Ballet, but she was also the former mistress of Nicholas II and the current mistress of Grand Duke Andrei Vladimirovich, and Halle was anxious about her security. He warned Kschessinskaya that the situation in town was very serious and advised her to save whatever she could from her house before it was too late. The revolution had begun. The ballerina looked at the possessions decorating her elegant style moderne house and felt that her situation was desperate: her most important diamond pieces were kept at Fabergé, but what was she to do with the incredible quantity of smaller items scattered around her house? When she sat down for dinner with her son, his tutor, and two dancers from the Mariinsky the following evening, shots could be heard next to her house. Kschessinskaya decided that it was time to leave. She put on her most modest fur coat, a black velvet coat trimmed with chinchilla, and threw a shawl over her head. Someone quickly lifted up her favorite fox terrier Dzhibi, whom she had almost forgotten, someone else carefully carried the traveling bag with her valuables, and they left. Kschessinskaya remained in Petrograd until July 1917, but she was not to live again in her house after that evening, finding shelter with friends and family instead. Driving past her former home, she once saw the most prominent female Bolshevik, the revolutionary Alexandra Kollontai, stroll around her garden in the ermine coat she had left behind:

FIGURE 1. Mathilda Kschessinskaya, her son, Vladimir, and her dog, circa 1910–1911.
© St. Petersburg State Museum of Theater and Music

the Bolsheviks had commandeered Kschessinskaya's former home as their headquarters.[1]

The absurd image of Alexandra Kollontai taking a stroll in Kschessinskaya's ermine coat is emblematic of the paradoxical situation Russia's imperial ballet found itself in after the October Revolution. Ermine is the fur of kings, and Kschessinskaya's ermine coat symbolized the symbiotic relationship between Russia's imperial ballet and its patron, the tsarist regime. More than any other art form, ballet was a child of aristocratic court culture, yet it not only survived the upheaval of the early revolutionary period but soon claimed its place in the official pantheon of Soviet cultural achievements. Just as Kollontai had put Kschessinskaya's ermine coat around her shoulders, the Soviet regime adorned itself with ballet.

But could the Soviet regime ever claim full ownership, or control, over ballet? Could the artistry of the imperial ballet survive and develop after a revolution that destroyed the social and political order of which ballet had formed an intrinsic part, a revolution that held the utopian promise of a new world and demanded before long that art should become an engineer of human souls, a propaganda tool serving the ideological needs of the state?

Under the tsars, several theaters had received the title "imperial," signifying their status as theaters operating under court supervision and on generous state funding. Russia's imperial ballet consisted of the ballet companies of two imperial theaters, the Mariinsky Theater of Opera and Ballet in St. Petersburg and the Bolshoi Theater in Moscow. Before the October Revolution, these two ensembles were the only public, state-supported ballet companies in Russia, even though from the late eighteenth century ballets were also performed by serf theaters maintained by aristocrats as part of Russia's flourishing private, aristocratic theatrical culture. In the last third of the nineteenth century, troupes of foreign ballet dancers began to perform in nongovernment-supported theaters springing up in the Russian provinces. After the ban on private companies in Moscow and St. Petersburg was lifted in the 1880s, touring companies also visited these two cities, especially in the summer. During the twilight years of imperial Russia, cabarets and "theaters of miniatures" emerged as centers for ballet experimentation. Strictly speaking, the Mariinsky and Bolshoi were thus not the only troupes performing in Russia, but as the only ballet companies with "imperial" status, they benefitted from the tsar's largesse and protection, enabling them to create those ballets at the heart of the classical canon that define our understanding of classical ballet to the present day. As this book is about the fate of Russia's imperial ballet after the revolution, it is therefore logical to focus on the former Mariinsky Ballet (known as Kirov Ballet for most of the Soviet period) and the Bolshoi Ballet and not on the numerous, but by comparison less significant, ballet ensembles created throughout the Soviet period.

How did Russia's formerly imperial ballet fit into the Soviet cultural project? I use the term *Soviet cultural project* to avoid the traditional emphasis on ideological control as a force that crushed artistic creativity in the Soviet Union and to emphasize instead the complexity of the relationship between art and politics in the Soviet Union as expressed in two central aspects of Soviet cultural policy. The first aspect reflects the utopian aspiration of the Russian Revolution to create a new, Socialist civilization. In its maximal definition, the Soviet cultural project aimed for nothing less than the total cultural transformation of society. This utopian vision soon began to pale before the complexity of reality, but throughout the Soviet period, the aspiration of reshaping, reeducating, and controlling the conscience of people lived on in the regime's dictatorial insistence on enlisting art to promote political and ideological allegiance.

The second aspect of the Soviet cultural project could be seen as the benign side of the educational impulse that also lay at the heart of the regime's dictatorial-utopian aspiration of social transformation and social control. The Soviet regime aspired to dispel the darkness of Russia's "backwardness" with the light of *kul'turnost'*, a broad term used to connote the general cultural level of a person. Initially, promoting kul'turnost' included an eclectic mix of activities, ranging from teaching workers how to brush their teeth, to increasing literacy, to making the bastions of high culture accessible to the masses, but before long a basic knowledge of Russia's cultural achievements was expected of every Soviet citizen. The Soviet emphasis on an education that required a knowledge of the most famous products of high culture was enshrined in one of Soviet civilization's central myths, its publicly promoted self-image as "the people who read the most [*samyi chitaiushchii narod*]" in the world. Similarly, during the Cold War between the East and West, the regime tried to use its cultural prowess to demonstrate the superiority of the Soviet system as a whole. The implications of the Soviet cultural project for high culture were thus complex. On the one hand, the arts benefited from strong state support and from a state-sponsored mindset that promoted a high regard for cultural achievements as a core value of Soviet civilization. On the other hand, constraints were put on artistic development by the regime's ideologically driven attempt to control artistic creation.

Ballet also benefited from the regime's promotion of high culture. It was transformed from an elite entertainment in Moscow and St. Petersburg to a widely popular object of national pride. But despite the regime's continuous demand for "Soviet" ballets that would shape the audience's "socialist consciousness," there was little in the work of the Kirov and Bolshoi Ballet companies that successfully contributed to the regime's dictatorial-utopian aspirations of social transformation and control. In the meantime, the "class-alien," prerevolutionary classical heritage of Russian ballet continued to flourish and to spread into remote areas of the Soviet Union.

The Soviet fate of Russia's imperial ballet forms an important part of Russian cultural history. Unfortunately, historians have largely ignored this subject, even though the fraught relationship between artists and political power under the Soviet regime continued to fascinate the public imagination in the West throughout the Cold War and beyond, notably within the context of the high-profile defections of dancers such as Rudolf Nureyev, Natalia Makarova, and Mikhail Baryshnikov. Each year, there seems to be a new book on Soviet history, reflecting the opening of archives to Western historians in the post–Cold War era and the continued interest of the general public in this part of twentieth-century history, but even though the Kirov and Bolshoi Ballet companies were among the most visible Soviet cultural ambassadors to the West during the Cold War, there is almost no new literature on this subject taking into account the opening of the archives in the 1990s. *Swans of the Kremlin* is the first archival study of the Kirov and Bolshoi Ballet companies during the first fifty years of Soviet power. While it analyses the specific problems that arose for ballet in the wake of the October Revolution and into the 1920s and 1930s, it focuses on the golden age of Soviet ballet, the 1950s and 1960s.

This book is about the remarkable resilience of artistic creativity under the Soviet regime. Despite the opening of the archives, the process of cultural production in the Soviet Union still seems to be poorly understood in the West. Often, this complex story continues to be reduced to the romantic but simplistic image of the lonely genius, cowed into submission by an omnipresent, dictatorial state. Today, almost twenty years after the end of the Cold War, Western conceptions of Soviet ballet continue to be almost exclusively based on the Cold War dictum that Soviet ballet was belligerently conservative, producing superlative performers who were tragically, maybe even hopelessly, trapped in a system that precluded any further development of the choreographic imagination, confining the artistic creativity of its star performers largely to the interpretation of the great classical repertoire. Without minimizing the ideological and political pressures on artistic creativity in the world of Soviet ballet, this picture requires revision.

Because the production histories of new ballets offer some of the best examples for the struggle for artistic autonomy, the focus of this book is not on the fate of the classical ballet repertoire in both companies, an unusually rich and complex topic that deserves a separate study. Similarly, I do not discuss the educational practice of the ballet schools of the Kirov and Bolshoi Ballet companies and their crucial role in passing on and developing Russia's prerevolutionary ballet heritage during the Soviet period. Thus *Swans of the Kremlin* is neither an exhaustive history of the Kirov and Bolshoi Ballet companies nor a comparative study of the two institutions. Instead, it uses examples from the experiences of both companies to discuss the wider issue of artistic autonomy within the field of Soviet ballet. In addition to reconstructing the struggles involved in staging new ballets, the book also puts key artistic debates within their wider political and ideological context and looks behind the scenes of significant events in Soviet ballet history, such as the Bolshoi Ballet's first tour to the West in 1956. The slight emphasis on the Kirov Ballet reflects the fact that during the period under investigation, Soviet choreography experienced a particular flowering at the Kirov.

What was the creative process in the world of Soviet ballet really like? Thanks to the enormous amount of paperwork created by the Soviet bureaucracies and the richness of this archival material, this book is primarily based on materials such as verbatim records of long debates held at the theaters and other venues, documenting the creative process at the time, although it also draws on memoirs by dancers and choreographers, most of which have been published in Russian only, and other sources. The quality of the archival records proved so high that they often offered a more reliable source for the debates of the time than oral history. Given the specific historical circumstances—the collapse of the Soviet Union and the tumultuous uncertainty of the immediate post-Soviet period—events of the past may take on a different meaning with the benefit of hindsight. For example, a well-known ballerina who was very critical of the Kirov Ballet's artistic director Konstantin Sergeev in the 1960s told me in conversation that now that she had been working in the West for several years, she realized the depth of Sergeev's knowledge of classical ballet and appreciated it. While such reevaluations offer fascinating insights, they are less suitable for reconstructing the artistic battles of the Soviet era. I hope to offer a more nuanced picture of creative life at the Kirov and Bolshoi Ballet companies than the one available at the present by combining extensive use of archival materials and other sources available only in Russian with an inside view into the world of Russian ballet gained through many informal discussions with former dancers of the Kirov and Bolshoi. *Swans of the Kremlin* benefited from many conversations with artists who danced with either the Kirov or Bolshoi Ballet company during the Soviet period, including Irina Kolpakova, Makharbek Vaziev (director of the Mariinsky Ballet from 1995 until 2008), Olga Chenchikova, and Evgeny Goremykin.

For the historian studying Soviet culture, questions concerning artistic autonomy and creative agency are arguably the most difficult and most interesting ones to answer. Even though ballet became one of the most celebrated Soviet cultural achievements, the glory of the Kirov and Bolshoi Ballet companies continued to rest on the "class-alien" heritage of the prerevolutionary classical ballet repertoire created under the patronage of the tsars. Time and again, the companies "failed" to live up to official demands for more Soviet propaganda ballets that were also popular with the public. What does ballet's resistance to being "Sovietized" tell us about the relationship between artistic thought and practice on the one hand and Soviet ideology and politics on the other hand? What does it tell us about the potential for artistic autonomy and continuity between Russia's pre- and postrevolutionary culture under the Soviet regime?

Swans of the Kremlin analyses how the Kirov and Bolshoi Ballet companies negotiated the restrictive and intrusive framework set for artistic creation by the Soviet regime. It shows how the ballet companies reclaimed artistic autonomy in a system that sought to deny it. Within the Soviet context, the struggle for artistic autonomy required the ability both to block out the system mentally and to play the system practically. Autonomy, in the sense of complete freedom of action, was made impossible by the regime's close supervision of cultural production. In the world of ballet, the quest for autonomy was complicated by the fact that writing, composing, or painting "for the drawer" was not an option.

Within the Soviet context, artistic autonomy needs to be defined more broadly as an exercised ability to maintain independent professional values, the continuity of artistic debates, and the ability to achieve purely artistic goals, such as pushing the boundaries of choreographic language. During debates that accompanied the struggle for implementing these goals, subversive artistic intentions could be hidden behind overtly orthodox ideological language. It is thus sometimes important to read between the lines of archival records. I use the term *Soviet system* to denote both tangible institutional constraints exerted on cultural production through bureaucratic oversight and censorship and less tangible mental constraints exerted by the omnipresence of ideology. The term *Soviet regime* refers to both the party and state apparatus.

I coin the term *artistic repossession* to grasp ways in which artists repossessed or creatively adapted and redefined what the Soviet regime sought to control: artists had no choice but to accept the political organizational structures and ideological frames that the regime imposed on cultural production, but they could learn to exploit them for their own artistic ends that had nothing to do with the regime's goals or the values these structures and ideological concepts were supposed to promote. Just as the owner of a house who was dispossessed might haunt the new owner and aim to repossess his property, artists in the Soviet Union tried to repossess their house of cultural production. Artistic repossession can be seen as a form of systemic subversion because it embodies tactics that operate within the system but seek to use the system to promote goals foreign to it. It demonstrates that sometimes constraints could become an enabling factor, inspiring extraordinary creativity to overcome the constraining pressure of circumstances.[2]

I build on some of the insights won by pioneering research in social history and ethnography like Stephen Kotkin's *Magnetic Mountain*, Sheila Fitzpatrick's *Everyday Stalinism*, and Alena Ledeneva's *Russia's Economy of Favors: Blat, Networking, and Informal Exchange* by applying them to the field of cultural history. All three of these books look at everyday practice or, in Sheila Fitzpatrick's words, "the forms of behavior and strategies of survival and advancement that people develop to cope with particular social and political situations."[3] As Kotkin has pointed out in his study of Magnitogorsk in the 1930s, ordinary people developed ways to resist the terms of daily life that developed within the crusade of building socialism: "One resists, without necessarily rejecting, by assessing, making tolerable, and, in some cases, even turning to one's advantage the situation one is confronted with."[4]

If Kotkin explicitly regards actions normally seen as passive or "deviant" as resistance and is guided by the belief that "the subject of inquiry should include not only what was repressed or prohibited but what was made possible or produced,"[5] Ledeneva goes one step further. In her study of *blat* and the Russian economy of favors, Ledeneva shows how practices that were necessary for the functioning of the Soviet system in economic and practical terms could ultimately be subversive of the system in terms of ideology and emphasizes the enabling power of constraints.[6] My work extends this approach to the study of Soviet cultural history by investigating strategies of resistance that ultimately subverted the ideology of the Soviet system within the context of the artistic life of the Kirov and Bolshoi Ballet companies.

I use the term *resistance* not in the sense of acts of outright, active opposition but in James C. Scott's understanding of everyday resistance as a "weapon of the weak" in face of political and practical restraints.[7] No matter how unequal the relationship between artistic creation and political power appeared to be in the Soviet Union, it was a two-way relationship of mutual influence that included the potential of artistic subversion of political-ideological power. My analysis of power relations thus reflects Michel Foucault's emphasis on the relationship between power relations and confrontation strategies and his contention that "there is no relationship of power without the means of escape or possible flight."[8]

In terms of political context, this book focuses on the Khrushchev era but also discusses events of the immediate postrevolutionary period, the impact of Stalinism on Soviet ballet, and closes with a ballet produced during the Brezhnev era, Yuri Grigorovich's *Spartacus*. Given the goal to assess everyday tactics developed by artists to reclaim artistic autonomy from an omnipresent regime, it does not discuss the extraordinary experience of the Second World War and the Kirov and Bolshoi Theaters' evacuations from Leningrad and Moscow but instead emphasizes the 1950s and 1960s, a golden era of Soviet ballet that witnessed a stormy reinvigoration of Soviet choreography, pitting defenders of Stalinist orthodoxies against innovators, the emergence of a new, highly talented generation of dancers, and the end of Soviet ballet's geographic isolation with the onset of Cold War cultural exchange.

It is important to add that the division of cultural history into neat political-historical units can be methodologically helpful, but the transition between different eras is in reality more fluid. While the cultural Thaw of the Khrushchev period undoubtedly provided an important impetus and crucial opportunities, the golden era of Soviet ballet at the center of this book should not be reduced to the political context of the Thaw. It extended well into a different period of Soviet cultural politics, which included Khrushchev's showdown with the creative intelligentsia in 1962 and 1963 and the early Brezhnev period. The year 1968 was chosen as cutoff date because the premiere of Grigorovich's celebrated version of Aram Khachaturian's ballet *Spartacus* within the context of the fiftieth anniversary of the revolution seemed an appropriately important historical occasion, especially because this production became, for many, synonymous with Soviet ballet. The 1970s and 1980s merit a separate study as they were defined by somewhat different problems and opportunities arising before the backdrop of Brezhnevite stagnation and Gorbachev's perestroika and glasnost.

By analyzing the struggle for artistic autonomy at the Kirov and Bolshoi during the first fifty years of Soviet power, I hope to help redress the neglect of ballet in the study of culture under the Soviet regime and to offer new insights in the complex relationship between art and power in the Soviet Union. *Swans of the Kremlin* focuses not so much on the repression of artists and the curtailing of artistic creativity by censorship as on the ways in which artists managed to navigate the Soviet cultural system and to shape the destiny of their art form despite systemic constraints. Ultimately, ballet proved stronger than politics. Even though the regime tried to impose ideological limits on artistic creation, even though there were borderlines that could not be crossed, the ambiguity inherent in any system created room for the artistic repossession of creative freedom. However hard the regime tried to control artistic life, artists at the Kirov and Bolshoi Ballet companies developed strategies to cope with the political-ideological realities of the life of an artist in the Soviet Union, reclaiming, to a certain extent, autonomy from a system they had no choice but to accept. By doing so, incremental adaptation could thus become a form of resistance, leading to a subversion of the system without necessarily presupposing its conscious rejection by the artists.

1 Survival

The Mariinsky and Bolshoi after the October Revolution

> Of all stage arts inherited from the past, ballet bore the largest
> quantity of "birth-marks" of the exploitative society. . . . One
> incontestable fact was preserved in the memory of each and
> everyone—ballet performances of the past were given only at
> the imperial theaters and they were held in the highest esteem
> by the tsar's family, by high officials, by the apex of the
> exploitative society.
>
> —YURI SLONIMSKY, *SOVETSKII BALET*

ON 25 OCTOBER 1917, as Bolshevik forces were besieging the Winter Palace,
the Mariinsky Theater was preparing for that evening's ballet performance
dedicated to the memory of Tchaikovsky.[1] Tamara Karsavina left her flat
near the Winter Palace around five o'clock in the afternoon. The ballerina,
who had achieved international fame with Sergei Diaghilev's Ballets Russes,
was dancing that night. By many detours she arrived at the theater an hour
later, but by eight o'clock, an hour after the scheduled beginning of the performance, about four-fifths of the cast were still missing. The performance
went ahead, even though "the few performers on the vast stage were like
the beginning of a jigsaw puzzle, a few clustered pieces here and there—the
pattern had to be imagined. Still fewer people in the audience. A cannonade
was faintly heard from the stage, quite plainly from the dressing rooms."[2]
The capture of the Winter Palace later that night concluded the Bolshevik
coup d'état and symbolized the beginning of a new era.

The Bolshevik Revolution struck the imperial theaters like a thunderbolt.
Ballet had been an entertainment for the elites of imperial Russia, and its
prospects were at best unclear during the assault on tradition and the clash

between the old and the emerging new order that followed the October Revolution. The political, ideological, and economic consequences of the revolution put the survival of ballet into question. Not only did the ballet companies have to cope with a mass exodus of leading figures of the stage and with nearly impossible working conditions but ideological pressures emerged from the cacophony of shouts by grassroots Communists, supporters of proletarian cultural movements, and the militant artistic avant-garde who were decrying ballet as an artificial, frivolous art form—a decadent playground for grand dukes hopelessly out of touch with reality. The question whether there should be a place for ballet in the proletarian, Socialist society Bolshevism was hoping to build was closely linked to an ideological-political debate involving the regime, Russia's prerevolutionary cultural elite, and the avant-garde: What should be the role of culture in a society that was supposed to build socialism? What should be the relationship between postrevolutionary culture and Russia's prerevolutionary cultural heritage? Would there be a place for ballet in the Soviet cultural project?

The Imperial Ballet in Prerevolutionary Russia

Born at Renaissance and absolutist courts in Europe, ballet's roots as an art form are firmly planted in aristocratic soil.[3] In imperial Russia, the sumptuous ballet productions at the Mariinsky celebrated the patrons of the imperial ballet companies, the tsars.[4] The first professional ballet performance in Russia is said to have taken place in 1736.[5] Two years later, Empress Anna Ivanovna granted permission to open a ballet school in the Winter Palace. Under continued royal patronage, ballet flourished and evolved into a well-established institution. In the nineteenth century, Russian ballet reached its golden age under the guidance of the Frenchman Marius Petipa.[6] Imperial St. Petersburg emerged as the undisputed international capital of classical ballet.

For the Romanov dynasty, architecture and ballet were means of cultural self-celebration. In many ways, the academic classicism of Petipa's choreography expressed in dance the grandeur and harmony of St. Petersburg's imperial architecture. Nowhere is this aesthetic symbiosis of imperial architecture and classical ballet more apparent than in the extraordinary harmony of proportion of Rossi Street, formerly known as Theater Street, which has housed the ballet school of the Mariinsky since 1836. Rossi Street is two hundred meters long, and its width of twenty meters corresponds exactly to the height of the identical buildings that occupy the whole length of the street on either side of it.[7] The yellow and white, strictly classical facades of arches and columns perfectly complement the color and style of the Aleksandrinsky Theater, located where Rossi Street meets Ostrovsky Square.

FIGURE 2. Mathilda Kschessinkaya as Aspicia in *The Pharaoh's Daughter*, 1898.
© Mariinsky Theater

For the dancers of the Mariinsky, life revolved almost exclusively around ballet from the day they entered the doors of the imperial ballet school on Rossi Street as small children. Until the end of their careers, they would cross these same doorsteps daily, first as students and then as dancers on their way to rehearsal.[8] Describing her student days around the turn of the

ℛ *Survival*

twentieth century, Karsavina remembers: "The fashion of our clothes belonged to the preceding century, but was well in keeping with the spirit of the institution, with its severe detachment from the life outside its walls. Vowed to the theater, we were kept from contact with the world as from a contamination . . . we were brought up in almost convent-like seclusion."[9]

The students of the imperial ballet school were considered members of the tsar's household. On the frequent occasions when students appeared in the Mariinsky's ballet productions, court coaches emblazoned with the double eagle accompanied by liveried coachmen transported the students from the school to the theater.[10] George Balanchine remembers how as a student, he appeared in Petipa's ballet *The Pharaoh's Daughter* on Nicholas II's name day on 6 December 1916.[11] Kschessinskaya was dancing the part of the pharaoh's daughter Aspicia. The twelve-year-old Balanchine played the part of a monkey jumping through branches above Kschessinskaya, who gracefully tried to shoot down the mischievous animal with her bow and arrow. After the performance, the students who had participated in it were presented to Nicholas II in the royal box. The tsar patted Balanchine's shoulder and gave him a silver box ornamented with the imperial crest and filled with chocolates.[12]

From childhood, the dancers of the Mariinsky were thus reared to take their place in a tsarist institution that occupied a central position in the social life of imperial St. Petersburg. Even if by the early twentieth century the ballet audience was not completely socially homogeneous, being comprised of representatives from the nobility, foreign diplomats, military officers, and the grand bourgeoisie but also lesser officials and students,[13] Kschessinskaya personified the ongoing symbiotic relationship between the ballet and its imperial patrons. Former mistress of Nicholas II, then mistress, and later wife, of Grand Duke Andrei, Kschessinskaya ruled the Mariinsky's stage. During the days of tsarist autocracy, the ballet companies of the Mariinsky and Bolshoi Theaters were jewels in the crown of imperial Russia, a dazzling entertainment reflecting the splendors of the regime. Some admirers of the ballet reached such ecstasy in their love for dance—or ballet dancers—that the term *baletoman* was coined to describe the delirious disciples of the imperial ballet. By declaring a war of annihilation on the political and social structure of imperial Russia, the Bolshevik Revolution aimed to turn the soil in which ballet had flourished into a wasteland.

The Mariinsky during the Civil War

Artists of the Mariinsky and Bolshoi Theaters reacted to the October Revolution with shocked hostility. By 27 October (9 November, O.S.) 1917, performances had stopped at both theaters. On 19 November 1917, the artists of the Bolshoi published a statement in *Rampa i zhizn'* condemning the violence of the Bolshevik takeover of power: "Aware that we are part of a great democracy, and grieving deeply over the spilled blood of our brothers, we protest against the violent vandalism that has not even spared the ancient holy of holies of the Russian people, the temples and monuments of art and culture. The State Moscow Bolshoi Theater, as an autonomous artistic institution, does not recognize the right of interference in its internal and artistic life of any authorities who have not been elected by the theatre and are not on its staff."[14]

The artists were not willing to readily accept new masters and sought to defend the theaters' artistic autonomy they had worked for since the February Revolution. The recently formed People's Commissariat of Enlightenment (Narkompros), responsible for education and culture, managed to establish contact with the theaters only after several attempts. Progress was faster in Moscow, where the Bolshoi resumed its performances on 21 November 1917 (O.S.). At the Mariinsky, some artists did not recognize Narkompros's authority until January 1918 and refused to perform. Resistance was firmest in the opera company, the chorus, and the orchestra. The ballet maintained a certain degree of neutrality: while the opera and chorus went on strike in January 1918, ballet performances continued.[15] This by no means meant that the ballet had come to terms with the new situation.

Most dancers were acutely aware that their art had flourished in a world that had now been destroyed. According to Fedor Lopukhov, a leading figure at the former Mariinsky,[16] director of the ballet company from 1922, and one of the most important choreographers of the 1920s, the Socialist revolution pushed the majority of ballet artists into confusion and dismay. Many dancers feared that soon they would be left without occupation in a country hostile to ballet, struggling for survival as the Russian Civil War was leading to a steady decline in living conditions: "The company seriously contracted—some grew seriously ill, some died, others left Petrograd in futile searches for a 'quiet haven.' Panic, terror tormented the artists of the former imperial theaters. Among them, numerous advisers from the ranks of 'former people' could be found who tirelessly repeated 'One has to flee abroad as soon as possible, death is awaiting everyone.' . . . There were famous ballerinas and dancers who fled abroad in secret, convinced that art was doomed to death in Soviet Russia, that the Bolsheviks were 'against art' and so on."[17]

In the years before the revolution, the Mariinsky's ballet company consisted of 212 to 228 members. By the 1919–1920 theater season, it had shrunk to 134 dancers.[18] In Moscow, fewer dancers left than in Petrograd.[19] The Mariinsky Ballet, however, lost approximately 40 percent of its dancers. Almost the entire Olympus of prerevolutionary ballet left Petrograd, including Mathilda Kschessinskaya, Tamara Karsavina, and Mikhail Fokine.[20] Without choreographers, ballerinas, and male principal dancers, the future of ballet seemed at best uncertain, even though time would show that some of the most talented choreographers of the younger generation, such as Kasian Goleizovsky and Fedor Lopukhov, had chosen to stay in Soviet Russia.

While the dancers worried about their professional and physical survival, the new program of the Bolshevik Party adopted in March 1919 already included the seeds of a cultural policy from which ballet would benefit throughout the Soviet period: the state-driven popularization of high culture, one of the cornerstones of the Soviet cultural project. The composition of the ballet audience changed in response to emigration, social and economic upheaval, and a government policy aimed to make the theaters more accessible to the masses. The new program of the Bolshevik Party adopted in March 1919 included a section on the enlightenment of the people, calling for open access to all treasures of art that had hitherto been inaccessible for the lower classes. During the civil war period, free theater tickets were given to organizations, factories, and army units. A Soviet source from 1950 gives the following statistics: at the Mariinsky, nine opera and ballet performances were given for free to trade unions in the 1918–1919 theatrical season, fifty-six in the 1919–1920 season, and eighty-six in the 1920–1921 season. In November 1921, workers of Petrograd received 21,110 seats for thirty-eight performances at the former Mariinsky. In Moscow, 577,434 tickets for the Bolshoi and its smaller branch stage, the Filial, were distributed in the 1919–1920 season, amounting to 84.5 percent of the full house. In the 1920–1921 season, 303,218 tickets for the Bolshoi were distributed (the Filial was not working that season), amounting to 96.8 percent of the full house. With the introduction of the New Economic Policy (NEP) in 1921, the distribution of free or subsidized tickets was—at least for the time being—abolished.[21]

The practice of distributing free or subsidized tickets introduced a new, unpredictable audience to the ballet, but given the iconoclasm and vandalism of the early revolutionary period, it was far from certain how this audience would react. According to Lopukhov:

> In the ballet this was a particularly dangerous moment. From time immemorial, the conviction existed that ballet is an art form "for the selected few"—for the apex of society, for the court and the aristocracy. Allusions were made that the ballet performance was born under the auspices of the courts of sovereigns; from this the conclusion was drawn that it was an integral component of tsardom. They

talked about ballet's isolation from life; it was thought that, in contrast to other art forms, ballet was unable to deal with reality's stirring questions, and that it could only serve as after-dinner amusement for satiated gourmets. There was no lack of such pronouncements in the press. The more terrifying it was to wait for the reaction of the new audience.[22]

Lopukhov also described the backstage environment before the first performance for the new audience:

> Everyone at the theater was tense to the breaking point. Some waited for the audience with agitation and hope; others—with terror; a third group calculated that this meeting would shatter all illusions and show that the artists of the ballet were not on the same path with the "rough bumpkins."
>
> When the auditorium, which had been intended for the "cream" of the capital's society, filled with workers and peasants in grey great-coats, in leather jackets, in shawls—in work and war clothes, now and then even with rifles in their hands—everybody's heart began to beat anxiously. . . . The new audience made its appearance silently, concentrated, gloomy, as gloomy as were its clothes. . . . At the beginning, this silence seemed to us a manifestation of suspicion and to some—of malevolence. Only then did we understand that an unprecedented attitude to the theater was manifesting itself in this way: to the old masters, the theater was a long-known vanity fair, to the new—a previously unknown, mysterious, and agitating church.[23]

Lopukhov's image of the masses entering the theater like a church might be exaggerated, but they were certainly crossing a threshold into the unknown. Before the revolution, ballet as a grand spectacle existed primarily in St. Petersburg and Moscow. The audience of the imperial ballet consisted for the main part of members of the nobility, ambassadors, military officers, and the grand bourgeoisie. Moving down the social ladder—and up in the theater auditorium—one could find lesser officials, students, and, on matinee days, children. Getting a seat was not easy, and balletomanes brought lawsuits against each other, challenging the right of a subscriber to bequeath his seat to a relative or friend.[24] Most simple Russians probably did not even know what exactly ballet was. After the revolution, parts of the new audience were perplexed by ballet's muteness, asking their more knowledgeable-looking seat neighbors whether the performers would soon begin to talk or sing. They marveled at the artifice of the movements and the scanty costumes of the dancers.[25] But as ballet reached the factories in

FIGURE 3. The new audience at the Mariinsky Theater, circa 1917–1918. © Mariinsky Theater

concerts for workers at their workplace, as free tickets for performances at the Bolshoi and former Mariinsky made ballet more widely available, awe, confusion, and maybe a desire to see skimpily dressed dancers turned into unrestrained, if at times unrefined, enthusiasm, leading a ballet critic to remark that "the nonsubscription public, which packed the theater to overflowing, applauded and howled with such violence that all the old theater rats scurried off in horror to the snuggest little holes."[26]

Government policy opened the bastions of imperial high culture to the masses, but the luxurious old-world charm of the ballets certainly did not contribute to awakening a "Socialist conscience" in this new audience. Far from galvanizing revolutionary fervor, ballet offered an escape from the horrors of revolutionary reality. In the civil war period, budgetary and artistic constraints, given the exodus of dancers and choreographers, made any serious attempts to stage new productions impossible. The starved, freezing populations of Moscow and Petrograd were flocking to see the same ballets that shortly before had delighted a bejeweled audience. The ballet repertoire of the Mariinsky for the 1918–1919 theater season consisted of old-time favorites such as *The Sleeping Beauty, Raymonda, Swan Lake, La Fille mal gardée, Le Corsaire,* and *The Little Humpbacked Horse.*

The famous Bolshoi dancer and ballet pedagogue Asaf Messerer, then a teenager, described watching a performance of the ballet *Coppélia* from the gallery at the Bolshoi in the harsh winter of 1919, a performance that convinced him he had to become a ballet dancer:

> It is cold in the theater, the audience sits in felt boots, in fur coats, under the cupola hangs a cloud of frost from the breathing of the spectators. The winter of 1919 was in general unprecedentedly fierce and hungry. Moscow was drowned deeply in snow, stiff dead horses were lying on the street, no one removed them. . . . And suddenly—the Bolshoi Theater! The red velvet of the stalls and the boxes, gold, the radiance of the light in the crystal pendants. All of this seemed almost unreal, and yet it was reality. The joyful luxury of the décor, the sound of the instruments being tuned in the orchestra, darkness slowly descending upon the auditorium after the chandelier had faded, the curtain flying up, and, finally, the bright stage, on which, not privy to the severe frost, stood a graceful ballerina in a short tutu and friskily gay.[27]

While the prerevolutionary ballet repertoire evoked the ridicule of the avant-garde, which envisioned a radically new culture reflecting the spirit of the revolution, the audience often preferred the entertainment offered by the old ballets to the experiments of the avant-garde that it did not understand. For example, ticket sales for the annual benefit performance for the corps de ballet of the Mariinsky in December 1918 widely surpassed ticket sales of the previous years, even though the ballet that was to be performed, Marius Petipa's *Talisman,* had actually been taken out of the repertoire five years ago.[28] *Talisman* was as removed from the reality of Soviet Russia in 1918 as possible and certainly did not carry any messages contributing to the social education of the masses. Created by Petipa in 1889, the ballet was known for its mass scene effects and for the rare simultaneous flight of two artists through the air. A fairy tale set in India, its sumptuous scenery evoked the mystery of ancient India and the fantastic world of the kingdom of spirits, reflecting the nineteenth-century predilection for the exotic and fantastic in ballet. Sales had exceeded twenty-thousand rubles only three days after ticket sales for *Talisman* had started.[29]

As early as January 1919, Anatoly Lunacharsky, head of Narkompros,

FIGURE 4. *Talisman*, circa 1925–1926. Olga Iordan and Aleksandr Pushkin, Rudolf Nureyev and Mikhail Baryshnikov's future teacher. © St. Petersburg State Museum of Theater and Music

remarked that the "old classical ballet" had turned out the favorite spectacle of the proletariat.[30] The ballet dancers of the former Mariinsky and Bolshoi continued to transport their audiences into a different world. At a party meeting, Lunacharsky somewhat defiantly commented: "We are far from the categorical program of Comrade Bukharin [who says] you must tear down the bourgeois theater. . . . Representatives of the workers often present different theatrical demands to me. Comrade Bukharin would wonder at the fact that not once have the workers demanded of me that I increase their accessibility to the revolutionary theater, but they ceaselessly demand opera and ballet. Perhaps Comrade Bukharin would be distressed at that. It distresses me little."[31] Some of the leading ballet figures of the day used the obvious success of the old classics with the new audience as an argument against accusations that ballet was inherently alien to the proletariat. In 1925, Lopukhov noted in *Rabochii i teatr* that the demand by workers' organizations for tickets for ballets like *The Sleeping Beauty* was so great that they were staged more than other ballets: the continued great success of the old productions in itself demonstrated their right to exist.[32]

In its struggle for survival in the immediate aftermath of the revolution, ballet not only had to prove its relevance but also had to overcome almost insurmountable practical obstacles. Reality backstage was the same harsh reality the spectators hoped to forget by going to the theater. Waiting for the magic of the stage to unfold, the audience had no idea what difficulties had to be overcome night after night in order for a performance to go on. The fact that performances continued uninterrupted throughout the civil war period is nothing short of a miracle.

In an interview given in January 1919, Ivan Ekskuzovich, the head of the Department of State Theaters in Petrograd and director of the Mariinsky, remarked that even though it was already 5:45 p.m., he was still not sure whether there would be a performance that night. Every performance depended on whether or not the theater had enough petrol in reserve. Assembling the set and props for each performance had turned into a daunting task. The state theaters had twelve storage houses located in different corners of Petrograd, but there were often no means for transporting the sets and props to the theater. Given the fuel shortage, it was difficult to operate the theaters, which were very complicated technical mechanisms, and temperatures inside often sank close to zero Celsius.[33] While the audience was able to keep on their fur coats, the dancers had to dance in their light costumes. After the performance, dancers and audience alike had to walk home to their unheated apartments on dark streets, as there was no tram after 6 p.m. and on holidays.[34]

The civil war also brought an acute food shortage. In December 1918,

Leonid Leont'ev, the chairman of the Committee of the State Ballet Company of the Mariinsky, explained how chronic malnourishment made it virtually impossible for the dancers to carry on their physically demanding work: "Even such a strong partner as Vladimirov complains that he supports the ballerina with difficulty. The adagio still goes well, but during the variation the legs of the artist usually weaken, turning into some kind of jelly. And that is natural, because it's impossible for one potato to satisfy one's hunger. Owing to this chronic undernourishment, one even has cases of fractured legs among the female dancers, dislocations, pulled tendons, and so on. The whole rank of female dancers on whom the repertoire depends, like Gerdt, Vill', Liukom, Spesivtseva, and others, have turned into invalids."[35] According to the season review of the *Biriuch petrogradskikh gosudarstvennikh teatrov* (Herald of Petrograd state theaters), "At the ballet, . . . nearly every performance hung by a thread. Before the curtain went up, the directors waited . . . for a telephone call or a note from one of the participants about illness and were prepared to cancel the performance."[36]

In these impossible working conditions, the continued functioning of the theaters depended to a large extent on the managerial and entrepreneurial skills of the theater directors. By the beginning of the 1919–1920 theatrical season, conditions had reached a desperate point. Given the continued lack of fuel, performances took place at a temperature close to zero Celsius, while the absence of electric light during the day made it impossible to rehearse. The Mariinsky was connected to a cable that provided the theater with light around the clock only in October 1919. According to the *Biriuch petrogradskikh gosudarstvennikh teatrov*, exhaustion and sickness might have led to the closure of the theater if not for two breakthroughs. At the end of November 1919, Ekskuzovich managed to obtain firewood and the theater began to be heated. On 15 November 1919, the united directory of the Mariinsky and Aleksandriinsky Theaters closed an agreement with the political department of the Seventh Army. In the agreement, the State Academic Theaters took responsibility to serve the cultural needs of the Red Army through journeys to the front. In return, all artists would receive a front ration of food, while staff and technical personnel were given rear rations. The distribution of the rations started at the end of November.[37] During those difficult years, dancers also tried to supplement their salary by taking part in concert performances in which they were frequently invited to perform. The organizers of such concerts paid in kind, for example, with raisins, sugar, bread or with things such as nails or even an axe, which could be exchanged for provisions on the market, thus proving more valuable than money, which was constantly loosing its value.[38]

The Threat of Closure, 1919–1922

Before long, an even greater threat to the ballet companies' survival than economic hardship and emigration emerged. The government and the creative intelligentsia were engaged in a heated ideological debate on the nature of revolutionary culture and its relationship with prerevolutionary culture. Central to this debate was the question if, and how, Russia's prerevolutionary cultural heritage could, and should, be adapted to the new cultural needs of Soviet Russia. On the extreme left, Communist iconoclasts and the radical artistic avant-garde argued that at the dawn of socialism, all remnants of prerevolutionary, bourgeois culture had to be destroyed to make way for a revolution in the arts. Already in 1912, the Russian futurist manifesto proclaimed with aggressive bravado that "the Academy and Pushkin are more unintelligible than hieroglyphs. Throw Pushkin, Dostoevsky, Tolstoy, etc. overboard from the steamer of modernity."[39] Radical party activists saw culture exclusively in terms of class and unequivocally condemned prerevolutionary culture as bourgeois, calling for the creation of a uniquely proletarian culture.

Proletarian and revolutionary stages sprung up in response to this vision of a radically new culture, providing colorful avant-garde experiments. Orchestras composed of factory horns were quite literally meant to herald a new age, but in the middle of dreams of proletarian culture and avant-garde experiments the academic stage of the former imperial theaters constituted a central topic of dispute in the era's artistic polemics. In December 1919, the former imperial theaters and selected prerevolutionary private theaters, such as the Moscow Arts Theater, received the title of "state academic theater," acquiring official and subsidized status. Their enemies denounced the academic theaters as politically dangerous relics, bastions of conservatism out of harmony with socialism. Workers' and avant-garde stages also coveted the large subsidies given to the academic theaters and envied the status of its artists.[40] On the other side of the debate were people such as Anatoly Lunacharsky. Lunacharsky was appointed People's Commissar of Education and head of Narkompros on 26 October 1917. Responsible for educational and cultural policies, Narkompros's jurisdiction also included the former Palace Ministry, which had controlled the imperial theaters.[41] Lunacharsky defended the academic theaters as academies, which would preserve the best of the prerevolutionary cultural heritage while providing standards of technical excellence, and protected them from militants within the party and their own artistic field. The state's policy toward the academic theaters became a major battlefield, pitting supporters of relative pluralism and the preservation of Russia's cultural heritage against proponents of stricter political guidance and transformation of the arts.[42] Many voices ranging from Communist Party members to avant-garde musicians and playwrights attacked the Bolshoi and former Mariinsky, arguing that ballet and opera were not only absolutely irrelevant to contemporary life but inherently incapable of adapting to it given their nonproletarian class origin. Others thought that maintaining the Bolshoi and Mariinsky was simply an economic luxury the state could not afford.

In the first years after the revolution, the Bolshoi and former Mariinsky were repeatedly under threat of closure. While numerous ideological attacks were directed against them, on the occasions where closing the theaters was seriously debated, events seemed to be driven primarily by economic considerations, reflecting the general commitment of the top leadership to preserve Russia's cultural heritage. At the same time, according to Lunacharsky, Lenin's "attitude toward the Bolshoi Theater was rather nervous. . . . He insisted that its budget be cut and said, 'It is awkward to spend big money on such a luxurious theater . . . when we lack simple schools in the villages.'"[43] While Lenin endorsed preservationist policies in the realm of culture, he considered them secondary to Narkompros's educational tasks, in contrast to Lunacharsky who could not bring himself to consider culture a matter of secondary importance. In 1921, an exasperated Lenin instructed Lunacharsky to "lay all the theaters in the grave" and to focus on fighting illiteracy.[44]

In the early 1920s, economic and ideological concerns repeatedly brought the Bolshoi and former Mariinsky Theaters dangerously close to being shut down. During the difficult winter of 1919–1920, many members of the Maly Sovnarkom (Small Council of People's Commissars; the Council of People's Commissars [Sovnarkom] was equivalent to the executive of the government) argued that given the acute fuel shortage in the country, it was criminal to give fuel to the Bolshoi, which was still so weak in its propaganda of new ideas. On this occasion, Lenin prevented the closure of the theater, arguing: "It is still too early for us to hand over the heritage of the bourgeois art to the archives."[45] In 1921–1922, the Bolshoi and former Mariinsky entered an extended crisis. By 1921, seven years of war, revolution, and civil war had brought Russia to the brink of ruin. The regime decided to adopt NEP, introducing a mixed economy that was partly Socialist, partly capitalist, in order to prevent the country's imminent collapse. Following the introduction of NEP, the state sharply cut back subsidies to both theaters. During a financial crisis in the summer of 1921, salaries were no longer paid at the Bolshoi. Just before the beginning of the new theater season, artists went on strike. On 5 November 1921, a notice appeared in *Izvestiia* announcing that the Moscow State Council of Trade Unions (MGPS) had decided to reorganize the company and administration of the Bolshoi and to close the theater if the reorganization turned out to be impossible.[46] Throughout November 1921, Lunacharsky engaged the MGPS in a debate in *Izvestiia* on this issue. At some point, the MGPS pointed out that it would be no sacrifice if the Bolshoi had to be closed during a period of reorganization as it served the proletariat least of all, adding acidly that speculators and the bourgeoisie would have to manage without the Bolshoi.[47]

In January 1922, Lunacharsky pushed a proposal for preserving the Bolshoi through Sovnarkom, but the decision was revoked by Lenin who wrote to Molotov that "having learned from Kamenev that the Sovnarkom has unanimously adopted Lunacharsky's absolutely improper proposal to preserve the Bolshoi Opera and Ballet, I suggest that the Politburo should resolve" to rescind the decision, to only leave a few dozen dancers and singers for Moscow and Petrograd, and to invest at least half of "the thousands of millions saved in this way" into the campaign against illiteracy and into reading rooms.[48] The decision was discussed anew. Lenin endorsed a proposal to close the Bolshoi made by a commission investigating how to reduce state expenditures in conjunction with the introduction of NEP, but two months later, on 13 March 1922, the Politburo declared the closure of the Bolshoi economically inexpedient, reflecting Lunacharsky's argument that it would be more expensive to pay compensation to those fired, and to guard and maintain the building of the Bolshoi without income from performances, than to keep it running.[49]

In the autumn of 1922, as the government sought to cut its expenditures because of NEP's impact on the state budget, the Central Committee once again discussed whether or not the Bolshoi and former Mariinsky should be closed. The Politburo voted to transfer funds from the academic theaters to primary schools, literacy campaigns, and libraries. On 17 November, the Bolshoi and former Mariinsky Theaters were ordered closed as of 1 December. Once again, Narkompros came to the rescue by presenting a plan to cut subsidies to the theaters by 350 million rubles per year. During the crisis, the government seemed primarily concerned with economic questions: the leadership's call for reforms focused on economic issues, and no demands for artistic reforms were made nor were any such reforms promised.[50]

The fact that the Bolshoi and former Mariinsky Theaters remained open did not signal an end to the ideological debate about whether or not they should continue existing. While the government might have focused its discussions on cutting costs, its deliberations took place in a climate of increasingly vitriolic ideological attacks on the two theaters, both in artistic debates and in the press.[51] Critics wrote about ballet's inevitable death as an art form socially alien to the revolution: "Ballet has grown numb like grass affected by frost and continues its existence as a foolish vestige. . . . Bal-

let isn't sick, it has sclerosis. Classical ballet as a form has become obsolete.
. . . Isn't this art form a hothouse plant? . . . Isn't this a museum art? . . . Attempts to express anything at least somewhat central to the life sensation
of the present through the means of classical ballet are absurd and doomed
to failure."[52]

Another critic stated laconically: "In order to rejuvenate the ballet . . .
one has to close the theater and begin from scratch."[53] In an article published
in 1923, Proletkult denounced ballet as "a thoroughly bourgeois art form, in
which only love, or some other simple feeling, is expressed through a special language of the legs, which specialize in erotic movements, and where
the head and separate parts of the magnificent human body are sacrificed to
the dance of the feet."[54] In an article in 1925, Lunacharsky, a firm supporter
of the ballet, remarked: "Ballet as a complete evening-filling performance
was preserved only in Russia. Of course, it also provoked a great number of
reprimands. The combination of dance, whose beauty and meaning no one
denies, with plots, expressed in extremely conventional mime and gestures
of the stylized choreographic element, seemed and seems to many unacceptable. The Communist comrades very often express their opinion from that
point of view that the Russian ballet is a specific creation of the landowner's
regime, a caprice of the court, that it, as such, carries in itself characteristics
antipathetic to democracy and the proletariat."[55]

In the late Stalinist period, the Soviet dance writer Yuri Slonimsky
summed up the "orthodox" view on ballet's "sociological flaws" as follows:

> Of all stage arts inherited from the past, ballet bore the largest
> quantity of "birth-marks" of the exploitative society. Therefore it was
> especially in need of the destruction of reactionary traditions of the
> gentry-landowner culture, of the greatest exposure to and development
> of democratic elements, . . . of the largest creation of new traditions.
> One incontestable fact was preserved in the memory of each and
> everyone—ballet performances of the past were given only at the
> imperial theaters and they were held in the highest esteem by the tsar's
> family, by high officials, by the apex of the exploitative society.[56]

Ballet and the Soviet Cultural Project in the 1920s

While the economic threat to the survival of the Bolshoi and former Mariinsky slowly abated, the ideological debate on the relevance of the two opera
and ballet theaters in a society that was supposed to build socialism continued throughout the decade. Lunacharsky's writings in defense of the two
theaters and of ballet focused not on economic issues but on proving their
contemporary relevance. In a 1925 essay, "For what purpose do we preserve

the Bolshoi?," he referred to economic objections to the theater's existence only in passing, calling them "less weighty concerns."[57] His defense of the theaters against persistent ideological attacks centered on a vision of a future Socialist culture in which ballet's pivotal role would demonstrate its artistic and social relevance. Lunacharsky was personally committed to preserving Russia's cultural heritage in this time of revolutionary upheaval. Dancers fondly remember him as the Bolshoi's loyal knight from the first days of the revolution, passing on numerous petitions on behalf of the Bolshoi to Sovnarkom.[58]

Lunacharsky occupied a middle ground between the defenders of the cultural tastes of the prerevolutionary, non-Bolshevik Russian intelligentsia and the supporters of proletarian culture. An amateur playwright, he was himself a product of the prerevolutionary intelligentsia. As someone who had become revolutionary primarily because of his interest in cultural change, he agreed with Aleksandr Bogdanov, the founder of Proletkult, that the proletariat could create its own culture, but Lunacharsky did not think that this would require a complete break with the achievements of prerevolutionary civilization. On the contrary, he thought that it would take a long time for a proletarian culture to develop and that the prerevolutionary intelligentsia could contribute to this process by passing on its skills.

For all his sympathy for the non-Bolshevik intelligentsia, Lunacharsky believed that bourgeois culture had to be adapted to the needs of the new Socialist state. His dedication to preserving Russia's cultural heritage reflected not just his personal affinity to the culture of the past but also a hope that preserving "bourgeois" achievements of the past would help accomplish "revolutionary" masterworks in the future.[59] Commissar of Enlightenment Lunacharsky supported a moderate, tolerant, and conciliatory policy toward the arts.[60] He was convinced that while each member of the government could respond personally to the cultural issues of the day, the government itself had to remain neutral; by tolerating a variety of artistic views and by maintaining its impartiality, the government would allow the Communist dialectic to run its natural course.[61]

Despite Lunacharsky's pluralist inclinations, the two policies that were to define the Soviet cultural project throughout the Soviet period—ideological control over artistic creation combined with an educational mission—were already discernible in Lunacharsky's ideas on cultural policy in early postrevolutionary Russia. They were reflected in his strategy for proving the social and cultural relevance of the Bolshoi and former Mariinsky Theaters, a strategy that rested on two arguments. First, as academic theaters, they should acquaint the masses with the best achievements of the past.[62] Second, opera and ballet had to be preserved not so much for their own sake alone but for what would emerge from them.[63] In an article written in 1925 on the occasion of the hundredth anniversary of the Bolshoi, Lunacharsky argued that the country needed to be convinced that the Bolshoi was not just a museum that was barely alive but that it had the potential to become an organic part of contemporary culture, a source of "revolutionary happiness" and of "revolutionary-artistic self-consciousness."[64]

Lunacharsky's cultural agenda envisioned art as a quasi-religious propaganda tool instilling enthusiastic revolutionary fervor in its audiences. There was a utopian streak to Lunacharsky's otherwise moderate personality. Before the revolution, Lunacharsky had been one of the main innovators in the Godbuilding movement that greatly irritated the more rational Lenin. In his book *Religiia i sotsializm* (Religion and socialism, 1908–1911), Lunacharsky argued that the essence of religion, its human spiritual bond, could be achieved without God, but Marxism and modern science alone would not be able to reproduce the ecstatic solidarity of religion. Lunacharsky envisioned a future where myths, sounds, and rituals would provide a spiritual support for the proletariat in its struggle, galvanizing the creative enthusiasm otherwise stimulated by religion: "Religion is enthusiastic, and without enthusiasm, people can create nothing great."[65] Lunacharsky believed in the fundamental importance of creating new rituals that would whip up active enthusiasm for the Soviet project. Art was supposed to play a central part in this transformational vision.

His idea of promoting the creation of revolutionary oratorios was central to his vision of transforming the Bolshoi into a center of Soviet culture. According to Lunacharsky, every great popular movement needed symbols, but Soviet Russia was short of symbols: revolutionary oratorios could provide the kind of evocative symbol the new regime needed, mythical expressions of desirable common ideas, feelings, and the historical experience of the Soviet people. They were supposed to play an important part in constructing the nation's new identity and creating a New Soviet Man (*novyi sovetskii chelovek*), the central aim of the Soviet cultural project. Lunacharsky envisioned a synthetic theater that would combine orchestral and choral music with dances. A plot expressed either in a poetic dialogue or rhythmic prose would alternate with arias, hymns, songs, and dance solos. For each public holiday, an oratorio would be written, which would be performed before a thousand people in a theater or, in summer, before tens of thousands of people in a huge amphitheater. According to Lunacharsky, only the Bolshoi and former Mariinsky Theaters, with their choirs, orchestras, singers, dancers, and set designers, possessed the artistic capacities to create such popular revolutionary ceremonies expressing the "rising sun of communism."[66]

In other words, the cultural and artistic know-how of the past should be turned into a transformative force paving the way into the future. Preserving opera and ballet was justified because it provided an artistic training ground for the future. Lunacharsky stressed the importance of ballet in staging synthetic oratorios: "It is here in particular that ballet finds its place. It seems to me it is not even worth to linger on this for especially long, for this element sets the masses on fire to an exceptional degree, and in any case, it is no less able than singing to give a keen expression to any experience. The harmony, precision of ballet movements, the full control over one's body, the full control over the lively mass—here is the pledge of the great role that ballet can have in the organization of such performances." Lunacharsky argued that before one could hope to stage revolutionary oratorios, adequate poets and composers had to emerge. In the meantime, it was important to maintain and further develop the technical standards of the performers by using old productions. In short, according to Lunacharsky, even if the Bolshoi was partially obsolete, the government preserved it not only because it still had some musical, theatrical, and cultural meaning but primarily because one day it would provide an arena for new works.[67]

From early on, visions for the Soviet cultural project were thus built around the ideological propaganda needs of the emerging dictatorial state and on a strong educational mission, reflecting the traditional educative impulses of the Russian intelligentsia. Lunacharsky pointed out that the "new theater" should not be light entertainment, but that it should play a role in the social education of the masses. Lunacharsky's ideas also have to be put into their wider European context. His thinking was influenced by Richard Wagner's early ideas of theater as an opera-ballet theater, a synthetic theater in which human words, music, dance, mime, painting, and architecture combine harmoniously. According to Wagner, this theater should give performances in which the people realize their highest ideals, the path of their suffering, and their struggles and victories.[68] Similarly, Lunacharsky envisioned revolutionary propaganda pageants that would galvanize the audience into one enthusiastic collective being.

Implicit in Lunacharsky's ideas is thus the belief in opera and ballet's potential as propaganda tools for shaping their audiences' consciousness, especially given the popular success of opera and ballet. During an address at the Bolshoi on 12 May 1930 on new paths of the opera and ballet, Lunacharsky asked: "Yet does it follow from what has been said that we, having inherited such a nice toy, such a golden rattle that the tsars and the tsarinas, the bourgeois and the bourgeoise once delighted in, can amuse ourselves with it and not do anything new in the field of opera and ballet? On the contrary. If it is such a great aesthetic force that it invigorates our audience notwithstanding even its alien content—now what a mighty weapon is it going to be in our hands if we insert into it our content?"[69]

Despite Lunacharsky's important status, his ideas on cultural policy in general and ballet in particular were not shared by all Bolsheviks. His dedication to ballet and the arts evoked criticism in some members of the party who thought that Narkompros was paying too much attention to culture while neglecting the fight against illiteracy. In response to a progress report on Narkompros's work at a session of the Central Executive Committee in 1926, a certain Comrade Kartashev caustically remarked: "It seems to me that the chief activity [of Narkompros] has been to search out old church monuments and develop the art of ballet."[70]

While the ballet companies survived the revolution, their future and artistic freedom was anything but guaranteed. Even in the tempestuous climate of early Soviet Russia, the question of how to fit the former imperial ballet into an embryonic Soviet cultural project was taken seriously. As the temples of Russia's prerevolutionary culture were opened to the masses to educate them in the civilization of the past, it was discussed how the cultural know-how of the past could be turned into a transformative force shaping the Socialist minds and civilization of the future. The fact that Commissar of Enlightenment Anatoly Lunacharsky repeatedly had to defend ballet's right to exist shows that ballet's role in this project was far from certain, and its survival after the revolution was not guaranteed. Lunacharsky's personal commitment to the Bolshoi and former Mariinsky Theaters and their ballet companies played a crucial role in preventing their closure. But even Lunacharsky's thinking focused on ballet's propaganda potential and the hope that the emotional energy created by the evocative power of propaganda pieces elevated to the status of common symbols would increase the audience's commitment to the state's project of building socialism and the spectators' loyalty to the regime.

Before the backdrop of political, economic, and social upheaval, the debate on ballet in early Soviet Russia was thus not confined to the question whether Soviet Russia needed ballet at all. As ballet demonstrated its resilience by continuing to exist day after day, attracting an enthusiastic audience, political pressures on its artistic development emerged, seeking to recast the formerly imperial ballet in a Soviet mold.

2🜚   *Ideological Pressure*

Classical Ballet and Soviet Cultural

Politics, 1923–1936

The main difficulty in Soviet ballet lies in the fact that dolls
are impossible here.

"BALETNAIA FAL'SH'," *PRAVDA*, 6 FEBRUARY 1936

~~~~~~

IF THE SURVIVAL OF Russia's prerevolutionary cultural heritage was put in
question by the violent political and social watershed of the October Revolution, the new political masters soon demonstrated that, in the sphere
of high culture, they were not so much fanatical iconoclasts as propagan-
dists seeking to capitalize on the power of Russia's prerevolutionary cultural
symbols by recasting them in their own image. Before long, discussions on
the future of the academic theaters focused on the political aim of giving
them contemporary relevance beyond contributing to the regime's educational mission of enlightening the masses. Reflecting the transformational
aspirations of the Soviet cultural project, art was supposed to help the regime shape a new civilization. The theaters were expected to build a repertoire that contributed to the state's ideological goals. In the 1930s, the Soviet
regime's desire to use art as a handmaiden of ideology and politics acted as
a catalyst for a process culminating in a dogmatic interpretation of the doctrine of socialist realism.

Socialist realism was not just an artistic style but a propagandistic ideology that promoted a view of Soviet life that had little to do with reality. If
nineteenth-century realism had tried to draw attention to real social problems by showing life as it was, socialist realism showed life as it ought to
be—a happy, Socialist utopia, where workers, peasants, and different na-

tionalities were united in brotherly comradeship, successfully constructing socialism and celebrating the fruits of their labor in a land of plenty. While socialist realism was initially used as a vague umbrella term extended from literature to all areas of cultural production, the actual meaning of this paradigm for each field of artistic expression was determined within each art form via a complex process.

Interpreting the meaning of socialist realism for classical ballet was complicated by several factors. If we distinguish between the substantial and formal aspects of a work of art, at least in theory, creating a ballet based on a plot showing Socialist life as it ought to be should be no more difficult than creating a dramatic play with a socialist realist plot. Finding a choreographic form of ballet production compatible with socialist realism from a formal point of view, however, proved problematic for at least three reasons. First, realism in art demands a representation of concrete things that is true to life, but as a medium of artistic expression, classical dance demands the acceptance of a highly formalized system of movement that has nothing to do with realism or the way "normal" people move. Like classical music, the nonrepresentational nature of classical dance makes it an allegorical or symbolic artistic medium whose meaning is not concrete and is difficult to verbalize, but unlike classical music, it is bound to the visual reality of the human body. Its very nature made classical dance vulnerable to the Soviet accusation of formalism, the focus on the formal elements of an art form at the expense of social content.

Second, classical ballet had formed an intrinsic part of imperial Russia's aristocratic court culture. Even before the revolution, in comparison to literature, music, and painting and among circles that believed in a social mission for art, ballet carried the stigma of a decadent entertainment that would never be able to make the social contributions of a "serious" art form. For this reason, many voices ridiculed ballet as a courtly hothouse plant irrelevant for a revolutionary society and condemned it as inherently incapable of contributing to the major discussions of the day. Third, if other art forms could orient themselves by taking nineteenth-century realism in their field as model, classical ballet had no nineteenth-century model of realism to fall back on. On the contrary, while Russian literature and art increasingly strove to depict real life in general, and social problems in particular, classical ballet had remained aloof from the social ills plaguing Russia, focusing instead on providing a dazzling entertainment for the elites of imperial Russia.

If it was difficult to determine the meaning of socialist realism for classical dance, the antiformalism campaign of 1936 provided ballet with a negative definition. The Pravda editorial "Baletnaia fal'sh'" (Balletic falsity), which was about the choreographer Fedor Lopukhov's production of Dmitri Shostakovich's ballet *The Bright Stream*,[1] demonstrated that creating a ballet based on a plot celebrating socialist life was simply not enough: Lopukhov's reliance on virtuoso classical dance to depict the life in a kolkhoz in the Kuban was branded as formalism.

A fear of virtuoso classical dance began to take hold over the ballet stage. In the wake of the antiformalism campaign, ballet became an apprentice of drama. The genre of *dramaticheskii balet*, or *drambalet*, became the only genre of ballet production deemed compatible with socialist realism. During the relatively tolerant era of the New Economic Policy (NEP), various artistic visions had competed on the ballet stage: short chamber ballets, symbolist or allegorical ballets, satires, abstract ballets, and traditional full-length productions. During the era of drambalet, which lasted from the mid-1930s until the cultural Thaw in the 1950s, full-length narrative ballets became the only acceptable type of ballet production. Dramatic content and narrative plausibility and coherence took precedence over choreographic inventiveness, leading to productions rich in realistic, elaborate sets and costumes and infused with folk dances supposedly answering calls for *narodnost'*, the promotion of folklorism as a way to create the illusion of an exhilarating Communist unity among all the peoples of the Soviet Union. The range of classical dance vocabulary used by choreographers became more confined, and more virtuoso dances had to be justified by the ballet's narrative plot, which was supposed to create occasions for dance such as weddings or other celebrations where "real" people in "real" life would also dance. The choice of ballet plots was largely confined to literary classics or contemporary propaganda topics.

Analyzing the multiple layers of debate that shaped the rise of drambalet in the late 1920s and 1930s is crucial for understanding the interaction between artistic thought and practice and ideology and politics that shaped the development of Soviet ballet and its position within the Soviet cultural project. The tenets of drambalet constituted an important part of the web of ideological, intellectual, and aesthetic constraints against which much of the struggle for artistic autonomy in the 1950s and 1960s was directed. But it would be a gross oversimplification of the complexities of Soviet cultural life to explain the ascendancy of drambalet by the ideological context of Soviet cultural production alone. The intellectual origins of drambalet had little to do with contemporary Soviet politics and propaganda. Instead, they reflected the inherent tension between the dramatic and nonrepresentational sides of ballet as a theatrical art, Russian debates about the meaning of art in society that had begun before the revolution, and wider European debates about artistic reform, ranging from Wagner's ideas of the Gesamtkunstwerk to experiments in Austro-German modernist music. The verbal requirements of the Soviet cultural project's ideological mission, however, explain why the genre of drambalet acquired a monopoly as the central paradigm for Soviet ballet productions and why its aesthetic requirements became more and more restrictive, running the risk of relegating the most important part of any ballet production—classical dance—to a secondary role.

The Dual Nature of Ballet

The debate that would pit defenders of the specificity of classical dance against those calling for ballet's dramatization in Soviet Russia in the late 1920s and 1930s had deep historical roots. The Soviet debate on the future of ballet reflected questions raised by the unique characteristics of classical dance as artistic medium and by the artistic tension inherent in the ballet production as a synthesis of several art forms. In ballet's evolution as a theatrical art form, ballet productions became tied to narrative plots, but the roots of classical dance as a nonrepresentational artistic medium lay in the allegorical spectacles performed at the courts of the Italian Renaissance.[2] Ballet evolved out of the *ballet de cour*, an entertainment for the nobility derived from Renaissance spectacles. Performed by aristocrats and royalty at the courts of Europe and combining dance with music and verse, the ballet de cour reached its height in France from the mid-sixteenth century until the reign of Louis XIV. Lavish spectacles that lasted for hours, ballets de cour usually illustrated mythological or allegorical subjects that often served as a metaphor glorifying royal power: Louis XIV, an accomplished dancer, acquired the epithet the Sun King following his appearance as the sun in a ballet de cour first performed on 23 February 1653, *Le Ballet de la Nuit*.

During the reign of Louis XIV, ballet moved from the court into the theater and became professionalized. The influential composer Jean Baptiste Lully collaborated with the choreographer Pierre Beauchamp and the playwright Molière to create *comédie-ballets* like *Le Bourgeois Gentilhomme* (1670) for the court. In 1669, Louis XIV founded the Académie d'Opéra, which was to become the Paris Opéra. Ballet had moved into the professional theater, and professional dancers replaced the aristocratic amateurs of the past. In 1713, a professional school of dance was established at the Paris Opéra. As ballet technique developed, the hybrid genre of opera ballets evolved, soon giving singing and dancing an equal place in opulent, loosely structured productions that provided a lavish feast for the eyes but were often thin in dramatic content.

The technical origins of classical ballet thus lie in courtly dances where the dignified, graceful deportment of aristocratic amateurs and their skilful execution of steps served as a visual metaphor of their position in the social hierarchy of absolutism. If dance had initially played a largely ornamental role in productions that combined dance with the spoken word, music, and singing, by the mid-eighteenth century choreographers began to explore dance's dramatic potential. Ballet evolved into a genre independent of opera. While several people explored a more serious vision of dance as an art form capable of expressing more complex meaning, the choreographer Jean-Georges Noverre is most commonly associated with the movement toward the ballet d'action, a ballet that tells a story through a combination of gesture and dance. In 1760, he published his highly influential *Lettres sur la danse et sur les ballets*, outlining his theory of ballet as dramatic spectacle that expressed dramatic action not in words but in dance and in which virtuosity for virtuosity's sake had no place. For the first time, Noverre's ideas designated the choreographer as the central creative force behind a ballet.

As we can see, the latent conflict between the ornamental side of ballet and its dramatic potential already existed when ballet as an independent theatrical genre was in its infancy. Noverre's reform program for ballet emerged during the Enlightenment. His criticism of ballet as a decorative divertissement and his plans to turn ballet into a more serious art form that told stories through dance reflect the general spirit of the age of reason and its emphasis on secular moral education. In the year of the French Revolution, Jean Dauberval, a student of Noverre, staged the ballet *La Fille mal gardée* in Bordeaux, a light-hearted comedy and the first ballet that had everyday characters—farmers—as its heroes. Like Noverre, Dauberval believed in the expressiveness of pantomime and gesture and in the power of ballet to tell a story: "I do not want just to please the eyes, I must interest the heart."[3] In early Soviet Russia, voices calling for the dramatization of ballet would refer to Noverre.

The ornamental side of classical dance was infused with spiritual meaning during the age of romantic ballet. Dressed in clouds of white tulle with little wings, the ballerina took center stage and began to dance on pointe. Expressing the spiritual and emotional yearning of the age, the ballerina symbolized an ethereal, unattainable ideal of female purity and beauty. Dancing on pointe, she created an illusion of weightlessness that removed her from the profanity of the real world into a kingdom of spirits. Ballets now alternated acts set in the real world that developed a dramatic plot expressed in pantomime and dance—which usually did not include pointe technique for characters that were regular mortals—with acts set in fantastical world in which the ballerina on pointe ruled supreme.

The dual nature of ballet as both a dramatic-narrative and musical-generalizing art form became apparent in this structural division of ballet productions. The formal division between narrative plot and acts set in a fantastical world led to the creation of the so-called white ballet, sections of pure dance that do not develop a dramatic plot but express emotional and spiritual longing and the core emotions of human existence in dance. The tension between the narrative, dramatic element of ballet productions and the specificities of classical dance as an artistic medium, which, like music, functions on an emotional, nonverbal plane, were also reflected in the second half of the nineteenth century in the structure of Marius Petipa's ballets, which alternated more pantomimic scenes illustrating a narrative plot with pure dance scenes expressing either the emotional landscape of the ballet's heroes or simply providing an opportunity for a beautiful divertissement of increasingly technical and complex dances.

Some of the most important names in early twentieth-century Russian ballet sought to overcome this division between dance and pantomimic drama, an aspiration that in early Soviet Russia was shared both by proponents of pure dance such as Fedor Lopukhov, who completely discarded the conventional mime and pantomimic scenes customary in the "old" ballet, expressing everything in dance enriched by new vocabulary, and by proponents of the dramatization of ballet, who wanted to discard the system of conventional mime and fuse a more natural pantomime with dance that was devoid of empty virtuosity. In prerevolutionary St. Petersburg, and with Diaghilev's Ballets Russes, Mikhail Fokine had already rejected the division of ballet's expressive means into pantomime and dance. He argued that in each new ballet, instead of just combining readymade, existing dance movements, a new form—a unique choreographic idiom—had to be found that corresponded to the ballet's subject. While Fokine predominately created ballets with a dramatic plot, he was also one of the first choreographers to experiment with plotless, musically determined ballets, most notably in his ballet *Chopiniana* (1907; also known as *Les Sylphides*). In Moscow, Aleksandr Gorsky, choreographer of the Bolshoi Ballet from 1902 until 1924, also sought to reform ballet and to overcome conventions of the nineteenth-century ballet, especially the division of pantomime and dance. The innovations of the Moscow Art Theater exerted an important influence on Gorsky in his search to increase the dramatic coherence and credibility of ballet productions.

Debates on ballet reform in early Soviet Russia reflected these prerevolutionary discussions among ballet professionals on how to overcome certain legacies of nineteenth-century ballet such as the formal division between pantomime and dance. Similarly, Soviet criticisms that ballet was a superficial after-dinner entertainment for the prerevolutionary establishment expanded on prerevolutionary criticisms of ballet's position within the hierarchy of arts. These criticisms were directly linked to the emerging conflict between pure art and social art in the Russian cultural debates of the second half of the nineteenth century. Nikolai Chernyshevsky, one of the most important thinkers of early Russian socialism and an advocate of the intelligentsia's social and political service to the people, contrasted Pushkinian principles of pure art with a Gogolian emphasis on depicting injustice and the suffering of humanity. In his *Esteticheskiye otnosheniya iskusstva k deystvitelnosti* (*Aesthetic Relations of Art to Reality*), published in 1855, he cast doubt on the intrinsic merit of art. Before long, the nihilist Dmitry Pisarev declared that a cook in St. Petersburg had done more for humanity than Raphael.[4]

It was only a small step from the radical nineteenth-century slogan "boots rather than Raphael" (or, in some versions, Shakespeare) to the futurists' call to throw Pushkin, Dostoevsky, Tolstoy, and other canonic prerevolutionary artists from the steamer of modernity. Turgenev, who left the journal *Sovremennik* (The contemporary) just after publishing *Fathers and Sons* in 1862, branded Chernyshevsky and Dobroliubov, who dominated the journal's editorial staff, as "literary Robespierres . . . trying to wipe from the face of the Earth poetry, the fine arts, all aesthetic pleasures, and to impose in their place mere seminarian principles."[5] In the meantime, the imperial ballet continued unabashedly to provide poetry and "aesthetic pleasure" to its audiences. Russian ballet was firmly entrenched in the camp of Pushkinian pure art. Pushkin had in fact been a great admirer of the imperial ballet, dedicating several stanzas of his *Eugene Onegin* to it and exclaiming that there was more poetry in the ballets of Charles-Louis Didelot, which had pushed ballet in St. Petersburg to new technical and dramatic heights, than in all of France's literature of the time.[6]

The Soviet cultural project incorporated into state policy the thinking of Russia's nineteenth-century progressive intelligentsia that insisted on the artist's social responsibility, seeing art, literature in particular, as a unifying, prophetic, and transformative social force. The ideological accusations hurled at ballet in early Soviet Russia echoed complaints and satirical comments made by members of Russia's progressive nineteenth-century intelligentsia that condemned ballet because, unlike other art forms, it ignored the social ills plaguing Russia. Like Mayakovsky in early Soviet Russia, Nikolai Nekrasov, poet and editor of *Sovremennik*, wrote satirical verses about ballet. Mikhail Saltykov-Shchedrin, a satirist and former member of the Petrashevsky group of intellectuals, whose members, including Dostoevsky, were famously condemned to be executed for subversion just to be pardoned by Nicholas I at the last minute, reflected: "I love the ballet for its constancy. New governments rise up; new people come onto the scene, new facts spring up; entire ways of life change; science and art follow these occurrences anxiously, adding to or partially changing their very substances—only the ballet hears nothing and knows nothing." Defenders of the ballet could claim that it was the ultimate expression of art for art's sake, but writing about the conservative, male ballet audience, Saltykov-Shchedrin insinuated that there was an element of erotic titillation lurking behind the spiritual elevation balletomanes claimed to experience: "they love to be carried to the transcendental sphere of the imagination at the sight of short gauze skirts."[7]

During the antiformalism campaign of 1936, the *Pravda* editorial "Baletnaia fal'sh'" firmly established the link between nineteenth-century and Soviet criticisms of ballet by quoting some ironic verses by Nekrasov from 1866, which made fun of "ballet peasants" in Petipa's ballets. The editorial claimed that far from having mastered realism in art, Soviet ballet displayed the same "false," "doll-like" attitude toward life as prerevolutionary ballet. But given the nature and conventions of ballet, how was one to represent reality in a realist way, all the while maintaining the specificities of the genre, without succumbing to naturalism? The theoretical issue of solving the tension between realism and ballet would preoccupy Soviet ballet historians and critics for decades.

Fedor Lopukhov's *Dance Symphony*, 1923

As the new Soviet regime sought to incorporate art into its dual cultural mission of education and indoctrination, the increasingly politicized context of artistic debates led to a fusion of internal discussions about artistic reform with the old complaint that ballet was too removed from social and political reality to be considered a serious art form relevant for contemporary society. Even though choreographers such as Fedor Lopukhov and Kasian Goleizovksy were able to conduct avant-garde experiments on the stages of the former Mariinsky and Bolshoi Theaters in the 1920s,[8] they did so in a political environment that questioned the right of ballet to exist and in a professional environment that was uncertain about ballet's future in Soviet Russia. While many dancers relished participating in Lopukhov's and Goleizovsky's experiments, there were also those who opposed such experiments as yet another threat against Russia's classical ballet heritage.

The ballet debates in early Soviet Russia should not be discussed only within their political-ideological context but need to be placed within the wider artistic conversations of the times. The exploration of the specificity of each artistic medium is one of the characteristics of modernism, leading, for example, to the emergence of abstract painting. Similarly, in classical ballet, Fedor Lopukhov tried to explore the musical, nonnarrative, abstract potential of classical dance during the artistically more permissive, experimental climate of the 1920s. Lopukhov occupies a unique position in early Soviet ballet, having shaped it in the 1920s both as a conservator and innovator. A committed supporter of Petipa's heritage, he ensured artistic continuity between the pre- and postrevolutionary era as the artistic director of the former Mariinsky from 1922 until 1930, even though his reconstructions of old ballets caused some controversy. His aim was to restore their choreography as closely as possible, but when neither he nor the old dancers could remember a part, or sometimes when he thought the original choreographer had made a serious mistake, he composed the missing parts, imitating the original choreographer's style as closely as possible. Probably the most famous example of this is his composition of the Lilac Fairy's solo in the prologue of *The Sleeping Beauty*. Some criticized him for adding his own choreography; others thought he did his best given the incomplete records of the old ballets. As choreographer, Lopukhov considered classical dance ballet's main expressive resource. His search for innovation focused not on substituting classical dance with something different but on developing its expressiveness by expanding its vocabulary. He invented new movements and introduced elements of other forms such as acrobatics, character dance, and the free dance movement.

Lopukhov was one of the first choreographers to experiment with nonnarrative, abstract classical dance. He theorized a kind of dance that seeks to visualize musical structure, an approach central for the development of twentieth-century classical dance. According to Stephanie Jordan, an authority on the relationship between music and choreography in the twentieth century, Lopukhov is of seminal importance for the development of dance as an autonomous, nonnarrative art form during the twentieth century. Jordan calls Lopukhov's *Dance Symphony: The Magnificence of the Universe* "a landmark in the history of ballet modernism," a work that "is viewed today as seminal to the development of twentieth-century works that were modernist, music based, and grounded in the classical vocabulary."[9] *Dance Symphony* was the first nonnarrative ballet built on a structural exploration of the relationship between dance and music and exerted an important influence on one of the young dancers in the premiere, George Balanchine. In 1924, Balanchine emigrated to the West and developed into arguably the most important choreographer of the twentieth century, shaping neoclassical ballet with its nonnarrative, musically sophisticated ballets.

Lopukhov's only partially implemented vision of choreography as nonnarrative, visualized music is important because it represents the artistic road of modernism that early Soviet ballet could not travel on. Lopukhov's unerring belief in the primacy of classical dance as main expressive resource in ballet was of great importance for Soviet choreographers in the 1950s and 1960s in their quest to lead Soviet choreography out of stagnation.

FIGURE 5. A group of artists of the former Mariinsky, early 1920s. Fedor Lopukhov is sitting in the second row, wearing a white bow tie. To his left are Elizaveta Gerdt and Mathilda Kschessinskaya's brother, Iosif Kschessinsky. © St. Petersburg State Museum of Theater and Music

Even though Lopukhov's experiments with choreography could be seen as a logical continuation of the nonnarrative, pure dance segments in the "white ballet" of the romantic era and in Petipa's ballets, there was a distinctly modernist edge to his approach to abstraction. His theoretical ideas about the genre of dance symphony go back to 1916 and were developed under the influence of Mikhail Fokine's ballets. Reflecting on the distinction in music between programmatic and nonprogrammatic music, Lopukhov called for a new form of ballet, the nonnarrative genre of dance symphony, which would express more abstract thoughts not connected to a conventional plot. Like a musical symphony, a dance symphony would be divided into several parts, developing several movement themes. The dance symphony would be the embodiment of a musical symphony and its themes in dance.[10]

If Petipa's ballets had alternated pantomimic narrative scenes and pure dance segments, Lopukhov wanted to discard dramatic narrative—and pantomime—in favor of choreographic, musical narrative. He wanted to choreograph ballets that danced the music, instead of dancing to music.[11] He believed that musical structure should serve as model for choreographic structure: the ideal relationship between music and dance was one of synthesis, the true integration of music and dance.[12] Traditionally, music had been secondary in the creation process of ballets. First, the story line, number, and character of the dances were determined, then the music required was ordered from a resident music writer. Tchaikovsky had opened the way for more complex musical scores to enter the world of ballet, and Lopukhov considered music of high quality a force that could push the development of choreography forward.[13]

The actual realization of Lopukhov's program for developing the genre of dance symphony was ill fated. His *Dance Symphony* to Beethoven's Fourth Symphony was performed only once, on 7 March 1923. Lopukhov had worked on the ballet with young members of the ballet company of the former Mariinsky.[14] The ballet's premiere took place under bad auspices. It was shown after a performance of *Swan Lake* preceded by long speeches. The pretentious, incomprehensible program notes did little to put the tired audience into the mood for an experimental piece. In addition to expressing Beethoven's symphony in dance, Lopukhov had intended to express several grandiose ideas about life. Different parts of the ballet were titled "Birth of Light," "Triumph of Life over Death," and so forth. While some critics pointed out the significance of the piece for the development of choreography at a meeting held at the Museum of the State Academic Theaters, the press harshly criticized the production.[15]

Why is a ballet that received only one performance considered a major turning point in the history of choreography? The ballet's theoretical ideas continued to influence debates on the future development of Soviet choreography in the 1920s. Lopukhov's theoretical explorations of developing nonnarrative, musically sophisticated dance are also highly significant because they anticipated the most important modernist developments in twentieth-century classical dance. Even if Lopukhov was not able to fully implement his program for nonnarrative dance, he stayed true to his belief in dance as the main expressive resource of ballet. Once a Soviet paradigm for ballet production focused on realism at the expense of classical dance, Lopukhov's beliefs would be condemned as formalism.

Between 1921 and 1931, Lopukhov staged ten new ballets and dances in operas at the former Mariinsky and revived approximately twenty old ballets.[16] His works emphasized developing the expressive means of classical dance, fighting those who argued that ballet was permanently stuck in the nineteenth century, that the revolution had made classical dance superfluous, or that the future of ballet lay in its dramatization. In his conclusion of *Puti Baletmeistera* (1925), Lopukhov firmly stated:

My third point is addressed to the government. . . . In view of the
growing number of attacks on choreography that have appeared in the
press recently, I and many other representatives of the art of choreography have formed the opinion that, in the eyes of the authorities, ballet is a flower cultivated by the bourgeois system, a flower that is both
useless in itself and also alien to the new . . . class of the proletariat.
However, this view is based upon a misunderstanding. Man's primitive
gestures . . . are the core of the art that goes by the name of ballet.
This art is the property of all mankind; it has elevated itself. . . to the
point where it can express the most abstract philosophical ideas, just as
primitive dance conveyed the first expressions of life.[17]

Ivan Sollertinsky's Campaign for Dramatizing Ballet, 1928–1930

During the 1920s, the artistic dividing line within the ballet companies ran
between innovators and traditionalists. For the most part, however, innovators and traditionalists were united in their belief in classical dance as the
main means of artistic expression in ballet. But dancers, choreographers, and
ballet pedagogues were not the only actors involved in the debate about ballet's future. Intellectuals such as the musicologist Ivan Sollertinsky and his
mentor, the theater specialist Aleksei Gvozdev, had an important impact on
the direction ballet took in Soviet Russia. They advocated a dramatization
of ballet where pantomime and danced recitatives would replace "empty"
virtuoso classical dance, supposedly elevating ballet from an entertainment
to a serious art form. While they rejected explorations of classical dance in
favor of its dramatization, they were by no means enemies of ballet. Their
program incorporated pre- and postrevolutionary criticisms of ballet as a
frivolous art form but also reflected intellectual-artistic ideas like Noverre's
program, Wagnerian ideas of the Gesamtkunstwerk, and contemporary developments in Austro-German modernist music that called for an opera reform based on a radically new relationship between libretto and music.

The discussion on ballet reform initiated by Gvozdev and Sollertinsky
in the leading cultural weekly *Zhizn' iskusstva* in the summer of 1928 demonstrates that in the cultural debates of the day, purely artistic concerns
fused with the ideological urgency underlying the Soviet cultural project.
If in nineteenth-century Russia art had come to be seen as a powerful force
of moral education and social transformation, this attitude was now incorporated into revolutionary politics. Gvozdev and Sollertinsky's program for
ballet reform gained prominence and influence in the belligerent climate of
the cultural revolution, which aimed to overthrow the old intelligentsia and
create a new proletarian intelligentsia in a virulent class war.[18] Their interest

in the dramatization of dance, however, predates the onset of the cultural revolution and its pressures on politicizing the ballet repertoire. Already in 1924, Sollertinsky began to translate Noverre's *Lettres sur la danse et sur les ballets*.[19] Published in 1927, it was edited by Gvozdev.

Despite their genuine interest in ballet, Gvozdev and Sollertinsky's preoccupation with the dramatization of dance and the dramatic composition of ballet productions reflected a severe underestimation of the importance of classical dance for the artistic value of ballet as an independent art form. Both condemned classical dance as decorative ornament incapable of any meaningful artistic expression. In their opinion, ballet's future lay in the dramatization of dance, in upgrading the dramatic content of ballet performances. They envisioned ballets that would rely not on virtuoso classical dance but on danced pantomime and character dance (stylized folk or national dances) to express a dramatic plot.

In the summer of 1928, coinciding with the onset of the cultural revolution, a turning point in Soviet cultural politics, their program for dramatizing dance was hotly debated in *Zhizn' iskusstva*. Gvozdev had opened his attack on classical dance half a year earlier by criticizing the lack of genuine reforms of the ballet theater, accusing ballet of existing outside contemporary arguments about the reevaluation of theatrical values. He then outlined his platform for ballet reform: "plot-based pantomime on new, contemporary topics—this is the basic and main task of contemporary ballet," as he believed that the future of ballet lay in expressing captivating dramatic action in danced pantomime, not in what he condemned as the abstract, purely decorative "tricks" of classical dance. Gvozdev essentially demanded that ballet become danced theater.[20]

The argument for the dramatization of ballet contradicted the position taken by choreographers like Lopukhov, who rejected pantomime, experimenting instead with pure dance. The debate centered on different opinions of ballet's artistic essence and its right to be a unique, independent medium of expression enjoying equality with music, drama, painting, literature, and so forth. If Lopukhov saw classical dance as the expressive resource that made ballet unique, Gvozdev put the artistic uniqueness of ballet into question by condemning classical dance as purely decorative, arguing that artistic content in ballet had to be an expression of meaning that could be verbalized, that is, of dramatic action: "Expressiveness can and should be demanded from pantomime, from pantomimic dance, from character dance, from the internal staging of the production, from the play of the actors in ballet and so forth. But one must not demand it from purely ornamental arabesques and flourishes. . . . No matter into what topic one inserts thirty-two fouettés, . . . they still don't acquire topical expressiveness, they still don't become intelligent actions of the dramatic order, but remain what they really are—a sparkling, turning, but purely mechanical display of physical dexterity."[21]

Sollertinsky was an equally passionate champion of the dramatization of dance. Given his professional involvement with the former Mariinsky as a member of the theater's artistic council from 1928 onward and as a teacher at its ballet school, Sollertinsky was an important force in shaping the emerging pressures on the ballet theater. His article "Za novyi khoreograficheskii teatr" (In favor of a new choreographic theater) came straight to the point: "Contemporary dance has lost the secret of direct expressiveness. Meaning nothing, it can only carry a concrete thought on condition of its theatricalization. Outside theatricality, it will only be an abstract ornament, an arabesque, a capricious ornamental pattern, where the play of moving lines will be considered a goal in itself. In order to become expressive once again, dance has to be turned into danced drama, and the dancer—into a choreographic actor."[22] Sollertinsky argued that in order to revive dance, it had to be made dramatically expressive by bringing it closer to contemporary dramatic pantomime, by connecting it with contemporary music, and by introducing new topics. Sollertinsky conceived expressive dance as plot-based pantomime, which, he contended, would not just "act" like dramatic pantomime but also "dance." In Sollertinsky's vision of a new ballet theater, dance, motivated by the action (for example, by ethnographic street scenes), would alternate with a choreographic "recitative," a distinctive, rhythmized form of pantomime.

The *Zhizn' iskusstva* debate shows a dividing line between Sollertinsky, the intellectual, on the one hand and the ballet establishment on the other hand. His battle cry for a new choreographic theater was followed by a questionnaire that *Zhizn' iskusstva* forwarded to several dancers, choreographers, and ballet teachers of the former Mariinsky. In the responses, there was a clear division between critics outside and members within the theater. N. V. Petrov, a director from the Leningrad Drama Theater, the only non-dance professional replying to the questionnaire, argued that pantomime and character dance had to be the main elements of contemporary ballet. Nine members of the former Mariinsky Ballet replied to the questionnaire, including Lopukhov and the celebrated pedagogue Agrippina Vaganova. In stark contrast to Gvozdev and Sollertinsky's rejection of classical dance, all but one respondent reconfirmed the role of classical dance as a vital element of contemporary ballet. All respondents considered it possible to create ballets on contemporary themes and welcomed the inclusion of acrobatic and physical culture movements in contemporary choreography, although within limits. Some respondents, including Lopukhov, firmly rejected pantomime and gestures used in the dramatic theater or cinema because they were based on the word, while in dance, gestures were based on music. Others did not oppose looking at the experience of the dramatic theater and the cinema for transforming ballet mime.[23]

The debate on ballet reform indicated that despite his love for ballet, Sollertinsky considered it inferior in the hierarchy of arts. In the field of music, in addition to promoting modernist, Western symphonic music, Sollertinsky was also at the center of a movement for opera reform propagating the celebration of everyday language, reflecting developments in Austro-German modernist music that had a major impact on Shostakovich's opera *The Nose* (1930).[24] By the time Shostakovich was working on the opera, Sollertinsky had become his friend and intellectual mentor.[25] Sollertinsky's vision of ballet reform mirrored his vision of opera reform: in both cases, he called for shifting the focus away from music and dance to the libretto, arguing for danced pantomime or recitatives based on the "musicalization" of everyday speech intonation.[26] But while he supported symphonic music, he considered pure classical dance an inferior means of artistic expression. Not all musicians shared this view of the musicologist Sollertinsky. Writing under the pseudonym Islamei,[27] the renowned conductor Nikolai Malko, who gave up his position as conductor of the Leningrad Philharmonic that same year, had defended "symphonic," nonnarrative dance in *Zhizn' iskusstva*: "After all, should the language of dance be removed from artistic circulation just because it cannot be translated into the language of verbal understanding? Wouldn't it follow from the same reasoning to cross out with a stroke of the pen all instrumental, chamber, and symphonic music? After all, it also doesn't possess direct verbal expressiveness!"[28] Sollertinsky replied that symphonic music and dance could not be compared because "next to the incalculable richness of music, and above all symphonic music, the language of the human dancing body proves to be too poor, qualitatively poor!"[29]

As Malko's comments and the response of ballet professionals to the *Zhizn' iskusstva* questionnaire show, there was significant opposition to Sollertinsky's program of dramatizing dance. The political context of the time, however, gave Sollertinsky's critique of classical dance clout. The debate on ballet reform took place during the era of forced collectivization, the First Five-Year Plan for industrialization and the cultural revolution that led to a complete reversal of the NEP concept of pragmatic cooperation with non-Communist bourgeois specialists. From the Shakhty trial in 1928 of engineers and technicians on charges of conspiracy and sabotage until a statement by Stalin signaling a reconciliation with the old intelligentsia in June 1931, Communist militants sought to gain absolute control over the arts and sciences, claiming that they were defending society against the "rightist danger" emanating from the old intelligentsia.

Policies aimed to increase ideological control over the repertoire of the Bolshoi and former Mariinsky. In 1929, Glaviskusstvo published a repertory index classifying plays, operas, and ballets into five categories: ideological works universally recommended for presentation were classified into category A; ideologically acceptable works into category B; works not completely ideologically sound and requiring a rehearsal for examination purposes into category C; ideologically acceptable but primitive works commemorating special political campaigns or historical dates into category D; forbidden works into category E.[30] Only four ballets were forbidden: *Fairy Doll, Smerch, The Vestal Virgin,* and *Number o, or the Wreck of the Council of Five. Smerch (Whirlwind),* by Goleizovsky, had actually been intended as revolutionary allegory. No ballet was classified under category D. The majority of ballets—thirty-four out of sixty-nine categorized ballets—including classics such as *Le Corsaire, Giselle, La Bayadère, Don Quixote, The Little Humpbacked Horse,* and *Vain Precautions (La Fille mal gardée),* fell into category C. Probably reflecting their higher musical quality, Tchaikovsky's ballets fell into category B.

Intellectual commentators and the political machine now joined forces to exert pressure on the ballet repertoire. In 1928–1929, the former Mariinsky responded to pressures to Sovietize its repertoire by announcing libretto competitions for a Soviet opera and a Soviet ballet. The ballet libretto competition was to a large extent initiated by Sollertinsky, who had joined the artistic council of the former Mariinsky in 1928. Sollertinsky worked out the competition's conditions and participated intensively in running it in the spring of 1929.[31] Published in *Zhizn' iskusstva,* the announcement of the competition stated: "The libretto of contemporary ballet is not just an accidental frame for the display of dance that lacks inner cohesion and does not issue from the basic activity—but the libretto is a choreographic drama, obligated to satisfy all the demands laid upon Soviet dramaturgy in general. . . . To write a really contemporary scenario for ballet is to take a first step along the way in the path of creating a Soviet choreographic theatre." The competition called primarily for a libretto based on a contemporary revolutionary theme. Themes should be developed according to a concrete perception of reality "and not by constructing abstract dance forms loaded with symbolic or allegorical meaning." The scenario had to be for an evening-filling performance.[32]

Calling upon ballet to finally make an ideological contribution to the Soviet cultural project, the competition's terms reflected Sollertinsky's campaign for upgrading elements of realistic drama in ballet, expressed through pantomime, and downgrading classical dance, especially any form of abstract choreography. A scenario written by A. V. Ivanovsky, a cinema producer, won the competition. Shostakovich composed the music for the ballet. Several choreographers worked on it, mainly Vasily Vainonen but also Leonid Iakobson. *The Golden Age* premiered in October 1930. Set in a capitalist city at an industrial exhibition, the ballet depicts a fight between a group of Fascists and a Soviet football team. It was not a success and disappeared after one season.[33]

Stalinist Culture and the Birth of Drambalet

While Sollertinsky's call for ballet's dramatization was reflected in some initiatives taken during the cultural revolution, the true birth of drambalet took place during the deceptive calm of the early 1930s. In June 1931, Stalin gave a speech that rehabilitated bourgeois specialists, marking the end of the cultural revolution and its militant call for proletarian dominance in art. The nonparty intelligentsia was no longer attacked by organized Communist groups or condemned because of its social origins. Old professional establishments won back their previous authority and traditional artistic institutions such as the Bolshoi Theater recovered their preeminence.[34]

Respect for Russia's classics constituted an important part of the emerging Stalinist cultural orthodoxies. Writers were supposed to emulate the style of Pushkin and Tolstoy, painters the nineteenth-century wanderers, composers Tchaikovsky and Rimsky-Korsakov, and Stanislavsky became the model for theater.[35] Nicholas Timasheff explained the revival of Russian tradition in the 1930s as symptom of the regime's "great retreat" from revolutionary ideology, arguing that the Communist regime had to abandon part of its utopia and allow a partial revival of the past to ensure its political survival. According to Timasheff, the masses had not enjoyed the Communist experiments in culture. The party therefore repudiated these experiments, focusing cultural production on the gratification of popular desires while forbidding anything that could undermine the regime. Folk art was given a place of honor, while literature, painting, music, and theater were forced to return to the mid-nineteenth century.[36]

The pressures on ballet in the 1930s indicate that the mechanism of Soviet cultural evolution was more complex and contradictory than that. On the surface, the withering away of the choreographic experiments of the 1920s and the emergence of drambalet, whose multiple-act, narrative ballets superficially resembled nineteenth-century ballets, seemed to follow the pattern of the great retreat hypothesis. Drambalet with its dramatic plots and melodramatic potential was also likely to find a more receptive, grate-

FIGURE 6. Kirov legends: Tatiana Vecheslova, Natalia Dudinskaya, Nina Anisimova, and Alla Shelest on Rossi Street, 1930s. At the time, the Kirov still rehearsed on the premises of the Leningrad Choreographic Institute, occupying the building on the right. © St. Petersburg State Museum of Theater and Music

ful audience than, for example, Lopukhov's modernist experiment *Dance Symphony*.

The logic of the great retreat hypothesis would predict that Petipa, the tsar of nineteenth-classical ballet, would become the unchallenged cultural authority for ballet, and his works, the model for all new ballets, especially given his close collaboration with Tchaikovsky, a musical model of this era. In fact, something much more complicated happened, indicating the highly complex and volatile position of ballet within the Soviet cultural project at the time. Instead of retreating out of a position of weakness, as Timasheff suggests, the regime had secured a position of relative power vis-à-vis the old intelligentsia and could now use the trappings of the old civilization as a provider of cultural legitimacy to the new elites. At the same time, these symbols of old civilization were supposed to acquire a new, "red" tint. *Swan Lake* certainly formed part of the cultural canon every member of the new Soviet elite striving for *kulturnost'* was supposed to know. In Sheila Fitzpatrick's words, "the wife of a manager who was ignorant of Pushkin and had never seen *Swan Lake* was an embarrassment."[37] Stalin himself loved the ballet and saw *Swan Lake* perhaps for the thirtieth time on the eve of his stroke in 1953.[38] But even *Swan Lake* was not safe from the demands of the time for more realism in ballet. In 1933, Vaganova, who succeeded Lopukhov as artistic director of the Kirov Ballet, staged a new production of the ballet. Inspired by Maxim Gorky's novels about *The Story of a Young Man in the Nineteenth Century*, Vaganova's production of *Swan Lake* was transformed into the story of a young, melancholic man from a declining noble family who falls captive to his own romantic fantasies.[39] During the Soviet period, in the spirit of socialist realism's preference for a clear-cut victory of good over evil, the Kirov and Bolshoi's productions of *Swan Lake* replaced the ballet's original tragic-romantic ending, which united Odette and Prince Siegfried in a victory of love over evil in their afterlife, with a life-affirming victory over evil in this life.

If the emerging conventions of drambalet led to adjustments in the classics, such as the removal of pantomime scenes using the old system of conventional mime gestures and a search for psychological depth and narrative realism, after the antiformalism campaign of 1936, drambalet became the only model for new ballets permitted on the Soviet stage. As a genre, it reflected Sollertinsky's call for the dramatization of dance and rejected Petipa's model for ballet productions that combined drama and lavish stage effects with masterly composed, complex dance compositions in opulent evening-filling ballets. In Petipa's ballet, pantomimic scenes driving the plot forward alternated with long sections of pure dance divertissements, but in the 1930s

FIGURE 7. Konstantin Sergeev as Siegfried in Agrippina Vaganova's production of *Swan Lake*, first act, first scene, at the Kirov Ballet, 1936. © Mariinsky Theater

and 1940s the emerging Soviet paradigm for ballet production condemned the most important achievement of Petipa's model as mindless, empty entertainment: long, complex classical dance segments involving a large corps de ballet, soloists, and principal dancers that did not advance a narrative plot were rejected as formalism. The Soviet paradigm for new ballet productions thus in many ways directly negated the most important element of Petipa's ballets: the complex use of classical dance.

Paradoxically, in the everyday practice of the theaters and their schools, Petipa's legacy survived as a cornerstone of Russia's classical ballet heritage, but it was seriously attacked in a book that must have constituted the first attempt to write an official history of Soviet theater. In 1933, the first volume of *Istoriia sovetskogo teatra* (A history of Soviet theater) was published in Leningrad. Ivan Sollertinsky wrote a seventy-page contribution on the musical theater on the eve of October and the problems of the opera and ballet heritage during the era of war communism.[40] He offered the following verdict on Petipa's legacy:

Indeed, the feudal-court conception of theater as effective, colorful spectacle, devoid of any serious ideological commitment and intended only to know and demonstrate the splendor and magnificence of the regime (and that was its function in the class struggle), was given completely undisguised in ballet. It found its highest and last expression in the creative work of Marius Petipa. His ballet was in essence nothing but gala, multi-act choreographic divertissements, demonstrating the virtuosity of dancers and corps de ballet masses, surrounded by a sumptuous, though often garish and tasteless set. The plotline, set forth in pantomime, is only stitches carelessly superimposed on the divertissement, with the goal of giving it something at least approximating unity. However, already toward the beginning of the last act, even the semblance of a plot is cast off and the divertissement principle reveals itself in full (for example, in *Raymonda*, *The Sleeping Beauty*, and so forth).[41]

According to Sollertinsky, not just his own ballets but the entire pre-Fokine ballet repertoire had been shaped by Petipa's "principle of dilution of plot action and transferral of the accent on self-sufficing, decorative classical dance." During his reign, the evil Petipa had laid his "imperious and heavy hand" on the entire repertoire, spoiling older ballets by choreographers such as Coralli, Perrot, Saint-Léon, and Dauberval, in which the tradition of narrative, pantomimic ballet had been stronger, by adding a profusion of his own dances, drowning in dances the dramatic action that even without this had been weak.[42]

The fact that classical ballet in general and Petipa's legacy in particular survived such ideological condemnations indicates that when analyzing artistic life in Soviet Russia, it is of paramount importance to distinguish between the level of ideological rhetoric and the level of artistic practice. Despite the power of ideological pressure, artistic practice demonstrated an astonishing level of resistance, testifying to the strength of tradition. As the experience of ballet in the Soviet Union shows, the inertia of tradition could be a powerful opponent to ideological demands.

Underneath the ideological accusations hurled against Petipa's ballets as mindless divertissements representing monarchic feudalism lies the question of whether classical dance is in itself expressive or purely ornamental, a question that centered on the more general aesthetic problem concerning the specificity of different artistic media. Is classical dance as an artistic medium meaningless because its meaning cannot be verbalized? Can content be found in nonverbal, nonrepresentative art? This artistic question acquired a particular urgency in the environment of a state that was increasingly trying to use art as vehicle for expressing the verbal content of its political propaganda.

Drambalet was an attempt to make the expressive nature of ballet more verbal by applying lessons from the dramatic theater. Vladimir Paperny's hypothesis that Stalinist culture emerged as an expression of cyclical cultural processes provides an interesting structural explanation for the emergence of drambalet's monopoly. Paperny's explanation of Soviet architectural aesthetics in the 1920s and 1930s is based on the theory that certain events in Russian history can be described in terms of a cyclical process during which either "Culture One" or "Culture Two" gains ascendancy. Paperny argues that Culture Two is based on the affirmation of the word, leading to a hierarchy of the arts according to their verbal possibilities and the emulation of literature by all other arts. The antiformalism campaign of 1936 was directed against an artistic approach—"formalism"—in which the verbal content was not clear: every art form was expected to reconstruct its language in order to be able to express a verbal text.[43] If one applies Paperny's model to ballet, the agenda to dramatize dance—to limit the use of the nonrepresentational language of classical dance while emphasizing danced pantomime—can be explained as an attempt to verbalize the quintessentially nonverbal art of ballet.

Applying his model to architecture, Paperny argued that in Culture One, the periphery is more important than the center and the authorities are not really concerned with architecture. Culture Two sees a transfer of values to the center; society ossifies. The authorities look toward architecture to control the movement of the population and to express a center-based value system spatially.[44] The static quality of Stalinist ballet, drambalet, could be seen as the ultimate expression of the government's desire to control population movement. Drambalet restricted the physical, gravity-defying freedom implicit in the ultimate bodily control of classical dance with the static monumentalism of gesture.

If verbalizing the art of ballet was the goal, the close involvement of dramatic directors in this process comes as no surprise. On 1 May 1931, the well-known theater director Sergei Radlov was appointed artistic director of the former Mariinsky. In the early 1920s, Radlov and Vladimir Soloviev, former collaborators of Meyerhold, founded the Theater of Popular Comedy in Petrograd on the principles of improvization and circus routine. The involvement of an avant-garde director like Radlov in the formulation of Stalinist ballet orthodoxies indicates that the origins of these orthodoxies are more complex than the great retreat hypothesis implies, an argument put forward by Boris Groys who contends that socialist realism in art derived from the spirit of the avant-garde, taking to its logical conclusion the idea of a fusion of life and art.[45] Radlov's vision of both ballet and opera centered on the creation of synthetic performances that would break down the division of genres in the performing arts. Similar to Sollertinsky's ideas, this vision included downgrading the importance of dance and music in ballet and opera productions.[46] Until his resignation in 1934, Radlov directed three ballet productions. Two of them, *The Flames of Paris* and *The Fountain of Bakhchisarai*, are important examples of this search for a fusion of genres and the dramatization of dance.[47]

The Flames of Paris, with music by Boris Asafiev, premiered in Leningrad on 6 November 1932, celebrating the fifteenth anniversary of the revolution. The scenario of the ballet, written by Nikolai Volkov and based on a novel by Félix Gras, foreshadowed a central element of drambalet: the adaptation of literary sources. Slonimsky's history of Soviet ballet published in 1950 hailed *The Flames of Paris* as the beginning of drama's central place in ballet, as the birth of heroic ballet, as the first time character dance achieved artistic equality with classical dance. The ballet later received the Stalin Prize.[48] Set during the time of the French Revolution, it contrasts the political fervor of the people of Marseilles with the treacherous, decadent evilness of the aristocracy. It tells the story of Jeanne and Pierre, the children of a peasant living not far from Marseilles. One day, Count Geoffrey, son of the local lord of the manor, the Marquis de Beauregard, tries to force himself on Jeanne in the forest but is pushed back by her. When her father tries to defend his daughter, he is arrested. Jeanne and her brother Pierre call upon the peasants to march to the marquis's castle. The angry peasants free the marquis's captives from a prison in Marseilles and unite with an attachment of citizens in the name of the revolution. Jeanne and Pierre are among them. The second act is set in Versailles: the dancers Mireille de Poitiers and Antoine Mistral are performing a ballet. A banquet follows; the Marquis de Beauregard and his son Geoffrey are among the guests and recount the peasant uprising and the march on Marseilles. The king and the queen appear, and the officers pay their homage and write a letter to royalist émigrés in Koblenz about plans to crush the revolution. Count Geoffrey is supposed to deliver the letter. When Mistral reads the letter while the count dances with Mireille, he wants to go into hiding, but the count kills him, fearing that the secret plans might be revealed. In the meantime, the volunteers from Marseilles have arrived in Paris and join forces with other volunteers on a central square. Workers begin to fill the square, young people parade puppets of the royal couple, and this is when Mireille runs to the square, exposing the plans to crush the revolution. Courtiers and officers cross the square, Count Geoffrey among them, but Mireille demands his arrest. He is surrounded by

FIGURE 8. *Flames of Paris*, third act, at the Kirov Ballet, 1936. © Mariinsky Theater

FIGURE 9. *Flames of Paris*, fourth act, at the Kirov Ballet, 1950. © Mariinsky Theater

the revolutionary crowd and led away. The crowd sets out to storm the Tuileries to the revolutionary song "Ça ira." A battle ensues inside the castle, the Marquis once again attacks Jeanne, but her brother kills him. The people are victorious and celebrate on the Mars Field, culminating in an impassioned, wild revolutionary dance, the carmagnole.

The revolutionary masses are the undisputed hero of the ballet. Crowds storm the stage with burning torches, singing revolutionary songs and dancing passionate character (folk) dances.[49] Radlov's concept for the ballet envisioned a dramatization of dance by upgrading the role of pantomime at the cost of actual dance. Vasily Vainonen's choreography was subordinated to Radlov's dramatic conception but nonetheless included wild character dances, court dances, and a virtuoso classical pas de deux during the final revolutionary celebrations, which, tellingly, is the only element of the ballet that was performed throughout the Soviet period until today.[50]

The second ballet Radlov was involved in, *The Fountain of Bakhchisarai*, is seen as the real birth of drambalet.[51] It premiered at the Kirov on 28 September 1934. Together with Leonid Lavrovsky's *Romeo and Juliet*, the two ballets also became the crowning achievements of drambalet. Of all the ballets of the drambalet era, only these two ballets have survived until the present day. Based on Pushkin's poem, and like *Flames of Paris* with music by Asafiev, the ballet was choreographed and directed by Rostislav Zakharov, under the general artistic supervision of Radlov. Zakharov emerged as one of the chief propagators of drambalet.[52] He graduated not just from the Leningrad Choreographic Institute but also from the director's department of the Leningrad Theatrical Technikum and believed that instead of "empty" virtuoso dance, pantomime, danced pantomime, and dance saturated with acting skills should form the expressive basis of ballets. In keeping with this philosophy, he chose only those steps from the wide vocabulary of classical dance that easily lend themselves to dramatization, resulting in ballets that were primarily danced dramas and not very inventive in terms of choreography. During the preparations for *The Fountain of Bakhchisarai*, he used his training as theater director and introduced the dancers to Stanislavsky's method of character development, which had been developed for dramatic actors, asking them to do "table work" and to study Pushkin's poem and materials on the period.[53]

The ballet tells the story of Maria, a Polish princess, who is abducted by the Tartar Khan Girei during a raid on her father's castle in Poland. Girei is smitten by her beauty and takes her to his harem in his Crimean palace. Though Maria does not return his love, she arouses the jealousy of his chief wife, Zarema, who stabs her. Zarema is thrown off the palace's walls to a certain death. The devastated khan builds a fountain of tears to Maria's

FIGURE 10. Galina Ulanova rehearsing the part of Maria in *The Fountain of Bakhchisarai* at the Kirov Ballet's rehearsal studio on Rossi Street, circa 1934. © Mariinsky Theater

FIGURE 11. Ulanova as Maria, Konstantin Sergeev as Vazlav, Maria's fiancé, and the choreographer Rostislav Zakharov rehearsing the first act of *The Fountain of Bakhchisarai* at the Kirov Ballet, 1934. © St. Petersburg State Museum of Theater and Music

FIGURE 12. Rehearsal of the final act of *The Fountain of Bakhchisarai* at the Kirov Ballet, circa 1934. Olga Iordan as Zarema offers her chest to the knife of Petr Gusev as Khan Girei. Ulanova as Maria is lying dead on the floor. © Mariinsky Theater

FIGURE 13. Tatiana Vecheslova as Zarema is pushed off the walls into a certain death in *The Fountain of Bakhchisarai*, fourth act, at the Kirov Ballet, 1936. © Mariinsky Theater

memory. The ballet entranced its audiences with the dramatic acting of the dancers. Maria was one of Galina Ulanova's most famous roles, and the moment when she leaned against a column after having received the mortal blow from Zarema, slowly sliding down to the floor as life was leaving her, became an iconic moment of Soviet ballet.

The Bright Stream and the Antiformalism Campaign of 1936

In the mid-1930s, there were still challenges to the idea that ballet's future lay in its dramatization. New ballets based on the innovative use of classical dance continued to be created by Lopukhov. After his dismissal as ballet director of the former Mariinsky in 1931, following his production of Shostakovich's ballet *The Bolt*, which was condemned as lampooning Soviet reality and the working class,[54] Lopukhov was asked by the Leningrad *obkom* (*oblastnoi komitet*; regional committee) of the Communist Party to organize a second ballet company at the Maly Opera House. It was decided that it would build its repertoire on comedies.[55]

In his memoirs, Lopukhov stressed that in his comedy ballets for the Maly he paid special attention to expressing action through dance. Commenting on his opposition to drambalet in those days, Lopukhov wrote: "At this time I was already definitely convinced that attempts to replace classical dance with . . . supposedly realistic pantomime was a grave mistake. In that way you throw out the baby with the bathwater. . . . To propagate pantomimic productions in Soviet ballet means that even under the most inventive directorship it will sooner or later lead into a blind alley."[56] On 4 April 1935, Lopukhov's ballet *The Bright Stream*, with music by Shostakovich, premiered at the Maly. A comedy, the ballet is set in a kolkhoz (collective farm) in the Kuban called "The Bright Stream." A brigade of artists arrives from the capital to participate in celebrations of the kolkhoz's production success but finds itself entangled in amorous intrigues. Zina, the wife of agronomist Petr, knows the ballerina of the group well because they used to study together at the ballet school. Petr is fascinated by the ballerina, a fascination shared by an old-fashioned dacha dweller who spends his summers in the kolkhoz. The dacha dweller's wife in turn falls in love with the ballerina's dancing partner. The kolkhozniks decide to play a trick on the dacha dwellers and the agronomist: Zina dresses up as the ballerina and goes to a rendezvous with her husband, the male dancer dresses up as the ballerina and meets the dacha dweller, while the ballerina disguised as her male dancing partner meets the dacha dweller's wife. The buffoonery culminates in a mock duel between the ballerina, dressed up as her male partner, and the dacha dweller, in which the ballerina "dies." The next morning, the misunderstandings of the previous night disentangle themselves. The dacha dwellers are being ridiculed, and the agronomist asks his wife for forgiveness. The friendship of the artists and the kolkhozniks is celebrated in a holiday in honor of the successful completion of the fieldwork.[57]

In his memoirs, Lopukhov wrote that he wanted to show in danced scenes a bright, youthful celebration of contemporary Soviet life. The ballet was a public success. In the autumn of 1935, Vladimir Ivanov Mutnykh, the director of the Bolshoi Theater, invited Lopukhov to become the artistic director of the Bolshoi Ballet and to stage *The Bright Stream* at the Bolshoi, where it premiered on 30 November 1935.[58] Within a few weeks, the ballet would become the symbol of everything socialist realist ballet should avoid; Lopukhov would be forced into creative silence.

In this ballet, Lopukhov wanted to demonstrate to the cultural-political machine that there was no inherent contradiction between classical dance and realism in art. The work was a challenge to those who claimed that ballet had to be dramatized, that danced pantomime had to replace classical dance as main means of expression in ballet. The authors of the ballet, Lopukhov and co-librettist Adrian Piotrovsky, declared that "the basis of the ballet art of our days remains classical dance. . . . We strove for our ballet to be a danced ballet, that dance was the basic and most important artistic-expressive means of the production. Such a demand by no means contradicts searches for a realistic style. But the fact of the matter is that realism in ballet has to be realized with its specific means, that is, above all with the means of dance and, in particular, of classical dance."[59]

If the enlightenment of the masses was one of the cornerstones of the Soviet cultural project, in the early 1930s, the masses were sometimes supposed to educate the cultural elites in the new ways of the peasant and workers' state. In January 1935, the current director of the Bolshoi Theater, Elena Malinovskaya, was sent into retirement. She was replaced by Mutnykh, formerly the head of the Central House of the Red Army, providing him with connections to the highest military echelons. Mutnykh's appointment had an immediate effect on the theater's repertoire politics. Before Mutnykh, the theater's emphasis had been on the nineteenth-century repertoire, but the new director wanted to focus on fulfilling the persistent official demand for a new Soviet repertoire. He also significantly increased the theater's practice of consulting with the worker and peasant audience within the framework of prepremiere and postpremiere discussions of new productions.[60]

The Bolshoi invited factory workers to comment on *The Bright Stream* in a series of rehearsals held shortly before its premiere on 30 November 1935, to test the intelligibility and "realism" of the production. The response of the workers was overwhelmingly positive, even though there were some critical remarks that were to be reflected in the *Pravda* editorial: some said the ballet didn't really show life on the kolkhoz, that the costumes did not reflect what people wore in the Kuban, that the ballet did not show enough amateur performances (*samodeiatel'nost'*), and that classical dances prevailed over character dances while the opposite should be the case. Significantly, given the impending accusation that the ballet had no intelligible content, the workers not only seemed to have understood the ballet but actually praised it as the first ballet produced by the Bolshoi that workers would understand and like. The worker Rama from the factory SVARTs commented: "I'm finding myself at the ballet for only the third time in my whole life, but I have to say, that even for me—an inexperienced person—everything in this ballet was clear and understood; if you want, the happy mood of the kolkhozniks celebrating their victory was even transmitted to me." The worker Belova from the Dinamo Factory added: "On the question, does the worker audience like this ballet, I think (all those present second this unanimously), that this is, if you want, the first ballet at the Bolshoi Theater that will be understood by and be interesting for the workers; everyone will have a great desire to go to it."[61] At one of the final rehearsals attended by the workers, the worker Danilov from the Ball-bearing Factory praised the Bolshoi for having taken some of the workers' comments onboard and exclaimed: "Nineteen thousand people work at the Ball-bearing Factory, the majority of them are young. I am convinced that our workers will attend this ballet, which is the most gratifying event in the history of the Bolshoi Theater, with pleasure."[62]

The ballet also left a deep impression with a group of Don Cossacks, who were visiting the capital from 30 November until 3 December 1935. Thirty-eight of the best singers and dancers had been chosen from fourteen kolkhozes to be shown the wonders of the Soviet capital. Of the four performances they attended, *The Bright Stream* left the strongest impression, last but not least because the awed kolkhozniks found themselves in the company of Stalin himself, who was attending the performance with Politburo members Lazar Kaganovich and Anastas Mikoyan. But even Stalin's presence could not distract the Don Cossacks from the action on stage, which was supposed to reflect their own experience as Cossacks constructing and celebrating Socialist life in a kolkhoz. Holding her breath and freezing in her seat whenever the dancers on stage were executing particularly difficult steps, Khoria Marynova from the kolkhoz Hammer and Sickle wondered: "But how did these people learn to dance this way, yes, to jump like birds? . . . Do they really not have some sort of springs in their shoes?"[63]

Everything pointed toward a bright future for *The Bright Stream*. It seemed to fit perfectly into the regime's propagandistic attempts to gloss over the harsh realities of Soviet life. Stalin famously said in November 1935: "Life has become better, comrades. Life has become more jolly." It was even performed at the Bolshoi in celebration of Stalin's birthday on 21 December, a special honor as performances for this day were always carefully chosen.[64] *The Bright Stream* presented the regime with a rare chance to offer audiences an artistically interesting yet entertaining, up-lifting ballet celebrating Socialist life on the kolkhoz, but the days of this "most gratifying event in the history of the Bolshoi Theater" turned out to be numbered. On 6 February 1936, a vicious editorial in *Pravda* struck the ballet like a bolt from the sky. Published nine days after the infamous *Pravda* article "Sumbur vmesto muzyki" (Muddle instead of music) on Shostakovich's opera *Lady Macbeth of the Mtsensk District*, the article "Baletnaia fal'sh'" marks the second in a series of unsigned *Pravda* editorials condemning formalism in Soviet opera, ballet, film, and the visual arts. The articles marked the beginning of the antiformalism campaign.

Nothing in the ballet's reception until this point had signaled that there would be an attack on *The Bright Stream*. Far from being predetermined and unilinear, Soviet cultural politics were shaped by a complex interplay of different factors. The ballet had been chosen for the Bolshoi only after its successful premiere at the Maly in Leningrad in April 1935. On 2 December, *Pravda* had published a very positive review of the ballet's premiere at the Bolshoi, and Stalin attended a performance of the ballet months before the crushing *Pravda* editorial without giving any indication that he disapproved of it. One plausible explanation of the antiformalism campaign and its unexpected attack on the Bolshoi Ballet's new "Soviet calling card," *The Bright Stream*, might lie in bureaucratic politics: in December 1935, the administration of Soviet cultural politics underwent serious structural changes and a new steering body was created, the Committee on Artistic Affairs, which was now trying to flex its muscles by starting a highly publicized, vicious campaign in the arts indicating that things could not continue as they had before its creation.[65] In 1953, the committee would unite with several other bodies to form a new Soviet Ministry of Culture.

A meeting between Platon Kerzhentsev, head of the Committee on Artistic Affairs, and leading cultural figures on 14 March made clear that the editorials were general policy pronouncements from which all fields of art should draw conclusions. At the heart of the antiformalism campaign stood the question of how to represent reality and how to define and produce "realism" in Soviet art. The antiformalism campaign identified formalism and naturalism as twin enemies of socialist realism. The *Pravda* editorials juxtaposed "formalist" art, which was stylized, modern, pessimistic, inspired by the West, with art that was realistic, traditional, optimistic, and inspired by folk art, and they disseminated the following policy directives: Soviet art condemned formalism (the focus on the formal elements of an artistic medium at the expense of social content, as in Western-influenced modernism and abstraction) and naturalism (vulgarity, pornography, tastelessness). They called for a classical, life-affirming and life-celebrating art of high seriousness.[66] The campaign unfolded before the backdrop of the Great Purges, in a climate where nobody could be sure whether they would be able to sleep through the night without being arrested.

It is surprising that Western scholars have analyzed the article "Baletnaia fal'sh'" primarily as a follow-up article on "Sumbur vmesto muzyki," interpreting it as a second attack on Shostakovich.[67] The article focused on the presentation of reality in ballet and echoed an old accusation hurled against the art form by some members of Russia's progressive nineteenth-century intelligentsia and by different groups since 1917: "Ballet—this is one of our most conservative art forms. It is more difficult for it than for all others to overcome the tradition of conventionality, cultivated by the tastes of the prerevolutionary audience. The oldest of these traditions—is a doll-like, insincere [fal'shivoe] attitude toward life. In ballet, built on such traditions, it is not people that act but dolls. Their passions—are the passions of dolls. The basic difficulty of Soviet ballet consists in the fact that dolls are impossible here. They would look unbearable, they would pierce the eyes with falsity."[68] Accusing ballet of a frivolous, false attitude toward life, the article demanded that if a ballet was to present a kolkhoz, its author and choreographer had to study a kolkhoz, its people, and its customs. Instead of relying on the artificial tradition of prerevolutionary ballet, they should take folk art as inspiration: "A serious theme demands a serious attitude, great and conscientious work. The rich sources of creativity in folk songs, in folk dances, and folk games should unfold before the authors of the ballet, before the composer."[69]

The article criticized the "unrealistic" use of classical dance as the ballet's main vehicle for artistic expression, stating that the authors had vulgarized life. On stage, there was neither a kolkhoz nor the Kuban, but "there are sugary 'paysans' who have leapt down from a prerevolutionary confectioner's box, who depict 'joy' in dances that had nothing in common with the folk dances in the Kuban or of anywhere else." A realistic, folk ballet had to take folk dances and games as its basis. According to the editorial, Lopukhov's reliance on classical dance had resulted in implausible, nonsensical confusion: "In the first act, doll-like 'kolkhozniks' appear. In the other acts any signs of such a, if one may say so, kolkhoz disappear. There is no intelligent content. Ballet dancers execute numbers between which there is no connection. Some people in clothes that have nothing in common with the clothes of the Kuban Cossacks jump on the stage, raving. Ballet nonsense in the foulest sense of the word reigns on stage. Under the pretence of a kolkhoz ballet, an unnatural mixture of false-folk dances with numbers of dancers in tutus is presented."[70] Contrary to the status of this editorial in Western literature as a follow-up attack on Shostakovich, only its last substantive paragraph talks about his music. It states that while it was simpler and less strange than the music of *Lady Macbeth*, it shared the librettist's and choreographer's devil-may-care attitude toward the Kuban's folk art.

In sum, the article called, in no uncertain terms, for realism in ballet by basing productions on a conscientious observation of reality adapted for the stage. The editorial branded the ballet's use of classical dance and the "inauthentic" character dances as formalism. Readers of the article could infer the following: reality and Soviet artistic realism do not include classical dance but include folk dance, which should become a major source of inspiration for the ballet theater. The article did not mention danced pantomime, but since it insinuated that classical dance was meaningless, the article was compatible with drambalet's aim to base choreography on something supposedly closer to the way people moved in reality than virtuoso classical dance, namely danced pantomime fused with elements of classical dance.

As a result of the antiformalism campaign, the debate on whether classical dance was an empty ornament or a nonrepresentational, highly expressive artistic medium akin to music was aborted. In a statement by the Bolshoi's director, Vladimir Mutnykh, the theater's leadership concluded that ballet's main shortcoming lay in its focus on pure classical dance at the expense of closer ties with the dramatic theater and folk dance: "You know the general evaluation of ballet. The evaluation given to ballet is very serious. *Pravda* gave the decision that out of all art forms, ballet is one of the most conservative art forms and that in this respect it significantly lags behind all art forms. What is the shortcoming of our ballet? The shortcoming of ballet lies in the fact that it rested on pure classical dance, it was cut off from the dramatic theater. The ballet actor doesn't think about his dramatic performance, and secondly, ballet is also cut off from folk dance."[71] The *Pravda* editorial exerted serious pressures on the ballet community. According to Yuri Faier, the legendary conductor of the Bolshoi Ballet: "The publication of the article about *The Bright Stream* had serious consequences for the art of ballet as a whole. . . . The desire of the authors to find new possibilities of classical dance in the embodiment of today's reality were sacrificed to a one-sided, narrow understanding of the plausibility of what was happening on stage, about the narodnost' of the musical and dance sources." A narrow understanding of realism left little place for the specific conventions of the genre and "the demand that the art of ballet should be plausible was turned into a prohibition for searches for new artistic forms, for the diverse use of the means of dance expression."[72]

The editorial reflected to a significant degree the view on classical dance propagated by some intellectuals in the 1920s. Nevertheless, for some members of the intellectual avant-garde, the editorial's criticism of classical ballet didn't go far enough. According to a secret People's Commissariat for Internal Affairs (NKVD) report on responses of the artistic intelligentsia to the *Pravda* articles, the director Vsevolod Meyerhold reportedly said that "the article 'Baletnaia fal'sh' isn't named correctly—it should be named 'Balet-fal'sh' [Ballet-Falsity]. This is an artificial [fal'shivoe] art, on stage the kolkhozniks in *The Bright Stream* look just as artificial as the sailors in *The Red Poppy*. One has to let amateur [samodeiatel'noe] art out on stage and not show a kolkhoznik in a tutu and with little wings."[73] It is ironic that even though Meyerhold supported the attack against ballet within the context of the antiformalism campaign, he himself was a hidden target of the campaign.[74] Even more ironically, Sollertinsky, intellectual architect of the program for dramatizing dance, was a victim of the antiformalism campaign in music.

Even if there was no explicit ban on classical dance, ballet professionals had to interpret the article as an ominous warning against using too much classical dance in new ballet productions. In the new ballets staged in the wake of the antiformalism campaign, danced pantomime, a limited selection of classical dance's rich vocabulary, and character dance became the main means of artistic expression, even if many drambalet productions included at least one virtuoso classical pas de deux that was justified dramatically, for example, by a celebration. By providing a basis for librettos, classical literature was supposed to replace ballet's "frivolity" with high-minded seriousness. Literary works by writers such as Pushkin, Gogol, and Shakespeare and contemporary propaganda topics—especially plots glorifying the freedom struggle of Soviet nationalities—became the libretto source of choice. Ballets on different nationalities in the Soviet Union provided a plausible excuse for using folk dance as inspiration and fulfilled the requirement of narodnost', contributing to the government's propaganda goal of creating a an image of brotherhood between the different nationalities.

At the Kirov, the first new ballet staged after the *Pravda* editorial was Zakharov's adaptation of Balzac's novel *Lost Illusions*.[75] The ballet took its "fear of dancing" so far that it seems to have consisted primarily of hardly intelligible pantomime.[76] In 1937, *Partisan Days*, by Vainonen, premiered at the Kirov. Based on pantomime and character dances and set in the area surrounding a Cossack village shaken by the struggle among Cossacks, partisans, and White Guards during the civil war period, the ballet revolved around a love triangle between a Cossack girl, her evil, rich Cossack fiancé, and a noble Bolshevik partisan. Probably fearful of repeating the mistake of *The Bright Stream,* Vainonen traveled to the North Caucasus to study folk dances on location, reproducing the original dances for the stage.

The increasingly rich use of folk dance–inspired choreography meant that ballets of the drambalet era could still be rich in dance, even though the use of classical dance had become more restricted. In 1938, the Kirov saw the premiere of Vakhtang Chabukiani's ballet *Heart of the Mountain*, a tragic love story between a knight's daughter and a simple peasant set in eighteenth-century Georgia before the backdrop of a peasant uprising against feudalism. Chabukiani, a native Georgian, drew his choreographic inspiration from Caucasian national dances. Unlike many other ballets of this period, the ballet relied primarily on dance to express the action, not on pantomime. In 1939, another ballet by Chabukiani premiered at the Kirov, *Laurencia*, based on an adaptation of a play by Lope de Vega. Like *Heart of the Mountain*, the ballet was unusually rich in dance compared to other productions of that period and incorporated many elements of Spanish dance. The ballet celebrates the brave Spanish peasant girl Laurencia, whose love, the peasant Frondoso, is mercilessly pursued by the Komandor, the local master, who wants Laurencia for his own enjoyment. At the ballet's climax, Laurencia incites the peasants to rise against their lord, who has thrown Frondoso into prison. Her fiancé is freed and kills the local tyrant, whose castle goes up in flames. In 1940, Lavrovsky's *Romeo and Juliet* premiered at the Kirov,[77] the most important ballet of the period and the biggest achievement of drambalet.[78]

During these years, the Bolshoi created fewer and fewer new ballets. According to both Faier and the dancer and pedagogue Asaf Messerer, one of the consequences of the article "Baletnaia fal'sh'" for the Bolshoi Ballet was the end of in-house experimentation: it was more and more often repeated at the artistic council and at meetings that the Bolshoi was an "exemplary" theater that should only show the best productions that had been tested by other theaters. This left no place for experimentation. The theater imported one ballet production from Leningrad after another.[79] The only "homegrown" ballet productions in these years were by the Leningrad choreographer Zakharov, who moved to the Bolshoi in 1938 and primarily created works based on Russian nineteenth-century literature for the theater, such as *The Prisoner of the Caucasus* (1938, based on Pushkin to music by Asafiev), *Taras Bulba* (1941, based on Nikolai Gogol to music by Vasily Soloviev-Sedoi), and *Mistress into Maid* (1946, based on Pushkin to music by Reinhold Glière). For the Bolshoi, he also choreographed the first production of Prokofiev's *Cinderella* (1945).

Drambalet undoubtedly made many positive contributions to the development of ballet by increasing the narrative coherence of ballet productions:

the dramatic logic of nineteenth-century ballets had sometimes been poor, resulting in convoluted plots that were difficult to follow. An increased focus on a ballet's dramatic conception, and the close collaboration of librettist, choreographer, composer, and set designer, potentially increased the work's artistic coherence. The emphasis on psychological development in the ballet artists' creation of their parts deepened the psychological aspect of ballet and developed the dancers' acting skills. The overall potential of drambalet as a viable form of choreographic theater, however, turned out to be limited. The demands of socialist realism put into question the specificity and uniqueness of classical dance as an artistic medium. By the late Stalinist period, the preoccupation of drambalet with narrative plausibility ran the risk of negating the essence of ballet as a unique artistic medium relying on complex classical dance as its main means of artistic expression. The path of drambalet turned out to be a blind alley.

The ascent of the genre of drambalet resulted from a combination of different but interlinked currents in the debate on the role of ballet in Soviet culture. Intellectuals like Sollertinsky and, to an even greater extent, members of the artistic avant-garde like Meyerhold criticized classical dance as frivolous, meaningless art incapable of expressing serious ideas. These accusations reflected a tradition within the Russian prerevolutionary intelligentsia that culture needed to go beyond being a goal in itself, that instead of celebrating *l'art pour l'art*, art was entrusted with the responsibility of philosophical, social, and political comment. In addition, artistic theories on a synthesis of genres reflecting Wagner's philosophy of the Gesamtkunstwerk influenced the thinking of many artists working in the theaters.

Politically, the Soviet cultural project reflected a view of art as a key agent of social transformation. Increasingly, the government demanded the creation of ballets on contemporary themes. The regime appreciated the propaganda potential of art, but political propaganda has a verbal message. From the point of view of some intellectuals and the government, it was seen as paramount to increase ballet's capacity to express verbal content. This required the development of an artistic method in ballet that could express verbal content in an easily comprehensible way. In a multilayered process of interaction, philosophical ideas and the propagandistic doctrine of socialist realism resulted in a pressure field that led to the emergence of the genre of drambalet as the paradigm for new Soviet ballet productions. The conclusion was reached that dance had to be dramatized; the full choreographic use of the complex, quasi-abstract vocabulary of classical dance became increasingly limited by the "realist" conventions of the genre.

Ballet professionals constituted of course a major force in this complex triangle of politics, intellectual ideas, and art. The tension between ballet's narrative potential and the nonrepresentational nature of classical dance had been reflected in debates about ballet reform since the eighteenth century. The idea of increasing the dramatic content of ballet productions was anything but alien to Russian ballet. Aleksandr Gorsky, the great reformer who led the Bolshoi Ballet out of a prolonged crisis in the early twentieth century, had already applied Stanislavsky's staging methods to his ballet productions at that time, emphasizing the dramatic content and the responsibility of every dancer on stage to act in character, two points that were also very important to Fokine. But the choreographic experiments of choreographers like Lopukhov show that there was also a strong movement away from dramatic narration to more symbolic or allegorical abstraction in Russian ballet. One can discern a straight line from Petipa and Ivanov, who composed long sequences of pure dance, to Mikhail Fokine's nonnarrative, musically based ballets such as *Les Sylphides*, to Lopukhov and George Balanchine.

The paradoxical situation of ballet in the Stalinist era illustrates the intricate web of interests and the complex mechanisms of interaction between different forces shaping cultural politics and production in the Soviet Union. The contrast between the rich choreographic language of classical ballets such as *Swan Lake*, which formed part of Russia's revered cultural heritage and revealed the new heights classical ballet training achieved in the Soviet Union under Agrippina Vaganova from the 1920s until the 1950s, and the impoverished choreographic language of drambalet shows that different processes were shaping the evolution of Soviet culture at the same time, sometimes leading to paradoxical outcomes. From the 1930s onward, the regime adopted Russia's nineteenth-century cultural heritage as a symbol of its high level of culture, a provider of cultural legitimacy to the regime. The acquisition of culture became an important goal of the new Soviet elites, the Bolshoi Theater became a symbol of the Soviet Union's status in the public imagination, and political leaders frequented the ballet. But despite the overall elevation of the status of ballet and the regular performance of a nineteenth-century classic like *Swan Lake*, other forces led to the emergence of a Soviet paradigm for ballet productions that diametrically contradicted the artistic essence of Petipa's ballets: the complex use of classical dance. After Stalin's death in 1953, dancers and choreographers would start to openly rebel against the dogmas of drambalet.

3🕭 *Art versus Politics*

The Kirov's Artistic Council, 1950s–1960s

> If I think that tonight I have to watch *Swan Lake* again, I feel sick. It's a wonderful ballet, but there is a limit to everything. . . . At night, I dream of white tutus alternating with tanks.
>
> —NIKITA KHRUSHCHEV IN A CONVERSATION
> WITH MAYA PLISETSKAYA

BY THE 1950S, the former imperial ballet had metamorphosed into an intrinsic part of the official pantheon of Soviet achievements. In his memoirs and at a speech given in Los Angeles in September 1959, Nikita Khrushchev reminisced about his generation's meteoric rise from uncouth ignorance to supreme power. During the bloody civil war that pitted defenders of the old order against Bolsheviks in the immediate aftermath of the October Revolution, Khrushchev was mobilized into the Red Army. On one occasion, he was housed with an intelligentsia family. One day, the lady of the house, a graduate of a school for daughters of the nobility, said "very bravely" to him, "'now that you Communists have seized power, you'll trample our culture into the dirt. You can't possibly appreciate a fragile art like the ballet.' She was right. We didn't know the first thing about ballet. When we saw postcards of ballerinas, we thought they were simply photographs of women wearing indecent costumes." Conceding that he and his Red Army comrades were "uncouth, uneducated workers," he stressed that they "wanted to receive an education, . . . wanted to learn how to govern a state and to construct a new society." He retorted to his hostess: "Just you wait, we will have everything including ballet."[1] A few decades later, Khrushchev's prophesy had not only fulfilled itself—at least with respect to ballet—but returned to haunt the prophet, who found himself watching *Swan Lake* more often than he would ever have imagined.

With the onset of the Cold War, another dimension was added to the Soviet cultural project: Soviet cultural achievements were enlisted to demonstrate to the West the superiority of the Soviet system as a whole. In a quest for cultural legitimacy, the Soviet ballet was shown off to foreign leaders and nations, and famous dancers rubbed shoulders with heads of state at official receptions. During the Thaw, foreign heads of state began to visit Moscow more and more frequently. The Bolshoi ballerina Maya Plisetskaya sarcastically remembers that:

> They were all taken to the Bolshoi to the ballet. And almost always—
> *Swan Lake*. . . . Khrushchev was always with the high guests in the
> loge. Nikita Sergeevich had seen *Swan Lake* so many times that he was
> sick of it. Toward the end of his reign, he complained to me at one of
> the receptions: "If I think that tonight I have to watch *Swan Lake* again,
> I feel sick. It's a wonderful ballet, but there is a limit to everything.
> After that, at night, I dream of white tutus alternating with tanks."[2]

In the 1950s and 1960s, the Soviet cultural project continued to combine the active promotion of high culture with demands that art contribute to shaping its population's Socialist conscience. What was the reality behind the glamorous propaganda picture of dancers gracefully greeting foreign notaries? Given the unusually close relationship between the Kirov and Bolshoi Ballet companies and Soviet power,[3] to what extent did politics infiltrate the daily artistic life of the companies?

The impact of the Soviet cultural project on ballet in the 1950s and 1960s was complex. On the one hand, the ballet companies benefited from a state policy that actively promoted high culture as a core value of Soviet civilization. On the other hand, political-ideological demands whose implementation was usually overseen by bureaucratic mediocrities limited artistic autonomy in a key area of cultural life, the formation of a theater's repertoire. But while the relationship between the Soviet regime and the Kirov and Bolshoi Ballet companies was in many ways one of dependence of the latter on the former, the state never succeeded in fully subjugating the artistic spirit of the ballet companies to its will. Loyalty was often simply nothing more than pragmatic accommodation to the system. Many artists compartmentalized between official demands that they had but little choice to fulfill and the artistic work they really cared about. This mindset provided a fertile ground for attempts to manipulate and renegotiate the tight system of ideological control imposed on the theaters.

Ballet and the Soviet Cultural Project, 1957

Despite ballet's uncertain future after the October Revolution, by the mid-1950s, it had secured an unusually central role in Soviet society and culture, especially in comparison to Western countries. Even in post-Soviet Russia, where state support for ballet has decreased, ballet continues to be an object of national pride, a symbol of Russian high culture whose iconic popularity is transmitted into Russian popular culture, where ballet is used for advertising products ranging from the national airline Aeroflot to chocolate and where pulp fiction has ballerina heroines.

By the late 1950s, reflecting its general attitude toward culture, the Soviet regime hoped to co-opt the ballet companies of the Kirov and Bolshoi for two purposes, offering strong state support in return. First, the regime looked to the ballet companies for providing cultural legitimacy by offering a continuum with the cultural glories of Russia's imperial past. Second, it tried to use the popularity of ballet for regime consolidation, urging the ballet companies to contribute to the Soviet cultural project by creating ballets on Soviet life and topics. The regime hoped that the celebrated Russian ballet could be used to educate and shape a New Soviet Man.

A decree issued by the USSR minister of culture on 31 December 1957, "O merakh po dal'neishemy razvitiiu sovetskogo baletnogo iskusstva" (On measures for the further development of Soviet ballet art), illustrates the complex relationship between officially sanctioned privilege and political tutelage characterizing ballet's position, vividly exposing the regime's central ideological concern vis-à-vis ballet: to use it as a propaganda tool through the creation of popular ballets on contemporary Soviet topics.[4] But year after year, the Kirov and Bolshoi Ballet companies failed to provide the desired successful propaganda ballets.

At the same time, the decree also identifies concrete measures to popularize ballet as an art form. The official attention lavished on ballet in the Soviet Union was thus a double-edged sword: it impeded the organic evolution of ballet by seeking to control the theaters' repertoire, yet government support for the popularization of ballet helped to make it one of the most popular art forms in the Soviet Union. In prerevolutionary Russia, the Mariinsky and the Bolshoi and their schools were the only state-funded public ballet theaters and schools; by 1947, there were thirty-one state opera and ballet theaters and fifteen state choreographic institutes (state ballet schools) across the Soviet Union. Eleven of the opera and ballet theaters were located in the Russian Soviet Federative Socialist Republic (RSFSR).[5]

The political value of cultural continuity is one of the themes implicit in the decree of 1957. Far from fulfilling the artistic avant-garde's iconoclastic dreams of creating a radically new culture, the Soviet state had retreated from the artistic experiments of the 1920s to a canonization of nineteenth-century culture. Its domestic cultural policy of popularizing Russia's nineteenth-century cultural achievements also served as an international political tool. In its competition with the West, the Soviet regime claimed time and again that the October Revolution had turned the Soviet masses into the most well-read, cultured people in the world.

The decree of 1957 started with praising Soviet ballet for continuing and developing the realistic traditions of the best masters of the Russian prerevolutionary ballet.[6] It implied that this continuity lay in Soviet ballet's content-rich dramaturgy and vivid performance style. The regime was creating its own historical fiction in this statement, illustrating the tensions underlying the uneasy marriage of cultural continuity and Soviet cultural ideology in the twin battle for cultural legitimacy and social reconstruction: even though there was a prerevolutionary Russian tradition of ballet reformers like Fokine and Gorsky, the greatest master of the Russian prerevolutionary ballet was a Frenchman, Marius Petipa, and realistic plot development was not his main concern.

Emphasizing and promoting Russia's great cultural legacy was only one aspect of the Soviet cultural project. Using this cultural legacy for consolidating and expanding Soviet power was arguably even more important from the regime's point of view. Consequently, the decree on the development of Soviet ballet focused on the state's desire to use ballet for propaganda. It emphasized that there were vital shortcomings in the creation of new Soviet ballet productions, reprimanding theater management and artistic directors of ballet companies for not attracting composers and writers to work on ballets dedicated to topics of contemporary Soviet life.[7]

Apparently, the regime realized that propaganda ballets would not inspire the population unless they were enjoyable to watch. It openly acknowledged that both the music and choreography of several ballets on contemporary topics were inferior to Russian classical ballets. The decree ordered all ballet theaters to include at least one new ballet "on a contemporary or historical topic from the life of the Soviet peoples" in their annual plans. In the Kirov's copy of this decree, this sentence is underlined by hand. The decree also prescribed several measures to stimulate the production of ballets on contemporary Soviet topics. For example, it ordered a public demonstration of the best ballets on contemporary themes in Moscow and the capitals of the union republics to be held in 1958–1959. Moreover, the ministries of culture and autonomous republics were told to allot to their theaters the funds necessary for concluding agreements with authors of new ballets, and the creation of new concert numbers and programs was ordered.[8]

Government pressure on the ballet companies to create ballets on contemporary Soviet topics was by no means new. Echoing the libretto competition held by the Kirov in 1928–1929, the decree of 1957 called for conducting a libretto competition for ballets, choreographic suites, and individual numbers on contemporary topics to be held in 1958. The competition was supposed to be organized in cooperation with the USSR Composers' and Writers' Union,[9] who, together with the Ministry of Culture's department for musical institutions, were to work out the conditions for the competition and the membership of the jury.

The decree enumerated several other measures to promote the production of Soviet ballets. For example, it ordered the department of musical institutions to send an annotated list of recommendations to opera and ballet theaters, listing Soviet ballets that were successfully running in Soviet theaters, and to ensure access to sheet music and recordings of the music of these ballets. It asked to inform theaters systematically about the most interesting ballets running in Soviet republics, in the "peoples' democracies" of the Communist bloc, and in foreign theaters and ordered theater directors to cooperate with the Composers' and Writers' Union in organizing a meeting to discuss problems in the further development of Soviet ballet art to be held in April 1958.

Significantly, the decree did not stop at commanding more ballets on contemporary Soviet topics. Almost half of the decree focused on measures to increase the popularity of ballet and to improve research on ballet and ballet criticism, illustrating that the Soviet regime's close involvement in culture was by no means always negative from the artists' point of view. Recommending ballet films as one of the most important means for popularizing ballet, the decree declared that the best ballet productions—especially by Soviet authors—needed to be put on screen and ordered specific actions: at least two ballet films with the participation of the greatest dancers were to be filmed in 1958; in 1958, the Kirov's *The Sleeping Beauty* and the Soviet ballet *The Red Poppy* with dancers from the Bolshoi were to be filmed; the ministries of culture of union republics and the Department for Film Production of the USSR Ministry of Culture were to ensure the wide dissemination of news on Soviet ballet in the cinematic journal *Iskusstvo* and similar programs; in 1958–1959, the Department for Film Production was to create two educational films on ballet based on the Moscow and Leningrad Choreographic Institutes (the schools of the Bolshoi and Kirov Ballet companies); the Department for Screen-Adaptation and Film Distribution and cultural bodies in the provinces were asked to ensure that the film ballets *Romeo and Juliet* and *Swan Lake* were shown more widely. The decree also touched on issues ranging from improving research and theoretical work on ballet, including the translation of foreign books on ballet, to improving the material base of choreographic institutes and increasing publications about ballet, chastising the journals *Teatr, Sovetskaia Muzyka*, and the paper *Sovetskaia kul'tura* for not paying enough attention to the problems of Soviet ballet.[10]

The mere existence of this detailed decree and its central points concerning the creation of ballets on contemporary Soviet topics and the popularization of ballet indicate the important place the art form occupied in the Soviet cultural project, leading to a very close relationship between Soviet power and ballet. The Bolshoi in particular became the quasi court theater of the Kremlin, creating an unusually close relationship between the fields of politics and ballet. Strong official support was hardly done in the name of a disinterested passion for the arts. The regime considered it politically advantageous to promote ballet because it was a major Russian cultural achievement with propaganda potential. The splendors of the Russian ballet were to be used for the aggrandizement and legitimization of the Soviet regime itself, reflecting the age-old use of art as glorification of a specific political order.

The Kirov's Artistic Council in the 1950s and 1960s

What did the close relationship between ballet and Soviet power mean in practical terms? To what extent did politics encroach on the daily artistic life of the Kirov and Bolshoi Ballet companies? Politics seeped into the theaters' life in many ways, ranging from the overarching cultural orthodoxies circumscribing the parameters of the artistically possible to vetting by the KGB-controlled personnel department and the existence of party and Komsomol (Communist Union of Youth) organizations within the theaters. Artists were elected to soviets and went on uncomfortable journeys to perform in collective farms in the distant provinces. It is questionable how much dancers enjoyed performing in front of slurping and burping party officials, but famous dancers could sometimes ask their political acquaintances for powerful patronage in artistic questions. Tours abroad offered a golden chance to travel beyond the Iron Curtain. The main financial beneficiary of foreign tours, however, was the Soviet state.

The working conditions at the Kirov and Bolshoi Ballet companies were similar, but the regime's approach toward the theaters differed. Throughout the Soviet period, the regime actively promoted the Bolshoi as the Soviet Union's premiere opera house, moving dancers such as Marina Semenova and Galina Ulanova from Leningrad to Moscow. Reflecting the regime's suspicious attitude toward Leningrad as a potential rival of Moscow and everything Moscow stood for, the Kirov was officially pushed into second place. Maybe this distance from the core of power contributed to the fact that the Kirov, and not the Bolshoi, emerged as the center for choreographic innovation during the late 1950s and early 1960s, providing a forum for a young Yuri Grigorovich and choreographers like Igor' Bel'sky and Leonid Iakobson.

Until the move of the Leningrader Grigorovich to Moscow, the Kirov contributed more to Soviet choreography than the Bolshoi, continuing the city's historical legacy as Russia's ballet capital. While choreographers like Gorsky and Goleizovsky worked at the Bolshoi in the 1920s, Leningrad had Lopukhov, and the most successful ballets of the *drambalet* era, such as Lavrovsky's *Romeo and Juliet* and Zakharov's *The Fountain of Bakhchisarai*, were created at the Kirov. Predictably, both Lavrovsky and Zakharov moved to Moscow, but the ballets they had created for the Kirov remained their most lasting creations. In their memoirs, Bolshoi dancers complained about the dominance of the "Leningraders" in their company in the 1930s. Despite these differences, both theaters were subjected to the same tight political oversight. The artistic councils of both theaters faced similar artistic and political dilemmas; the experience of the Kirov's artistic council can therefore serve as a general example of the conflict between art and politics in the world of Soviet ballet.

A theater's life revolves around the staging of productions. The state's insistent clamor for more ballets on contemporary Soviet themes offers one of the most illuminating examples of the relationship between Soviet power and ballet and the regime's direct infringement on a theater's crucial prerogative to decide its own repertoire. Repertoire plans had to be approved by the Ministry of Culture, a theater's general director was a political appointee answerable to the authorities, representatives of either the Ministry of Culture or other government or party bodies were gray eminences at discussions whether or not new productions could be released to the public, and so forth. The persistently low number of ballets on contemporary Soviet themes and the comparatively short stage life of most of them indicate, however, that even though formally the theaters had no artistic autonomy from the Soviet regime because repertoire decisions were contingent on political approval, the state never managed to fully control the artistic spirit of the Kirov and Bolshoi Ballet companies.

The Kirov, for example, tried to dutifully fulfill the government's command for one new Soviet ballet per year, but, far from expressing active support for the regime by enthusiastically creating propaganda ballets, this task was primarily an ideological obstacle that had to be surmounted to enable the company to focus on its "real" work, such as the meticulous nurturing of its prerevolutionary artistic heritage. The Kirov thus managed to preserve artistic norms that were autonomous of the political-ideological desires of the regime by compartmentalizing its work.

While many important artistic questions concerning the ballet company were decided behind closed doors, in unreported discussions and telephone calls, the artistic council of the Kirov occupied a central role in the formulation of the theater's repertoire politics, given its official status as final arbiter of artistic questions. As its discussions were recorded in detailed minutes, it provides an important window into the inner workings of the Kirov's artistic life.

In early 1955, the Ministry of Culture tried to use the artistic councils within Soviet theaters to reinvigorate the Soviet Union's theatrical landscape, which had fallen into a creative stupor in the late Stalinist period. The theaters were ordered to widen the membership of artistic councils from a small group of artistic leaders within the theaters, such as the director, principal conductor, principal director, and the artistic director of the ballet company, to a much larger body offering wider representation of the theaters' artists. By widening the artistic councils' membership, the new regulations reflected a more general trend in the country toward replacing one-man fiefdoms in all areas with more collective leadership.

The Kirov's new artistic council was confirmed by the Ministry of Culture on 21 July 1955. Comprising twenty-eight members, it consisted of the theater's director (chairman of the council), its principal conductor (deputy chairman), its principal (stage) director (*rezhisser*) (deputy chairman), its principal designer, the artistic director of the ballet, the chief choirmaster, the concertmaster, the chairman of the theater's trade union (a musician from the orchestra), the secretary of the theater's party organization (a soloist opera singer), the head of the set design and production department, six soloist opera singers, five soloists from the ballet company, one corps de ballet dancer, one artist of the orchestra, and one member of the choir. It also included several people who were not working at the theater, namely two art historians (A. N. Dmitriev and Iu. V. Kelgyn), the ballet historian and librettist Yuri Slonimsky who was also a member of the Writers' Union, and the popular composer Vasily Solov'ev-Sedoi.[11] Apart from one dancer of the corps, the representatives of the ballet company were well-known representatives of the older generation and consisted of the company's artistic director Fedor Lopukhov, the former ballerina Tatiana Vecheslova, the character dancer Nina Anisimova, the leading male dancer Konstantin Sergeev, and Natalia Dudinskaya, Sergeev's wife and dance partner.

It is not clear how the membership of the council was decided at this

point, but a decree issued by the USSR minister of culture on 13 December
1956 revoked the system in place and prescribed the annual election of the
council's members "from the numbers of the most authoritative members of
the collective" at the beginning of each theatrical season at a general meeting of the theater's "creative workers." If a theater chose to, the elections
could be by secret ballot. In addition to the elected members, the director
of the theater, its principal conductor, principal director, and the ballet company's artistic director would automatically become members of the artistic
council. "Representatives of the public and cultural figures" could also be
elected. "In the interest of widening the initiatives of creative collectives,"
the decree left it to the theaters to decide the specifics of implementing the
decree, "taking into account the peculiarities and traditions of the given theater, on the basis of the standard regulations." Similarly, the decree gave theater leadership the right to decide independently how to assign the yearly
allocation by the state to individual productions.[12]

On 21 March 1957 a general meeting of the "creative collective" of the
Kirov—the theater's singers, dancers, musicians, and its mime ensemble—
met to decide how to implement the decree. Out of 554 artists, 420 were
present. It was decided to conduct elections to the artistic council by secret
ballot.[13] As long as members of the artistic council were elected, voting
seems indeed to have been secret. A report on elections to the Kirov's artistic council held in October and November 1958 states that the ballet had

FIGURE 14. A general meeting of the Kirov Theater, 1950. © Mariinsky Theater

elected only three members because all other candidates did not receive the necessary number of votes, even though three meetings had been dedicated to this question.[14] At the same time, membership of the council was subject to final approval by the Ministry of Culture and thus politically controlled.

Since each artistic ensemble within the theater elected its own representatives, representatives of the ballet company were elected by the dancers only. In addition to the four automatic members (theater director, principal conductor, principal director, artistic director of the ballet), the council would have twenty-two members (six representatives from the opera, seven from the ballet, five from the orchestra, three from the chorus, and one from the mime ensemble). The meeting rejected the Ministry of Culture's suggestion to elect "representatives of the public and cultural figures" to the artistic council as "the practical work of previous members of artistic councils had shown their weak interest and participation in the work of the artistic council."[15]

This by no means meant that the theater managed to exclude "outsiders," namely officials, from its debates. The management of the theater was expressly given the right to invite "representatives of the public and cultural figures" to meetings of the artistic council to discuss important creative questions.[16] "Representatives of the public" in this case probably referred primarily to representatives of party and government. Before a new production was released, it was shown to the artistic council at the so-called *priem* (reception) or *prosmotr* (viewing; examination), where it was decided whether or not the production was artistically and politically ready to be shown to the public. Representatives of the Department of Culture of the Executive Committee of the Leningrad City Soviet, of bodies such as the city or oblast committee of the Communist Party of the Soviet Union (CPSU), or of the Ministry of Culture were usually present at the prosmotr of new productions. A report on elections to the artistic council elected in October and November 1958 shows that the secretary of the party bureau and the chairman of the theater's trade union committee were also automatic members of the artistic council, joining it without election.

Membership rules changed slightly during the period discussed here. In the early 1960s, members were no longer elected but appointed. For the first time in years, the membership of the Kirov's artistic council confirmed by the RSFSR Ministry of Culture on 2 January 1961 also included members from outside the theater, namely two representatives of the Leningrad branch of the Composers' Union (the composer Solov'ev-Sedoi and the musicologist Druskin).[17]

Presided over by the theater's director, the Kirov's artistic council was supposed to look into all basic creative questions and into certain organi-

FIGURE 15. Artistic Council of the Kirov Theater, 1968. From left to right: Petr Rachinsky (general director), Roman Tikhomirov (principal stage director), Konstantin Sergeev (artistic director, ballet), Ivan Sevast'ianov (principal designer), Konstantin Simeonov (principal conductor), and Aleksandr Murin (choirmaster).
© Mariinsky Theater

zational questions such as evaluating the qualification of artists, hiring new artists, and retiring old ones. A report by the Kirov's artistic council about its work in 1957–1958 stressed the council's focus on artistic questions, stating that management decided organizational questions on its own, turning to the artistic council only in extreme cases.[18] Most importantly, under the chairmanship of the theater's director, the artistic council decided the fate of new productions. Without the artistic council's approval, a proposal for a new production could not enter the rehearsal stage, and all aspects of new productions were subjected to the scrutiny of the artistic council throughout the rehearsal process. Without the artistic council's agreement, no production would be released to the public.

Formally, the artistic council played a consultative role.[19] Ultimate authority lay with the theater's director, a political watchdog who reported directly to the Ministry of Culture. The decree of 1956 on artistic councils reflected this hierarchy: it stated that taking into account the opinion of the creative collective and of the artistic council, the director of the theater had the right to confirm repertoire plans, to decide whether new productions were ready to be released, to determine expenses, to confirm estimates for each production within the limits of annual allocations, and to decide personnel issues.[20] But even though the theater's director possessed such decision-making powers, the role of the artistic council should not be underestimated. Within the theater's management, artistic expertise and authority rested within this body.

Artistic Repossession and the Artistic Council

Since the chair of the artistic council, the Kirov's director, was primarily a political administrator who reported to the political organs in charge of the Kirov, namely the Ministry of Culture of the RSFSR,[21] the framework for discussions held by the artistic council was by definition political. At the same time, the artistic council included some of the theater's most authoritative artistic voices. There was therefore an inherent tension between the council's function as a body providing political oversight over the theater's work, personified in more political members of the council such as the theater's director and the secretary of the theater's party bureau, and its important artistic role. As a consequence, one needs to read between the lines of the council's minutes to discern the true meaning of statements made during discussions, gaining fascinating insights into the multiple layers of meaning astute Soviet artists managed to infuse into their words. In this climate, an overtly straightforward debate on whether or not the Kirov should show the ballet *La Bayadère* on a visit to Moscow reveals complex layers of intention, where ostensibly ideologically orthodox opinions are in reality acts of artistic repossession shielding the potentially ideologically subversive legacy of St. Petersburg/Leningrad's prerevolutionary ballet heritage from Moscow's gaze.

Who were the representatives of the ballet company on the artistic council? While the membership varied slightly over the years, Konstantin Sergeev and his wife, Natalia Dudinskaya, were permanent fixtures. Sergeev and Dudinskaya were the gray eminences of the Kirov Ballet, even during the short period when Sergeev was not its artistic director.[22] They belonged to the same legendary generation of Kirov dancers as Galina Ulanova and Vakhtang Chabukiani, who had enchanted audiences during the Stalinist period. In the 1950s and 1960s, both combined a deep respect for St. Petersburg's classical ballet tradition with an innate hostility and suspicion toward innovation. Natalia Makarova's verdict on Sergeev is fairly typical:

> The artistic policy in the Kirov was formed under the strong dictatorship of Konstantin Sergeyev. At the beginning of the sixties it became a sort of patrimonial estate, and he ruled over it as a great landowner.
> . . . From the time Sergeyev became the main choreographer at the Kirov, he tried to protect the stronghold of the classical dance from any modernistic or simply contemporary trends, and this policy was

both stimulating and disastrous. Sergeyev was extremely professional, flesh and bone of the Petersburg balletic culture. . . . He could rehearse the entrance of the court ladies in the Prologue of *The Sleeping Beauty* for hours, polishing each detail. . . .

Ambitious, intelligent, and shrewd, Sergeyev was far from being "an ordinary guy." He combined a high degree of professionalism and knowledge of the classical dance with reactionary attitudes and a rigid aesthetic presentation. Because he had got stuck in the aesthetics of the thirties and forties, he was rather militant against accepting anything newer than the standard classics. . . .

The Kirov needed Sergeyev and the authorities were pleased with him because his conservative tastes coincided with theirs. Afraid of intruders in their bureaucratic calm, they could sleep peacefully at night, secure with Sergeyev.[23]

Overtly, Sergeev and Dudinskaya were reliable members of the Soviet artistic establishment, but their artistic conservatism was less politically motivated than a reflection of their love for St. Petersburg's classical ballet tradition. They were not so much loyal pawns in the government's hands as shrewd operators who observed the rules of the game in order to promote their own artistic priorities, which for them lay not in innovation but in nurturing impeccably high standards of academic classical dance and in preserving the Kirov's purity of style.

The following episode of artistic repossession illustrates the distinction that needs to be made between Dudinskaya and Sergeev's public-political and private-artistic personalities. The Kirov planned to visit Moscow in 1959, a visit that inevitably had strong political overtones. As Dudinskaya stressed at the artistic council's discussion of the visit's repertoire, the trip should be interpreted as an official report of the theater's activities to the authorities in Moscow, and the repertoire should be chosen accordingly. Dudinskaya emphasized that the theater needed to demonstrate that it was working on productions dedicated to Soviet topics.[24] The uneasy relationship between Moscow, the Soviet capital, and Leningrad, the former imperial capital, gave a special meaning to this discussion. Even though there was a certain comfort in the greater geographic distance from the Kremlin, the Kirov Theater's position was defined by the regime's general suspicion of Leningrad and its determination to turn the Bolshoi Ballet into the premier company of the country, leading to a diversion of artistic talent from the Kirov to the Bolshoi.

Discussing the repertoire to be shown in Moscow, Dudinskaya was troubled by the inclusion of Petipa's ballet *La Bayadère*. At that time, *La Bay-*

FIGURE 16. Natalia Dudinskaya and Konstantin Sergeev rehearsing Sergeev's *Path of Thunder* at the Kirov Ballet, circa 1958. © St. Petersburg State Museum of Theater and Music

adère was not in the Bolshoi's repertoire.[25] From an artistic point of view, it was a crowning achievement of the prerevolutionary St. Petersburg ballet, especially in its third act, known as the "Kingdom of the Shades," an exemplary showcase of the academic purity of the St. Petersburg school. But from the point of view of Soviet cultural ideology, the ballet was deeply flawed: revolving around a beautiful temple dancer in an India of half-naked fakirs and bejeweled maharajas, the sumptuous ballet reveled in luxurious exoticism and included many elements that Soviet ideologues could condemn as class-alien entertainment favored by St. Petersburg's nineteenth-century aristocracy. Even though it is not clear whether this index was still relevant in the 1950s, in the classifications of ballets in the 1929 repertoire index mentioned in chapter 2, *La Bayadère* was rated a *C* ballet, a ballet that was "not completely supportable ideologically but not forbidden. Rehearsal for examination purposes required."[26] Dudinskaya warned: "We have to approach the compilation of the list of ballets that we are taking to Moscow correctly. It is imperative that there are Russian classics as well as Soviet composers. I am against the ballet *La Bayadère*. I love dancing this ballet very much, but I think that we ought not take it. It is such an archaic ballet, it is possible to make fun of it. The last act is good and can be included in the concluding concert, but I think one should not take the ballet as a whole."[27] Sergeev fully agreed with her.[28]

Dudinskaya's comments on *La Bayadère* show the extent to which a public image of regime loyalty could mask ideologically suspect artistic loyalties. A student of Vaganova, Dudinskaya had joined the Kirov Ballet in 1931. Emerging as one of the stars of this era, she had come artistically of age during the Stalinist era of drambalet, when prerevolutionary ballets like *La Bayadère* were ideologically criticized as superficial trifles. But even though Dudinskaya was part of the official Soviet cultural establishment, the values of her professional identity provided a strong alternative to her Soviet identity. From approximately the age of eleven, she had been reared for a career as a ballet dancer at the Leningrad Choreographic Institute, where for about eight formative years during her adolescence she underwent hours of painstaking daily training rooted in centuries of practical experience that had nothing to do with the new Soviet state.

In many ways, her teachers were handing down not just the technique but the spirit of the imperial ballet to a new generation of Soviet children. From the day they entered the ballet school as small children at the age of nine or ten, these "children of the revolution" lived in a double reality where the political and ideological education and demands of the Soviet regime had to coexist with the different, much older set of values, traditions, memories, and professional schooling handed down to them by their teachers.[29] In her memoirs written in the West, Natalia Makarova, who graduated from the school of the Kirov in 1959, stressed that "the most significant thing about the Vaganova School was very likely the daily, unobtrusive feeling of contact with the great ballet of the past, its traditions and unwritten laws, which nourished us like mother's milk. You simply could not get away from it."[30] Fondly remembering some of her dance teachers, she pointed out that:

> Their roots went back to St. Petersburg, and they escaped the fate of millions who rotted in the camps of the Gulag. They were permitted to live and to work, passing on, with inspiration, the tradition of the St. Petersburg ballet, which many of them had known personally, for they had begun in the days of Petipa and Ivanov. . . . Nikolai Ivanovich Ivanovsky[31] . . . always wore spats and patent leather shoes and would say "my respects" to us kids and doff his hat when he met us on the street. And this was a better lesson for us than any of the sermons on Communist morality we heard. Ivanovsky taught as traditional dances, and working with him turned into excursions to the France of the Sun King or Spain during the time of the Hapsburgs. He did not simply show us how to move in the gavotte or the pavane; to the movements themselves he supplied stories of the temper of those distant periods.[32]

According to Makarova, this spirit of old St. Petersburg was present not just in the dance teachers who taught them the specialized subjects of their profession but also in many of the teachers who provided the general academic schooling at the Vaganova school, which provided a normal school education alongside the specialized ballet training.[33]

Once the students graduated into the company, this double reality of the Kirov's imperial past and its present existence in Soviet Russia continued in their daily lives as artists. Irina Kolpakova, one of the leading Kirov ballerinas of her generation who graduated from the Vaganova School in 1951, enthusiastically remembers her coach, the former ballerina Elena Liukom, who had started her career at the Mariinsky in 1909. Unlike Makarova, who defected, Kolpakova built a successful career as a dancer and as a loyal member of the Soviet cultural establishment who did not shy away from politics. Her identity combined different sets of values: in addition to being a prominent Soviet citizen, she had a strong professional identity as a leading classical ballerina taking her place in a long line of St. Petersburg ballerinas in full awareness of her artistic responsibility to keep alive the precious artistic past her teachers and coaches had handed down to her. Comparing the strong sense of ballet history and continuity at the Kirov during Soviet times to the lack thereof she had noted in many places in the West since she started working there in the 1990s, she recalled how Liukom coached the classics, how she "was telling us how much she liked to dance and how much she liked kissing the grand princes, for example after a concert in Pavlovsk, when they were walking with the grand dukes. We thought this was wonderful. This was about her own life, but it is life on the stage too, it is life. And then you begin to realize that this movement belongs to you, you are in it, you perform it."[34] Dudinskaya's opposition to taking the "archaic" *La Bayadère* to Moscow should be interpreted not as her objective judgment of the ballet but as the politically astute, pragmatic avoidance of trouble. As an act of artistic repossession, it attempted to shield some of the prerevolutionary ballet traditions nurtured in Leningrad from Moscow's gaze, a gaze that might ridicule, or do something even worse, to a ballet close to the heart of the Kirov's tradition.

Preserving St. Petersburg's classical ballet legacy in Soviet Leningrad could provide a defense against Sovietization. Conservatism in ballet didn't necessarily reflect loyalty to a regime with conservative artistic tastes. On the contrary, it could indicate a dedication to artistic and aesthetic ideals that were completely alien to Soviet ideology, ideals that in their symbolic value as remnants of a bygone era could potentially subvert the official, Soviet values propagated by the regime: on the ballet stage, aristocratic beauty and glamour continued to reign, in striking contrast to the official Communist condemnation of either as class-alien and anti-Soviet. In their long years of training and during rehearsals of the classics, Soviet ballet dancers were not likely to be told to carry themselves like a proletarian worker at the factory assembly line; instead, they would be admonished to maintain the aristocratic bearing of a princess.

While ever the perfect "Soviet" artist in public, behind the closed doors of the rehearsal studio, people like Dudinskaya could forget the rules of the political game. *La Bayadère* was in fact one of her favorite ballets. In a documentary on Dudinskaya filmed in 1988, her assessment of *La Bayadère* is strikingly different from her "official" verdict of the ballet as too archaic, which in the Soviet ballet discourse implied "decorativeness" at the cost of intelligent content and dramaturgy. In the documentary, Dudinskaya and Sergeev are shown teaching the pantomimic jealousy scene between Nikiya and Gamzatti to students at the Vaganova School. Dudinskaya explains: "One of my favourite ballets was *La Bayadère*, in which there are not only Petipa's remarkable dances but also very deep content, requiring great acting skills. I strive to teach my students to dance well and to become good thinking artists."[35] Tellingly, the material chosen by her to do so was not taken from a Soviet propaganda ballet but precisely from one of the "archaic" acts of *La Bayadère*.

FIGURE 17. Natalia Dudinskaya as Nikiya and Vakhtang Chabukiani as Solor in *La Bayadère*, third act, at the Kirov Ballet, 1950. © Mariinsky Theater

Astute catering to the regime's demands could serve as an artistic survival strategy aimed at repossessing the house of art from its political intruders by lulling the ideological watchdogs into a false sense of security. While such actions should by no means be taken as conscious subversion of the system, they inadvertently did subvert the system by creating two realities. In the Potemkin village of a fictitious reality for official consumption, ballets like *La Bayadère* were declared remnants of an archaic prerevolutionary age while ballets on themes of contemporary Soviet life were promoted. In the artistic reality of the closed rehearsal studios of the theater and its school, ballets like *La Bayadère* were treasured as important links in an uninterrupted chain of classical ballet tradition bridging the prerevolutionary and Soviet eras, as lifeblood for tomorrow's artists.

Conservatism as Resistance

The Soviet cultural project sought to enlist art as an agent promoting political allegiance and contributing to the regime's goal of social transformation and control. The efficacy of the regime's attempt to usurp the artistic life of the Kirov Theater can be tested by evaluating to what extent, and how, the theater fulfilled the regime's demand for ballets on contemporary Soviet topics. Discussions of prospective repertoire plans by the Kirov's artistic council inevitably identified the creation of operas and ballets on Soviet material as the theater's "basic task,"[36] but the regime repeatedly criticized the Kirov for not producing enough operas and ballets on contemporary Soviet topics. For example, at the Eighth oblast' conference of the CPSU, the secretary of the Leningrad *obkom* (*oblastnoi komitet*; regional committee) of the CPSU reprimanded: "we can't be satisfied with the work of this theater, which is one of the most prominent musical theaters in the country. The theater does not use the huge potential of its creative collective." At this meeting, Galina Kirillova, a soloist of the Kirov Ballet and a member of the theater's party bureau, engaged in the popular Communist game of self-criticism, identifying the failure to stage enough new productions in general, and Soviet productions in particular, as the ballet company's main shortcoming.[37] Similarly, in 1960, the *gorkom* (*gorodskoi komitet*; city committee) of the Leningrad CPSU criticized the theater for bad work regarding the creation of productions on contemporary topics, noting that recently only one ballet on a contemporary topic had been created, *The Coast of Hope*.[38]

The repertoire plan of the Kirov Theater was as much a response to official requirements as a reflection of genuine artistic aspirations. Each season, the Kirov Theater had to submit a repertoire plan for approval to the Ministry of Culture. Responding to the ideological propaganda demands of the regime, each annual plan had to include at least one new opera and one new ballet on a contemporary Soviet topic. Prior to its submission, the repertoire plan was discussed by the theater's artistic council. It is not clear from the archival documentation how repertoire plans were formulated in the first place, but it seems likely that they were the outcome of discussion between the director of the theater, the artistic leadership of the opera and ballet companies, and the theater's repertoire literature department.

When trying to determine to what extent the Soviet regime managed to control the repertoire of the country's leading ballet companies, it is instructive to compare the situation in Russia to the fate of ballet in China. The history of Chinese ballet illustrates how classical ballet had in some bizarre way become a "Communist" achievement in the minds of Soviet leaders. In the 1950s, the Soviet government dispatched ballet teachers from the Bolshoi and Kirov to the young People's Republic of China to help establish classical ballet in Communist China. After the Sino-Soviet split and the onset of the Chinese Cultural Revolution in the mid-1960s, Soviet ballet teachers were kicked out of the country and classical ballet was denounced as politically alien. During the Cultural Revolution, the nascent Chinese ballet was set on a strict diet of a handful of "revolutionary model ballets," most notably The Red Detachment of Women, set during the civil war of 1927–1937 and telling the story of a peasant girl who becomes a heroic fighter after having been liberated from her tyrannical master by a Red Army leader. Madame Mao controlled the creation of China's revolutionary model ballets. Lasting for hours, the ballets abounded in dancers parading around with guns, reflecting the tastes of Madame Mao who commented on a performance by the Beijing Dance Academy in 1972: "The dancing looked all right, but where are the guns? Where are the grenades? Where are the political meanings?"[39]

In contrast to the performance monopoly of revolutionary model ballets in China during the Cultural Revolution, the Kirov's and Bolshoi's rather feeble response to the official demand for Soviet ballets throughout the Soviet period suggests that the Soviet regime's control over artistic production was limited by four factors. First, unlike in China, ballet was firmly rooted in Russia. Its resistance to Sovietization demonstrated the power of tradition. The comparatively low number of ballets on contemporary Soviet themes and discussions at the artistic council indicates that underneath their lip service to the great goal of creating Soviet ballets, even the most loyal dancers and choreographers frequently saw this task more as a chore than as a worthy mission. "Loyalty" was probably often nothing more than pragmatic accommodation to the prevailing system and included a readiness to manipulate the system to achieve completely nonideological, artistic goals. Underneath the official rhetoric celebrating the "union" of ideology and art, independent professional values continued to flourish in the Soviet cultural sphere. Second, the audience proved to be fairly uncooperative with the state's attempt to "educate" it, avoiding productions on Soviet themes that it found boring. Third, as will be shown in detail in the following chapters, some of the innovative choreographers of the 1950s and 1960s, such as Bel'sky, Grigorovich, and Iakobson, hijacked the official call for Soviet ballets for the advancement of their own artistic agendas, challenging the ideologically informed orthodoxies imposed on choreography under the mantle of providing ballets on Soviet themes. Fourth, the Kirov's and Bolshoi's exceptionally strong tradition of passing on performance traditions and knowledge from one generation to the next kept the legacy of the imperial ballet alive in the bodies and artistry of the Soviet dancers and developed it.

The limited number of long-lived ballets on contemporary Soviet themes is one of the main indicators that the regime's power to control artistic creation was in the final analysis limited: the theaters might be forced to create productions celebrating the virtues of Soviet labor, but their short life span shows that they were often created simply to "fulfill the plan." At the discussion of the Kirov's prospective repertoire plan for 1962, the following statistics were given. The Kirov's active repertoire comprised forty-five works of classical heritage, not including a whole range of classical operas and ballets that had fallen out of repertoire and that the theater wanted to revive. In contrast, in all the years of Soviet power, spanning by now four decades, only ten Soviet operas and eleven Soviet ballets had been shown on the Kirov's stage.[40]

A look at the Kirov Ballet's repertoire and performance statistics for a number of selected years shows that the classics continued to form the backbone of the Kirov's repertoire, together with Soviet ballets based on literary sources or fairy tales. Ballets on contemporary Soviet topics were clearly in the minority.[41] It is often argued that the conservatism of the Kirov's repertoire was a symptom of Soviet cultural malaise, but the opposite argument can be made. Far from signifying "ideological loyalty," the conservatism of the leading ballet companies' repertoire could be interpreted as resistance to the regime's pressures to Sovietize.

Even though Stalin died in March 1953, the repertoire of the year 1954 still gives a good indication of the Kirov's repertoire during the late Stalinist period, a time of artistic paralysis. It is useful to look at the repertoire performed during this specific year since the revolt against artistic director Sergeev in 1955 discussed in the following chapter was partially a response to it. Of the nineteen ballets performed in 1954, seven were from the classical repertoire: Petipa's *Swan Lake*, *The Sleeping Beauty*, *La Bayadère*, *Don Quixote*, and *Raymonda*; Fokine's *Chopiniana*; and Coralli, Perrot, and Petipa's *Giselle*. I am also including Vainonen's *Nutcracker* in this category because of Tchaikovsky's music, even though the Kirov's production was a product of the drambalet era. The remaining twelve ballets were by Soviet authors and, with the possible exception of Leonid Iakobson's fairy-tale ballet *Shurale*, exponents of the ruling genre of drambalet. Tellingly, of these twelve ballets, two were fairy-tales (*Shurale* and *Cinderella*) and six were based on Russian or world literature (*The Bronze Horseman* [Pushkin], *Esmeralda* [Victor Hugo's *Hunchback of Notre-Dame*],[42] *Laurencia* [Lope de Vega's seventeenth-century play *Fuente ovejuna*], *The Fountain of Bakhchisarai* [Pushkin], *Flames of Paris* [on themes of Félix Gras's *Les Marceliers*], and *Romeo and Juliet* [Shakespeare]). Only two of the ballets based on literary sources had revolutionary topics (*Flames of Paris*, the French Revolution, and *Laurencia*, a peasant uprising in a Castilian village). Only three ballets performed by the Kirov in 1954 were on themes of Soviet "contemporary" life (*The Red Poppy*, dealing with the Chinese people and their Soviet comrades, *Gayané*, revolving around a cotton picker in an Armenian cotton collective, and *Native Fields*, based on kolkhoz life and engineering).

Classical ballets and ballets of the drambalet genre based on literary themes constituted the vast majority of performances given by the Kirov in 1954. Of a total of 125 ballet performances, ballets from the Kirov's prerevolutionary heritage received 55 performances (including Vainonen's *Nutcracker*). Ballets by Soviet authors based on literature or fairy tales were performed 45 times. The Kirov's three ballets on Soviet contemporary topics were performed 25 times. The most performed ballet was *Swan Lake* (21 performances), followed by *The Bronze Horseman* (18), *The Red Poppy* (13), and *The Nutcracker* (10). All remaining ballets perceived less than 10 performances. About 44 percent of the performances were dedicated to the classics, 36 percent to ballets of the drambalet genre based on world literature, and 20 percent to ballets of the drambalet genre reflecting Soviet propaganda.

The performance statistics for 1956 and 1957 show the changes in the Kirov's repertoire at the dawn of the Thaw and after Sergeev was—at least temporarily—replaced as artistic director. Compared to one genuinely new ballet staged during the period of Sergeev's leadership from 1951 until 1955 (the drambalet propaganda ballet *Native Fields* in 1953), there were three ballet premieres between June 1955 and the end of 1957 (*Taras Bulba* [based on Gogol], *Spartacus* [about the Spartacus uprising in ancient Rome], and *The Stone Flower* [based on a fairy tale by Bazhov]). Of 124 performances in 1956, prerevolutionary classics received 58 performances (*Swan Lake, The Sleeping Beauty, Don Quixote, La Bayadère, Raymonda*, Vainonen's *Nutcracker, Chopiniana, Giselle*). Ballets by Soviet authors on literary themes or fairy tales received 53 performances (*The Bronze Horseman, Shurale, The Fountain of Bakhchisarai, Taras Bulba, Laurencia, Cinderella, Romeo and Juliet*, and *Esmeralda*). The number of performances in this category is higher in 1956 than in 1954, probably reflecting that one new ballet had recently been added to this category (*Taras Bulba*). Ballets on Soviet themes (*The Red Poppy, Native Fields*, and *Gayané*) received only 12 performances, compared to 25 in 1954. Premiered toward the end of December in 1956, Iakobson's experimental ballet *Spartacus* received a single performance. The most performed ballets in 1956 were *The Bronze Horseman* (17), *Swan Lake* (16), *The Sleeping Beauty* (12), *Shurale* (10), and *The Fountain of Bakhchisarai* (10).

The quick disappearance of ballets on contemporary Soviet topics probably reflected both the artists' and the audiences' attitude toward these ballets. By 1957, only one ballet on a contemporary Soviet topic remained in

FIGURE 18. Corps de ballet dressing room before a performance of *Swan Lake* at the Kirov Ballet, 1961. © Mariinsky Theater

the repertoire (*Native Fields*), receiving only 3 performances. Similar to previous years, out of a total of 123 performances, the classics received 50 performances. Ballets of the drambalet genre based on literary themes and fairy tales were performed 41 times. Pointing choreographically in a new direction, the new ballets *Spartacus* and *The Stone Flower* together received 29 performances. The most performed ballets in 1957 were *The Bronze Horseman* (16), *Spartacus* (16), *Swan Lake* (14), *The Stone Flower* (13), *The Nutcracker* (10), and *The Fountain of Bakhchisarai* (10). Compared to 1954, ballets of the drambalet genre, ranging thematically from world literature to Soviet propaganda, had decreased from twelve ballets in 1954 to six in 1957 (including *Shurale* and *Taras Bulba*).

To what extent did the repertoire of the Kirov Ballet of the early 1960s differ from its repertoire in the early 1950s and, in particular, from the 1954 repertoire discussed above? Looking at the ballet repertoire from 1961 until 1964, several observations can be made. The prerevolutionary classics continued to provide the backbone of the Kirov Ballet's artistic identity. *Swan Lake* was firmly established as the most performed ballet, receiving 86 performances out of a total of 567 ballet performances given between 1961 and 1964. *Swan Lake* accounted for 15 percent of all ballet performances given at

FIGURE 19. *Swan Lake*, first act, second scene, at the Kirov Ballet, 1965. Photographer: Nina Alovert. © St. Petersburg State Museum of Theater and Music

the Kirov from 1961 until 1964. The drambalet pageant *The Bronze Horseman* was the second most performed ballet during this period, receiving 50 performances. Of the ballets of the drambalet genre, only a select few survived: *The Bronze Horseman, The Fountain of Bakhchisarai, Romeo and Juliet,* and *Laurencia*. All ballets created on Soviet contemporary themes during the drambalet era had disappeared from the repertoire, as had the ballets *The Red Poppy* and *Flames of Paris*. As Konstantin Sergeev said laconically in 1959, when the revival of *The Flames of Paris* was discussed: "The ballet has played its role. . . . The third act is very interesting but as a whole production—it has become antiquated."[43]

New ballets by choreographers like Igor' Bel'sky (*The Coast of Hope* and *Leningrad Symphony*), Yuri Grigorovich (*The Stone Flower* and *The Legend of Love*), and Leonid Iakobson (*Spartacus, Choreographic Miniatures, The Bedbug,* and *The Twelve*) broke with the conventions of the Stalinist drambalet era. Reflecting the government's demand made explicit in the decree of 1957 that at least one new ballet on a Soviet theme had to be staged per year, several new ballets on Soviet themes had been created. But, as will be discussed in more detail in the following chapters, not all of these ballets were simple propaganda fare. On the contrary, choreographers such as Iakobson and Bel'sky used the government's and theater's support for ballets on Soviet themes to advance their own, convention-breaking artistic agendas, often to the consternation of cultural bureaucrats and conservative elements within the theater.

Staging Soviet Ballets

Discussions by the Kirov's artistic council suggest that while the theater accepted the creation of operas and ballets on contemporary Soviet themes as its basic official task, it did so without much enthusiasm. Again and again, the theater's leadership dutifully defined the creation of Soviet operas and ballets as its primary task. For example, commenting on the role of the artistic council within the Kirov Theater in 1957 and 1958, Director Orlov noted that "primary attention is now devoted to the creation of Soviet operas of full value, reflecting the image of our contemporaries." But "unfortunately, one ought to point out with all self-criticism, that the creative efforts of the theater and the artistic council with respect to the creation of monumental Soviet operas of full value don't yet yield the required result."[44] Similarly, discussions of the theater's prospective repertoire plan for 1962 identified the creation of productions based on Soviet and contemporary topics and the attraction of Soviet composers as the theater's basic task. At the same meeting, Sergeev, artistic director of the Kirov Ballet, also emphasized that the company was striving to stage ballets on topics of contemporary life.[45]

Judging from discussion of prospective repertoire plans by the Kirov's artistic council, the repertoire plans were maybe primarily intended to keep the Ministry of Culture happy and only secondarily as realistic work plans. A discussion of the prospective repertoire plan for 1960 to 1962 held on 31 March 1959 opened with the clarification that the theater's leadership had taken as its starting point the necessity to stage more new productions and to produce two new operas and two new ballets each year.[46] Dutifully, the ballet company's plans did indeed include two new productions per year, including one production on a contemporary topic per year, for example, a ballet called *Friendship* by the Soviet composer Solov'ev-Sedoi about friendship between the democratic youth of this world congregating in Moscow for the Sixth International Youth Festival.

Apart from their provisional titles, however, little was known about these productions, boding badly for the plan's realization given the long production period required for new ballets. As one member of the artistic council, F. P. Sukhov, member of the orchestra and chairman of the theater's trade union committee, remarked:

> About the plan for the ballet one wants to say that there is no purpose
> in it. We also don't yet know anything about the ballet *Friendship*. . . .
> As with respect to the opera, so with respect to the ballet the production brigades are not indicated—which choreographers, conductors,
> and so forth will be involved. In my opinion, one must not approach

putting together plans for three years in this way. We have outstanding choreographers—Sergeev, Iakobson, and others. One should have consulted with them before putting together the plan. One can give a commission to Soviet composers and interest them. We don't take this into account—someone takes up something somewhere, but there is no ideological content. Three years—this is not a lot of time and one has to work with the composers. Intensive work with the choreographers, with specialists is also necessary in order for our plan to be realistic. So far I don't see such reality.[47]

There is ground for suspicion that it was the same ballets on "contemporary Soviet topics" that were included year after year, never to see the blaze of the limelight. As M. N. Iatsko, member of the orchestra and secretary of the theater's party bureau, complained: "One wants to reproach the leadership of the ballet for including *Avrora, the Piper from Strakonshch* from plan to plan. . . . I fully support those who said that before confirming the plan, one should at least listen to the piano score of the music, but it would be better to include already finished works in the plan." The closing remarks of Director Korkin illustrate the somewhat artificial character of the repertoire plans, which primarily reflected constant pressure to produce operas and ballets on Soviet topics and the Kirov's failure to deliver, especially with respect to the creation of contemporary operas. Korkin reiterated: "The obkom of the party all the time puts this question to us—where are the contemporary topics? . . . The plan for the ballet even has a defined quality in comparison with the opera—contemporary composers are more included." During the exposition of the plan at the beginning of the meeting, it was pointed out that new operas by Soviet composers on contemporary subjects would be included in the plan as they appeared, indicating how, in theory, absolute priority was given to productions on contemporary life.[48]

Given the haphazard manner in which the Kirov's repertoire plans were formulated, reflecting official demands for Soviet operas and ballets more than realistic artistic possibilities, it is no surprise that the plans were rarely implemented in their first version. Remarking on the discrepancy between plans and reality, Director Korkin pointed out that "the plans of past years have changed about five times. At the beginning there was one thing, and in the end there is something completely different. . . . The plan has to be approved in principle, but the leadership should discuss it further, taking into account the remarks said today. The production brigades and the start and finish dates of work on productions need to be defined."[49] The production history and failure of the ballet *"Russia" Has Come into Port*, mentioned in the discussion above under the provisional title *Friendship*, illustrate how

FIGURE 20. *"Russia" Has Come into Port*, third act, at the Kirov Ballet, 1964. © Mariinsky Theater

the Kirov sometimes had to stage propaganda ballets on contemporary topics against better artistic judgment to fulfill the regime's demands. A serious lack of genuine Socialist enthusiasm is apparent in the theater's persistent difficulties in finding librettos on contemporary topics and choreographers and composers interested in staging them. The Kirov's prospective repertoire plans discussed on 31 March 1959 included *Friendship* in the list of ballets to be staged in 1960, but it took another four painful years until the unsuccessful premiere of this ballet with a convoluted plot about noble Soviet sailors, Italians traveling to a youth festival in Moscow, their Fascist enemies, and the vulgar West, under the name *"Russia" Has Come into Port*.[50]

Ideological requirements forced the Kirov to waste precious time on an artistically unpromising production, seriously restricting the theater's artistic autonomy of action. From the beginning, the ballet ensemble had serious doubts about the quality of the ballet in general, and its libretto and choreography in particular, but persistent difficulties to find ballet librettos on contemporary Soviet topics and the need to respond to the official demand of one contemporary Soviet ballet per year to keep the regime happy overruled any artistic doubts. More concrete discussion of the ballet by the artistic council started in January 1962. Vasily Solov'ev-Sedoi and Rostislav Zakharov, the composer and choreographer in charge of the production, were dinosaurs of the Soviet artistic establishment. Solov'ev-Sedoi had composed popular Soviet songs and headed the Leningrad Composers' Union at some point. In the polemics of the Thaw era surrounding the experiments of the choreographers Bel'sky, Grigorovich, and Iakobson, Zakharov, who had created one of the most successful ballets of the drambalet era, *The Fountain of Bakhchisarai*, and who had subsequently become a politically well-connected member of the ballet establishment, represented the camp of archconservatives who hailed the drambalet conventions of the Stalinist era as the Holy Grail of Soviet ballet.

At the Kirov Ballet, now comprising many dancers who had come of age with Grigorovich's and Bel'sky's works that explicitly challenged the tenets of drambalet, many looked upon Zakharov's project with suspicion. Bel'sky voiced these concerns at a discussion by the artistic council of the Kirov's repertoire plan for 1962: "Doubt is arising in the ballet company concerning the ballet *"Russia" Has Come into Port*. The ballet collective knows neither the music, nor the libretto. But if in this case the musical material can be accepted on faith, many know the libretto and rate it negatively. The art council absolutely has to acquaint itself with the libretto and the music before work begins. The ballet collective—even more so."[51] The theater was interested in the production primarily for one reason—no matter how bad the libretto was, it was on a contemporary topic and had a realistic chance of being staged. Judging by Sergeev's comments, in its desperation to heed the government's call for Soviet operas and ballets, the theater's leadership often included the names of productions in its plan that were unlikely to ever see the stage:

> We (the former director Comrade Korkin, I, and Comrade Dovlatova) listened to the music and content of the ballet for the first time at the composer's apartment. We liked it, but we also had serious reservations about the libretto. Solov'ev-Sedoi and Zakharov have said that during the process of creation, the director's exposition, the libretto will be reworked. Sometimes in our chase for a contemporary topic we include in the plan works, not guaranteeing the supply of a single note. And in this case—the music is ready, the theme is contemporary, it would be strange not to jump on this work from the very beginning.[52]

The opera soloist Laptev brought the debate to a simple point, as finally there was a realistic project for a production on a contemporary topic: "It seems to me that the question is clear; the music is ready, the libretto will be reworked. . . . There is no basis for sowing doubts, we have waited for this ballet, we have hurried the composer. A contemporary topic doesn't come so easy, and one can't reject it so easily."[53] The ballet was included in the repertoire plan for 1962.

As rehearsals for the ballet proceeded, artistic concerns became increasingly difficult to ignore. By January 1963, the production of the ballet had not progressed much. At an artistic council discussion of the theater's repertoire plan for 1963 and for the 1963–1964 theatrical season, several representatives of the ballet company raised concerns about the ballet's quality. The principal dancer Askol'd Makarov commented that "we like the music of *Russia*, but the dramaturgy we don't like. Where do things stand now? The collective is worried about this." Another principal dancer, Irina Kolpakova, was more outspoken, stating point blank that it had been a mistake to invite Zakharov to stage the ballet.[54]

As rehearsals progressed, even conservative contemporaries of Zakharov became increasingly worried about the ballet's artistic merit: in December 1963 the artistic council discussed the ballet's severe shortcomings, and Sergeev gave a dismaying account of the production's dramaturgical weakness and general incoherence, suggesting numerous cuts and changes. Iakobson's evaluation was even more damning:

> Concerning the production as a whole—there is little that is intelligible and there is little that is interesting. Is our theater, a theater of international standing, following the right path in creating this production? As a whole, the music is not dramaturgical, even though in details it is excellent. The choreographic language is weak, uninteresting. The director's work also doesn't make one happy with innovation and originality. . . . Many aspects of the plot are naïve and primitive. The dramaturgy is weak. Realizing the Soviet theme on stage in this way does not constitute a solution to this problem. In this shape the production will not be intelligent, it will not be artistically elevated. We have to make productions taking into consideration a mature, demanding audience. One has to seriously reconsider this production from a dramaturgical, musical, and directorial-choreographic point of view.[55]

The regime's demand for productions on Soviet topics seriously compromised the theater's artistic autonomy by giving it almost no choice but to waste time and resources on staging a ballet like *"Russia" Has Come into Port* against better artistic judgments. But despite the political circumstances that limited the theater's artistic autonomy of action, at least in the case of this ballet, ideological demands did not manage to compromise its autonomy of artistic judgment. There were few illusions about the ballet's artistic value, but some members of the council simply adopted a pragmatic, yet painful point of view: in a system where cultural institutions were controlled by an ideologically driven state, the Kirov Theater needed to keep the government happy. Regardless of artistic merit, the ballet needed to be staged to keep the theater in good graces by fulfilling the government's demands for ballets on contemporary Soviet themes. As Sergeev pointed out: "If we put our stakes on completing only the production of stage masterpieces, then very many works would never have seen the light. In its searches for topics for a contemporary production, the theater has the right to experiment, it even has the right for a failure. We must not reject this work, we absolutely have to complete it." Even more poignantly, Vladimir Tomson, the administrative director of the ballet company, stated outright: "We need this production, it is on a Soviet topic. Work on it absolutely has to be completed." It was decided that work on the ballet would continue but concrete measures needed to be taken to rework it.[56]

The artistic council's final discussion whether or not the ballet should be allowed to premiere highlighted several issues. Nobody in the artistic council questioned the need to fulfill the government's demand for ballets on contemporary Soviet themes, but most seemed to think that little of artistic value was to be expected of such enterprises. The artistic verdict on Zakharov's ballet was resoundingly negative, uniting artists from usually conflicting artistic camps such as the conservative classicist Sergeev and the Kirov's innovative enfant terrible Iakobson. In the final analysis, artistic standards could not be appropriated by the regime, making a purely ideological production lacking any artistic value such as Zakharov's ballet unacceptable to most artists on artistic terms, even if political considerations made the ballet's release necessary.

On 11 February 1964 there was a final debate whether or not *"Russia" Has Come into Port* was ready to be shown to the public. The artistic council's assessment of the ballet's artistic quality was unanimously scathing, but it was still recommended that the ballet be shown to the public. The artistic council basically accepted the ballet as a necessary evil reflecting the demands that the Soviet cultural project made of ballet. A pragmatic assessment of the more tiresome aspects of Soviet cultural life lay at the heart of the council's decision, but even though such pragmatism was unavoidable, it did come at an artistic cost. Iakobson was one of the few, if not the only one, who demanded outright that the ballet not be shown to the public because its artistic worthlessness could compromise the image of the theater. He warned: "Friends of the theater do not advise releasing this production. . . . This production does not have the right to exist in our theater." Others resigned themselves to the fact that the theater sometimes ended up staging rubbish in its quest to heed the regime's call for Soviet operas and ballet. The secretary of the party organization of the theater, Z. N. Strizhova, dryly noted that "one cannot consider this work our victory. Yet another production is added to the number of mediocre productions of the theater. It is very sad that they are mainly productions on a contemporary topic that become common."[57]

Similarly, someone else remarked that there was little that was interesting in the ballet's choreography but that "few perfect productions are created on a contemporary topic. If one puts one's stakes on masterpieces, the repertoire of our theaters will be very meager. One ought to try." Dudinskaya considered the ballet beyond hope. Even though the ballet should be released, she warned that it was impossible to demand any more from the company by trying to redo some elements of the production. Tomson, the ballet company's administrative director, agreed with Dudinskaya: the ballet should be shown as it was, but there was no point in doing any corrections.[58]

Members of the company were frustrated to have wasted their time on a politically motivated production of such minimal artistic value. Nurturing the classical repertoire must have seemed like an artistic haven from such realities of Soviet cultural life. A Ms. Kabarova complained: "It is very sad that the theater took to work on such an imperfect work. The work on this ballet has taken away much spare time, which has hindered the preparation and release of productions of the classical repertoire." Not surprisingly, ballet artists and the authorities approached this artistically worthless but "Soviet" ballet differently. Unlike many of the representatives of the theater who wanted to release the ballet that they considered artistically beyond repair and get it done and over with, the representative from the Department of Culture of the Executive Committee of the Leningrad City Soviet was not satisfied by the fact alone that the ballet was on a contemporary topic and demanded higher quality. T. A. Shubnikova of the Department of Culture stated unequivocally: "The production doesn't make one happy. In terms of dramaturgy and in terms of choreography, this is a very weak work. The theater has the right to experiment, but Soviet ballet has passed through the initial stage of coming into being a long time ago. There are numbers in the production that are tainted with bad taste (cancan dances, the number 'Loshadki'). It did not succeed in showing convincingly the shady sides of Western art, its corruption. The artistic council has to weigh everything and decide the fate of the production."[59] In this case, the official representatives of the Soviet regime seem to have left the final decision to the theater.

Ultimately, the theater's leadership would be held responsible if the Kirov failed to deliver productions on contemporary Soviet topics; the theater's and the ballet's leadership supported the production of this ballet throughout its rehearsal stage despite serious artistic misgivings. Unencumbered by the burden of official accountability, the dancers themselves were less willing to accommodate the creation of an artistically completely worthless ballet. A general atmosphere of opposition pervaded the ballet company throughout the production's rehearsal period. In his closing remarks, Sergeev pointed out that "more could have been achieved if the company had been eager and if it had helped. The choreographer did not inspire the company, he did not get it to stand behind him. . . . It is absolutely inadmissible to switch off during the performance because of one's mood, as happened today with the artist Gensler."[60] The meeting unanimously decided to show the ballet to the public on 14 February 1964. It was shown four more times in 1964, but not a single time in the following year.[61]

If artists were the regime's tools in projects like this, its target were the spectators' souls, but the audience sometimes proved stubbornly unwilling to accept the propaganda fare presented to it in the shape of Soviet operas and ballets. On 13 April 1963 the Kirov Theater held a conference for its audience to gauge its opinion on the theater's work. Approximately five hundred people assembled in the foyer of the third circle of the auditorium, including representatives of the most important enterprises in town, workers, engineers, teachers, students, servicemen, pensioners, and housewives.[62] The comments made by a certain worker Nikazov provide a clue to how audiences responded to the Soviet operas and ballets the regime was pressuring the theaters to stage. Nikazov had been going to the Kirov for the past eight years and had seen all classics of the opera and ballet repertoire. He preferred opera to ballet: "I can watch a ballet once or twice, but the opera *Carmen* I watched fifteen times." A simple worker who had fallen in love with the Kirov Theater, Nikazov embodied the regime's ideal audience for Soviet operas and ballets, but unfortunately Nikazov was anything but convinced by the theater's attempts to stage Soviet operas and ballets. Judging by his comment, and by the enthusiastic response it inspired in the audience, large parts of the audience were about as keen on watching the kind of Soviet operas and ballets produced as many artists were on creating them:

> I very much want to listen to a real Soviet opera, to be exact, one about
> the present day and not to a parody. Let the Soviet composer learn
> to write an opera in the way in which Tchaikovsky does. [Laughter.
> Noise.] Let there be only one Soviet opera to which one could listen
> if only five times. One would want there to be a real opera, and not
> *The Desperate Road.* [Applause.] I don't even consider this an opera, one
> could watch a dramatic play on this topic. For example, at the Bolshoi
> Theater, the play *Story from Irkutsk* is running, and today we heard that

FIGURE 21. The auditorium at the Kirov Theater, 1961. © Mariinsky Theater

the Kirov Theater wants to stage an opera *Story from Irkutsk* or a ballet.
I don't want to see one or the other. [Applause.][63]

The impact of the Soviet cultural project on ballet in the 1950s and 1960s
was complex. As the decree of 1957 illustrates, ballet benefited from a state
policy that promoted high culture as a core value of Soviet civilization, but
the artistic autonomy of the Kirov and Bolshoi Ballet companies was seriously compromised by the regime's demand for ballets on Soviet contemporary themes. The tension between state-sanctioned privilege and stifling
political tutelage was reflected in the artistic council, which had to reconcile
artistic standards with political considerations.

Even though the ideological demands of the Soviet cultural project se-
verely circumscribed artistic autonomy of action in fields such as repertoire
formation, independent artistic norms continued to exist. Members of the
artistic council flatly rejected Zakharov's ballet on artistic terms. One can
read between the lines that many of them didn't expect anything else from
those Soviet ballets staged primarily to fulfill the government's demands.
Many artists of the Kirov applied a double standard to the productions of
the theater, distinguishing between "real" work and tiresome "official" work
that had to be completed one way or the other to keep the regime's goodwill
on which the theater's ability to focus on "real" work—such as maintaining the classical repertoire—depended. As principal choreographer of the
Kirov, Sergeev himself created several ballets on contemporary themes, but
in the assessment of Natalia Makarova, who defected to the West during
Sergeev's leadership of the Kirov:

> Under [the authorities'] pressure [Sergeev] had to stage ballets on
> contemporary themes, reflecting the victories of the Soviet people in
> agriculture or space flight. . . . But I still don't think that, given his rare
> professionalism in relation to the classics, Sergeyev really believed in
> the artistic value of such ballets. He was forced to obey the dictates of
> his bosses, and it was probably against his will that he included in the
> repertoire ballets of his friends, such as Zakharov's *"Russia" Has Come
> into Port*, about how Soviet sailors are so noble and Western ones are so
> corrupt. He didn't want to jeopardize his own position. He lived under
> pressure and simply accepted the rules of the game, squandering the
> energy of the world's best dancers on this kind of junk.[64]

Given the omnipresence of the regime in an ideologically based, dictatorial state like the Soviet Union, the Kirov Ballet had little choice but to
be responsive to the regime's demands. But the reality of cultural produc-

tion in the Soviet Union was complex. The Kirov's repertoire politics and discussions at the artistic council demonstrate that pragmatic considerations pushed the Kirov to erect a "Potemkin village" of Soviet productions for the regime's consumption in which neither the artists nor the audiences believed. Artists didn't hide their boredom and irritation at having to stage an artistically worthless ballet like Zakharov's *"Russia" Has Come into Port* in order to tick the box "Soviet ballet" on their official repertoire plan.

Statements made by astute Soviet artists could have multiple layers of meaning. In this environment, Dudinskaya's ostensibly ideologically "orthodox" opinion on whether or not the Kirov should perform *La Bayadère* in Moscow was in reality a rhetorical weapon aimed to shield the potentially ideologically subversive legacy of St. Petersburg's imperial ballet. Circumstances turned artists into masters of Orwellian doublespeak, a mindset that provided a fertile ground for more drastic attempts to manipulate the Soviet system and renegotiate the limits for artistic autonomy set by the Soviet cultural project.

4 ♫ ℬ*allet Battles*

The Kirov Ballet during
Khrushchev's Thaw

What on earth is Grigorovich doing? Among his semiprecious
stones there is a jasper. But there are no jaspers in these
regions! I, for example, am now staging a ballet about the
underwater kingdom of the Baikal. What would happen,
comrades, if instead of an omul, I showed some sort of sprat?

—A CHOREOGRAPHER FROM THE URALS CRITICIZING
GRIGOROVICH'S BALLET *THE STONE FLOWER*, 1960

AFTER STALIN'S DEATH in March 1953, the new leadership of the country
had to face the wide-ranging consequences of Stalinism. The Khrushchev
era was marked by the dilemmas that arose out of this complex process. If
late Stalinism had sucked the life out of the Soviet utopia, the reforms of
the Khrushchev era sought to revive the Soviet project by renegotiating the
country's Stalinist legacy. Despite the enormous range of economic and social problems, the field of culture emerged as one of the areas most emblematic of the struggle between reform and continuity, which is characteristic
of this era. As Polly Jones has pointed out, the question of how to revitalize
Soviet culture became one of the principal, most public predicaments of de-
Stalinization: how could one replace the dogmatic and repetitive culture of
the Stalinist period with a culture that offered a relevant means of communication between the party and the people?[1] Within the context of Khrushchev's reforms, culture was supposed to play a pivotal role in the revival of
the Soviet project by infusing the population with a new sense of purpose,
by rekindling popular enthusiasm for the Soviet utopia, and by bestowing
a mantle of legitimacy on the new leadership. In order to revive the Soviet

project as a whole, the Soviet cultural project needed to be infused with new life.

At the dawn of the Thaw in Soviet culture, the fields of politics and art worried about the same phenomenon—stagnation in cultural production—albeit for different reasons. If some segments of the political establishment were concerned about cultural stagnation because they realized that low-quality art unpopular with the public could not make any meaningful contribution to ideological propaganda, artistic circles worried about cultural stagnation as a symptom of the limitations imposed on artistic expression and development.

This coincidence of political and artistic concerns created a potent opportunity for artistic repossession, a form of systemic subversion that exploits the system for goals foreign to it in order to creatively adapt or re-define the ideological limits imposed on the field of cultural production by the regime. Artists of the Kirov Ballet managed to exploit the wider political environment of de-Stalinization for their own, artistic goals. It is not necessarily outright rejection or explicit resistance that undermines attempts of collective control over individuals the most but the almost subconscious subversion of a system from within by people who simply try to forge their own destinies within the parameters set by the system.[2] The relationship between artistic practice and politics in the Soviet Union of the Thaw was anything but straightforward, illustrating Foucault's assessment of the relationship between power relations and confrontation strategies and his contention that "there is no relationship of power without the means of escape or possible flight."[3]

The Revival of the Soviet Cultural Project

In the late Stalinist period, the specter of creative asphyxia haunted the world of ballet. By the late 1940s, *drambalet* had turned into a dogmatic restraint on choreographic development. While the artistry and virtuosity of dancers like Ulanova, Dudinskaya, and Sergeev continued to push the artistic limits of ballet performance, Soviet ballet had reached a dead end in terms of choreography. Some of the most respected voices in the Soviet dance world began to speak out publicly against this stagnation, most notably Igor' Moiseev, the choreographer and founder of the USSR Folk Dance Ensemble, and the ballerina Galina Ulanova.

In April 1952, about a year before Stalin's death, Igor' Moiseev published a lengthy article on the state of Soviet choreography in *Literaturnaia gazeta*. According to Moiseev, ballet was plagued by stagnation, conservatism, and a fear of the new.[4] While Moiseev spent a considerable part of his article analyzing reasons for the lack of ballets on contemporary topics, his comments illuminated why many felt that drambalet had reached a blind alley: it relegated dance to an auxiliary role in ballet productions.

> Soviet ballet is trying hard to enrich its content. Where in the old ballets the theme was habitually merely a peg on which to hang a dance entertainment, in most Soviet ballets the subject is the core of the ballet. At the same time all our latest productions suffer from a common fault, the poverty of dance form; the striving after content and the depiction of it are taken as a denial of the leading role of the dance.
>
> This is a dangerous symptom, which indicates that, while preserving any number of the outmoded canons of the classical ballet, we are breaking with one of its most fruitful traditions, the unfolding of content and feeling through the language of the dance. . . . We have justly criticized many old ballets because they did not combine the dance with healthy thought, but we cannot permit new ballets to have healthy thought uncombined with the dance.[5]

Moiseev used two recent productions by the drambalet choreographer Rostislav Zakharov to illustrate the consequences of this trend, namely Zakharov's productions of Prokofiev's *Cinderella* (Bolshoi, 1945) and of Pushkin's *The Bronze Horseman* (Bolshoi, 1949; music by Reinhold Glière). As the choreography became more and more monotonous, stage effects and sets became more elaborate to capture the audience's interest. In *The Bronze Horseman*, a technically elaborate scene depicting the flooding of St. Petersburg became the ballet's central episode:

> To change the dance until it becomes the dullest part of the ballet, as for example is done in *Cinderella* and in *The Bronze Horseman*, to convert ballet into a selection of technical stage effects in which everything is demonstrated except the abilities of the ballet company and the powers of the choreographer, in which scenery undergoes a more complex evolution than the dancers themselves, and in which the confusion of styles leads to the worst possible eclecticism, is to discard the best traditions of the classical ballets without infusing anything new into them. The classical ballet in its time knew the fairy tale ballet, but that was dance plus fairy tale and not fairy tale minus dance, as is the case with the Bolshoi Theater productions of *Cinderella* and *The Bronze Horseman*.[6]

If the quality of choreography was a major concern, the general lack of new productions was the most obvious symptom of stagnation. In April 1953, Galina Ulanova published an article titled "S khudozhnika sprositsia" (The artist is answerable) in *Sovetskaia muzyka* that criticized and analyzed the absence of new ballet productions at the Bolshoi: for the past three years, the Bolshoi had not staged a single new ballet.[7] According to Ulanova, timidity and indifference, or the professional incompetence of the personnel of the Committee for Artistic Affairs and the leadership of the Bolshoi Theater and its ballet company, were among the main reasons why composers did not come to the Bolshoi with their new compositions. Ulanova asked:

> Where does this timidity come from? Can timid, fearful people create passionate, life-affirming art? The principle "better nothing than something new," which some of the leaders of the Committee for Artistic Affairs and figures of our theater adhere to, is a useless principle. . . . At times it seems to me that the time of comrades N. Bespalov, M. Chulaki, A. Anisimov, L. Lavrovsky, and S. Orechnikov passes in agonizing suspense as to when the "ingenious work," the finished model of the new art, will finally appear. But in our days, one mustn't live so complacently in art, "waiting" until "someone" gives us a finished recipe for the creation of new art. One must search hard, strive, dare, experiment; one must work.[8]

A fear of the new had pervaded the Bolshoi, a fear that probably reflected the bitter lesson of official attacks on new works in the past. One cannot blame those likely to be held accountable to conclude "better nothing than something new." According to Asaf Messerer, this fear of experiments beset the Bolshoi Ballet in 1936, after the *Pravda* editorial "Baletnaia fal'sh,"[9] but the problems were symptomatic of the general crisis of Soviet culture in the early 1950s. A memorandum on the state of Soviet culture sent on 20 June 1955 by the Minister of Culture of the USSR N. Mikhailov to Khrushchev offered a summary of the current situation in film, theater, music, the fine arts, and printing. It called for measures to raise the ideological and artistic level of cultural production but primarily criticized the arts for their insufficient ideological contributions. Out of the memorandum's eleven sections, four alone were dedicated to the cinema, an artistic medium considered particularly important for propaganda.[10]

The memorandum focused on the propagation of Soviet culture in general and works on Soviet topics in particular. It concentrated on the contribution of Soviet culture to the ideological education of the Soviet population but acknowledged that an ideological message would not successfully reach the population unless it was attractively presented. For its own reasons, the government was thus concerned not just about the type of topics presented to the audience but also about the quality of cultural production. Soviet theaters were criticized for staging few productions on the most topical issues of Soviet life that were both ideologically and artistically valuable: over the past nine years, more than one thousand new plays had been produced but only about thirty had survived on stage for a longer period. Many theaters faced exceptional difficulties in their search for good new plays. The report noted that problems in repertoire formation had a direct impact on the level of theater attendance, which was unsatisfactory, especially at the local level where in 1954 the average attendance was 59 percent of the capacity of venues. The memorandum acknowledged that attendance levels were a direct function of the repertoire, the quality of performance, and the general standard of a theater's work.[11]

There were also practical issues that hampered the work of performing artists. In particular, under current legislation theaters were not allowed to dismiss artists who could not perform at the necessary level, which in turn made it impossible to hire artists who would be able to do so.[12] For the Kirov Ballet, this legal issue caused serious problems because numerous dancers who were past their prime refused to retire and make way for their younger colleagues.[13] In ballet the general problem of artists losing their professional abilities was exacerbated by the fact that a dancer's professional life is comparatively short, at the time usually not continuing much beyond the age of forty.

Exploiting the Political Climate: Konstantin Sergeev's Dismissal

For the Kirov Ballet, the era of the cultural Thaw and de-Stalinization coincided with a generational shift within the company. A confrontation between different artistic generations reinforced by general trends within the country lay at the heart of the dynamics of change that led to the invigoration of the Soviet choreographic scene in the second half of the 1950s. In 1955, stars of the drambalet period such as Konstantin Sergeev, Natalia Dudinskaya, and Tatiana Vecheslova had been dancing at the Kirov for approximately twenty years, the average length of a dancing career in those years, even though many of the most well-known dancers of this era danced significantly longer.[14] A new generation of talented dancers in their twenties or early thirties was looking for wider artistic opportunities in general, and the opportunity to create new parts in new ballets in particular.

Both at the Kirov and Bolshoi, interesting new ballet productions had become a rarity. At the Kirov Ballet, principal dancer Konstantin Sergeev had stood at the helm of the company both as its chief choreographer and artistic director since 1951. In the spring of 1955, his leadership style led to a palace revolt by several young members of the company. The episode culminated in a decision by the USSR Ministry of Culture to remove Sergeev from the posts of chief choreographer and artistic director. In the generational struggle within the Kirov Ballet, the young challengers benefited from the general official support given to the young as a force potentially capable of revitalizing the Communist project within the context of the wider process of de-Stalinization.

On 23 February 1955, *Pravda* published a letter to the editor by three Kirov dancers, Askol'd Makarov, Konstantin Shatilov, and Nikolai Zubkovsky.[15] According to the letter, Sergeev stifled creative initiative, didn't nurture young talents, and jealously preserved a monopoly over leading parts for himself and his wife and dance partner, Natalia Dudinskaya. The letter contrasted the Kirov's earlier contributions to the development of Soviet ballet both in terms of ballets and dancers with the creative stagnation of recent years, lamenting that the company had primarily been busy with the restoration of old ballets. Moreover, Sergeev and Dudinskaya's monopoly over certain principal roles led to the cancellation of performances if one of the two dancers was unable to perform, and talented young artists were stifled in their development by not being cast. If young dancers were cast in new parts, they danced them infrequently and were not given adequate rehearsal time. Young dancers were not only forced to substitute for sick principal dancers at short notice but pushed onto stage without being given the chance to rehearse systematically and sufficiently.[16]

The article thus highlighted two issues. The first related to the problem of repertoire renewal, the lifeblood of any ballet company. Since Sergeev had assumed the position of artistic director in 1951, the only new ballet, the propagandistic drambalet *Native Fields,* had proved a disastrous failure. The remaining three new productions had all been restorations of old ballets. If Ulanova had highlighted the lack of new productions as a problem particularly acute at the Bolshoi in her article for *Sovetskaia muzyka,* the situation at the Kirov did not seem to be any better. The second problem related to the company leadership's attitude toward promoting young talents. These two issues were by necessity related. If young dancers were to fully develop their talent, they needed new roles to challenge them. The article accused Sergeev of lacking a coherent strategy for nurturing young talent, both in terms of introducing them to the running repertoire of the company and in terms of offering them opportunities to dance in new ballets.

Even though the selection of articles surrounding the dancers' letter to *Pravda* may have been coincidental, it illustrated the ideological emphasis placed during the Thaw on "youth" as a beacon of hope shining into a bright, Socialist future, a climate that the instigators of the campaign against Sergeev used to their own, artistic advantage. Two of the three main articles printed on the same page as the letter were related to the Komsomol (Communist Union of Youth). One of the articles reported on the plenum of the Central Committee of the Komsomol, calling upon the young to dedicate all their strength to fulfilling the decisions of the January plenum of the Central Committee of the Communist Party. In the other article, the Central Committee of the Komsomol called upon all Komsomol members and village youth in the Soviet Union to promote the cultivation of corn. Printed within the vicinity of these drives to promote the participation of the young in building communism, the Kirov dancers' provocatively titled article "What hinders the growth of young talents" stuck out as an eyesore.

The article's publication in the central party organ, *Pravda,* implied that there was official support for the Kirov's "young Turks" against Sergeev. At first sight, this might seem surprising. Artistically conservative, Sergeev was not only one of the most celebrated male dancers of his generation but also a loyal member of the Soviet establishment. Dutifully fulfilling his public role, he was a member of the committee of the Stalin Prize and served as deputy of the Soviet of Worker's Deputies of the Oktiabr'skii district in Leningrad. In 1955, however, the Soviet regime apparently required more of the artistic director of the Kirov Ballet than loyalty and a highly professional artistic conservatism. The regime was concerned about cultural stagnation and worried about the Kirov Ballet's failure to stage new ballets in general and ballets on Soviet topics in particular. On 7 March 1955, Deputy Minister of Culture of the USSR Kemenov attended a general meeting of the Kirov Theater to acquaint it with new regulations concerning artistic councils and to discuss the letter to *Pravda* about the Kirov Ballet.

Artistic and political concerns had for a moment fused. Both politicians and artists were worried about creative stagnation, even if their reasons were different. Kemenov was supposed to explain one of the measures the government had taken to address this issue. In early 1955, the Ministry of Culture tried to use the artistic councils of Soviet theaters to reinvigorate the Soviet Union's theatrical landscape. New regulations issued by the ministry ordered the theaters to widen the membership of artistic councils from a small group of artistic leaders within the theaters to a much larger body.

The Soviet government must have been seriously concerned about the creative lethargy of the Kirov, taking the rare decision to send a deputy minister of culture to Leningrad to look into the situation.[17] At the meeting, Kemenov stated that "theater" was a collective art, that decisions had to be decided by a collective, and that the artistic council provided the organizational forum for doing so. The Kirov was given until mid-April to decide upon the particulars of renewing its artistic council. Like the dancers who had written to *Pravda,* the government was worried about the lack of new productions at the Kirov. Discussing the Kirov's shortcomings, Kemenov asked, "Why did the theater propose only two [new] productions in its plan instead of four? Because of this, the plan was rejected and it was ordered to submit a new one. The theater can and must produce more productions." Moving on to the situation of the ballet company, Kemenov declared that if man had a "golden age," then this "golden age" was very short in ballet and great talents could be ruined if young artists didn't get the chance to create new roles, "and it's for this reason that we don't understand why such a strong collective like the ballet of your theater plans only one [new] production per year." The deputy minister concluded that bad planning was the source of the problem because in terms of capacity, the ballet company should be able to stage two new productions per year. He firmly stated that if the theater's artistic council had functioned better, "a whole range of questions would not have been put in the newspaper article. A correct expression of public opinion and a well-working artistic council would not have permitted such a situation."[18] For once, the regime and many artists agreed: there were not enough new productions and creative life was in a rut.

But while the dancers lamented the lack of opportunity to grow artistically with the creation of interesting new parts, Kemenov's speech showed that the government was primarily concerned about the lack of operas and ballets on Soviet themes. The regime's decision to reform the artistic councils was based on the hope that more collective leadership would improve the theaters' contribution to the regime's ideological machine. Kemenov elaborated the reasons behind the government's urgent call for reforming the artistic councils: "Why is this so important? . . . The Central Committee of the party says that now, in our conditions of a difficult and conflictual international environment, the great educational role of Soviet literature and art is of particular significance." Kemenov called upon the artistic councils to help the theaters to work on the basis of socialist realism, lecturing that "to be at the height of the tasks of socialist realism—this means to possess deep knowledge of the real life of the people, their feelings and thoughts, to show heartfelt sensitivity toward their experiences, and the capability to depict this in absorbing, intelligible artistic form."[19]

Remarkably, Kemenov's comments on artistic form combined the usual battle cry against those diverging from the path of socialist realism with a call for more individuality, indicating that the government might have realized that an endless repetition of the same dogmas lay at the heart of Soviet cultural stagnation. Commenting on socialist realism, Kemenov stressed:

This method ought not to be understood as something standardized. Such an understanding is harmful dogmatism. We are talking about a diversity of forms and style. . . . If one thinks about the productions of our theaters, surely the phenomenon exists that a young director shapes a production, and instead of giving him the possibility to approach a new form, the principal director arrives and completes it in his own manner. The production loses the individuality of its creator, becomes commonplace, even though at a professionally high standard. The result is the leveling of individuality.[20]

Tapping the vitality of the young was seen as pivotal to carefully reinvigorating creativity and to opening a meaningful path of cultural communication between the regime and the people. Kemenov stressed that introducing young artists to the membership of the artistic council was particularly important: "Stanislavsky and Nemirovich-Danchenko and Vakhtangov did this daringly in their time. . . . The artistic council has to be formed on the principle of combination of old and young cadres."[21]

In his closing remarks, Kemenov concluded that many speakers had confirmed the content of the letter to *Pravda*. He reiterated the government's concern about the lack of Soviet ballets, emphasizing that no one reproached the theater for staging classical ballets, but that it should not stop working on Soviet productions. Kemenov concluded that Orlov, the director of the theater, and Sergeev had not been sufficiently self-critical in their assessment of the theater's attitude toward nurturing young talent. Young dancers were indeed busy dancing in the running repertoire, but this was not enough:

> Comrade Orlov said that things are satisfactory with regards to this question at the ballet, and Sergeev explained that work with the young proceeded like a torrent in spring. One mustn't confuse the question of production commitments of the young with the big and serious task of the education and cultivation of young talents. . . . We are talking not about this, but about a more important question. For many years, young performers haven't known the word *première*. Is this normal? This is absolutely not normal. How can one talk here about a rapid spring torrent?[22]

Regardless of whether or not Sergeev was to blame for the situation at the Kirov, Kemenov's condescending and schoolmasterly attitude toward him was typical of the humiliating tutelage Soviet artists were constantly subjected to in their dealings with predominantly ignorant but powerful Soviet cultural bureaucrats. Referring to the accusation that Sergeev and his wife, Dudinskaya, had built an artistic monopoly, Kemenov offered Sergeev— a living legend in the Soviet ballet world—some words of artistic advice:

> Zubkovsky said that Sergeev doesn't dance with other ballerinas. But this would be very interesting for the young ballerinas and for you,

Konstantin Mikhailovich. . . . As a master, Konstantin Mikhailovich Sergeev belongs to a greater number of people than to one Natalia Mikhailovna. And for you, Konstantin Mikhailovich, it is more interesting to meet with other creative individuals and to create an image with them. This is necessary for your development as well as for the education of young ballerinas and for the audience. If you are a leader, you have to be an example for others in your personal behavior.[23]

Kemenov concluded that both Sergeev and Dudinskaya had more to learn from the article and from the statements made at the meeting.[24]

The meeting concluded that the letter to *Pravda* correctly pointed out several shortcomings in the work of the ballet company. All materials of the meeting were to be passed on to the Ministry of Culture of the USSR.[25] Nine days later *Pravda* published a short notice that stated that the discussion at the theater had shown that Sergeev was responsible for the Kirov Ballet's shortcomings. In order to overcome these shortcomings, the Ministry of Culture ordered the formation of an artistic board of the ballet.[26] The Ministry of Culture abolished the post of chief choreographer; the board was to be headed by Fedor Lopukhov, the newly appointed artistic director of the company, and the Ministry of Culture confirmed Tatiana Vecheslova, Konstantin Sergeev, Konstantin Shatilov, and Alla Shelest as members of the artistic board.[27]

The protocol of the meeting indicates that its outcome had been a foregone conclusion. The meeting closed before many of the people who were on the list of speakers had had a chance to speak. In response to a complaint that not everything was clear and that many "comrades" still had something to say about Sergeev's leadership, Kemenov merely replied that he had to leave for a meeting at the dramatic theater: those who had not had a chance to speak could submit their speeches for inclusion in the meeting's protocol, but they would have no bearing on the decision.[28] Judging by the protocol, opinions on both Sergeev in particular and the state of the company in general were divided. Most of the attached statements by dancers who did not get to speak at the meeting supported Sergeev and complained about the meeting's undemocratic nature, but this could be interpreted both ways: either Sergeev's supporters were speaking up because they were in the majority and protested the outcome of the meeting, or they were speaking up as an embattled minority that felt mistreated.

Choreographic Symphonism versus Drambalet

Sergeev's dismissal and Lopukhov's appointment were a harbinger of the ensuing paradigm shift in Soviet choreography from drambalet to choreographic symphonism (*khoreograficheskii simfonizm*) and symphonic dance (*simfonicheskii tanets*). Even though it never went as far as Lopukhov's radical experiment with abstract dance, his *Dance Symphony* of 1923, choreographic symphonism was closely related to Lopukhov's creative agenda of pushing forward choreographic development by exploring the structural relationship between music and dance and by focusing on the expressiveness of pure dance movements, in contrast to drambalet's focus on dance's dramatic-pantomimic potential. Lopukhov lost no time in reclaiming the Kirov's stage as a platform for innovative choreography. Soon after his appointment, he invited the shunned choreographer Leonid Iakobson to stage Khachaturian's ballet *Spartacus* and championed the young, inexperienced choreographer Yuri Grigorovich by entrusting him with a new production of *The Stone Flower*.

Pierre Bourdieu has observed that stylistic breaks in the field of culture are often accompanied by a rediscovery of previously discarded artistic trends. An absolute break of a new generation with the immediate preceding generation of "fathers" is often supported by a return to the traditions of the next generation back, the "grandfathers."[29] This certainly applied to the realm of Soviet culture during the Thaw, which saw a partial rediscovery of cultural endeavors of the 1920s. Lopukhov uses the image of "grandfathers" and "grandsons" to describe his relationship with the "symphonic" choreographers emerging in the 1950s: "The people say that children sometimes resemble their grandfathers more than their fathers. I flatter myself with the hope that this will be true with respect to my 'grandsons' in ballet. Grigorovich and Bel'sky, not having seen my best works, but knowing about my cherished desires from conversations with me, inherit from me the most important thing, which I in my turn tried to inherit from my predecessors— from Lev Ivanov, M. Fokine, and, of course, M. Petipa."[30]

Lopukhov's emphasis on a chain of artistic continuity linking Petipa, Ivanov, Fokine, himself, and the symphonic choreographers of the Soviet cultural Thaw, and the historical roots of the debate juxtaposing drambalet and choreographic symphonism, indicate the continuity of artistic thought across periods of drastic political and social change in Russia. In many ways, the choreographic battle that pitted proponents of symphonic dance against defenders of drambalet continued the old debate about ballet's nature: Is ballet's expressive nature closer to the dramatic theater or to music? Should ballets be danced, narrative dramas, or does the nonrepresentational nature of classical dance make ballet most artistically persuasive as a general allegory of human emotions? The language of some of the reviews of Petipa's *The Sleeping Beauty* published after the ballet's premiere in 1890 bears a striking resemblance to Soviet demands for content-rich ballets and condemnations of dance as empty ornament unless intimately linked to a dramatic plot:

> The first condition for the ballet to be a *ballet,* and not a féerie with dances, is that (a) the dances correspond to at least the basic needs of the choreography and (b) that these dances must necessarily be a *direct consequence* of the ballet's plot. Without this, a ballet isn't a ballet but something absurd and incomprehensible. . . . In *The Sleeping Beauty* there is nothing of the sort. The line of action doesn't *illustrate* the dances at all. The dances are neither here nor there and in the majority of cases come as an unexpected surprise, like a hair that fell into the soup.[31]

Similarly, a vocal defense of *The Sleeping Beauty* in 1895 anticipated some of the criticisms made of drambalet in the 1950s. Hermann Laroche, a music critic and friend of Tchaikovsky's, contrasted the striving for the "certainty of verbal speech" and realism in other contemporary ballets with the more generalized, mythological level on which *The Sleeping Beauty* takes place: "In contrast to opera, which is capable of representing contemporary, everyday, middle-class existence, the ballet is destined to carry us to the kingdom of the fantastic and the impossible, the incomprehensible and the inexpressible. . . . It's absolutely true that the dramatic action in *The Sleeping Beauty* is slow and elementally simple. But it's the same in the *Odyssey* and in Aeschylus's *Prometheus* and in Boccacio's *Griselda* and in Wagner's *Parsifal*."[32] In the 1950s, some Soviet dance writers began to voice similar complaints against drambalet and its attempt to depict everyday situations in the pseudo-verbal realism of dance pantomime, emphasizing instead the ability of symphonic music and classical dance to express profound but generalized truths that cannot easily be captured in words.

But the paradigm shift in Soviet choreography should not be discussed solely in terms of old artistic debates continuing across different historical periods. In the 1950s, the reemergence of symphonic dance was accompanied by loud polemics that pitted representative of the drambalet establishment against their artistic challengers. The reemergence of choreographic symphonism was primarily an artistic reaction to the monopoly of drambalet within the wider context of Soviet ideological-cultural dogmatism.

In the early 1950s, Soviet ballet discourse revolved around several key terms and dichotomies. Like all Soviet art, Soviet ballet was supposed to embody the principles of *narodnost'* (nationality), *ideinost'* (ideological content), and *partiinost'* (party spirit). The call for narodnost' translated into an abundance of modified national dances in Soviet ballets, while ideinost' and partiinost' meant that ballet librettos should have social and educational propaganda value. Even librettos of classics such as *Swan Lake* were not safe: instead of its traditional tragic ending, the Swan Queen Odette and Prince Siegfried live happily ever after in the Soviet version, personifying the victory of good over evil.

The contrast between nonrepresentational and narrative art was a crucial determinant for the development of Soviet choreographic language. While this dichotomy is not peculiar to the Soviet context, it was defined in uniquely ideological terms and, to the detriment of artistic autonomy, acquired ideological and political significance as a symbol of the struggle between the Soviet Union and the West. In the 1930s and 1940s, attacks that ballet was a pretty after-dinner entertainment for the upper classes incapable of addressing humanity's fundamental concerns metamorphosed into the claim that in the Soviet Union ballet had acquired a brain, a social conscience, and *soderzhatel'nost'* (content-richness). According to Soviet ballet rhetoric, every second in a truly *Soviet* ballet expressed important ideas, while ballet in the bourgeois West was empty entertainment devoid of intelligent content. Reflecting the Soviet emphasis on art's social mission and the implicit requirement that its message could be put into words, socialist realism precluded any flirtation with modernism and abstraction, condemning such attempts under the blanket term *formalism*. If we define *abstraction* as the absence of easily verbalized narrative content, similar to music, classical dance is by definition an abstract language, but unlike music, it is bound to the physical reality of the human body. Soviet ballet had to find a way to bridge the gaping chasm between classical dance's nonrepresentational, highly conventionalized nature and the demands of socialist realism. It did so by declaring dramatic content its new god, relegating imaginative choreography to a secondary role.

Rostislav Zakharov's book *Iskusstvo baletmeistera* (The art of the choreographer), published in 1954 in Moscow, was intended as a practical bible for the drambalet choreographer. Zakharov identified folk art and Stanislavsky's realist school of dramatic theater as the two guardian angels that led Soviet ballet from the erroneous paths of formalist experimentation pursued in the 1920s and early 1930s to the right path of socialist realism. The adaptation of Stanislavsky's method—including "table work," preparatory rehearsal work that is conducted sitting around a table—to ballet was supposed to ensure that instead of a formalist pursuit of dance technique as a goal in itself, Soviet dancers created realistic, convincing characters who acted in narrative dance dramas. In drambalet terminology, they achieved *tanets v obraze*, dance inside a character's figure. Zakharov distinguished between *deistvennyi tanets*, dramatic dance, and *divertismentnyi tanets*, divertissement dance. He defined deistvennyi tanets as those dances in a ballet that disclose the plot of a ballet and the character of its heroes. Zakharov repeatedly warned against seeing classical dance technique as a goal in itself, stating that it was merely a means for expressing content: a choreographer should only use those movements of classical dance that corresponded to the plot of a specific ballet.[33]

The genre's theoretical premises were flawed. Drambalet tried to bring the content of ballets closer to the content of dramatic plays while lacking the most important element of the dramatic theater: the power of the spoken word. By limiting the diversity of classical dance vocabulary, drambalet limited the scope of its expressiveness. Its mistrust of complex classical choreography meant the end of large classical ensemble pieces for a corps de ballet and soloists so typical of Petipa's ballets. In *Iskusstvo baletmeistera*, Zakharov provided his own version of Russian ballet history—which does not mention Marius Petipa—in which he condemned complex classical choreography for not pushing forward a plot and as mindless entertainment for decadent courtiers and declared that Soviet ballet had parted with this "tradition" for good. In addition to deistvennyi tanets, Zakharov identified another form of dance permissible in drambalet, divertismentnyi tanets, which should characterize a ballet's location and milieu and take its inspiration from national dances.[34]

Drambalet was essentially a condemnation of pure dance in the name of logically developed and realistically presented dramatic content. In the 1950s, pure dance tried to fight its way back into Soviet choreography under the guise of the term *choreographic symphonism*. The rhetoric of the term *choreographic symphonism* as used in Soviet discussions from the 1950s onward needs to be analyzed as a shrewd response to the ideological dead end into which pure dance had been pushed by drambalet's ideologically termed condemnation of choreographic experiments of the 1920s and early 1930s.[35]

If drambalet looked toward the lessons of the dramatic theater to give the "frivolous" art of ballet some "socialist realist substance," the proponents of symphonism sought to relegitimize pure dance by stressing dance's artistic kinship to symphonic music, a genre well respected in Soviet Russia, and by evoking the choreographic achievements of romantic nineteenth-century ballet in the effective use of pure dance as epitomized in the swan scenes of *Swan Lake*, the dance of the Wilis in the second act of *Giselle*, and the "Kingdom of the Shades" act in *La Bayadère*.

In 1957, the year Grigorovich's production of Prokofiev's ballet *The Stone Flower* marked the rebirth of choreographic symphonism on the Soviet stage, the Russian ballet critic and historian Vera Krasovskaya wrote an article that eloquently put forth the theoretical argument of those who saw the salvation of Soviet choreography in a return to choreographic symphonism.

Quoting Pushkin, who said that he loved poetry without plan better than a plan without poetry, Krasovskaya lamented that today's dramatic ballet often resembled a plan without poetry.[36] By drawing parallels to symphonic music, which might be programmatic but never express a narrative, quasi-verbal dramatic plot, the term *choreographic symphonism* was supposed to pave the way for the return of the kind of dance that had been branded as formalist for the past two decades. Within the context of Soviet constraints on artistic discourse in general, and the taboo placed on anything approaching abstraction in particular, the term *symphonism* should be understood as a code word for quasi-abstract dance that does not narrowly illustrate a dramatic plot but expresses more general concepts and emotions in complex, even virtuoso, classical choreography. Proponents of choreographic symphonism argued that, similar to symphonic music, the expressive strength of classical dance lay not in the representation of concrete situations but in its capacity to operate on a level of poetic, nonverbal generalization.

The specific use of the terms *choreographic symphonism* and *symphonic dance* in the debates of the 1950s and 1960s should not be confused with statements on Tchaikovsky's contribution to making ballet *music* symphonic. Choreographic symphonism was achieved primarily through *choreographic* means and could be attained even in a ballet such as *La Bayadère*, which was not blessed with music of high quality. Petipa's choreography in the ballet's "Kingdom of the Shades" for a large female corps de ballet of forty-eight dancers, three female soloists, and Solor and Nikiya is one of the treasures of the nineteenth-century repertoire. Krasovskaya describes "Kingdom of the Shades" as an "example of genuine symphonic dance," emphasizing that "symphonism here arises exclusively in the sphere of plastic imagery," as Minkus's music was "not in the least symphonic": in the best case, it did not disturb the impression made by the dance, while in the worst case, its jaunty rhythms clashed with the poetry of the plastic action.[37] Judging by the examples Krasovskaya used, Soviet dance writers defined choreographic symphonism as the choreographic development of different movements' themes, the creation of polyphonic ensembles that juxtapose different voices in the corps with soloists, the visual reconstruction of musical images.[38] The ideologically acceptable language of symphonic music was used to return legitimacy to the complex, nonnarrative segments of classical choreography for a large corps and soloists typical of Petipa's ballets.

The call for the return of choreographic symphonism was an appeal for the return of complex choreographic compositions using the classical vocabulary in all its virtuosity and a plea to free choreography from the constraints of drambalet, which limited dance to a primarily illustrative function tied to a narrative. Krasovskaya warned that if a ballet was staged as if it

FIGURE 22. *Native Fields*, third act, third scene, at the Kirov Ballet, 1950. © Mariinsky
Theater

were a dramatic play or movie, where dance is not the center of action but
fulfills only an illustrative role, the ballet stopped being a ballet, and not
possessing the narrative possibilities of a prose drama, it ended up resembling "a mute opera, a spectacle that, to tell the truth, is not one of the most
fascinating ones." To illustrate the point that, like music, ballet could express
minute shades of feeling but not "everyday and prosaic action,"[39] Krasovskaya contrasted *Swan Lake* with the ballet *Native Fields*, a drambalet by the
choreographer Aleksei Andreev created for the Kirov in 1953:

> Odette dances the aspiration toward freedom, the heroine of *Native
> Fields* has to express in dance the desire that her fiancé will arrive to
> construct an electric power station in the native kolkhoz. Siegfried
> dances a confusion of feelings, the struggle between spiritual and
> carnal love; and the hero of *Native Fields* dances agitation before the
> defense of a diploma and the pleasure on account of its success, he
> chooses between the possibility to stay on as graduate student and the
> necessity of going to work on the kolkhoz. Far from the generalizing
> imagery of dance, straightforward "kitchen-sinkism" gives rewarding
> material for parody. Realism of ballet action lies in the area of poetic
> generalization.[40]

The debate also concerned the development of choreographic vocabulary. Krasovskaya argued that symphonic dance led to the development and perfection of choreographic language because it made choreographers introduce more movements to increase their ability to express any shade of emotional imagery, while "the very rejection of symphonic dance inevitably led to and resulted in the poverty of the dance palette[, and] . . . many classical dance movements are today mistakenly forgotten by the majority of Soviet choreographers."[41]

Using the Komsomol for Pushing Choreographic Innovation

Like any paradigm shift in artistic production, the victory of symphonic dance over drambalet was not an easy one. The ability of artists to exploit political forces played a crucial role in overcoming resistance within the Kirov Ballet to those who wanted to challenge the choreographic boundaries set by drambalet. Work on *The Stone Flower* and on two other ballets central for the rise of "symphonic dance," Igor' Bel'sky's productions of Andrei Petrov's *Coast of Hope* (premiering at the Kirov Ballet, 16 April 1959) and of Shostakovich's *Leningrad Symphony* (premiering at the Kirov Ballet, 14 April 1961), proceeded parallel to work on the theater's main production plan, leading to serious problems in getting the necessary allocation of rehearsal space, rehearsal time, and pianists. The artists involved in creating *The Stone Flower* repossessed the field of cultural production by using ideological rhetoric (the emphasis on youth during the Thaw) and instruments of ideological education (the Komsomol) for the attainment of artistic, non-ideological goals.

The designation of Grigorovich's production of Prokofiev's *The Stone Flower* (premiering on 25 April 1957) as a "youth production" played an important role in ensuring the ballet's successful staging. The involvement of the Kirov's Komsomol organization and the decision to dedicate the ballet to the Sixth International Youth Festival to be held in Moscow and Leningrad facilitated the creation of adequate working conditions, culminating in an order by USSR Minister of Culture Mikhailov in February 1957 instructing the Kirov Theater's leadership to do everything necessary to ensure the ballet was finished in time.

The young Grigorovich owed his commission to stage *The Stone Flower* to Lopukhov. Grigorovich was barely thirty at the premiere of the ballet, his first major work, and the decision to entrust him with the production was far from unanimous. Originally, Konstantin Sergeev had been tasked with choreographing a new version of the ballet, after Lavrovsky's production for the Bolshoi under the title *Skaz o kamennom tsvetke* had proven a failure at its premiere in February 1954. Lopukhov initially insisted that Sergeev take Grigorovich as his assistant, but according to Lopukhov, when it became clear that Sergeev was not able to propose anything interesting while the young Grigorovich had an attractive plan, Grigorovich was entrusted with the ballet.[42] It is not clear when exactly Grigorovich took over the production from Sergeev, but he did so at the latest by the end of the 1954–1955 theatrical season.

It was a battle waged by innovators—supported by Lopukhov—but the defenders of the choreographic status quo sought to obstruct the project both secretly and openly. Grigorovich's opponents shook their heads, complaining that an "obscure" choreographer ought not to be preferred over a People's Artist, and they doubted whether Grigorovich's and the artist Simon Virsaladze's plans were realistic. Furthermore, they did not like that young dancers were brought into the project, and some criticized the introduction of changes of Prokofiev's score necessitated by alterations in the stage action.[43] The young dancer Alla Osipenko created the part of the Mistress of the Copper Mountain, choreographically the most innovative and controversial part of the ballet. Her sleek costume made her probably the first dancer in the Soviet Union to wear just a revealing leotard on stage, and she was threatened by Sergeev and others: "If you will dance like you dance *The Stone Flower*, you will no more be able to do anything. Not *Swan Lake*, not *Raymonda*."[44] In this environment "every step of Grigorovich was under the threat of 'fire' by numerous skeptics 'out of friendship' and 'out of duty.' But the choreographer as well as the artist manifested extraordinary endurance and worked productively. They succeeded in the most difficult thing—to fight opponents with the weapon of creative work. With every month, the number of foes and skeptics dwindled, the quantity of those sympathizing with the new cause grew, although many obstacles remained right up to the premiere and even after it."[45]

The Stone Flower is an allegory about the problems of artistic creation, the pursuit of discovering the secret of beauty. Set in the Urals, it tells the story of the stonecutter Danila who dreams of creating the perfect malachite vase, the semblance of a real flower, but he can't discern the mystery of nature, the secret of its beauty, and the secret of artistic creation. He gets engaged to Katerina, who is threatened by the evil steward Sever'ian. In his pursuit for the secret of art, Danila ends up in the subterranean kingdom of the Mistress of the Copper Mountain. Katerina goes in search of Danila, pursued by Sever'ian, who is swallowed by the earth by the command of the Mistress of the Copper Mountain. In the meantime, the mistress has disclosed the creative secret of beauty to Danila. She admits her love to him, but he

FIGURE 23. *(above)*
Indoor scene with
Katerina in *The Stone
Flower* at the Kirov
Theater, 1957.
© Mariinsky Theater

FIGURE 24. *(left)*
Irina Kolpakova as
Katerina and Aleksandr
Gribov as Danila in
The Stone Flower at the
Kirov Theater, 1957.
© Mariinsky Theater

FIGURE 25. *(above)*
The kingdom of the
Mistress of the Copper
Mountain in *The Stone
Flower* at the Kirov
Theater, 1957.
© Mariinsky Theater

FIGURE 26. *(right)*
Alla Osipenko as the
Mistress of the Copper
Mountain and Aleksandr
Gribov as Danila in *The
Stone Flower* at the Kirov
Theater, 1957.
© Mariinsky Theater

confesses that he loves Katerina, and the mistress turns him into stone. Katerina enters her kingdom. Impressed by her love, the mistress lets Danila and Katerina go.

The ballet also marked the beginning of Grigorovich's collaboration with the set and costume designer Simon Virsaladze. Even though as a narrative, evening-filling ballet, *The Stone Flower* by no means signified a complete break with drambalet, both the ballet's choreography with its emphasis on dance over mime and the much more modern designs appeared radical to Soviet eyes because they broke with the ossified conventions and slavish realism of recent drambalet productions such as *Native Fields*, something that was entirely lost to Western audiences when they first saw the ballet. For example, in addition to introducing the type of large, classical ensemble criticized as formalist in a scene depicting the kingdom of the Mistress of the Copper Mountain, Grigorovich tried to escape drambalet's performance conventions by insisting that his dancers concentrate the maximal impact of their expressiveness in their movements and gestures, their dancing, and not in dramatic mime with their facial expressions. The angular choreography for the Mistress of the Copper Mountain and her figure-hugging costume looked especially revolutionary on a Soviet stage. Alla Osipenko, who created the part of the Mistress of the Copper Mountain, remembers the long period of private, incredibly creative rehearsals in Grigorovich's flat in a strange room that was fully tiled, and after working hours in the rehearsal studios of the company, as the golden age of her creative life. After Grigorovich had shown the results of their private "Komsomol-youth work" to the company, they gave him an ovation and he was granted permission to proceed with rehearsals as part of the theater's normal working plan.[46]

It is difficult to assess to what extent work on *The Stone Flower* was deliberately obstructed or whether certain problems were simply caused by overstretched work schedules and insufficient planning. *The Stone Flower* was designated to be staged by the young artists of the theater, and rehearsals were to proceed parallel to Iakobson's work on *Spartacus*.[47] While the idea to work on two productions simultaneously might have been good in theory, especially given the government's call to "increase the production" of new operas and ballets, it created serious problems for the secondary, "youth production," which was supposed to have its premiere only after the premiere of *Spartacus*. Until the premiere of *The Stone Flower* one-and-a-half years later, in April 1957, the Kirov Theater's newspaper repeatedly reiterated the same concerns. Initially, uncertainties about the production of *Spartacus* prevented the *The Stone Flower* team from working at full speed.[48] Once work on *Spartacus* had begun in earnest by the end of 1955, hardly any rehearsal

FIGURES 27 AND 28. Alla Osipenko as the Mistress of the Copper Mountain and Aleksandr Gribov as Danila during the first demonstration of *The Stone Flower* to the Kirov Ballet at the rehearsal studio of the Kirov Ballet on Rossi Street, circa late 1956, early 1957. © St. Petersburg State Museum of Theater and Music

time was left for *The Stone Flower*. If Grigorovich had previously been able to rehearse with the soloists in the studio for two hours, he no longer had even this little time at his disposal.[49] Over the next few months, less and less rehearsal time was given to *The Stone Flower*. Instead of being able to rehearse with three different casts, Grigorovich had only two incomplete casts at his disposal.[50] *The Stone Flower* team was not given the necessary rehearsal time, rehearsal space, and pianists.[51]

Whoever was to blame, the Komsomol organization of the Kirov began to lobby for political support for the production in the hope that it would translate into better working conditions. It would be too much to argue that the young artists of the Kirov consciously thought of subverting the Soviet system by exploiting the Komsomol organization within the theater for their own, artistic purposes. Instead, they simply played according to the rules of the game. Artistic innovation that challenged Soviet cultural ideology should not be equated to outright political opposition to the Soviet system as a whole, even though some artists were surely led to reject the system because it infringed on their artistic autonomy. Some of the dancers involved in staging *The Stone Flower* were perfectly loyal Soviet citizens playing the political game successful artists usually had little choice but to participate in, but they nonetheless tried to push the boundaries imposed on cultural production. It is also important to remember that membership in the Komsomol did not necessarily say anything about the private political inclinations of a dancer: talented young dancers were often simply told to join the Komsomol. The Bolshoi ballerina Ekaterina Maksimova—who writes in her memoirs that she never had particular faith in the official party ideals because her grandfather had been arrested and shot—remembers that she was pushed into the Central Committee of the Komsomol after she won the All-Union Ballet Competition in 1957 without anyone ever asking her whether or not she wanted to join the organization.[52] At the Kirov, fifty-eight dancers were members of the Komsomol, including two young dancers creating leading roles in *The Stone Flower*, Irina Kolpakova (Katerina) and Alla Osipenko (Mistress of the Copper Mountain).[53]

Subverting the Komsomol was not the intention of the artists, who neither rejected nor wished to alter the organization as such. But the ambiguity inherent in any social structure or organization led to a situation where they subverted the organization subconsciously by using it to promote artistic goals alien to it. De Certeau's description of the ambiguity that allowed the indigenous peoples of the Americas to subvert Spanish colonization of the region from within offers an interesting structural parallel. It is not necessarily outright rejection of or explicit resistance to a system that undermines any attempt of collective control over individuals the most, but rather it is the almost subconscious subversion of the system from within by people who simply try to forge their own destinies within the system's parameters: "submissive, and even consenting to their subjection, the Indians nevertheless often *made of* the rituals, representations, and laws imposed on them something quite different from what their conquerors had in mind; they subverted them not by rejecting or altering them, but by using them with respect to ends and references foreign to the system they had no choice but to accept."[54]

Seeking political patronage was a powerful strategy in the game of Soviet life. Finding that the theater was not providing them with satisfactory working conditions in general and those necessary to stage *The Stone Flower* in particular, the theater's Komsomol appealed to higher political organs for intercession with the theater's management. On 20 May 1956, *Za sovetskoe iskusstvo* published an open letter by the Kirov Theater's Komsomol Committee to USSR Minister of Culture Mikhailov. The letter reiterated some of the complaints that had led to Sergeev's removal in 1955, protesting that there still did not exist normal conditions for the artistic growth of the young generation. If the earlier *Pravda* letter had primarily blamed Sergeev, this letter turned to Mikhailov because G. N. Orlov, the director of the Kirov, did not "solve the questions" that worried the Komsomol Committee.[55] The unresolved pension question was one of the main obstacles to the professional growth and systematic promotion of young dancers. Old dancers refused to retire, and young dancers were forced to remain in the corps de ballet because there were too many soloists in the company's rooster. In practice, many of the older soloists could no longer perform. Corps de ballet members were de facto dancing solo parts, even though formally, also in terms of salary, they were members of the corps. This led to a chronic "nonfulfillment of norms"—de jure corps de ballet dancers were not fulfilling the higher number of performances members of the corps were supposed to dance because they were cast as soloists. In order to avoid this, the management tried to let corps members dance solos only when it was necessary, which meant that young dancers, as a rule, prepared their parts quickly and did not dance them systematically.

While the pension issue was a major problem, the letter's comments on *The Stone Flower* are more relevant. The letter emphasized that the ballet ensemble had exerted a lot of effort on ending the creative stagnation of past years, but work was constantly hampered by the "defective system of allocation and utilization of creative cadres."[56] The Komsomol of the ballet had happily taken up Lopukhov's suggestion of a youth performance, *The Stone Flower*, and dreamt of showing the ballet at the International Youth Festival in Moscow. Mikhailov was then told that the young choreographer and his young dancers had prepared all parts to music played from a tape recorder, that they had been given almost no studio space and no pianists to rehearse. The support of the theater's Komsomol helped improve working conditions.[57] Grigorovich told *Za sovetskoe iskusstvo* on 19 June 1956 that more than half of the ballet had been staged despite difficult working conditions and that it was especially important to finish the ballet according to plan in order to show it at the International Youth Festival. He pointed out that the theater's Komsomol organization and its secretary Guliaev were now helping him in every possible way to put conditions in order—but at every meeting, the theater's management continued to move the ballet's place in the theater's performance plan.[58]

By October 1956, rehearsals were proceeding regularly and more productively, because the dancers creating the leading roles—Alla Osipenko, Irina Kolpakova, and Aleksandr Gribov—were released from participating in rehearsals for *Spartacus*.[59] The most decisive progress, however, was made after the premiere of *Spartacus* on 27 December 1956, in the months leading up to the International Youth Festival to be held in Moscow and Leningrad in 1957. *Za sovetskoe iskusstvo* now wrote about *The Stone Flower* as a youth production dedicated to the Sixth International Youth Festival, adding that this obliged everyone in the theater to adopt a more serious attitude toward the ballet.[60] The production was hailed as a present by the young artists to the International Youth Festival and as the first production created with the force of the young in the history of ballet theater. A third cast of more experienced dancers was now added to the two youth casts, and the Komsomol committee appealed to the whole company, especially the "older comrades," working with them on the production to help the young achieve their goal.[61]

Using the Komsomol as a tool to increase artistic autonomy by ensuring working conditions necessary for staging an artistically innovative but ideologically insignificant work finally paid off. In a masterstroke of artistic repossession, the involvement of the Soviet government was now used to the advantage of the young innovators. It even led to the minister of culture's direct involvement, something that would have been beyond imagination in any state where the fields of cultural production and politics were less intimately linked. On 15 February 1957, the USSR Minister of Culture Mikhailov issued an order "about the creative initiative of the young ballet artists of the Leningrad State Academic Theater of Opera and Ballet named after S. M. Kirov."[62] In the order, *The Stone Flower* had metamorphosed into an initiative by the Komsomol organization of the Kirov Ballet. Pointing out that the production was about to be finished, that it was dedicated to the international youth festival, and noting the worthy initiative of the youth

FIGURE 29. Alla Osipenko as the Mistress of the Copper Mountain and Aleksandr Gribov as Danila rehearsing *The Stone Flower* with Tatiana Vecheslova. © St. Petersburg State Museum of Theater and Music

of the Kirov Theater, Mikhailov ordered Orlov to provide comprehensive help to the production team for the production's release. Directors of other opera and ballet theaters were ordered to emulate the youth initiative of the Kirov dancers and to organize youth initiatives for new operas, ballets, and concert programs running parallel to the theaters' basic production plan. Ministers of cultures of union republics were told to encourage such youth initiatives by ensuring good working conditions and by offering all necessary help.

Mikhailov's order paved the way for ensuring that the ballet's premiere would no longer be postponed. In response to Mikhailov's order, the ballet's production team held a special meeting with the theater's leadership. Grigorovich would now have the stage fully at his disposal for rehearsals from 1 March onward, the premiere was earmarked for 10–12 April, and the director of the theater's workshop assured the team that the ballet's sets would be ready in time, even though the workshop was working at full capacity to fulfill the Ministry of Culture's order to produce sets for a Tadjik and a Tatar *dekada*.[63] On 19 March, *Za sovetskoe iskusstvo* reported that the Komsomol Committee of the theater had called on the Komsomol of the workshops to organize Komsomol youth posts in all the workshops involved in the mounting of *The Stone Flower*. Both committees agreed to publish a report on the work of the "festival production."[64]

If the party saw the Komsomol as a force of youthful ideological reinvigoration, then within the context of *The Stone Flower*, politics and ideology are conspicuous in their absence from the rhetoric of the Kirov Theater's Komsomol. On 31 March 1957, *Za sovetskoe iskusstvo* published an article by B. Gudkov, the secretary of the Komsomol's Oktiabr'skyi district committee. Gudkov emphasized that preparations for the Sixth International Youth Festival had to be infused with profound political content. Instead, he pointed out, "in the preparation period for the festival, very serious mistakes were made on the side of the Komsomol organizations, which mainly consist in the fact that no serious attention was spared for the political side of the festival and people were carried away by the cultural enterprises among the masses."[65] In a way, the Komsomol of the Kirov Theater thus subverted the official purpose of the Komsomol. As the youth wing of the Communist Party, it was in theory responsible for instilling Communist values and introducing young people to political life. Unconcerned by the political purpose of the organization, the Kirov Theater Komsomol used the organization's clout for the purely artistic goal of producing *The Stone Flower*: dedicating the ballet to the International Youth Festival helped generate official political support for the production, which in turn contributed to creating the working conditions necessary for the ballet's timely completion.

Ideology as Artistic Weapon

The premiere of *The Stone Flower* marked the beginning of an open confrontation between the defenders of drambalet and the supporters of symphonic dance. Different views on the correct path for choreographic development in the Soviet Union lay at the heart of this conflict, but the confrontation was intensified by the tensions inherent in any generational shift and by the usual animosities and jealousies between competing artists. The struggle between the different camps was exacerbated by the Soviet attempt to impose an ideological framework on the arts, making possible a negative form of artistic repossession: artists could use the weapon of ideology to defend their position against challengers. It should not be precluded that some artists sincerely believed in the ideological rhetoric they used, but, given human nature, it is equally likely that others used the weapon of ideology to further their own ambitions, not to defend the Soviet system as such.

In the fight to maintain their leading position within the artistic hierarchy, defenders of drambalet tried to delegitimize their challengers by branding them as ideologically suspect. They accused Grigorovich of being a "modernist" using "Western" methods because unlike his drambalet colleagues, and more like choreographers in the "decadent" West, he sought to incorporate much more challenging technical elements in his choreography that had a more modern aesthetic. At the same time, they also tried to brand his colleague Igor' Bel'sky as a formalist flirting with abstraction. Bel'sky's ballets showed that within the complex climate of Soviet cultural production, artistic innovation that subverted Soviet cultural dogmas could go hand in hand with ideologically sound, even propagandistic, contemporary plots. Bel'sky's ballets on contemporary Soviet themes illustrate that the dividing line between official and unofficial art in the Soviet Union could be extremely blurred: the ballets' themes were ideologically orthodox, but especially in the case of *Coast of Hope*, Bel'sky's artistic interpretation of them was condemned as abstract by defenders of the artistic conventions of drambalet, an accusation that came dangerously close to attaching the anti-Soviet label of formalism to the choreographer. Bel'sky tried to be much more metaphorical than narrative or literal in his choreography, even if it told a story, and the set and costume designs for ballets such as *Coast of Hope* looked so minimalist to Soviet eyes that they did indeed bear a dangerous resemblance to Western abstract works.

His first major ballet, *Coast of Hope*, to music by the young composer Andrei Petrov, premiered at the Kirov on 16 April 1959. *Coast of Hope* was a choreographic allegory of patriotism and loyalty: a fisherman is stranded on an alien shore and thrown into prison, but neither threats nor temptations can weaken his loyalty to "his shore." The prison walls give way to the power of his loyalty to "his shore," and the fisherman and his friends return home. Bel'sky's next major ballet, the one-act ballet *Leningrad Symphony*, had its premiere at the Kirov in 1961. Set to the first movement of Shostakovich's Seventh Symphony, it was dedicated to the struggle of Leningrad's population against the Nazi invasion. The ballet is almost the only Soviet ballet on a contemporary topic still performed today. While expressing a concrete idea, the struggle against the Nazi invasion, it told the story in a more abstracted way that broke with drambalet's emphasis on dramatic narrative development, on very concrete characterization of a ballet's heroes down to small biographical details, and on realistic set designs that paint a detailed image of locations. In *Leningrad Symphony*, the ballet's main characters are symbolic types, simply named "Girl," "Young Man," and "Traitor"; sets and costumes are minimalist and abstracted. The ballet is about the general heroism of the population's resistance and does not follow an intricate dramatic plot. Like *The Stone Flower*, *Leningrad Symphony* was produced outside the Kirov's normal performance production plan, relying on young dancers who dedicated their time to the productions on top of their regular workload.

If for some, *The Stone Flower* represented the dawn of a new era where music drove the dramatic structure of choreography and where complex classical dance returned to the ballet stage, others looked at it askance, observing serious violations of the conventions of drambalet. Gavriela Komleva, a Kirov ballerina who joined the company a few months after the ballet's premiere, remembers the stormy atmosphere within the company at the time:

> *The Stone Flower* revealed the dissatisfaction of a part of the company with the repertoire and offered a new direction for searches. A split appeared within the company: some thirsted for novelty, the usual suited the rest. . . . "Like-mindedness" existed neither among the dancers nor among the choreographers. The theater was boiling. The trade union meetings of the company in those years were eventful, each time they returned to heated debates about the fate of art and our ballet. . . . The meetings lasted for hours and . . . were often continued on the following day.[66]

Many talked about a crisis, and Komleva realized only later that she had participated in one of the Kirov's most fruitful periods, but despite illusions of increased freedom during the Khrushchev Thaw, borders continued to exist, not just in party doctrines but also within the artists' minds: passionate convictions often fused with intolerance into narrow-mindedness. The

FIGURE 30. *Coast of Hope* at the Kirov Ballet, 1959. © Mariinsky Theater

FIGURE 31. *Leningrad Symphony*, first act, at the Kirov Ballet, 1961. © Mariinsky Theater

company was divided into two camps, corresponding not just to aesthetic preferences but also to egoistic interests and human sympathies.[67]

Although the arguments ran high, Grigorovich by no means rejected all the characteristics of drambalet, notably "content-rich" drama and a focus on the psychology of a ballet's heroes. His artistic credo thus mirrored both the goals and limitations of de-Stalinization. If de-Stalinization aimed to renegotiate the country's Stalinist legacies to relaunch the Soviet project without challenging the core of the system itself—an ideologically driven one-party state with a planned economy—Grigorovich's ballets infused new life into the Soviet formula of content-rich, plot driven, full-length dramatic ballets by returning dance to its rightful place at the center of choreographic expression without challenging the fundamental premise of Soviet ballet as narrative art form.

Even though *The Stone Flower* did not challenge the most basic, narrative demand made of Soviet ballet, Grigorovich's determination to develop the plot by means of dance alone and his refusal to obsess about presenting a realistic image of life in the drambalet manner bore the signs of Western heresy to some. Proponents of drambalet accused their symphonic challengers of a casual attitude toward a realistic presentation of reality, coming dangerously close to a flirtation with abstraction. The defenders of the established Soviet choreographic order tried to present the aesthetic struggle between choreographic symphonism and drambalet as a Manichaean battle between Western-style formalism and Soviet realism. Framing the debate in these terms had potentially lethal ideological implications for the choreographic innovators. At the All-Union Choreographic Conference held in Moscow in 1960, Grigorovich and Bel'sky were declared leaders of formalism. The criticisms hurled at the two choreographers were at times preposterous and illustrate the absurd distortions of artistic debates by ideological dogmatism. For example, a choreographer from the Urals decided to take Grigorovich to task for the geological nonauthenticity of *The Stone Flower*: "What on earth is Grigorovich doing? Among his semiprecious stones there is a jasper. But there are no jaspers in these regions! I, for example, am now staging a ballet about the underwater kingdom of the Baikal. What would happen, comrades, if instead of an omul, I showed some sort of sprat?"[68]

At the conference, a stormy debate between defenders of Grigorovich's and Bel'sky's choreographic innovation and the drambalet old guard broke loose. Leonid Lavrovsky gave the keynote address at the meeting. In an effort to defend the tenets of drambalet—and his own position in the choreographic hierarchy—Lavrovsky railed against the so-called theory of the world of agitated feeling. Singling out the second act of *The Stone Flower*, set in the subterranean kingdom of the Mistress of the Copper Mountain,

Lavrovsky, whose own production of the ballet for the Bolshoi in 1954 had widely been declared a failure because of its faithful observation of dram-balet dogmas, accused Grigorovich of using the formal means of modernized acrobatics typical for this "theory of the world of agitated feeling" to express this hallowed topic of Russian nature.

Using typical Soviet rhetoric, Lavrovsky contrasted Soviet ballet's elevation to a serious art form rich in content with the pointless demonstration of dance technique. He stressed that there were some people who had a simplistic view of ballet as something where one needed to jump around nonstop from curtain up to curtain down. Lavrovsky stated that the champions of this "danciness" had a confederate in the West, George Balanchine, who led a technically accomplished company that didn't dance to music but to naked rhythm without any content. In his concluding remarks at the end of the conference, Lavrovsky stated that there was a struggle between two directions in ballet, a realist one and a formalist one. Lavrovsky called the ballet scholar and librettist Yuri Slonimsky and the ballet historian and critic Vera Krasovskaya, who had given talks strongly supporting recent innovations, the theorists of formalism, and branded Grigorovich and Bel'sky as the practitioners of this formalism.[69]

The Leningrad journalist Nina Alovert contended that it was precisely the creative searches of Iakobson, Grigorovich, and Bel'sky that had overcome the dangers of naturalism and the excessive preoccupation with everyday themes and with details of daily life. Bel'sky tried to rebut the accusation of Westernism hurled at him despite his choice of Soviet themes: "What is a 'Western' performance? It is above all a vague, ideologically uncommitted performance. How can a performance that carries our idea be in its essence 'Western'?" In the ideologically framed diatribes of the drambalet establishment, the importance of safeguarding the Soviet Union's ideological weapons for its struggle with the capitalist West mixed with an absurd preoccupation with biographical and other "realistic" details in ballets. Sergeev declared that it was especially important to keep the Soviet Union's ideological weapons in order in the struggle with the West and that he was worried that some choreographers displayed modernist tendencies, surrendering themselves to bourgeois aesthetics. He was disturbed by theories put forth at the conference that tried to rally everyone to the "'world of agitated feeling,' the world of emotions, the world of abstract images, devoid of biographical particulars, biography and profession." Sergeev then established the link between the contemporary call to "the world of agitated feeling" and Lopukhov's "abstract" ballet *Spring Fairy Tale*, once again illustrating the wide meaning of the abusive term *abstraction* in Soviet parlance: Sergeev stated that Ostrovsky's *Snegurochka* could hardly be recognized in Lopukhov's "abstract" ballet, where heroes had no names and lacked realistic detail, living somewhere doing something in complete separation from concrete surroundings. Sergeev added that tendencies of "abstract" ballet could be seen in *The Stone Flower*.[70]

Along similar veins, Zakharov declared that "two currents were outlined in the discussion: one defends ideinost', narodnost', realism in the art of dance, the other—antirealistic tendencies adversarial to these concepts. After all, the most agitated feelings, if they are separated from ideas, lead to a completely incorrect abstract conception—'the world of feelings' in general." Even though Grigorovich and Bel'sky were attacked from many sides at the conference, the power of the old guard was waning. In his closing remarks, the chairman of the conference, Deputy USSR Minister of Culture A. Kuznetsov, emphasized that contemporary topics should take the center of attention, but that that did not mean depicting a man with a portfolio. Warning against abstraction and deviations to Western European modernism and American jazzism, Kuznetsov also cautioned against demagogic attacks against those searching for new paths: "One ought to protect our principles of socialist realism in every possible way from attempts to distort them ideologically. But one mustn't attach labels and subject some comrades who are searching for new paths in art to demagogic criticism."[71]

The conference proceedings were published in 1962, incidentally the year that George Balanchine and New York City Ballet visited the Soviet Union for the first time. According to the editors, the appeal to take into account the specificity of choreography, the struggle against naturalistic imitation of everyday life and against the mechanic transfer of literature's and the dramatic theater's laws to ballet, had raised concerns among some conference participants that choreography would be turned into a fetish, cut off from life and from the realist basis of Soviet art. According to the editors, some of the comments at the conference underestimated Grigorovich's and Bel'sky's achievements, illegitimately trying to separate them from the principles of narodnost', partiinost' and realism.[72]

In the same year when the proceedings were published, the grand dame of Soviet ballet, Galina Ulanova, published an article in *Izvestiia* that argued that it was the duty of the older generation to support the young generation in its progressive artistic experiments that were bound to include some blunders: there ought not to be any antagonism between the generations— the older generation should be happy when the young generation tried to find its own voice. Ulanova explicitly condemned any attempts to brand Bel'sky as abstractionist and Grigorovich as modernist: "It is easiest to stick a label on somebody. For example: Igor' Bel'sky is sick with abstractionism, Yuri Grigorovich is a modernist. That's it." Ulanova pointed out that the literal meaning of the word *modern* was positive; it only became negative when used in its metaphorical sense as designating bourgeois art. She defended *Coast of Hope* and Grigorovich's *The Stone Flower* and *The Legend of Love*. Pointing out that older generations had committed their own errors, she pleaded for the right of the young generation to commit their own artistic mistakes on a path that would lead to new discoveries.[73]

In her review of Grigorovich's most modernist work, *The Legend of Love,* in *Za sovetskoe iskusstvo* in April 1961, the ballet critic Valeria Chistiakova put the debates on choreographic searches within the wider context of the reassessment of socialist realism during the Thaw. Criticizing the attempts of some to pass off artistic complacency as defense of realism in Soviet choreography, she emphasized that the understanding of realism in Soviet art was not unchangeable and that it developed with the times, giving as example a famous cinematic expression of the Thaw in culture, Grigory Chukrai's popular movie *Ballad of a Soldier* (1959).[74] Within a year, however, the limits of this development became painfully clear: during the showdown between Khrushchev and the creative intelligentsia in 1962–1963, *The Legend of Love* would be singled out for criticism.

The dynamics of the paradigm shift in Soviet choreography during the Thaw show the complex relationship between artistic development, politics, and ideology in the Soviet Union. There was significant continuity of artistic thought across the Russian Revolution, showing that the development of ballet maintained a dynamic of its own even within the intrusive ideological context of the Soviet experience. The question of modernism and realism in art, rendered explosive within the context of Soviet cultural ideology, added an additional layer to the artistic reaction against the Stalinist dogmas of drambalet, illustrating the complex, interactive relationship between artistic thought and practice on the one hand and Soviet ideology and politics on the other hand.

A confrontation between different artistic generations reinforced by general trends within the country that favored the young acted as catalyst for the invigoration of the Soviet choreographic scene in the second half of the 1950s. The climate of the Thaw created new opportunities for artistic repossession. The involvement of the Komsomol in the successful staging of Yuri Grigorovich's *The Stone Flower* shows how the ambiguity inherent in any social structure or organization enables ordinary persons to reclaim autonomy from all-pervasive political-ideological forces by subverting the system from within. At the same time, the confrontation between supporters of the old drambalet order and supporters of symphonic dance shows how regular animosities, jealousies, and differences of opinion between competing artists were exacerbated by the Soviet attempt to impose an ideological framework on the arts, offering the opportunity to delegitimize competitors by attempting to brand them as ideologically suspect. Ideological dogmatism sometimes led to absurd distortions of artistic debates.

The choreographic battles of the 1950s and early 1960s were by necessity intimately linked to ballet's position within the Soviet cultural project. Within the context of the Khrushchev reforms, which were supposed to breathe new life into the Soviet project, a pivotal role was ascribed to culture as a powerful means of communication between the regime and its people. Since the 1930s, socialist realism had been much more than merely a method of cultural production: it was supposed to ensure that art was an ideological tool successfully contributing to the Soviet cultural project, whether in its maximal definition of striving for a transformation of society and the creation of a Socialist civilization or in its minimal definition of promoting loyalty to the regime. By the early 1950s, the definition of socialist realism had ossified into strict dogmas that not only stifled creative freedom but ultimately limited art's capacity to serve as a meaningful conduit of communication between the authorities and the people.

Even if the meaning of socialist realism for each art form was to a certain extent renegotiated during the Thaw, the preeminent position of the doctrine as the defining factor of Soviet cultural production was not. The limits of de-Stalinization therefore also became apparent in the renegotiation of realism in art. In the world of ballet, Grigorovich's talent ultimately managed to silence those who tried to sideline him as "Western" or a modernist danger to realism in Soviet ballet. But despite accusations of modernism, in the final analysis, Grigorovich's innovative ballets did not challenge the core definition of Soviet ballet as a content-rich art form that narrated stories in full-length, dramatic ballets.

5🕭 ‍ *Beyond the Iron Curtain*

The Bolshoi Ballet in London in 1956

> I've never seen any magic like that in my entire life. It was the
> sort of miracle that it is to have a baby. . . . This was exactly
> the same, theatrically, to me. We couldn't believe it.
>
> —ANTOINETTE SIBLEY'S MEMORIES OF GALINA ULANOVA
> AS JULIET, 1956

The Cold War struggle for victory between democratic capitalism and Soviet socialism took place on several battlefields. In the nuclear age, as the
consequences of military action became unfathomable, the ideological battlefield assumed increasing importance. With the onset of the Cold War,
artists metamorphosed into frontline soldiers in the ideological showdown
between East and West. Slipping across the Iron Curtain, they were sent by
their regimes, overtly to foster understanding between the enemy nations
and covertly to win over the hearts and minds of the enemy's civilian population with the potent weapon of cultural mastery.

The Cold War added an international dimension to ideological constraints imposed on every art form's ability to define its identity within
the Soviet cultural project: art produced under the Soviet system had to
be clearly differentiable from—and superior to—art produced under democratic capitalism. The culture of each camp turned into a metaphor for
the different systems themselves, and victory on the cultural front became
equated with overall victory in the showdown between the conflicting
world views of the two superpowers. As David Caute has argued in his
study of the struggle for cultural supremacy during the Cold War, "never
before had empires felt so compelling a need to prove their virtue, to demonstrate their spiritual superiority, to claim the high ground of 'progress,' to

win public support and admiration by gaining ascendancy in each and every event of what might be styled the Cultural Olympics."[1]

Many studies analyze how culture was used as instrument of Cold War propaganda.[2] While providing fascinating insights into the politics of Cold War culture, some of them risk reducing art produced during the Cold War era into political tools. As exemplified by the debate surrounding CIA involvement in the rise to supremacy of American abstract expressionist painting, any discussion of culture within the Cold War context has to strike a careful balance between putting art in its political and cultural context without socially overdetermining the sources of artistic inspiration and success.

Similarly, the Soviet artists sent across the Iron Curtain were not just pawns of the Kremlin. The messenger should never be confused with his master. During the tours of the Kirov and Bolshoi Ballet companies, the regime sought safety in numbers. Dancers were herded together in groups supervised by KGB watchdogs, supposedly to prevent any dangerous thoughts that might come to the artists' minds if left to confront the corrupting influences of the West on their own. But no matter how hard the regime tried to manage the impressions gained by its artists abroad, it could never exercise complete control over the minds of its cultural ambassadors and the evolution of artistic thinking. For the first time in decades, the inauguration of cultural exchange programs in the late 1950s enabled Soviet dancers to directly compare the artistic outlook of Soviet ballet with ballet in the West. Was direct contact with the Other a constraining or an enabling factor in the evolution of Soviet ballet's self-understanding?[3]

The Politics of Cultural Exchange

The internationalization of the Soviet cultural project reflected an increased internationalization of Soviet politics as a whole. Unlike Stalin, who had only ventured abroad twice during his long rule to attend the conferences of the war-time allies at Tehran and Potsdam, Khrushchev soon began to appear on the world stage in an effort to revitalize Soviet foreign policy. Following an invitation by Prime Minister Anthony Eden, Khrushchev and Prime Minister Nikolai Bulganin visited Great Britain in April 1956, barely two months after Khrushchev's secret speech to the Twentieth Congress of the Communist Party of the Soviet Union (CPSU) marked the beginning of de-Stalinization. Although the state visit led to hardly any substantive results,[4] the Bolshoi Ballet's visit to London in October 1956 could be counted as one of them. Sir David Webster, the general administrator of Covent Garden, had issued an invitation to the Bolshoi Ballet in 1946, the year Covent Garden reopened after the war. Ten years had passed since then, leading to nothing but a recurring nightmare haunting Sir David's dreams: just as a cycle of Wagner's *Ring* was under way, he would receive a telephone call from the Russian embassy saying that 280 dancers had arrived and were ready to perform.[5]

In the wake of Khrushchev and Bulganin's visit to England, the Soviet government reassessed the cultural ties between the two countries. In May 1956, the Soviet Minister of Culture Nikolai Mikhailov reported to the Central Committee of the CPSU on measures taken by his ministry to develop cultural ties between the Soviet Union and England. While the official rhetoric of cultural cooperation stated increased understanding and friendship between the Soviet and British people as its goal, it was hoped that cultural "friendship" would ultimately lead to political sympathy. In the competition between the United States and the Soviet Union, Western Europe was the main battleground and the souls of Western Europeans were the coveted prize. It is clear from Mikhailov's comments to the Central Committee that cultural cooperation was to be a conduit for Soviet propaganda. Following his enumeration of areas of cultural cooperation between England and the Soviet Union, Mikhailov concluded that the Soviets were conducting propaganda in England badly and compared Soviet propaganda negatively with American activities in England.[6]

The Bolshoi's visit to London in October 1956 was planned within this political-ideological context. Mikhailov concluded his report with a program for developing artistic contacts between the Soviet Union and England. As the first item on this agenda, he informed the Central Committee that, in principle, an understanding had been reached on an exchange between the Bolshoi Ballet and the Sadler's Wells Royal Ballet in autumn 1956: the Bolshoi Ballet would visit London and Sadler's Wells Royal Ballet would visit the Soviet Union.[7] While the Bolshoi's visit to London took place, the return visit of Sadler's Wells was cancelled because of the Soviet invasion of Hungary.

Russian ballet was about to become a cultural ambassador of the Soviet Union. Hopes were high that the artistic mastery of Soviet ballet would stun the world, symbolizing the cultural peaks reached by Soviet civilization and proving not just the superiority of Soviet ballet but of the Soviet project as a whole. But the Soviet government was not so naïve as to think that this victory was necessarily an easy one. In the months leading up to the tour, every detail of the preparations was scrutinized by the powers that be.

Much more than the reputation of Soviet ballet was at stake. For the majority of the London audience, the Bolshoi's dancers would offer them their first glimpse of the "Red enemy." The Soviet government probably assumed that Western audiences would scrutinize every aspect of Soviet ballet, extrapolating from their observations general conclusions about life in the Soviet Union. In this environment, ballet tights became a matter of state. In a letter updating the Central Committee of the CPSU on the preparations for the tour, Minister of Culture Mikhailov pointed out that the quality of ballet costumes took on a special importance within the context of foreign tours. Lamenting the unsatisfactory quality of ballet tights produced by the Soviet textile industry, Mikhailov asked the Central Committee for permission to order sixty ballet tights from Czechoslovakia.[8] Maybe the Soviet government feared that the low quality of Soviet tights would indicate to Western audiences the paltry state of the Soviet Union's production of consumer goods.

For the London audience, the Bolshoi would embody Soviet culture. The Soviet view on art would be apparent in its choice of repertoire for the tour. Soviet ballet was to be represented by the two best ballets of the *drambalet* era, Lavrovsky's *Romeo and Juliet* and Zakharov's *The Fountain of Bakhchisarai*. The theater argued that these two productions had not only had a tremendous impact on the development of Soviet ballet but that they were also very popular in the USSR, thus making them interesting both for foreign audiences and for dance professionals. *Swan Lake* was taken to London as a symbol of Russian ballet, as the best ballet of Russia's prerevolutionary classical heritage. Originally created in France during the romantic era, *Giselle* was included in the repertoire as an international treasure of choreography. The Bolshoi Ballet's repertoire in London was thus supposed to reflect the highest achievements of Soviet ballet and the best examples of nineteenth-century Russian and Western ballet.[9] Wisely, Western audiences were spared the more pedestrian products of the late drambalet era in general and failed attempts to create propaganda ballets on Soviet contemporary life in particular. In the months leading up to the tour, the theater not only replaced decrepit sets and costumes but set designs and the productions themselves had to be adapted to Covent Garden's stage, which was significantly smaller than the Bolshoi's and could accommodate only a scaled-down version of the sets and a smaller number of participants.[10] The Bolshoi also staged a new production of *Swan Lake* for its visit to London.

Even before the Bolshoi's first tour to the West had become a certainty, one of the side effects of international touring on the life of the Bolshoi Ballet during the Soviet era became apparent in whispered conversations in the theater's corridors. The prospect of foreign travel tempted some artists to focus less on their jobs than on the possibility of traveling abroad. In March 1956, Viktorina Kriger, a famous former dancer now in charge of the Bolshoi Museum, published a satirical article in *Sovetskii artist*, the Bolshoi Theater's newspaper, mocking how the theatrical rumor kitchen led to the wildest ideas about future tours and who would get to go on them, creating an unhealthy atmosphere within the theater.[11] A few years later, in March 1959, shortly before the Bolshoi Ballet's first tour to the United States, at a time when the Bolshoi Ballet was already regularly undertaking major tours abroad, Leonid Lavrovsky, artistic director of the Bolshoi Ballet, chastised his dancers for forgetting about their work while obsessing about who would be taken abroad:

> I would also like to talk about the unhealthy hullabaloo around our tours abroad. We don't live for the tasks faced by the theater, we only live for these tours. "OK, I managed to go on this tour, but what do I have to do now in order to elbow my way unto the next tour, where to call, whom to call, whom to beg, whom to write to"—now this is what our artists' life is like. When abroad, we have to defend the honor of Soviet art. And what we see when abroad, . . . this is not what is most important. We are not enriching ourselves on these tours, but we are sent on them.[12]

Abroad, dancers were representatives of the Soviet people who would be scrutinized by curious and not always sympathetic eyes. Lavrovsky warned:

> I have heard a proverb there: "You in Russia have some kind of saying 'a drunken swine,'" but there people say: "a drunken Russian swine." We sometimes underestimate the attitude of enemies toward us and behave somewhat freely. I happened to be at one of the receptions and saw how people look at us, when they pour you cognac. I don't think that it would be a sacrifice from your side if you didn't empty ten glasses but have half a glass of wine. Abroad, one has to keep the strictest control over oneself in all aspects of everyday life.[13]

Tours abroad were a matter of state, adding a highly political dimension to the question of who would be taken. Commenting on the impending tour of the Bolshoi Ballet to the United States in 1959, G. A. Orvid, director of the Bolshoi Theater, explicitly stated the purpose of these tours: "You are doing a necessary, big governmental task. Moiseev's ensemble and 'Berezka' have gone on tour to America. We have friends there. We know how this exchange of cultural values changes the attitude of the simple American toward us, because the propaganda there paints us in rather unattractive colors." Only those who seemed politically reliable could be entrusted with this diplomatic mission. Orvid ominously warned: "We can't have resentments and conversations: why am I again not going? The party organization has discussed each candidature very seriously, who can travel and be of use over there, so that we won't have 'tourists' as happened on past tours."[14]

The fear of sending "tourists" whose interest in foreign life expressed an ideologically embarrassing curiosity about life outside the Soviet Union paled next to the fear of sending politically untrustworthy artists who might undermine the entire project of promoting the Soviet Union by defection. Even before highly publicized defections of Soviet dancers started with Nureyev's flight to the West in 1961, high artistry and international fame by no means protected dancers from humiliating ideological scrutiny. The intrinsic paranoia of the Soviet regime made it ban one of its most celebrated dancers from the Bolshoi Ballet's first major international tour. In 1956, London impatiently awaited Maya Plisetskaya, but despite initial indications that Plisetskaya would participate in the tour, she was withdrawn from the list of participants as politically suspect. The KGB had put a red X on her name, banning her from foreign travel. Despite Plisetskaya's international fame and repeated invitations to perform abroad, the travel ban was lifted only in 1959, on Khrushchev's personal intercession. Until then, before each tour, she would be assured that this time she would be allowed to travel abroad only to see her name removed from the travel list at the last moment.[15]

Born into a Jewish family that included many famous theatrical artists, her family had suffered heavily during the Great Terror of the Stalinist era. In 1938, Plisetskaya's father was executed by the GPU, the security organ that would later become the KGB, and her mother, an actress, was thrown into prison for eight years. In her memoirs, Plisetskaya stipulates that contact with foreigners was one of the reasons for her father's arrest and execution in 1938. Her father's brother had emigrated to America before the revolution but visited the Soviet Union in 1934 and sent numerous letters upon his return to the United States.[16] Assuming that there was any logic in such bans on foreign travel, the fact that Plisetskaya's maternal uncle Asaf Messerer, ballet master at the Bolshoi, was allowed to travel while her brother, also a dancer at the Bolshoi, was not indicates that the "problem" lay indeed with her father's family, even though her mother's family had also suffered during the purges.

There was an ugly, inhumane side to international tours. If it was in its interest, the regime didn't shy away from treating even its most celebrated artists like they were property of the state. An episode indirectly linked to the travel ban imposed on Plisetskaya shows how political, artistic, human, and—considering the amount of money flowing into state coffers as a consequence of the tours—financial concerns were hopelessly entangled. Both from an artistic and political point of view, the Bolshoi Ballet wanted to show its best face to London audiences. Its star dancers were crucial to ensure the success of the tour. Striking Plisetskaya from the list of participants could thus potentially have serious consequences for the tour's success. On

13 August 1956, John Tooley, assistant to the general administrator of the Royal Opera House, sent a letter to Mr. V. Stepanov at the Soviet Ministry of Culture expressing Covent Garden's dismay that Plisetskaya's name had been omitted from a recent list of the tour's participants sent by the Ministry of Culture:

> This is a great blow to us and will cause considerable disappointment to the vast number of people who were looking forward to seeing her dance here.
>
> It was understood during conversations with Mr. Shashkin last May that Madame Plisetskaya would come with the company, and it was agreed that her name should be included in the statement to the press both here and I believe in Russia on the completion of our negotiations. . . . Furthermore, we have been given no reason at all for her withdrawal and are therefore quite unable to explain to the public why she will not be appearing.
>
> I must protest about the withdrawal of one of your leading dancers without explanation and ask you to reconsider this decision. The box office opens on Monday, 27 August, for the sale of tickets for this season, and it is essential that we should be in a position to give the public full information about dancers and the repertoire.[17]

Initially, three of the Bolshoi's leading female principals were supposed to carry the repertoire of the tour: Galina Ulanova, Raisa Struchkova, and Maya Plisetskaya. Provisional casting lists had included repertoire statistics for these leading principals, showing how they would share the artistic burden between them. For example, in a plan dated 24 May 1956, Ulanova was scheduled to dance nine of the ten planned performances of *Romeo and Juliet* and three out of the four planned performances of *Giselle*. She was not scheduled to appear in either *The Fountain of Bakhchisarai* or *Swan Lake*. Plisetskaya, in turn, was cast to dance every single one of the six performances planned for *Swan Lake* and all performances of the second female lead, Zarema, in *The Fountain of Bakhchisarai*. Struchkova was supposed to dance *Romeo and Juliet* one time, the lead in *The Fountain of Bakhchisarai* six times, the lead in *Giselle* one time, and the second female lead in *Giselle*, Myrtha, three times.[18]

Less than a month after this plan had been formulated, A. S. Tsabel', the administrative director of the Bolshoi Ballet, asked the director of the Bolshoi Mikhail Chulaki to intercede with the Ministry of Culture so that an additional female soloist, Velita Viltsin', could join the tour because Ulanova's health would not allow her to dance more than five to six performances of *Romeo and Juliet*. This would have an impact on the casting of the entire tour: "It is perfectly obvious that the workload of such ballerinas as R. S. Struchkova and M. M. Plisetskaya will change—Struchkova will be allotted more performances of *Romeo and Juliet*, Plisetskaya will be allotted more performances of *Swan Lake*."[19] Viltsin' was supposed to ease the burden on these ballerinas by taking over some of the performances of Zarema in *The Fountain of Bakhchisarai*, a part usually danced by Plisetskaya, and the role of Juliet, danced by both Ulanova and Struchkova.

The decision to ban Plisetskaya from the tour was to have grave consequences for the star of the tour, Ulanova, illustrating the high human costs inflicted by the regime on its cultural ambassadors, reducing them at times to little more than the regime's slaves. A few days before the tour, the British press reported that for unknown reasons, neither Plisetskaya nor Ulanova would come to London.[20] It is not clear whether Ulanova's cancellation was a false rumor or whether there were last minute debates in Moscow whether or not Ulanova should be sent, perhaps because of health reasons. But in the end, Ulanova not only participated in the tour but, with Plisetskaya staying behind in Moscow, the burden of success weighed even more heavily on her shoulders. Instead of dancing only five or six performances of Juliet, the technically least challenging female leading role of the ballets taken on tour, Ulanova, at the very ripe dancing-age of forty-six, also danced *Giselle* and the second act of *Swan Lake* for a BBC broadcast. All in all, she led thirteen performances in London, almost three times the number of performances recommended by Tsabel'. On 25 October, after having danced *Giselle* in front of the Queen, Ulanova and the company danced the ballet again from 2:30 am until daybreak so that the ballet could be filmed.[21]

Ulanova's drastically increased number of performances had serious health consequences. The Bolshoi's visit to London ended on 29 October 1956. On 17 November, during a performance of *Giselle* at the Bolshoi, Ulanova injured her calf. *Sovetskii artist* reported that the injury had been caused by overwork during the preparations for the tour in London and during the tour itself.[22] It helped the exhausted Ulanova little that she was widely praised for her superhuman efforts upon her return to the Soviet Union, leading Deputy Minister of Culture of the USSR V. I. Pakhomov hailed her as a "hero of labor" for the thirteen performances she had given in London at a meeting dedicated to the tour held on 21 November 1956 at the All-Russian Theatrical Society's (VTO) House of the Actor in Moscow, a meeting that Ulanova was too sick to attend.[23]

Ulanova and Plisetskaya were, however, not the only ones adversely affected by the politics surrounding the tours abroad to the West. In the lead up to the Bolshoi's visit to London, the fragility of Soviet-British relations underpinning the possibility of cultural exchange was demonstrated by a diplomatic incident that seriously jeopardized the Bolshoi's visit. Mutual suspicions continued to hide under the rhetoric of increasing understanding through exchange in ostensibly apolitical areas such as sports and culture. On 29 August, Nina Ponomareva, a Soviet discus thrower who was in England for a British-Soviet athletics match, was apprehended by a store detective on Oxford Street and accused of having stolen five hats.[24] The Soviets interpreted the incident as a deliberate provocation.

On 21 September 1956, twelve days before the scheduled opening night at Covent Garden, *Izvestiia* published a letter signed by eleven leading artists of the Bolshoi, including Chulaki, Ulanova, Asaf Messerer, and the conductors Aleksandr Melik-Pashaev and Yuri Faier. The artists wrote that the provocation directed against Ponomareva was completely incomprehensible and that they had assumed that the English authorities would immediately cut short this provocation. This had not happened, and the ensemble was deeply worried that one of them would be subjected to a similar provocation if they traveled to London. Could the company travel to London under such circumstances?[25]

The letter sparked anxious, indignant speculations in England whether the Bolshoi would cancel the visit that had promised to be the biggest cultural event in England in years. All the tickets for the visit, over fifty thousand, had been purchased, many of them by people who had queued outside Covent Garden for three days and nights in order to secure a coveted seat.[26] While the Russian side expected the British authorities to order the court to drop charges against Ponomareva, the English insisted on the independence of its judiciary from executive interference. An editorial in the *Times* called the entire affair "deplorable and almost incredible," emphasizing that Ponomareva's case probably originated in a misunderstanding and that, if this was indeed the case, "her reputation and liberty are safe in an English court." This understanding of law, the editorial pointed out, was foreign to Russians, and the dancers therefore probably honestly believed that the charge had been "concocted" and that they themselves were threatened by similar dangers if they came to London, insisting therefore on an intervention by the British authorities to prove the absence of political malice. The editorial asked rhetorically: "Is there any means of convincing the Russians that, just as the lowliest English court would indignantly repudiate the demand that it should convict at the will of the executive, so it is beyond the utmost authority of the State to stop the process of justice once it has been set in motion?"[27] Despite the public posturing on both sides, both parties were keen to avoid a cancellation, last but not least for financial reasons. A flurry of notes was exchanged between Moscow and London in order to find a diplomatic way out of the crisis. On 22 September, Soviet Deputy

Minister of Culture Pakhomov wrote to the chairman of the Soviet Relations Committee of the British Council, asking him to use all his authority to remove the reasons that were threatening the Bolshoi's visit.[28]

On 23 September, Soviet Prime Minister Bulganin received a telegram from the National Council of the British-Soviet Friendship Society, informing him that the council had asked British Prime Minister Eden to ask the director of public prosecution to review all facts related to the charge against Ponomareva in order to end the affair or to look for some other just resolution. The society now asked Bulganin to convince the Bolshoi Ballet not to cancel its visit. The letter stressed that no one would understand a cancellation of the tour because of the Ponomareva affair, emphasizing that a cancellation would damage mutual trust and cultural exchange, satisfying only the enemies of British-Soviet friendship.[29]

Officials were not the only ones who were worried. The feverish interest of the English public in the Bolshoi's visit indicates the powerful impact of the Bolshoi Ballet on the public imagination of the Soviet Union's ideological foe. Political calculations to use cultural exchange as an ideological tool reflected a reality where high culture played a greater public role than it does today. Numerous letters were sent to the editor of the *Times* on this issue.[30] Emotions in England ran so high that letters by indignant Englishmen ranging from ballet lovers to Soviet sympathizers and Communist Party members began to trickle across the Iron Curtain onto desks at the Bolshoi, all equally eager to advise the theater on the right course of action.[31] A certain D. M. Ross, an Englishman living in Naples, admonished the director of the Bolshoi Ballet that it would be foolish to cancel the Bolshoi's tour because of the Ponomareva incident: "It would be an example of childish stupidity without parallel, and all it would achieve would be to prove that provocations directed against the Soviet Union are extremely successful because Soviet diplomats, and apparently Soviet artists too, rise to the bait and what might have been small insignificant incidents become magnified out of all proportion." Instead, Mr. Ross imploringly lectured:

> The way to deal with insults is to rise above them, to be too big, too dignified, to notice them. The only way to deal with provocations is to refuse to be provoked. This is elementary common sense, elementary tactics. . . . Treat the Ponomareva incident as a mountain climber would treat a mosquito bite received on the way. He knows that there will be more mosquitoes but he doesn't abandon the climb because of that! Change your minds and come to Britain. We need the experience of seeing your wonderful ballet. And your country hasn't got so many friends in the West that it can afford to throw away those that it has

or refuse an opportunity like this to make many new ones. You must come. Those people who spent three days in a line waiting to buy tickets will never forgive you if you don't.[32]

A "staunch supporter of the USSR," Molly Bland from Tufnell Park in London felt "compelled to inform" the director of the Bolshoi of her "bitter disappointment and anger after [the] decision to cancel the Covent Garden booking." Ms. Bland continued, stating that "by this stupid action [the Bolshoi] undo the good that has been done by the visits of Soviet artists during the past years thereby playing into the enemy's hands."[33] Mrs. Sheila Kleiman expressed the bitter disappointment of English balletomanes:

> I cannot express to you the pleasure we really derived from knowing that we had a seat for what we considered to be the greatest dancers in the world, and now so many thousands of us will be disappointed. We had queued through rain and sunshine and talked of nothing else for weeks on end. Our disappointment is tremendous.
>
> Anna Pavlova to us younger ones is now just a dream who unfortunately was never real to us because of our young years, but now we have the opportunity of seeing Galina Ulanova—the world's greatest, and we are going to be deprived of this pleasure.
>
> Please show us just how wonderful you can be and send your company here, so that we may give them the great welcome they will so richly deserve.[34]

In the meantime, preparations for the visit continued in Moscow.[35] On 27 September, the *Times* reported that Russia's decision to allow the Bolshoi Ballet to go to London was expected to be announced the following day. According to the *Times*, Chulaki had stated after consultations with the Ministry of Culture that the decision to go to London was a personal one that had been influenced by the British Council's message to the Ministry of Culture assuring the Russians that their fears of provocations in London were groundless.[36] On 28 September, the Soviet Ministry of Culture finally announced that the Bolshoi would come. The announcement did not mention the Ponomareva case but referred to the many appeals received from British organizations, members of Parliament, and individuals and stated that "Britain is sincerely striving to create a favorable atmosphere for the performances of the Bolshoi Theater Ballet in London."[37]

This whole episode illustrates the overarching context of Cold War confrontation between two fundamentally different political and social systems that overshadowed any attempt to increase mutual understanding through cultural exchange. While the Soviet side feared a loss of face by having one of its celebrated athletes prosecuted for the petty theft of consumer goods, the English side was keen to demonstrate the independence of its judicial system, even at the cost of creating a major diplomatic row. After the resolution of the crisis—but not of the Ponomareva case—an editorial in the *Times* emphasized:

> Everything will be done, and would always have been done, to make the company welcome. Everything, that is, except interference with the independent and impartial system of justice which protects all British citizens and visitors, great and humble, alike. That is the point of view which Moscow has now sought to understand, though law courts and charges against foreign visitors mean to them something very different from what they mean to us. This episode has been unhappy, but in some ways it may do good. It has been a salutary reminder that the differences between the Russian and British systems are real and that the gulf between the two peoples will not be narrower without care or without occasional friction.[38]

In fact, the proceedings could apparently have been dropped at any time by the attorney general, a member of the Eden Cabinet, as "not in the public interest." Instead, the decision to pursue the charge was taken at cabinet level.[39] Ponomareva, who had "disappeared," probably into the safe haven of the Soviet Embassy in London, failed to appear in court on 3 October. Embassy officials claimed they did not know about her whereabouts.[40] On 12 October, she finally appeared in court, pleading not guilty. The magistrate, however, found the sentence proved. That same day, Ponomareva finally left for the Soviet Union by boat.[41]

Western Preconceptions of Soviet Ballet

While Cold War politics at times threatened to overshadow the cultural significance of the Bolshoi Ballet's first visit, the importance of the tour for both Soviet and English ballet from an artistic point of view cannot be overstated. For the Bolshoi, it was the first time its artistic credo of dramatic ballet would be judged by a Western audience whose sensitivities had been shaped by the different aesthetics of Diaghilev's Ballets Russes. While Soviet ballet tried to emulate the conventions of realistic dramatic theater in evening-filling danced dramas, the Ballets Russes had presented ballet evenings consisting of a combination of several shorter pieces created in a collaborative, often artistically revolutionary vision by visual artists, composers, and choreographers.

For the nascent English ballet and a Western audience that, since the Ballets Russes, equated greatness in ballet with Russia, the Bolshoi's visit to

London offered the first real chance to see Russian ballet since the revolution had pushed it into isolation. Individual Russian dancers had toured to the West with concert programs, but this could not compare to seeing the Bolshoi Ballet in its own productions. A few months before the Bolshoi's visit, in July 1956, the Stanislavsky Ballet, Moscow's second best ballet company, visited Paris, but a conclusive verdict on Soviet ballet could not be made before seeing either the Bolshoi or Kirov. Was Russian ballet still as great as before the revolution?

In order to put the Bolshoi Ballet's 1956 visit to London into the right artistic context, it is important to remember that twentieth-century ballet in Western Europe and North America received its initial impetus from Russia, from Diaghilev's Ballets Russes. At the time of the arrival of the Ballets Russes in Paris in 1909, ballet in Western Europe had been in steady decline for decades. The Ballets Russes sparked a new interest in the art form and radically reshaped expectations of the genre's artistic possibilities. Former members of Diaghilev's company went on to found schools and companies all over Europe and America. The roots of England's national ballet can also be traced to the influence of the Ballets Russes. Compared to Russia's over two-hundred-year-old ballet tradition, English ballet in the 1950s seemed ridiculously young. Barely twenty years old, it had been established in the 1920s and 1930s by two women, Ninette de Valois, who in 1931 founded Sadler's Wells Ballet, the company that was to become the Royal Ballet, and Marie Rambert, who in 1926 established Britain's oldest ballet company, Ballet Rambert. Both Rambert and de Valois had worked with Diaghilev.

The formative impact of the Ballets Russes on the two founding mothers of British ballet exemplifies an important dimension of the meeting between Western and Soviet ballet in 1956, the question of artistic lineage as the defining factor of artistic identity. Diaghilev did not return to Russia after the revolution and was promptly denounced by the Soviet authorities as a promoter of decadent art profiting from the tasteless craving of Europe's bourgeoisie for colorful novelties. In the West, however, it was argued that Diaghilev had imported everything that was great and innovative about Russian ballet to the West. If figures such as Fokine, Nijinsky, Pavlova, and Karsavina had shaped the early Diaghilev enterprise, in later years, dancers, who were to define Western ballet for years to come, including the young George Balanchine, flocked to the Ballets Russes from revolutionary Russia.

Political hostility influenced Western assessments of the arts in the Soviet Union, often precluding a priori the possibility that something of great artistic value could be created in a country that until recently had been held in the tight grip of Stalinism. Such perceptions were often rooted in and confirmed by the opinions and personal experience of émigrés living in the

West. If in literature the argument was made that Russian literature had split into a "Soviet" and an "émigré" branch, before the Bolshoi's arrival in London the English press put forward the parallel argument that Russian ballet had split into two branches after the revolution, one in the Soviet Union and one in the West. While the enormous impact of Russian ballet on Western ballet through participants of the Ballets Russes cannot be overstated, it is misleading to equate this with a formal "split" of Russian ballet. Many important Russian ballet figures emigrated after the revolution and imparted their knowledge to new generations of Western dancers, but the flowering of these seeds developed its own dynamic, reflecting the foreign soil in which they had been planted. Meanwhile, the work of the great institutions of Russian ballet, the schools and companies in Petrograd/Leningrad and Moscow, continued.

The expectations sparked in London by the Bolshoi's visits were complex. Russian dancers were still expected to be the greatest, a belief engrained in Western audiences and dancers since the Ballets Russes. But while Soviet Ballet was seen as successor of the imperial ballet in terms of tradition and academic classical schooling, many believed that the artistic lifeblood of innovation had permanently emigrated with Diaghilev's enterprise from Russia to the West. British expectations reflected the importance of tradition as a force of artistic legitimization in ballet: the British insistence on a formal split in Russian ballet probably reflected a psychological desire to increase the artistic credibility of the nascent British ballet by claiming its direct descent from Russia. As the *Times* mused in anticipation of the Bolshoi's arrival:

> There is a danger that exaggerated conceptions of what is coming will produce in the event an exaggerated disappointment which would do less than justice to the visitors. We should remember that Soviet ballet, particularly the companies in Moscow and Leningrad, represents the tradition against which Diaghilev and Fokine rebelled. The great choreographic revolution initiated by Fokine in large measure passed the Soviet ballet by. . . . The Soviet dancers we have seen already in this country are the products of a system which has descended nearly unchanged from Ivanov and Petipa, and the strengths and weaknesses we saw in them are in fact the strengths and weaknesses of Soviet ballet as a whole. British ballet, which no one claims is yet better than the Soviet variety, also descends from Petipa and Ivanov, but it is a descent by way of the mind and genius of Fokine and Diaghilev.[42]

Britain's most authoritative dance magazine, the *Dancing Times*, offered some predictions of the Bolshoi's strengths and weakness. After emphasizing the Russians facility in big and bold movements but noting the quasi-disappearance of batterie—jumps where the legs are beaten together in the air—and of "tiny, rapid brilliant steps," the magazine noted: "choreography, partly because of this absence of small detail, is limited in invention by our standards. The actual soli and pas de deux when they come are all rather similar. The Russians are not, of course, familiar with developments in this art outside the Soviet Union. Fokine, Massine, Balanchine, Ashton, and Petit are known to them mainly by repute and have had no influence whatsoever on Soviet choreography." While noting the poverty of Soviet choreography, the *Dancing Times* did not outright reject the Soviet genre of dramatic ballets: "we may be proud of our choreographers, and we think that decoratively we are far ahead of the Russians, but where we shall see a revelation is in the actual theatrical production. There, it is agreed by everyone who has seen the Soviet Ballet, they leave us standing." The *Dancing Times* was referring both to the dramatic handling of ballet productions and to the performance style of Russian dancers, who "carry everything before them on a tide of theatrical conviction that [British dancers] seldom approach"; the corps de ballet participated in a way unknown in England, "in style and mood they are as much part of the ballet as the ballerina." It was assumed that settings and costumes would be old-fashioned.[43]

The leadership of the Bolshoi Ballet's tour to London was more than aware of Western preconceptions. The artistic leadership of the tour fell on Leonid Lavrovsky's shoulders, the choreographer of *Romeo and Juliet*. Talking about the London tour to an audience at the House of the Actor in Moscow on 21 November 1956, Lavrovsky described the Bolshoi Ballet's anxieties before its departure for London: "In a number of newspapers, the kind of notices crept in . . . that said that those English spectators who expect a lot of new and interesting things from the Soviet ballet, well, they will be disappointed, that already for thirty years, Soviet ballet has been cut off from everything big and significant that is happening here in the West, it boils in its own juice and therefore can't surprise us with anything." Judging from Lavrovsky's comments, however, the Bolshoi was more concerned about defending the reputation of Russian dancers as the best in the world than about the question of innovation.[44]

Drambalet as Innovation

Given this pressure of expectations, the Bolshoi's tour started under less than ideal circumstances. Because of the Ponomareva affair, the company arrived not seven or eight days early as planned to allow for rehearsal time, but on 1 October, leaving one day before the opening night performance of *Romeo and Juliet* on 3 October. The first rehearsal lasted for eighteen hours without intermission. After a long night, at 2 p.m. on 2 October, the Bolshoi could officially confirm that the tour would open as scheduled.[45]

Contrary to predictions that even though the dancing would be good, the Russians would not be able to teach the West anything in terms of artistic innovation, the artistic impact of the Bolshoi's visit was enormous. The night before opening night, the Bolshoi Ballet was rehearsing *Romeo and Juliet*. That evening, the Sadler's Wells Ballet had danced in Croydon, but around 11:30 p.m. the company made it back to Covent Garden to watch the rehearsal. As they crept into the stalls circle of the Royal Opera House, Raisa Struchkova and Aleksandr Lapauri were rehearsing the balcony pas de deux, but the English dancers were about to see one of the tour's revelations, Galina Ulanova. The English ballerina Antoinette Sibley remembers the moment:

> And then at the end this little old lady in the stalls got up, short greyish hair and wrapped in layers of wool—we all thought she was the ballet mistress. She went up and chatted to them both, and then she went up on the balcony and said something to Yuri Fayer, you know, the amazing blind conductor. And then she took off her woollies and in front of our very eyes, no makeup, no costume, no help from theatrical aids whatsoever, she became fourteen years old. I've never seen any magic like that in my entire life. It was the sort of miracle that it is to have a baby, that minute when the baby's born and you realize what's actually happened—to you, to your baby, to your husband— this God-given thing. This was exactly the same, theatrically, to me. We couldn't believe it.[46]

After decades of isolation, the pressure to succeed was enormous. It was further amplified by the ideological mission the Soviet regime had mapped out for the company to symbolize Soviet civilization as a whole. Backstage during opening night, the agitation was so intense that Leonid Lavrovsky thought it almost impossible to express even the memory of it in ordinary human speech.[47] Back in Moscow, he attempted to give words to his emotions at a meeting dedicated to the London visit held at the VTO Central House of the Actor. The Bolshoi had confronted an unknown, unpredictable foreign audience:

> The auditorium was not filled with the kind of "people" that we have in mind when we use this word. Essentially, all of London's high society was present. . . . And the performance began from the very beginning under incredible tension. . . .
> And the act is running. Romeo and Juliet are on stage. Usually,

FIGURE 32. The Bolshoi Ballet's *Romeo and Juliet* at the Royal Opera House, Covent Garden, 1956. © 1956 Royal Opera House

FIGURE 33. Curtain call for the Bolshoi Ballet's *Romeo and Juliet* at the Royal Opera House, Covent Garden, 1956. Third from the left: Leonid Lavrovsky (choreographer), followed by Yuri Faier (conductor), Yuri Zhdanov as Romeo, and Galina Ulanova as Juliet. © 1956 Royal Opera House

their appearance is greeted with applause. The entire leadership of the company and all artists not taking part in the performance sat and waited—when will there finally be some movement in the auditorium? But it is quiet in the auditorium. Fifteen, twenty minutes pass, forty-five minutes pass, and you feel that your pulse is stopping and, if this continues, you will have a heart attack. It's like a psychological attack. And even when the curtain went down there was absolute silence in the auditorium.

"So they didn't receive the performance well? This means it's a flop?" Several agonizing seconds passed. The agitation was such that the hands of the stage workers were shaking. I looked at them and saw completely white faces. Then, when these several seconds had passed and an explosion of applause resounded, everyone began to smile at each other. The whole auditorium that was packed to the full with 2,400 people begins to applaud and scream at the same time. I haven't heard a similar explosion of applause. And the atmosphere around us began to ease, everyone began to congratulate each other, to smile.[48]

The success of the Bolshoi's tour demonstrated that ballet could indeed be a powerful tool in a cultural Cold War for the hearts and minds of ordinary people. Ballet fit perfectly into this new, international dimension of the Soviet cultural project. For the next month, London was in Bolshoi fever. In addition to 55,000 people who saw the Bolshoi at the Royal Opera House,[49] 9.5 million viewers, constituting more than half the adult television audience in Britain, watched the BBC's broadcast of Ulanova dancing the second act of *Swan Lake* on 21 October.[50] The *Times* dedicated a long editorial to the problem of rampant black market speculation with tickets for the Bolshoi.[51] The Bolshoi extended its stay for a few days, adding three evenings of divertissements at the Davis Theater in Croydon, which held 3,500 people.[52] Of the thousands of people who queued outside the Davis Theater to secure a ticket, only about one in four was successful, no one who joined the queue later than 4 a.m. stood a chance. More than 1,500 people were turned away.[53]

The public success of the Bolshoi was beyond question, but what was the professional verdict? In addition to English dancers, many French dancers and members of New York City Ballet and American Ballet Theater who were visiting the continent came to London to watch the Bolshoi.[54] The Bolshoi's visit shook Western preconceptions that political-ideological circumstances had completely stifled the artistic development of ballet in the Soviet Union. The renowned ballet critic Mary Clarke exclaimed: "What a lot we have to learn! Each night I went to the Bolshoi ballet I felt more ignorant and more lacking in theater experience. I had been so complacent in advance, thinking that because I had seen some concert performances, some films and another Soviet company in Paris, I knew precisely what the Bolshoi had to offer. The first night of *Romeo and Juliet* proved me wrong, and each succeeding production drove the lesson home."[55] Even though the impoverishment of Soviet choreography and the heaviness of the Soviet sets were widely noted, contrary to expectations that Soviet ballet in general would seem hopelessly old-fashioned, many saw the Soviet concept of full-length dramatic ballets as an innovative alternative to the Western predilection of one-act ballets. A. V. Coton wrote in *Ballet Today* that during the Bolshoi's first performance of *Romeo and Juliet*: "we were aware of watching the results of a completely new conception of ballet. At almost no point does it resemble the Western idea of what ballet is for, how it is best made, what kind of subjects are most suitable, what kind of personality the dancer should acquire in order to realize the character most completely."[56] England's great ballerina Margot Fonteyn remarked that, watching *Romeo and Juliet*, "the very weight of the production, criticized by some as old-fashioned, was what impressed me. No doubt it was just such realism that Diaghilev had discarded when he presented his innovations early in the century, taking Europe by storm. Now it burst on me as new and completely valid."[57]

For some, acquaintance with the Soviet ballet led to a serious reconsideration of Western ballet. Coton argued that the Russian dancers "produce a kind of effect we have rarely, if at all met before," an effect that he put down to the more serious Soviet attitude toward ballet:

> In Russia, ballet has been manipulated so that it is, within their culture, a major art, not a minor one as it has always been in Europe. Part of this process of rethinking ballet into a new shape has been the development of a style of dance acting . . . that emanates from the Stanislavsky method of actor training. . . . Their choreographers have analyzed every second of the action. . . . They have then ruthlessly trimmed, clarified, adjusted, or simplified it so that the continuous action of any phase of any ballet . . . never fails to open out the plot, reveal significant aspects of the characters, or in some way keep the spectators' attention on the continuous unfolding of the story.[58]

In contrast, the Western "development of ballet for forty-odd years has been along the lines of Fokine's principles and . . . ensnared by, as well as legitimately fascinated by, the formula of the one-act, short ballet. We have made a kind of ballet which must necessarily have scenery, costumes, music, staging, and dance-style in key with the theme or idea or plot—which accounts for all the cleverness, the touches of genius, and the banality, repetitiveness and vulgarity, that one sees in so many works by Western choreographers today."[59]

The success of the Soviet concept of dramatic ballet in London was primarily based on Lavrovsky's *Romeo and Juliet*, a success far from guaranteed given that the ballet was based on Shakespeare, one of England's cultural treasures. The Bolshoi dispelled any doubts whether the poetry of Shakespeare's play could be transformed into a mute ballet. The critic of the *Times* ecstatically wrote after the opening night: "mime is older than poetry, prior even to dancing or music. Mime, dance and music can spell poetry. . . . But can a mime ballet sustain the poetry of *Romeo and Juliet* with Shakespeare left out? It can. For the Bolshoi Ballet's performance of the long setting of the tragedy . . . was a translation almost of Shakespeare's very words into sheer poetry."[60] Mary Clarke emphasized the dramatic continuity and extraordinary musicality of Lavrovsky's production:

> Some people have objected that the choreography is limited and, in itself, not interesting. This is a criticism beyond my comprehension. If a sequence was detached from the ballet and set beside that created by Ashton for the Royal Danish Ballet's production—for example, the balcony or bedroom pas de deux—then we should in every case applaud Ashton. But the whole point of a Soviet production is that you cannot detach a sequence. Viewed as a part of the whole beautiful, wonderful, complete realization of Shakespeare's play then, in my opinion, the Lavrovsky choreography is not only masterly but right.[61]

Constructive Criticism

Created during the height of Stalinism, *Romeo and Juliet* showed that great art could be produced even during the most difficult times. Its librettist, Andrian Piotrovsky, had also been the coauthor of the libretto for Lopukhov's ill-fated ballet *The Bright Stream,* singled out during the antiformalism campaign of 1936. Piotrovsky was arrested in 1938 and died in prison. Piotrovsky had written *Romeo and Juliet*'s scenario together with the theater director Sergei Radlov, who was artistic director of the Kirov Theater from 1931 until 1934. Radlov was arrested and sent to the Gulag for eight years in 1945, to be rehabilitated in 1957, the year after *Romeo and Juliet*'s resounding success in London. Despite the complex climate at the time of the premiere at the Kirov in 1940, the ballet's score, which had been considered undanceable upon completion in 1935, had retained its modernist dimension: it was Prokofiev's first score after returning to Soviet Russia in 1935 after having lived in the West for several years, composing three scores for Diaghilev.

FIGURE 34. The Original Kirov production of *Romeo and Juliet*, first act, second scene, with Galina Ulanova as Juliet in a scene with her nurse, 1940. © Mariinsky Theater

FIGURE 35. The original Kirov production of *Romeo and Juliet*, first act, fourth scene, 1940. © Mariinsky Theater

If *Romeo and Juliet* was an almost unqualified success, the limitations of drambalet became more apparent in the second drambalet production presented in London, Zakharov's *The Fountain of Bakhchisarai.* Mary Clarke called the scene in the harem of the khan "the only languor of the season" and Asafiev's music "thin, poor stuff."[62] The *Times* wrote that if you took the Polish scene in *Boris Godunov* and added Fokine's *Polovtsian Dances* from *Prince Igor,* you had the ingredients of *The Fountain of Bakhchisarai*: "But Diaghilev did this sort of thing better. The missing ingredients are choreographic invention, distinguished music, and décor of character. . . . What the ballet discloses is the loss to Russia of Fokine, for the actual vocabulary of steps provided for the dancers is limited to the basic classical pas on which Fokine, Balanchine, and our own Ashton have since built up a whole language of expressive steps."[63] The response of the English ballet establishment to the two drambalet productions presented in London, *Romeo and Juliet* and *The Fountain of Bakhchisarai,* was thus complex. The emphasis on dramatic coherence and expressiveness was admired by many, but the absence of choreographic invention and the disappearance of some aspects of ballet technique from Soviet choreography, resulting in limited, repetitive choreographic vocabulary, were widely noted. Arnold Haskell, the influential English ballet writer, was struck by the impoverishment of female technique, pointing out that brilliant rapid steps and batterie had almost disappeared, even though elevation in jumps had increased tremendously.[64]

Before long, the disappearance of certain elements of the classical ballet vocabulary from Soviet choreography was discussed not just by Western observers, showing the impact of international cultural exchange on internal Soviet ballet debates. In 1962, reflecting upon the first visit of New York City Ballet to the Soviet Union, the Bolshoi dancer Aleksandr Lapauri commented on the rich choreographic vocabulary used by George Balanchine and criticized the limited vocabulary used by Soviet choreographers: "We repeat all elements with which G. Balanchine creates his intricate combinations daily in our training classes, but, for some reason, we bashfully call them 'naked technique,' from the whole enormous arsenal of movements we use several 'letters,' out of which we create a limited number of phrases, repeating them from ballet to ballet. The monotony of male dance is especially striking. Whole sections, such as, for example, batterie, have dropped almost completely from the field of vision of our choreographers."[65] The elimination of certain classical steps from the Soviet choreographic vocabulary was a direct consequence of the ideological tenets of drambalet. Certain Soviet dance circles had branded some elements of the traditional ballet vocabulary as "naked technique," which should not be used in Soviet choreography because it was supposedly incapable of expressing anything serious.

Why some elements of ballet technique were thus branded and other no less technically challenging steps were not is open to conjecture. Both Western and Russian comments on this issue seem to refer primarily to the impoverishment of petit allegro vocabulary, small but intricate steps and jumps performed at a quick speed.

From a superficial point of view, expansive movements such as powerful jumps, enabling the dancer to cover the stage in mighty leaps, corresponded to the heroic utopianism the Soviet state was propagating. Sky-borne dancer aviators covering a wide space with soaring leaps were certainly more likely to express a teleological ideology premised on the strategy of "catch up and overtake" than dancers performing small, complex steps whose understated charm lay in accuracy and detail. Within the aesthetic ideology of dram-balet, soaring jumps and turns were maybe more easy to justify dramatically than intricate small jumps and steps. To put it somewhat simplistically, big, heroic jumps seem more overtly suited to express strong emotions like love and despair than small steps. Judging by the reaction of average ballet audiences, they are also more likely to evoke a quick emotional response. Maybe they were also seen as more "realistic" and closer to the common woman and man than some of the complex batterie jumps, whose virtuoso technique of beating one's legs together in the air had originated in the early days of ballet, when the ankles were the most visible and mobile part of the dancer's body dressed in heavy court dress, exemplifying the finesse of ballet as a court art.

Constraining and Enabling Aspects of the Other

Despite these criticisms, on the artistic balance sheet of the cultural Cold War, the Bolshoi's visit clearly scored points for the Soviet side. In addition to stimulating a debate about the respective merits and artistic identity of Russian and Western ballet, the press predicted that the enormous public success of the Bolshoi's London visit would have implications for the future of ballet in Britain. The *Times* argued that the Royal Opera House had "gained in national esteem from the Bolshoi visit" and speculated that the visit might have won a new audience for ballet in England, pointing out that "the Bolshoi . . . has made more propaganda for the art of ballet in a month than dancers, critics, and balletomanes usually manage in a year." If only a small fraction of these people continued to go to the theater to watch the British ballet after the Bolshoi left, "the effect upon the future will be every bit as powerful as the influence the visit has already had on critics and dancers."[66]

From an artistic point of view, despite criticisms of the lack of innovative choreography, the theatrical concept behind drambalet, and Lavrovsky's

Romeo and Juliet in particular, had a lasting impact on the development of British ballet, demonstrating that, contrary to Western expectations, not all artistic creativity was stifled and some art of value had been created under Stalin. The artistic influence of the Bolshoi's dramatic ballets on choreographers such as Kenneth MacMillan, John Cranko, and maybe even Frederick Ashton is undisputed and has been pointed out by their biographers.[67] Lavrovsky's *Romeo and Juliet* deeply impressed and influenced Kenneth Mac-Millan, one of the Royal Ballet's defining choreographers. MacMillan's first full-length ballet for the Royal Ballet, his own version of Prokofiev's *Romeo and Juliet*, created almost ten years after he had first seen Lavrovsky's ballet, exemplifies the impact of the psychological character development and general dramatic coherence of the Bolshoi's production. Ninette de Valois wrote in 1985, almost thirty years after the Bolshoi's 1956 visit, that "any production of *Romeo and Juliet* owes much to Lavrovsky and Prokofiev. Scenically and choreographically the original may have been surpassed many times, yet all of today's productions bow, intentionally or unintentionally, to the basic craftsmanship and unified development of the original Russian production. . . . Prokofiev's *Romeo and Juliet* is a yardstick by which composers, choreographers, designers and scenario-writers may well study the *structure* of a full-length ballet for some time to come."[68]

Today, MacMillan's *Romeo and Juliet* is a favorite in the international ballet repertoire, but at the time it stood in the shadow of Lavrovsky's production. After the Bolshoi's Covent Garden season in 1963, the Royal Ballet had hoped that Lavrovsky might mount his *Romeo and Juliet* for the Royal Ballet, while the Bolshoi might in turn acquire Frederick Ashton's *La Fille mal gardée*.[69] After discussions led nowhere, MacMillan was commissioned to create the Royal Ballet's own version of *Romeo and Juliet*. Premiered in 1965, MacMillan's *Romeo and Juliet* was a big success. Margot Fonteyn and Rudolf Nureyev received forty-three curtain calls at the premiere, but the defining impact of Lavrovsky's *Romeo and Juliet* at the time is reflected in the closing remarks of a positive review in the *Times* that evaluates MacMillan's ballet as a passable "second best" in light of the unavailability of "the original": "forty-three calls and forty minutes of applause is obviously triumph enough. Yet it is still perhaps true, without disparagement of Mr. MacMillan, that the Royal Ballet might have done better to have waited a couple of years until it could have mounted the definitive Lavrovsky production. But, in all conscience, this new MacMillan should serve well enough."[70]

The Bolshoi thus returned triumphant from London, but on the other side of the Iron Curtain the end of Soviet ballet's isolation started a thought process that fed into internal debates about the artistic identity and future of Soviet ballet. On the surface, the overwhelming public success of the visit vindicated the realist path chosen by Soviet ballet, namely, the prioritizing of dramatic narrative in choreography and dramatic expression in dancing. According to the official eulogies, the success of the Bolshoi Ballet with English audiences signified nothing less than the victory of truth over deception: on the stages of Covent Garden, life-affirming Soviet realism had vanquished the bourgeois phantasmagoria of modernist art.

Deputy Minister of Culture V. Pakhomov announced that the acquaintance with Soviet choreographic art had led to a highly significant turning point in the minds of the audience after the reign of modernism and that its pursuit of form for form's sake and dance for dance's sake had deprived Western European audiences for decades of the chance to see realist art that was true to life: "In Western ballet art, form gained self-sufficient meaning, turned from a means to express an idea, profound content, the meaning of human struggle and of life—into an end in itself, into a means to cover up the lack of ideological content, into a method to distract the attention of the spectator from the unsightly capitalist reality surrounding him, to embellish contemporary bourgeois society." Pakhomov painted an ideological picture of the Bolshoi Ballet as bearer of light into the darkness of capitalist society: the Bolshoi had appeared in London as the carrier of the idea of life-affirming truth, changing the notion of what constituted the essence of ballet for many. The implementation of the principles of socialist realism had helped the masters of ballet at the Bolshoi to make their productions "profoundly content rich, lively, and exciting."[71]

The response by the English ballet world to the performances of the Bolshoi showed that at the time, notwithstanding the widely noted shortcomings of Soviet choreography, the Bolshoi was indeed seen as offering an alternative path for the development of ballet. To put it simply, Soviet ballet was distinguished from Western ballet by its "rich content"—its focus on telling a story—and the emotional absorption and conviction of its technically superb performers. The almost ecstatic response of the English audiences, critics, and dancers to the dramatic and emotional conviction of every member of the Bolshoi Ballet dancing in London in 1956 confirms that there was something uniquely expressive about the Russian performance style.

Within the Soviet Union, a phrase from Aleksandr Pushkin's *Eugene Onegin* was time and again invoked like a magical chant to conjure up this unique quality of Russian dancers: "the soulful flight of the Russian Terpsichore."[72] When comparing Western and Russian ballet, Soviet commentators repeated this phrase over and over again, elevating it to the main paradigm of Russian ballet. Igor' Moiseev couched his good luck wishes for the Bolshoi Ballet before its departure for London within this paradigm: "The English spectator, who knows the at times virtuoso technique and discipline peculiar to French and English ballet well, will see the animation and thrill, 'the soulful flight' characteristic of Russian choreography."[73] Within the context of the cultural Cold War, the emphasis on emotional depth as the defining characteristic of the artistic identity of Soviet performers in comparison to their Western counterparts was not unique to ballet. On 6 October 1959, a group of theater personalities comprising V. T. Komissarzhevsky, V. A. Kandelaki, N. P. Akimov, and P. A. Markov reported on their impressions of theatrical and cinematic life in the United States at a meeting at the VTO Central House of the Actor in Moscow. Commenting on the reception of Russian and Soviet art in the United States, Markov declared that:

> The Bolshoi Ballet, the dances of Moiseev, the Moscow Art Theater—all these cultural phenomena enjoy enormous, completely unique respect there. There is not a single cultural personality that does not treat Russian, Soviet art with enormous respect. When I read about our performances, about the fact that they have such success, it at times seemed to me to be an exaggeration. As a matter of fact, there is no exaggeration. This is really a recognition of the strength of Russian art, of the strength of the spirit of Russian art. When we say, for what does one love and value Russian art there, then it is for enormous soulfulness and depth. There, you are not amazed by eccentricity, you are not amazed by leftist forms. But when the "soulful flight" of the Russian Terpsichore makes its appearance, when the art of the Art Theater makes its appearance, then one celebrates the victory of our Russian and Soviet art.[74]

The political architects of the Soviet cultural project hoped to use art to demonstrate the superiority of socialism and the Soviet system, but far from carrying a distinctly "Socialist" message, the message of the regime's cultural ambassadors often focused on the nonpolitical, spiritual depth of the Russian soul—an amorphous quality whose nonpolitical essence could also be understood as potential locus of resistance against Sovietization, offering audiences at home and abroad a safe haven of nonpolitical meaning. Maybe the emphasis on the extraordinary soulfulness of Soviet performers also reflected a veiled recognition that the comparative advantage of Soviet art often lay in the area of performance.

Despite the official propagandistic rhetoric that hailed the Bolshoi Ballet's visit to London as an ideological coup and loudly reaffirmed Soviet ballet's identity as the antithesis to Western ballet, the tour showed that cultural exchange offered the possibility of earnest artistic exchange after years of Soviet isolation. Underneath the political context, the artistic meaning of cultural exchange was significant. The reaction of Western audiences offered

Soviet ballet an outside appraisal of its strengths and weaknesses that fed into domestic debates about the further development of ballet in the Soviet Union. Given the political purpose of cultural exchange, it is remarkable that even in public comments Soviet officials discussed Western criticisms that Soviet choreography was not innovative and sometimes even lacked dances. In his assessment of the tour, Pakhomov announced in the spirit of Communist self-criticism:

> However, we, Soviet people, have not gotten used to rest on one's laurels, even after a completely deserved and undoubted victory; we can and must draw the necessary conclusions from those sensible critical remarks that were made about our performances during the tour.
>
> Figures in the world of ballet and, above all, choreographers, are obliged to think about how to strengthen the role of dances in future ballet productions. The language of ballet is dance, and it must be allotted a fitting place in choreographic productions. After all, it's not a secret that quite often ballets emerge here where pantomime occupies a significantly bigger place than dance.[75]

Pakhomov was not the only one who argued that Western criticisms of Soviet ballet in London should be discussed in earnest. At a Komsomol meeting of the Bolshoi Ballet held on 23 November, Ia. Sekh criticized the theater's leadership for having failed to organize a meeting to discuss the London tour. At the same meeting, the secretary of the party bureau of the ballet, Iu. Gerber, seconded this opinion: full attention should be paid to the criticisms voiced in London.[76] At a meeting of the party organization of the ballet, A. Varlamov stated that the "tour to London passed by with a triumph but we don't have the right to close our eyes to just criticism, which was occasionally heard among the series of foreign reviews. The management and party committee should have gathered the company and seriously talked about our achievements, as well as about our shortcomings."[77]

Some artists tried to use the response of Western audiences as "objective outsider opinion" to vindicate some aspects of ballet that in the Soviet Union had been assaulted for ideological reasons. Leonid Lavrovsky tried to use the enthusiastic response of the London audience to the character dances in *Swan Lake* to "relegitimize" the character dances performed in nineteenth-century classical ballets that had been looked at with suspicion since the revolution, as they were seen as too far removed from actual folk dances. One of the main points of criticisms hurled against Lopukhov's *The Bright Stream* during the antiformalism campaign of 1936 decried its dances as sugary concoctions that had nothing in common with the real folk dances danced in the Kuban, where the ballet was set. Commenting on the unanticipated success of the character dances in *Swan Lake*, Lavrovsky wrote in *Sovetskii artist* that this unexpected applause made him think about something they had earlier been skeptical about—academic character dance:

> I think that in connection with the development of the culture of folk dance in our country, figures in the world of choreography began to somewhat underrate the culture of academic character dance, which is extremely important, complex, and vitally necessary for the creative solution of new ballets.
>
> The masters of the past, creating this genre of stage dance, of course spurned genuine folk dance, but they based themselves at the same time on the distinctive features, style, manner of the ballet production and accordingly adapted such a dance. . . . Academic character dances are an integral part of our whole repertoire. One must not dismiss them and replace them with folk dance, copying the performance manner of genuine folk dance in one ensemble or the other. This would be a mistake, because the creative solution of the subject of a ballet requires from the choreographer a corresponding adaptation of folk dance in conformity with the manner and style of the given production.[78]

The most important artistic aspect of cultural exchange between East and West was undoubtedly the opportunity for Soviet and Western artists to critically look at the artistic development of ballet "on the other side." Within a few years, some dancers compared the opportunities offered by the West's artistic pluralism and freedom favorably with the officially circumscribed artistic possibilities in the Soviet Union. To others, the choreographic experiments of Western choreographers looked like a pointless heresy not worth wasting much thought on. The artists of the Bolshoi Ballet visiting London in 1956 did not have much of a chance to sample Western ballet. Lavrovsky, for example, had not been able to see a performance by the Sadler's Wells Ballet, but together with Chulaki, he had attended a rehearsal of Anton Dolin's Festival Ballet, the precursor of today's English National Ballet. Lavrovsky's assessment of the company at the meeting of the House of the Actor was scathing, as he thought it was so bad that it didn't even deserve to be called a company.[79] The rehearsal consisted of three fragments: a fragment of *Coppélia*,[80] a new ballet, and a piece by the nineteenth-century choreographer August Bournonville. Lavrovsky remarked about *Coppélia*: "There was a pas de deux; in principle, it was a classical pas de deux, but in its form, it had absolutely nothing in common with what we got used to seeing in our old production. This is an illiterate execution of a series of classical movements."[81]

It is striking that Lavrovsky and other Soviet establishment artists compared contemporary Western choreography or art with artistic experiments
they themselves had conducted in the 1920s, always concluding that even
though their experiments had been "sinful," they were superior to current
Western experimentation. Regarding Festival Ballet's new ballet, Lavrovsky
stated: "I remember my infantile trials around 1924–1925, when the new
ballet existed, but I also remember Marius Petipa. Remembering these sins,
I have to say that there was high professionalism, because we were all lit-
erate people; there was an idea. But here this doesn't exist. Imagine that a
female dancer appears in front of you with a manifestly meaningless assort-
ment of movements—classical movements together with acrobatics. This
isn't even Duncan, but some tenth school of the twenty-fifth student of
Duncan. Something has been collected from all movements." Vadim Ryndin,
chief artist of the Bolshoi Theater and Galina Ulanova's husband, remarked
on some sketches shown to him for operas at *La Scala,* "this is a phase we
passed through a long time ago: in the 1920s, we saw something similar in
Rabinovich's work, in Petrovsky's work, I did something along these lines.
But for us, this is the past."[82]

With the onset of cultural exchange, the contrast between Soviet and
Western choreography soon began to be epitomized by New York City Ballet and its founder Balanchine's neoclassical, abstract choreography, the aesthetic and ideological antithesis to Soviet ballet. In his searing remarks about
the new work rehearsed by Festival Ballet, Lavrovsky emphasized that "to
all this, a theoretical basis was given by the choreographer Balanchine. . . .
His credo is that there should be absolutely no guiding principle, absolutely
no idea in the art of ballet, and absolutely no content is necessary. He sees
his task in the following: taking a work, the idea and feelings are not the
essence but only the ornamental pattern of the work and on the basis of this
musical pattern he sees the pattern of the dance."[83] The biographical prox-
imity between the drambalet establishment and George Balanchine added
a unique psychological dimension to the comparison between Western and
Soviet ballet: George Balanchine had graduated from the ballet school of
the Mariinsky in 1921, only a year before Lavrovsky. While Balanchine's
and Lavrovsky's paths had diverged in diametrically opposed directions,
their roots were the same. They had been contemporaries at school and had
both been involved in choreographic experiments in Soviet Russia in the
1920s that were so vocally rejected by drambalet in the 1930s. In 1923, both
had participated in a precursor of Balanchine's abstract ballets, Lopukhov's
Dance Symphony: The Magnificence of the Universe, discussed in chapter 2. In
1962, Balanchine returned to the Soviet Union during New York City Ballet's first tour to the Soviet Union, bringing with him an artistic vision of

ballet that completely clashed with the official Soviet definition of ballet's essence. To some, the ballets of Soviet ballet's "lost son" provided a vision of what could have been, had political circumstances been different.

If the ideological warning against "Western" influence runs like a red thread through the attacks against the supporters of symphonic dance discussed in chapter 4, in the long run the exposure to Western choreography within the context of Cold War cultural exchange probably helped to cement the position of symphonic dance, the return of complex classical dance to the center stage of Soviet choreography. The archival notes of the all-union meeting of ballet figures on problems of Soviet choreography held in June 1963 refer to concerns raised at the last all-union meeting on Soviet choreography,[84] that American ballet might overtake Soviet ballet. In Soviet rhetoric at the time, American ballet as embodied by Balanchine's New York City Ballet was usually condemned for its abstract, purely technical nature, but the inventiveness and technical accomplishment of Balanchine's choreographic style were also often noted. Within this context, the remarks made by Mikhail Chulaki at the conference in 1963 are interesting. Chulaki, the composer who was the Bolshoi's director from 1955–1959, its director and artistic director from 1963–1970, and head of the artistic council on choreography under the auspices of the USSR Ministry of Culture, started his remarks by praising Soviet ballet, emphasizing its great effect when traveling abroad, hailing it as carrier of great ideas, distinguished by its unique capacity to express complex topics. One of the main points of Chulaki's remarks, however, focused on the poverty of dance and dance inventiveness in Soviet ballets, pointing out that dance had started to occupy a modest place in the synthesis of different art forms in ballet productions, when it should in fact take the main place. He criticized performances where 80 percent of the time was dedicated to pantomimic explanations of plot as opposed to dance, urged choreographers to exchange timidity for new, daring searches, and called for restoring dance's rights and primacy in the synthetic art of ballet.[85]

Dancers were sent across the Iron Curtain as ambassadors of the Soviet cultural project on an official mission to demonstrate the superiority of Soviet civilization to the world at large. In the final analysis, international cultural exchange demonstrated less the superiority of one political system over the other than the unifying force of art across cultural and ideological chasms. The impact of international cultural exchange on the artistic self-understanding of Soviet dancers in the 1950s and 1960s was complex: for some, it resulted in an identity crisis that led to a questioning of the aesthetic foundations of Soviet choreography; for others, it confirmed the superiority of Russian soulfulness over cold Western technical prowess; for a third group, the truth might have been somewhere in the middle.

The first major international tour of Soviet ballet, the Bolshoi's visit to London in 1956, already indicated that the impact of international tours on Soviet ballet would be multilayered, reflecting the tension between the ideological context of Cold War cultural exchange and the onset of an international exchange of artistic ideas. The enormous success of the tour increased the prestige of ballet at home, last but not least in the eyes of the Soviet government. The international awe at the expressive artistry of Soviet dancers confirmed for some Soviet ballet circles that compared to the "soulful flight" of Soviet performers, Western dancers were artistically inferior, cold technicians whose performances had nothing to do with the existential questions faced by mankind, while ballet in the Soviet Union had been elevated to a more serious plane, and that the narrow focus of Soviet ballet on narrative ballets was therefore artistically fully justified. The wider ideological confrontation between East and West sometimes reinforced a rigid form of artistic nationalism on both sides of the Iron Curtain, acting as potential constraint on further artistic development by insisting on defining artistic identity as antithesis to the Other.

At the same time, Soviet ballet circles were not immune to Western criticism of Soviet choreography. The end of Soviet ballet's international isolation provided an outside appraisal of its strengths and weaknesses, preparing the ground for comparisons between the artistic pluralism and choreographic experimentation of ballet in the West with creative opportunities at home. As evident from discussions at the artistic council of the Bolshoi and at the all-union meeting on problems of Soviet choreography held in 1963, contact with choreographic developments in the West in general, and with Balanchine's choreographic genius in particular, convinced some personalities within the Soviet ballet world that Russian ballet would be pushed to the sidelines if it did not reform itself artistically. Both admiration for and fear of competition by the Other could serve as inspiration for change and as a positive force acting on domestic constraints on artistic evolution.

The consequences of international cultural exchange were by no means one-sided. The artistic dimension of Cold War cultural exchange often cancelled out the ideological-political dimension of the so-called Cultural Olympics, allowing the Other to metamorphose from antithesis into inspiration. Just as a closer acquaintance with Western choreography influenced the development of Soviet choreography, the dramatic coherence and theatricality of the Soviet productions presented in London in 1956 during the Bolshoi's first major international tour had a profound impact on the development of modern narrative ballet in the West. The dancers' artistry and *Romeo and Juliet* in particular demonstrated that not all artistic creativity had been stifled under Stalin: ballets had been created that offered an innovative alternative to Western ballet, and dancers had emerged that inspired Western dancers with their virtuosity and artistry.

Enfant Terrible

Leonid Iakobson and *The Bedbug*, 1962

> For every new production, Iakobson wangled, begged,
> implored the authorities. And then—he defended himself,
> returned abuse, brushed it aside. An Iakobson premiere was
> always, without fail, a negotiation, a scandal, the jitters.
>
> —MAYA PLISETSKAYA

IN HER AUTOBIOGRAPHY, Natalia Makarova remembers that in her first year at the Kirov, she was "fabulously lucky"—she fell into the hands of the choreographer Leonid Iakobson, the choreographic enfant terrible of Soviet ballet, a person of notoriously difficult character who was known as the "Chagall of ballet" because of his fertile and unique choreographic imagination. For the young Makarova, creating the role of Zoya Berezkina in Iakobson's ballet *The Bedbug* was a turning point: "In *The Bedbug*, I sensed for the first time just how constrained I had felt in the romantic vein. . . . I am eternally grateful to Iakobson for believing in me and, little by little, as it were incidentally, drawing out my nature and myself."[1] Dancers like Plisetskaya and Makarova considered Iakobson a rarely gifted choreographer and, in their memoirs, mourn the persistent persecution of his work as one of the tragedies of Soviet ballet.[2] But far from everyone shared their enthusiasm for his works that broke with the tradition of classical dance, replacing it with a unique choreographic idiom that combined diverse elements like pantomime, newly invented movements, classical dance vocabulary, movements rejecting even the basis of classical dance—the en dehors position of the hips—and so forth. Many dancers and members of the ballet establishment looked at his creations as the dangerous ravings of a madman threatening the citadel of classical dance, while the authorities opposed his works as ideologically questionable testimonies to nonconformism.

The acrimonious debates surrounding Iakobson's ballet *The Bedbug*, created for the Kirov in the early 1960s, show both the remarkable concessions that strategic persistence could wring from the system and the interplay of artistic and political-ideological pressures that ultimately imposed limitations on choreographic experimentation—and artistic autonomy—both during the Thaw and during the ensuing period of official reassertion of ideological control over the arts. The ballet's history spans a period that includes the height of cultural tolerance during the Thaw, symbolized by the publication of Solzhenitsyn's *A Day in the Life of Ivan Denisovich* in autumn 1962, and the hasty reaffirmation of the borders of the culturally permissible in the winter and spring of 1962–1963.

The ballet seemingly responded to the government's impatient call for ballets on Soviet topics, but Iakobson's choice of topic reflected his artistic strategy of stubbornly fighting for an uncompromised implementation of his highly individualistic vision of choreography and art. Iakobson did not choose a simple propaganda plot but a literary source open to interpretation. In June 1962, after a five-year-long battle, Iakobson's ballet *The Bedbug*, based on Mayakovsky's play of the same name, premiered at the Kirov. The ballet received fifteen performances and then became one of two ballets staged by the Kirov singled out for attack during Khrushchev's showdown with the creative intelligentsia in 1962–1963.[3]

The interaction of artistic criticisms made by the more conservative ballet establishment with politically based aesthetic-ideological concerns shows how nonconformists like Iakobson often faced a two-front battle in the field of Soviet cultural production: in a system where the state controlled cultural production, highly individualistic artists like Iakobson remained dependent on large, state-sponsored—and state-supervised—ensembles like the Kirov. At the same time, Iakobson's choreographic style, artistic vision, and character doomed him to the role of an outsider within his own profession. Iakobson was in many ways an "antiestablishment" choreographer who, if he had been born in the West, would arguably have been more likely to found his own company than to work for a big classical ensemble. Within the Soviet context of state-controlled cultural production, however, it was virtually impossible to create one's own company. Until Iakobson finally managed to found his own ensemble, Choreographic Miniatures, in Leningrad in 1969 toward the end of his life, he remained dependent on the conservative ballet establishment not just for infrastructure like a stage and rehearsal space but also for access to the highly professional dancers he needed. In addition, and also once Iakobson had his own ensemble, the political and ideological controls imposed on artistic creation in the Soviet Union continued to make his life as a creative artist unfathomably difficult. The limits imposed on artistic autonomy and on the potential for artistic repossession reflected this dual pressure on artists who did not fit into the established system. The combination of artistic and ideological pressures on Iakobson exemplifies the complex interplay between the creative intelligentsia and the political machine in setting the parameters for cultural production within the Soviet Union.

Iakobson and Vladimir Mayakovsky's *The Bedbug*

Even though by the late 1950s and early 1960s ballet occupied a position within the Soviet cultural project that was, at least in theory, supposedly equal to traditionally more "serious" art forms such as classical music or the dramatic theater, people both outside and within the ballet profession continued to believe that there were some topics that ballet could not express. Much of the initial opposition to Iakobson's *The Bedbug* reflected resistance to the idea to create a ballet based on Mayakovsky. When Iakobson first approached the Kirov with his plan in 1956, his idea was met with ridicule and derision. Not only his enemies within the theater but even his friends laughed in his face. When he tried to explain that he envisioned a ballet in which Mayakovsky would be shown composing the play *The Bedbug*, that the ballet would be about Mayakovsky and his creative process, he was declared insane.[4]

Written in 1928, Mayakovsky's shattering satire of Communist society consists of two parts. The first part of the play is set in 1929 and condemns the profiteering and proletarian philistinism of the Soviet bourgeoisie. Ivan Prisypkin, a former party member and a former worker of immaculate proletarian background, fulfills his dream of bourgeois comforts by marrying Elzevira Renaissance, manicurist and cashier of a beauty parlor. The drunken wedding party ends with a disastrous fire that presumably kills everyone. The second part of the play is set fifty years later, in 1979. In Mayakovsky's nightmarish vision of the Communist millennium, Prisypkin's excesses are unthinkable; sex, vodka, tobacco, dancing, and romance have ceased to exist.[5] Prisypkin's frozen body is found in an ice-filled cellar: instead of having died, he survived his wedding party as a body frozen in the water firemen had pumped into the beauty parlor after the blazing culmination of his wedding. In this world of Communist utopia, Prisypkin is exhibited in a cage as a zoological curiosity, together with a bedbug. According to the director of the zoo, the *bedbugus normalis* and Prisypkin, the *bourgeoisius vulgaris*, "are different in size, but identical in essence," both are parasites feeding on mankind.[6] But in this dehumanized world of communism, Prisypkin suddenly looks the most human.[7]

Iakobson initially planned to use both parts of the play and conceived three acts, dedicating the third act to the second half of Mayakovsky's play. According to Iakobson, his production was met with such disbelief that he barely managed to preserve the first two acts, giving the ballet a sense of incompleteness.[8] The ballet culminated in the wedding cortege deriding the petty-bourgeois philistinism of Prisypkin's world. After the wedding, Prisypkin and his bride were shown frolicking like two insects on a giant bed with pink satin covers. The ballet ends with Mayakovsky setting his heroes on fire.

Iakobson wanted to make Mayakovsky the real hero of the ballet, an idea that was considered unusually daring, if not outright impudent. Mayakovsky and his creative process were at the heart of the ballet. Before the music started, the curtain rose on Mayakovsky, caught deep in thought. He took one giant step, then another, and a third. Transposing the poet's creative writing process into the realm of the ballet theater, Mayakovsky created the ballet's different characters by showing them how to move, making the ballet a product of the poet's fantasy. Iakobson fused the first half of Mayakovsky's play with episodes from the First World War, the revolution, the civil war, and the construction of socialism. For example, in a scene called "Gulliver and the Lilliputians," Iakobson juxtaposed a Red Army soldier, danced by grown-ups, with children dressed as factory owners, financiers, and officers, expressing different national characteristics. The Red Army soldier could lift up each of them with one hand and looked down on them like the Red Army soldier on one of the propaganda posters Mayakovsky had designed for the windows of the Russian Telegraph Agency (ROSTA) in the early days of the revolution.

Iakobson used Mayakovsky's drawings, and his ROSTA posters in particular, as inspiration for the production's style. He called his ballet a "choreographic poster" (*khoreograficheskii plakat*). Iakobson returned to the ideals of his youth in *The Bedbug*: the expressive language of the ballet was not classical dance but *svobodnaia plastika*, free movement, using the grotesque for the creation of a danced satire, a genre that is rare in ballet.[9] Natalia Makarova described the choreography of the part she created in the ballet, Prisypkin's jilted lover, the working girl Zoya Berezkina:

> The choreography of my part called for me to utilize the movements, transformed by Iakobson, of rock and the twist. I did not play a part; I was simply myself and felt no discomfort at being a romantic ballerina who was dancing on heels, with knees knocking, a springy step, awkward lines, and crossed arms. My friends said to me: "So you are

FIGURE 36. *(right)*
Askol'd Makarov as
Mayakovsky in *The
Bedbug* at the Kirov
Ballet, 1968. © Mariinsky
Theater

FIGURE 37. *(below)*
The Bedbug at the Kirov
Ballet, 1968. © Mariinsky
Theater

FIGURE 38. Natalia Makarova as Zoya and Konstantin Rassadin as Prisypkin in *The Bedbug* at the Kirov Ballet, 1968. © Mariinsky Theater

eager to distort your beautiful body in those ugly poses!" I loved it, especially my last solo, my "talk with the stars," after my chosen one, Prisypkin, . . . has married the heavyset Elzevir[a] Renaissance. I run about, unaware, as if borne along by unbearable pain, tossing my legs back, knees giving way, dropping, writhing, and clutching with my hands in the air, and cold, indifferent stars are burning high overhead. Then I stop, helpless, and commit suicide, putting my head in an imaginary noose and swinging in the wind.[10]

The creative conception of the ballet did not conform to standard expectations of a Soviet ballet at the time, instead combining elements of the 1920s Soviet avant-garde with a radically nonclassical choreographic language. It is thus not surprising that Iakobson's implementation of his idea proved controversial, but why were people so taken aback by Iakobson's idea even before he implemented it? Ballet was by no means alien to twentieth-century Russian poets. As the Russian ballet writer Vadim Gaevsky has pointed out, when St. Petersburg descended into a dark age under its new name Leningrad, some of the city's most important cultural standard bearers—most notably Anna Akhmatova and Joseph Brodsky—used the city's fabled ballet as a nostalgic cipher for the cultural glory of St. Petersburg/Leningrad.[11]

Of all twentieth-century Russian poets, Mayakovsky was probably one of the least likely candidates to find himself transformed into the hero of a ballet. He detested Russia's classical ballet heritage and everything it represented. In the 1920s, he loudly ridiculed ballet as the epitome of bourgeois culture. In 1930, Meyerhold's production of Mayakovsky's last comedy, *The Bathhouse,* included a parody of the recent ballet *The Red Poppy.*[12] Mayakovsky's sarcastic reference to the ballet in *The Bathhouse,* produced three years after the premiere of *The Red Poppy,* was typical of the disdain some members of the avant-garde felt for Russia's classical ballet, which they perceived as symbol of the vulgar taste of the philistine bourgeoisie: "You were at *The Red Poppy?* Oh, I was at *The Red Poppy!* Amazingly interesting! The flowers flitting about everywhere, the singing, the dancing of all sorts of elves and . . . syphilids."[13] By combining the words *syphilis,* the venereal disease plaguing nineteenth-century prostitutes and their debauched gentlemen customers, with the word *sylph,* the airy spirits epitomizing the spiritual yearning of nineteenth-century romantic ballet, Mayakovsky's memorable *syphilids* evokes a visceral disgust for ballet as something akin to a decomposing body wracked by disease. By putting this word into the mouth of a ballet spectator, Mayakovsky ridicules the ballet audience as a naïve and uneducated group reveling in cheap spectacle. Similarly, in the opening scene of his play *The Bedbug,* ballet is repeatedly evoked as a metaphor for the vulgarity of Soviet society during the New Economic Policy, a society that Mayakovsky saw dominated by a new Soviet bourgeoisie for whom the attainment of bourgeois comforts was the highest goal in life. The play opens in front of a state department store in Tambov, private peddlers are walking around. The second character to speak in the play is a man selling dancing dolls who praises his wares by shouting: "Dancing dolls! Straight from the ballet studios! The best toy for indoors and outdoors! Dances to the order of the People's Commissar!"[14] When Prisypkin hears the vendor praise his dancing dolls from the ballet studios, he orders his future mother-in-law to buy one:

MAN SELLING TOYS: Dancing dolls from the ballet studios. . . .

PRISYPKIN: My future children must be brought up refined. There, buy one, Rosalie Pavlovna.[15]

For Mayakovsky, ballet was synonymous with the bourgeoisie he detested.

The shocked laughter that greeted Iakobson's suggestion to base a ballet on Mayakovsky probably reflected primarily a fear that it would be impossible to successfully express this topic choreographically and not a general recognition among the ballet community that Mayakovsky had detested ballet, especially as Mayakovsky's comedies with their scornful references to ballet had not been performed between 1930 and 1955. Moreover, a choreographic interpretation of the poet's work could be politically dangerous, especially in the hands of a provocative choreographer like Iakobson. During the Thaw, cracks began to appear in the death mask of ideological orthodoxy that had been forced onto the poet's memory. For the past twenty years, Mayakovsky had been officially hailed as the "poet of the revolution." In 1935, five years after the poet's suicide, Stalin elevated Mayakovsky to the "best and most talented poet of our Soviet epoch." Mayakovsky's official transformation from a complex, radical avant-garde poet to the Soviet poet laureate led to the forced mass consumption of an ideologically sanitized version of the poet's work, a process that Boris Pasternak lamented as the poet's second death.[16] His satirical plays criticizing the hypocrisy of Soviet society were banned. In 1955, Mayakovsky's comedies returned to the stage after a twenty-five year ban. *The Bedbug*, one of the most biting satires of Soviet society, was produced by several directors in the manner of Meyerhold. Valentin Pluchek's somewhat constructivist and grotesque staging at the Theater of Satire was particularly important.[17] Iakobson seems to have conceived his idea for a ballet on Mayakovsky and *The Bedbug* soon after the play had returned to Soviet stages.

There was certainly some artistic affinity between Iakobson, the choreographic nonconformist, and Mayakovsky, the radical avant-garde poet. Iakobson had a special talent for satire paired with a predilection for grotesque, making a play like *The Bedbug* particularly attractive to him. Like the poet, Iakobson had been in search for radically new expressive forms since his youth. In the 1920s, there had been a vibrant free dance scene in Soviet Russia where non- or semi-classically based movements could flourish, but in the 1930s, this scene was repressed, to the detriment of choreographers such as Iakobson. Even though Iakobson firmly believed in the classical school for training dancers, he challenged its monopoly as choreographic style. In his youth, his biting comments on classical ballet were not far from the snorting disdain showered on classical ballet by avant-garde artists like Mayakovsky. In 1928, as a twenty-four-year-old dancer with the former Mariinsky Ballet, Iakobson belligerently proclaimed in *Zhizn' iskusstva* that "in no art form is there such artistic stagnation as there is in the art of choreography. The classical style, looming like a certain fate and prevailing over all other currents, at the present represents no artistic value whatsoever. A blend of French affectation (which we call for some reason grace) with soulless Italian virtuosity—that is the basis of classical dance. No ray of feeling whatsoever, no progress whatsoever. What beauty can there be in complete and utter unnaturalness?"[18] In 1931, Iakobson published an article in *Rabochii i teatr* urging that all classical ballets be thrown out of the repertoire, with the exception of *Swan Lake* and *The Sleeping Beauty*.[19]

At that time, his program for dance reform propagated the replacement of the existing classical dance system with "active gesture" (*deistvennyi zhest*) and pantomime. According to the Soviet dance theorist and critic Galina Dobrovol'skaya, pantomime did become his main expressive means, but his understanding of the term was decidedly different from everyone else's: instead of imitating everyday movement, Iakobson's pantomime lived inside dance. Like his drambalet contemporaries, he rejected abstract dance technique in favor of choreographic narration and the conventional pantomime of old ballets in favor of a merger of dance and pantomime into a new stylistic whole, but in contrast to the propagators of drambalet, Iakobson's view on the specific expressive nature of dance never put him at risk of turning ballet into an apprentice of the dramatic theater. Iakobson was unique because he sought to develop a new plastic language within a philosophy of dance as an independent voice of artistic expression bound only by its own laws and conventions and not by those of other forms of artistic expression, such as the dramatic theater.[20] In Russian, Iakobson's choreographic style is often described by the term *svobodnaia plastika*, free movement, which differs both from dance and pantomime and is characterized by movement not subject to the laws of classical dance. The term is also used to describe Isadora Duncan's dances and some of Mikhail Fokine's ballets.[21]

Iakobson was part of the Soviet classical ballet elite by virtue of his Leningrad training and professional affiliations. He remained reliant on the classical elite because of his need for dancers who had the physical control and coordination that only classical ballet training of the highest caliber can give, but he always found himself swimming against the predominant choreographic style of any given period of Soviet ballet. At the outset of his career, Iakobson's experimental choreographic aesthetics did not fit within the paradigm of drambalet. For most of the 1930s and 1940s, his work was confined to the provinces. In 1950, Iakobson staged the ballet *Shurale* for the Kirov, a highly successful narrative ballet based on a Tatar fairy tale. In 1951, Iakobson and some of the dancers received the Stalin Prize for *Shurale*, but disaster struck only a few weeks later when a central newspaper printed an article by the highly conformist choreographer Aleksei Andreev under the polemic title "Kosmopolit v balete" (A cosmopolitan in ballet)." At a time when the anticosmopolitan campaign had created an atmosphere of paranoid xenophobia and rising anti-Semitism, Andreev denounced Iakobson—who was Jewish—as a cosmopolitan enemy of Soviet choreography who since his schooldays had rejected the pure classics of the Russian ballet school. While *Shurale* continued to be shown at the Kirov, Iakobson was thrown out of the theater. For the next six years, basically no one—not even in the provinces—was prepared to close a contract with Iakobson.[22] He created only one ballet during this period, the classically based fairy tale ballet *Solveig* at the Maly Opera Theater in Leningrad in 1952. Championed by Lopukhov, he returned to the Kirov as experimental choreographer in 1956 to choreograph the first production of Aram Khachaturian's ballet *Spartacus*. Iakobson was back, and so were the polemics about his work. In the words of Maya Plisetskaya: "For every new production, Iakobson wangled, begged, implored the authorities. And then—he defended himself, returned abuse, brushed it aside. A Iakobson premiere was always, without fail, a negotiation, a scandal, the jitters."[23]

Artistic Opposition to Iakobson and *The Bedbug*

Many people at the Kirov were hostile toward Iakobson's work. Iakobson's unorthodox aesthetics and his character combined into an explosive mixture that condemned him to the status of eternal outsider within his own profession. Within the narrow confines set by both the wider Soviet cultural context and by the dedicated traditionalism of large segments of the Soviet ballet establishment, Iakobson continuously had to confront irritated incomprehension. According to Makarova, "most dancers did not like Iakobson. Used to the standard classics, they felt uncomfortable in his contorted, expressively sharpened poses, which, in addition to everything else, Iakobson demanded they imbue with emotional content."[24] Paradoxically, despite the hostility of many toward his style and character, Iakobson was considered a highly original choreographic talent. It is for this reason that he continued to create works for the Soviet Union's premier ballet companies. Thirty years after his death in 1975, the former Kirov ballerina Irina Kolpakova summed him up with the following words: "he was a genius, but a person with a horrible character, but that is not important."[25]

Iakobson's artistic position probably reflected his personality: maybe the combination of a difficult character with an unusual artistic talent would have predestined him to embark on an opposition course with the establishment in any society. Iakobson's artistic nonconformity formed an explosive mixture with his uncompromising stubbornness, his cruel professional honesty, and his dictatorial rehearsal habits. According to Iakobson's widow, the dancer Irina Iakobson, the choreographer did not listen to anyone's advice, instructions, or requests.[26] His brutal honesty alienated artists who were working with him. Makarova remembered "beautiful but sluggish bodies capable only of serving as props on stage made him furious, and at rehearsals he often tossed off caustic remarks to this effect, remarks for which the dancers could not forgive him."[27] The nature of Iakobson's creative process as described by Irina Iakobson, and his literary collaborator Vladimir Zaidel'son, did not contribute to making the dancers feel comfortable in the rehearsal studio. Some choreographers arrive at rehearsals with a clear idea of what they plan to do, and some involve the dancers in the composition process; Iakobson did not share his creative process with anyone. He arrived at the studio with only a general idea in his head. While he used the individuality of the dancer he was working with as a springboard to create an image, he often did not know himself how things would turn out. Like working on a block of stone that is steadily hewn into shape, he would create an image by working in minute, intricate brushstrokes, changing a dancer's hand and only then seeing what needed to be done with the whole body. Unless they were used to his fragmented, mosaic-like working method and trusted him, the dancers would become irritated and, having no idea where any of this was leading, thought they were wasting their time on trifles.[28]

Iakobson's unusual working method reflected the peculiar nature of his choreography. He strongly believed in classical dance as the only training that could give a dancer the professional balletic coordination of movement necessary for being able to dance his choreography, with its highly complex requirements. His choreographic style, however, was far removed from classical ballet choreography. In each of his compositions, Iakobson created new movements that were completely his own. According to Irina Iakobson, the dancer would be shown one movement for one note and another for the next, but the artist would not yet know how to connect the movements: Iakobson always used unfamiliar movements, an unfamiliar way of physical coordination, and no preparatory movements. Irina Iakobson explains that her husband's work could be compared to the work of an animation artist who draws many images that by themselves mean little but taken together create a moving, living image on screen. As a result, his choreography was saturated with movement and technically highly complex, at first sometimes seemingly impossible to dance.[29]

Iakobson's character made him anything but easy to work with. People at the theater called him a quarrelsome, unintelligible dictator with whom it was difficult to get on. At rehearsals, Iakobson typically tended to tell the dancers to "be quiet and do what I tell you."[30] Iakobson's difficult nature was probably exacerbated by the mocking hostility of many dancers at the Kirov toward his work. The first ballet he staged for the Kirov after the war, *Shurale*, was by all accounts very classical by Iakobson's choreographic standards, but many dancers initially rejected his work and felt offended by it. Denunciations and humiliating letters were written. Irina Iakobson remembers that the following lines were making the rounds at the theater:

> A horrible groan is audible on stage.
> Iakobson is staging a ballet there.

Arms, legs, faces flit by.
A grand pas is danced on buttocks.

. . .

All evil spirits have been consumed by fire,
The whole stage is left in shit,
And in the center on the biggest heap,
Our stinking Iakobson is standing.[31]

It is not surprising that in this atmosphere, whenever someone smiled or whispered during a rehearsal, Iakobson started shouting and threw the artist out of the rehearsal, assuming that he had been the target of the smile and the whisper. In general, Iakobson found it difficult to rein in his temperament. Several years later, when he had finally managed to establish his own company, Choreographic Miniatures, he once became so frustrated at a rehearsal that he shouted at his main persecutor, Tamara Andreevna Petrova, the head of the cultural department of the Leningrad gorkom (city committee), and threw her out of the studio, screaming after her: "I'm sick of you! You and your dark passions," alluding to her anti-Semitism.[32]

An uncompromising, temperamental choreographer who loudly challenged the aesthetics and conventions of both the ballet establishment and the authorities was bound to run against walls in the climate of Soviet cultural orthodoxies. Iakobson's position at the Kirov during the production process of *The Bedbug* was further complicated by wider developments within the company and the country's creative climate. Compared to the choreographic reawakening at the Kirov in the late 1950s, by 1962, the general artistic climate within the company was becoming increasingly hostile to experimentation. To a large extent, the conservatism of the company during these years reflected the personal artistic credo of Konstantin Sergeev, who returned to his previous post of artistic director in 1960, a position he lost in 1970 following Makarova's defection. If Sergeev's removal from this post in 1955 had reflected the government's support for the young and a desire to revive the arts, Sergeev's reinstatement in 1960 presaged a reaffirmation of limits imposed on artistic innovation. Sergeev replaced Boris Fenster, who had died at the Kirov on 29 December 1960 during the dress rehearsal of his last ballet, *Masquerade*. The political leaders felt comfortable with Sergeev's conservative taste. After the theater's director announced that the minister of culture had appointed Sergeev artistic director of the Kirov Ballet, Sergeev's remarks reflected his deep dedication to the Kirov's classical heritage—and his hostility toward experiments: "I am grateful to the party and the government for their concern about Soviet ballet, for the trust shown to me personally. I have become older, I have become wiser. I love our classical art very much and will do everything to guard its tradition. I am, of course, not against experiments, but we will transfer them to the rehearsal studio, and on stage, we will release only what is worthy of the tradition of our theater."[33]

Many at the Kirov strongly opposed Iakobson's proposal for a Mayakovsky ballet. At a meeting held at the All-Russian Theatrical Society (VTO) in Leningrad on 22 February 1963, Askol'd Makarov, the dancer who created Mayakovsky's role in the ballet, pointed out that more than five years of dogged struggle had to pass until Iakobson's *The Bedbug* saw the limelight.[34] Iakobson first approached the Kirov's leadership with his idea for a ballet on Mayakovsky in 1956, at a time when the company was still rehearsing his *Spartacus*.[35] For two and a half years, the Kirov Theater did not allot time to Iakobson to present his creative concept.[36] Iakobson was not a person to give up easily. Trying to beat the system by its own rules, he sought political patronage and appealed to Nikolai Mikhailov, the Soviet minister of culture, to press his case with the Kirov's leadership. On 17 May 1957, Iakobson wrote to Mikhailov:

> I am sorry to trouble you. But I am compelled to turn to you again in connection with the fact that the instructions given by you to the Kirov Theater to listen to the choreographic exposition and music on the theme of Mayakovsky's comedy *The Bedbug* within five days have until now not been fulfilled. Since then, two months have already passed. My repeated requests for a report to the artistic council of the theater or a meeting with the ballet company to read through the exposition and to play through the music have been turned down. Having lost hope and faith, I again turn to you in agitation, that the disinterestedness of the artistic leadership in this production may lead to a nonobjective decision. Therefore, we (the composer O. Karavaichuk and I) beg you to spare us some time and to call us to Moscow, so that we can report to you and play our new composition with the aim of a decision concerning the possibility of its staging.[37]

Whether or not Mikhailov interceded on Iakobson's behalf this time is not known, but things clearly did not progress. Iakobson turned to the second ballet company in Leningrad, the Maly Opera and Ballet Theater. In September 1958, the Maly agreed to include *The Bedbug* into its plan for productions for 1958–1959.[38] The response to Iakobson's exposition and Karavaichuk's music at the discussion held at the Maly was overwhelmingly positive, but the theater was also concerned about the combination of the proposal's potential political-ideological pitfalls and Iakobson's unruly artistic nature. The theater's director, B. Zagursky, remarked that some notes of discontent could be heard among the ensemble's members and made clear that he would not allow Iakobson's fantasy to gallop completely freely.

Despite the Maly's reputation as a company more open to experimentation than the Kirov, a "Soviet" ballet based on Mayakovsky was expected to fit within official parameters and to contribute to the task of ideological education that the Communist Party (CPSU) had set for the country's theaters to accomplish. Zagursky was concerned that Iakobson's understanding of Mayakovsky would clash with the narrow ideological confines imposed on the poet's work after his death. Already at this first discussion, Zagursky warned Iakobson that his ballet could not be based just on grotesque. When Iakobson pointed out that the piece was on the whole a satire and had to be resolved accordingly, Zagursky warned Iakobson to remember that Mayakovsky's writings on Communist society were not satirical but full of deep revolutionary enthusiasm.[39]

Over a year later, the ballet had still not been staged. Iakobson now went back to the Kirov with his plans. On 10 December 1959, the Kirov's artistic council discussed Iakobson's concept for a ballet on themes by Mayakovsky under the new working title *Misteria-Buff/Oktiabr'*.[40] The ballet was included in the repertoire plan, but another two and a half years passed until its premiere under the title *The Bedbug* on 24 June 1962.

It was by no means unusual for the Kirov to allow several years to pass after a ballet had in principle been approved for production. It takes time to create and rehearse a new ballet, especially in a company with a large running repertoire and substantial touring commitments. For example, the Kirov's artistic council approved Arif Melikov's music for Grigorovich's *The Legend of Love* at a meeting held on 13 January 1959, and the ballet was included in the provisional repertoire plan for the 1960–1961 season.[41] The premiere of the ballet took place two years and two months later on 23 March 1961. The two and a half years that passed between the artistic council's decision to include Iakobson's Mayakovsky ballet in the prospective repertoire plan and the ballet's premiere thus don't seem to have been excessive. It is important to remember though that it took Iakobson three years of constant lobbying and fighting to convince the theater to include his ballet in the prospective repertoire plan in the first place.

If the delay in the production was not entirely unusual, the specific circumstances of *The Bedbug's* creation were definitely unfortunate. From an organizational point of view, the ballet was planned for a season that was heavily interrupted by the ballet company's international touring commitments: in 1961, the Kirov toured to Paris—where Nureyev defected—London, the United States, and Canada. In January 1962, when the whole company found itself reunited in Leningrad, rehearsals for the ballet recommenced, but according to Askol'd Makarov, the ballet was in essence created in one and a half months. From late 1961 until April 1962, Iakobson was busy adapting his production of Khachaturian's *Spartacus* for the Bolshoi. Work on *The Bedbug* began in earnest in mid-April. In May, the dancers had to simultaneously prepare for a trip to Moscow.[42]

Even though the delays and scheduling conflicts affecting the production process of *The Bedbug* were not unique, the overwhelmingly hostile attitude toward Iakobson's ballet was unusual, demonstrating artistic limits imposed on choreographic experimentation in the Soviet system of state-sponsored and controlled art, where choreographers who wanted to swim against the current remained dependent on the state-sponsored artistic establishment and its institutions. According to Iakobson, the ballet was created in an atmosphere of "absolute distrust, incomprehension, and open mockery."[43] Askol'd Makarov was one of the few who defended the work and apparently believed in it, but Iakobson pointed out that even Makarov

> believed more in me than in what I was doing. He said—I believe in you, but in what you are doing—I don't. The day before the dress rehearsal, when an audience was supposed to come for the first time after all sort of arguments, he said—it is shameful to appear in this part, there is no character and no dance. I walk around the stage like an idiot and everyone tells me that. This was the day before the dress rehearsal. And the majority felt this way about their parts. There were few who believed, few who understood, and the theater expected a complete, serious flop from this work.[44]

Playing the System: How Iakobson Got to Stage *The Bedbug*

Considering that many people at the Kirov and most cultural bureaucrats had a strong aversion to Iakobson, and given Sergeev's hostility toward experiments, it seems surprising that Iakobson was able to stage *The Bedbug* at all. The explanation probably lies in the fact that, at least on paper, the ballet answered the government's constant call for ballets on contemporary, Soviet topics. As there was a persistent lack of proposals for such ballets, the theater ultimately could not really afford to reject a proposal like Iakobson's. Less than a month after Sergeev's appointment in April 1960, a closed party meeting at the Kirov discussed a resolution by the Leningrad gorkom of the CPSU on the theater's work and the tasks of its party organization. The decree criticized the theater's work on creating productions on contemporary topics as the theater's main shortcoming. At the Kirov's closed meeting to discuss the decree, Korkin, the theater's director, pointed out that recently, the Kirov had produced only one ballet on a contemporary topic, Bel'sky's *Coast of Hope* (premiering 16 April 1959).[45]

It is striking that quite a few of the most artistically innovative ballets created at the Kirov in the late 1950s and early 1960s were those that responded to the authorities' call for ballets on contemporary topics with propaganda potential, for example, Bel'sky's *Coast of Hope*. Hoping to increase artistic autonomy in terms of choreographic language, choreographers tried to artistically repossess the field of Soviet choreography while providing the Soviet regime with ballets on Soviet topics that were supposed to contribute to the Soviet cultural project. It is unlikely, however, that Iakobson suggested ballets on contemporary topics solely to trick the authorities and the theater into allowing him to stage a ballet. In the case of *The Bedbug*, the multiple layers of the original literary sources and the complex official attitudes toward Mayakovsky's play make it safe to assume that Iakobson was attracted to his source for its complex artistic qualities. At the same time, Iakobson certainly hoped that composing ballets on Soviet topics would coax the authorities into a more favorable attitude toward him.

Unfortunately, Iakobson's treatment of Soviet topics usually did not coincide with the authorities' interpretation of a given topic. For example, Iakobson once created a miniature called *Levyi marsh*, seeking to depict the revolutionary sailors who had transformed themselves from an anarchic mass into a genuine revolutionary actor, only to be pushed off the stage of Soviet history soon after the revolution. Iakobson considered the sailors' fate a genuine tragedy and tried to depict it as such, but the party bureaucrats rejected Iakobson's interpretation of early Soviet history, demanding that the sailors be shown as revolutionary heroes and asking for a happy end. Iakobson refused to budge and maintained that he had depicted the sailors as he remembered them from his youth. As with many of Iakobson's ballets, a dead end was reached. Vladimir Zaidel'son remembers that Iakobson looked like he had a bad toothache when he reported that the miniature had been forbidden: he had seriously calculated that far from exposing him to ostracism, this miniature on a revolutionary topic would elevate him in the eyes of the authorities.[46]

From the theater's perspective, the fact that *The Bedbug* was on a Soviet topic undoubtedly played a decisive role in its decision to allow Iakobson to stage it. Askol'd Makarov, who thought that *The Bedbug* was released unfinished, explicitly stated that the theater decided to release the ballet not long before the season's end in order to fulfill its financial plan: "The leadership needed a birdie, so that there would be a new ballet in the season. This is necessary for the financial plan. It turns out that such organizational barriers play a role in art." *The Bedbug* helped the theater to fulfill two such organizational hurdles: the norm set for new productions per season and the expectation that the theater should stage productions on Soviet topics. At meetings at the Kirov, *The Bedbug* was commonly mentioned in the same breath with reiterations that the theater needed ballets on contemporary topics. For example, on 17 May 1960, the Kirov Theater's newspaper reported on the closed party meeting discussing the Leningrad gorkom's decree on the theater's work mentioned above and published an article by Sergeev on the tasks of the ballet company. Predictably, Sergeev declared that the theater needed ballets on contemporary topics. Next, he pointed out that since January, the company had been working on Iakobson's Mayakovsky ballet. Similarly, on 26 April 1961, at a meeting by the Kirov's artistic council discussing the theater's prospective repertoire plan for 1962, Sergeev stressed the company's aspiration to create ballets on contemporary Soviet life. After this statement, he immediately referred to the work done on Iakobson's *Misteria-Buff* (the working title of *The Bedbug*).[47] In an article published in *Za sovetskoe iskusstvo* on 23 January 1962, Sergeev was even more explicit about the connection between the theater's duty to stage ballets on contemporary Soviet themes and Iakobson's Mayakovsky ballet. He declared that the year 1962 was impregnated with the ideas of the Twenty-Second Congress: "literature and art are called upon to resolve the task of Communist education with their specific means, enthralling man with the truth and beauty of artistic images, awakening the desire not only to live better but also to be better." He later mentioned that Iakobson's ballet would be the first new ballet in the following season: "Basing the ballet on motives of Mayakovsky's work, the authors castigate the petty bourgeois world of the Prisypkins and those like them and affirm the New Man of Communist society."[48]

Artistic and Ideological Responses to *The Bedbug*

Sergeev's grand statement that Iakobson's ballet would affirm the New Man of Communist society turned out to be debatable. On 22 February 1963, the Leningrad branches of the VTO and of the Union of Soviet Composers held a meeting to discuss *The Bedbug*. The debate reflected how in the Soviet Union artistic and ideological concerns interacted and shaped each other. One of the main points of argument centered on the tension between the state's ideological requirements and an individual artist's personal vision. It revolved around the question of whether or not Iakobson had infused the ballet with enough ideological and revolutionary zeal, a debate that reflected different attitudes toward Iakobson's artistic style and different perceptions of Mayakovsky's poetry.

The majority of speakers stated that the ballet's satirical side was stronger than its heroic side. Far from everyone thought that Iakobson's understanding of satire coincided with the official interpretation of Mayakovsky's intentions: Iakobson was accused of having failed to infuse the ballet with enough revolutionary pathos and teeth-grinding ideological satire. Once again, ballet was accused of creating a false, potentially subversive "puppet reality" on stage instead of glorifying the Soviet project. The musicologist Leonid Entelis, the meeting's chairman, opened the discussion and, after some positive remarks, set out to criticize the revolutionary scenes Iakobson had interpolated into the ballet:

> There are a number of extremely unsuccessful episodes in this ballet, above all the civil war episode. This is not a poster cartoon, but rather a caricature, puppets. When a Red Army man grabs some White general on a poster, it is one thing, but when he begins to move and seizes the white general—it's a totally different matter. And a feeling of triviality arises. The pathos of the civil war—the romanticism of the civil war—and instead, red puppets and conventional white puppets show up. . . . The episode of the construction of a new world seems extremely unsuccessful to me. These are not Soviet people constructing a new world, but gigantic ants carrying away bricks. There is no constructive work taking place, no construction, but deconstruction. This leaves an impression that is not just bad but simply insulting.[49]

M. A. Gukovsky, who declared himself a passionate admirer of Mayakovsky, provided the harshest ideological criticism of Iakobson. Echoing Entelis's opinion that the civil war scenes didn't work, he complained that "there is no ideological enthusiasm in them and they create the impression of marionettes—of puppets . . . and not heroic figures of the civil war."[50] Seconding the musicologist S. Katanova's opinion that the comic and entertaining side of the ballet's satirical images sometimes prevailed over the seriously satirical, he formulated a biting critique of Iakobson's work:

> Heroic spirit doesn't become heroic spirit, and satire is reduced to entertaining grotesque and the combination of these two qualities makes the aesthetics of the ballet mistaken, because Mayakovsky is possible only in powerful enthusiasm and in savage satire, which is never turned into a little smile and mockery, into giggling. It is fierce hatred. You will excuse me, but when you watch this performance, you think all the time—when will the nonsense with the heroes stop . . . and when does the entertaining variety show begin? It is interpreted as an entertaining grotesque and not Mayakovsky's horrifying satire.[51]

The perception lingered that it was beyond ballet's artistic possibilities to express more complex topics in general and satire in particular. In his introductory remarks, Entelis emphasized that satirical topics rarely appeared on the ballet stage and that Iakobson had therefore faced an extremely difficult task, made even more complex by the interpolation of topics such as war, revolution, the construction of socialism, and Zoya Berezkina's tragedy. The comparison of the rhetoric used in 1936 in the *Pravda* editorial "Baletnaia fal'sh'" on Lopukhov's ballet *The Bright Stream* with the rhetoric used by some of *The Bedbug*'s critics shows that, almost fifty years after the revolution, even a ballet combining Mayakovsky with revolutionary episodes could find itself accused of filling the stage with empty-headed puppets incapable of expressing serious issues. In both cases, the Russian word *kukly*, puppets, is used to describe ballet. Despite its place in the official pantheon of Soviet achievements and its role as the Soviet Union's cultural ambassador, ballet still found itself subject to the prejudice that classical dance was an innately unserious ornament removed from Soviet *obshchestvennost'*, the Soviet community. Gukovsky concluded that hasty work and alienation from the community were at the heart of the shortcomings not just of *The Bedbug* but of much that ballet did in general.[52]

The debate whether or not Iakobson understood Mayakovsky's essence highlights an important aspect of Soviet cultural life and the limits imposed on artistic autonomy. All too often, artists had to position themselves in relation to the official ideological interpretations and evaluations imposed on art. This also led to a personalized form of ideological artistic conflict where artists had to choose sides—and bear the potential political consequences of their artistic allegiances. At *The Bedbug* debate, Shostakovich's friend, the literary and drama critic Isaak Glikman, who never wavered in his support for the embattled Shostakovich during the antiformalism campaign in 1936, sprang to Iakobson's defense and said that Gukovsky was wrong to accuse the choreographer and the theater of not sensing the essence of Mayakovsky's work. Glikman stressed that one shouldn't overstate the depth of Mayakovsky's play and that one shouldn't be frightened by or reproach the choreographer for the production's entertaining side, reminding the participants of the debate that Mayakovsky himself didn't fear the entertaining and amusing:

> One should not think that the fire of hatred blazed incessantly in
> Mayakovsky's plays. . . . By all love for Mayakovsky, by doing this you
> are watering him down. . . . You are appearing as a fanatic and ascetic
> of one idea and . . . you take a very narrow position today and say that

> The Bedbug is sometimes even made likeable and one looks at him with
> a smile. That's the charm of the actor. . . . We shouldn't just grit our
> teeth in class hatred, looking at the stage. This will be uncomfortable.
> I think that poetics is the crux of the matter. . . . The spirit of *The
> Bedbug* is transmitted in a talented way.[53]

Glikman also defended Iakobson's representation of heroic episodes of Soviet history in the ballet: even though the civil war had been more sublime,
heroic, and tragic, the artist had a right to show only one facet of the civil
war—Iakobson's ballet was not a Soviet encyclopedia. Glikman added that
the scene about the First World War had made such an impression on him
that he had watched with a gaping mouth, only closing it halfway through
the ballet because it was so interesting to watch.[54]

Opinions on whether or not Iakobson's ballet was filled with enough
ideological zeal were divided. On balance, more people seemed to be
against than for Iakobson, but several people defended his interpretation of
Mayakovsky's writings as truthful to the poet's spirit. Commenting on criticisms that Iakobson's depiction of the civil war was not heroic enough, the
musicologist M. Bialik asserted that there was also no heroic spirit in Mayakovsky's civil war: Iakobson's representation of the civil war had convinced
him. Bialik then described some episodes of the ballet to demonstrate that it
was not just a caricature but a genuinely Mayakovskian satire.[55]

If the question whether or not Iakobson had correctly represented the
essence of Mayakovsky's work provided the debate's main topic, conflicting
opinions on Iakobson's overall artistic vision for the ballet and his choreographic language in particular shaped the discussion of the ballet's ideological content. According to Entelis, Iakobson's use of ballet's expressive
means to bring across Mayakovsky's satire and interpolated topics like war,
revolution, and the construction of socialism had met with mixed success.
He focused on the artistic core of the ballet, the nature of Iakobson's choreographic language: "There is a big controversy about the plastic language
of *The Bedbug*. Maybe the general controversy is even precisely about this.
I saw the production twice, the second time I liked it much better than the
first time. The first time I thought—why is this production not running at
the BDT [Bol'shoi Dramaticheskii Teatr], at the Satirical Theater, at Akimov's, but at the Kirov Theater."[56] Entelis was not even sure whether to
consider *The Bedbug* a "ballet" at all. Tellingly, he posed the hypothetical
question how Konstantin Sergeev or Yuri Grigorovich would have staged
the ballet and concluded that either of them would have created a ballet that
was more based on dance. This comparison indicates aesthetic limits imposed on choreographic experimentation on the Soviet ballet stage: within

the field of Soviet choreography, no matter how dangerously "Western" or modernist Grigorovich might have seemed to some, his classically based choreographic language was recognizably balletic and thus more acceptable than Iakobson's idiosyncratic lexicon. At the same time, it is difficult to hypothesize whether Iakobson would have been more welcome on the stages of traditional, classical ballet companies in the West. Maybe Iakobson's tragedy was less the conservatism of the Soviet ballet establishment than the lack of a highly professional, alternative modern dance scene as it existed in the West.

Iakobson's choreographic language, which broke with classical dance, was incomprehensible to some. In Entelis's eyes, *The Bedbug*'s aesthetic problems began as soon as Iakobson's characters started to move: "One of the essential problems of this ballet originates here. The problem of aesthetics and dynamics. When Iakobson stages something statically, resembling the ROSTA windows—it is more or less convincing. When static turns into movement, into dynamics—then something completely different emerges." Others praised the originality of Iakobson's choreographic language. Glikman hailed the production as something genuinely new and stated that Iakobson did not have many rivals in the field of movement, possessing an unusual sensitivity for all nuances and gradations of a plastic image and the ability to seemingly create images from nothing. Similarly, pointing out that *The Bedbug* could not be called a ballet in the normal sense of the word, the former Kirov Ballet character dancer Shmyrova praised Iakobson for his special choreographic language, his special kind of rhythmized pantomime based on grotesque plastic movement and his expressive originality that was full of fantasy.[57]

The discussion of *The Bedbug* shows that even in the 1960s there was still no consensus on whether or not ballet was capable of expressing any topic in general and any literary topic in particular. There were still people who tried to measure ballet's artistic value by its ability to approximate the verbal expressiveness of literature. Many of the speakers emphasized that Iakobson's experiment was both daring and important precisely because it tried to expand the thematic horizons of ballet: some hoped that now that the ballet theater had received its baptism of fire in the area of contemporary social satire, classical dance would be used in further attempts in this field. Within this context, some of Gukovsky's comments about *The Bedbug* sound particularly odd. Even though Iakobson's choreographic language in *The Bedbug* was far removed from traditional classical dance, Gukovsky used the ballet as an illustration that classical dance was incapable of expressing certain topics. Condemning *The Bedbug* as a nonsensical, entertaining vari-

FIGURE 39. *(above)*
Askol'd Makarov as
Mayakovsky in *The
Bedbug* at the Kirov
Ballet, 1968. © Mariinsky
Theater

FIGURE 40. *(left)*
The Bedbug at the Kirov
Ballet, 1968. © Mariinsky
Theater

ety act, he concluded: "A very serious problem arises—can one give a deeply hateful satire in the language of pure classical dance? I think one mustn't. The whole alphabet of classical dance always makes its heroes attractive for the audience. I don't want to say that Rassadin [Rassadin danced Prisypkin] coped badly with his role. He coped with it splendidly, but this is a positive hero. He is attractive and not repulsive. . . . Apparently, in order to find a satirical language, it is necessary to break up the classical language more."[58]

One wonders how Gukovsky could possibly consider Iakobson's choreography, with its knock-kneed dancers in heels, "pure classical dance," but the comment reflects one of ballet's main ideological predicaments in the Soviet context. Time and again, ballet was called upon to Sovietize and to create ideologically sound ballets on contemporary Soviet life, but often, when it tried to do so, it was chastised for being incapable of doing justice to Soviet topics. For example, at a meeting of the Kirov's artistic council on 13 November 1963, the Kirov included a ballet on the civil war hero Chapaev in a prospective repertoire plan that specifically took account of the upcoming fiftieth anniversary of the revolution in 1967. The ballet *Chapaev* was planned for the 1966–1967 theatrical season.[59] On 13 March 1964, the head of the Kirov's literature repertoire department wrote a letter to the Z. Vartanian, the head of the department for musical establishments at the Ministry of Culture: the theater had heard that two years ago, a libretto for a ballet on Chapaev had been submitted to a libretto competition and judged favorably. The letter informed the ministry that the Kirov planned to create a ballet on Chapaev for the celebrations of fifty years of Soviet power and asked for help in obtaining a copy of the libretto.[60]

Considering that the Ministry of Culture called for competitions for librettos for ballets on Soviet topics in order to stimulate the Sovietization of ballet, it should have been pleased that the Kirov was actually interested in staging one of those librettos. Instead, Vartanian sent a rather curt reply to the Kirov, informing the theater that there was no such libretto among the librettos that had received awards and been approved at the competition and adding that "moreover . . . the subject and figure of the legendary military leader V. I. Chapaev can hardly be convincingly disclosed with the means of ballet art."[61] On the one hand, the government wanted ballet to Sovietize, but on the other hand, it still considered certain Soviet topics off limit and beyond ballet's expressive powers. Being "Soviet" was thus clearly not just a matter of content—it was also very much a matter of form, and the form of classical dance continued to be suspect.

Surprisingly, given these lingering doubts concerning ballet's expressive abilities and given the shocked disbelief Iakobson encountered when he proposed to make Mayakovsky the main hero in his ballet, most people were convinced by the choreographer's transformation of the poet into a choreographic image. Iakobson's task was greatly helped by the specific talent of Askol'd Makarov, a dancer who was a gifted actor and also physically resembled the poet. Many of Mayakovsky's former friends, colleagues, and admirers who came to the theater to watch *The Bedbug* had the greatest misgivings before the curtain went up. Before the *prosmotr*, the pre-premiere review, an incensed Viktor Shklovsky walked up to Moldavsky and asked him whether he had anything to do with this outrage. During the intermission, Shklovsky ran around the theater looking for Moldavsky and told him ecstatically that what he saw on stage was the real Mayakovsky, the Mayakovsky he had loved.[62] According to Moldavsky, many of Mayakovsky's old friends watched the production, all of them liked it, and the poet Olga Berggol'ts published a rapturous article about the ballet in *Literaturnaia gazeta*.

It is difficult to determine whether or not the general public liked the ballet. At the discussion held by the VTO and the Soviet Composers' Union, contradictory statements were made. For some members of the public, Iakobson's *The Bedbug* provided a welcome breath of fresh air and evoked associations with the flowering of the Soviet avant-garde in the 1920s. A few members of the audience wrote an ecstatic letter to Iakobson on 26 June 1962, two days after the ballet's premiere: they had been stunned by *The Bedbug* and thanked him and the dancers for having put on a daring production that shattered everything that was stagnant in ballet. In the late 1920s and early 1930s, they had seen Meyerhold's productions of *The Bedbug* and *The Bathhouse* and wrote that Meyerhold would have been ecstatic about Iakobson's *The Bedbug*. The letter strongly distanced itself from the many conservative ballet lovers: "Many and many spectators are sick, if not worse, with the self-admiration of conservatism and caution—it will come to no good, the many stagnant connoisseurs of ballet. Therefore, when new and daring art appears on stage, one is sincerely happy and the troubled sleep of the guardians and keepers of accurate and circular art already doesn't trouble you. One doesn't feel sorry for these people because they are very far from art."[63]

The Bedbug and the Regime's Showdown with the Intelligentsia, 1962–1963

Responses to *The Bedbug* demonstrated from the outset the interaction between artistic, ideological-aesthetic, and political-ideological pressures on the autonomy of art. Before long, political-ideological pressures began to weigh on the ballet in a much more immediate form. Barely half a year after the premiere of *The Bedbug*, the CPSU embarked on an open collision course with the liberal intelligentsia, proving wrong expectations that the publication in November 1962 of the first book to openly describe the life in Soviet labor camps, Aleksandr Solzhenitsyn's *A Day in the Life of Ivan Denisovich*, signaled the second round of de-Stalinization promised at the Twenty-Second Party Congress. As Priscilla Johnson has pointed out, the issue of authority and control was at the heart of the leadership's confrontation with the intelligentsia. De-Stalinization had eroded the authority and infallibility of the party in the eyes of many, and the showdown with the intelligentsia became a symbol of the party's attempt to reclaim its absolute authority over society. The party had tried to enroll literature in its de-Stalinization drive, but this had led to unwanted consequences: artists had tentatively begun to express unorthodox thoughts and to experiment.[64]

On 26 November 1962, a semiprivate exhibit of paintings considered avant-garde by Moscow standards opened in the studio of the art teacher Eli Belyutin. Within a few days, the works presented at the studio were summoned to the Manezh Gallery, where a retrospective exhibit of socialist realist art was taking place, and hung in three rooms separate from the rest of the exhibition. On 1 December 1962, Khrushchev, four presidium members, and several members of the party secretariat paid a surprise visit to the Manezh Gallery. When Khrushchev reached the nonrepresentational paintings and sculptures, he broke out into a crude diatribe, comparing modern art to a child doing his business on a canvas and then spreading it around with his hands and announcing that listening to jazz made him feel like he had gas in his stomach.

Only hours later, a campaign for ideological purity in art was under way. On 17 December 1962, about half a year after *The Bedbug's* premiere, a meeting between party leaders and 400 writers, artists, and other intellectuals took place at the Pioneer Palace on Lenin Hills. Central Committee Secretary Leonid Ilyichev, chairman of the Central Committee's Ideological Commission, delivered the main speech, reportedly lasting ten hours, thundering that art must be militant and inculcate Communist Party spirit. Like a leitmotif, he lamented Western influence on Soviet art. On 24 and 26 December, Ilyichev held a second meeting with 140 writers, artists, and cinema workers at the Central Committee headquarters. On 7 March 1963, 600 writers, artists, and other intellectuals again met with the leadership, this time at the Kremlin's Sverdlov Hall. Khrushchev delivered the main speech.

The artistic repercussions of the leadership's showdown with the creative intelligentsia were also felt within the walls of the Kirov Theater. On 19 December 1962, the party organization of the theater held a meeting to discuss the theater's tasks in light of the decisions taken at the November plenum of the CPSU's Central Committee. Once again, it was emphasized that the theater had to actively participate in the aesthetic, Communist education of the Soviet people. The secretary of the theater's party bureau, Z. H. Strizhova called for a battle against alien influences on Soviet art: "We have to fight for a new ascent of the art of socialist realism, for the affirmation of Communist ideology, against alien influences of decadent, bourgeois art, of which N. S. Khrushchev reminded art workers during his attendance of the exhibit of young artists and also at the meeting with the creative intelligentsia."[65] As was to be expected, the theater's party secretary identified the creation of productions on contemporary topics as decisive.

Not surprisingly, two of the most innovative choreographers, Iakobson and Grigorovich, were soon singled out as the creators of works tainted by "alien influences." On 22 March 1963, the Kirov Theater held an open party meeting. R. I. Tikhomirov, principal stage director of the Kirov, delivered a report. Socialist realism was confirmed as the method lying at the heart of Soviet art. Tikhomirov expanded on the combative mission of art in the age of Cold War ideological confrontation: "In the period of full-scale construction of communism, the responsibility of the artistic intelligentsia for the development of the ideological, spiritual life of Soviet society has increased as never before. At a moment when the struggle of two ideologies—Socialist and bourgeois—is taking place in the entire world, an acute battle for the minds and souls of people, it is essential that such a mighty ideological weapon as literature and art is kept in purity, in constant battle readiness. No machinations of bourgeois ideology must impede our progressive movement forward." Tikhomirov pointed out that false tendencies had appeared in a number of works by artists and writers, even of very talented ones. He proceeded to analyze the mistakes in the Kirov's work. For example, he noted that compared to some foreign classics such as La Traviata, the theater rarely showed the best Russian operas about the country's heroic past. He then turned to ballet: "The creators of several ballet productions have a non-critical attitude to the formalist searches of Western choreographers, borrowing from them a predilection for erotic and naturalistic dances and unaesthetic dance movements (The Legend of Love, The Bedbug)." Tikhomirov then criticized the appearance of some abstract elements in the designs of some operas and emphasized that the development of art was incompatible with abstraction and formalism: it was the duty of every member of the creative intelligentsia to stand firmly on the position of socialist realism in art. The party meeting later decided that the party bureau and the theater's leadership should review The Bedbug, The Legend of Love, and several other— unnamed—productions in order to raise their "ideological-artistic level."[66]

The question of whether or not The Bedbug was consistent with socialist realism had also come up at the previously analyzed discussion of the ballet held by the VTO and the Soviet Composers' Union on 22 February 1963, just a few weeks before the ballet was accused of "alien tendencies." When the former Kirov dancer Shmyrova declared that Iakobson's path was the path of socialist realism, a lady in the audience made a disdainful sound. Moldavsky later criticized this reaction, reflecting the hopes of many artists during the Thaw that there would finally be a move away from the narrow Stalinist interpretation of socialist realism toward more artistic autonomy:

> When Shmirova was speaking and said the phrase about Iakobson's socialist realism, some lady let out a strange sound. I am not against sounds made by ladies. But in the years of the cult of personality, we got very used to considering socialist realism some narrow path in the theater of a sham MKhAT [Moskovskii khudozhestvennyi teatr (Moscow Art Theater)], having nothing in common with the genius of Stanislavsky. And in music correspondingly. This happened probably in all art forms. We are paying terribly for this in literature and art. One can talk about the degree to which Iakobson managed to put in big ideas, but in any case, this work is in the system of socialist realism, I am convinced of this.[67]

During the regime's 1962–1963 showdown with the creative intelligentsia, it became clear that contrary to hopes raised during the Thaw, the regime planned to maintain tight control over artistic "autonomy." On 14 March 1963, Leningrad's creative intelligentsia was called to the Tauride Palace to discuss the results of the meeting between the leadership of party and government and the creative intelligentsia held in Moscow on 7 and 8 March 1963. A large group from the Kirov participated at the meeting, including Konstantin Sergeev, who spoke about major questions concerning the development of choreographic art. The main report at the meeting was delivered by Vasily Tolstikov, member of the Central Commitee of the CPSU and first secretary of the Leningrad industrial regional committee of the CPSU.[68] In his report, Tolstikov singled out *The Legend of Love* and *The Bedbug* for their ideological aberrations.

Over the coming months, political-ideological pressures on choreographic development were amply demonstrated. *Za sovetskoe iskusstvo* continuously referred to the necessity to remove elements of eroticism and naturalism from *The Bedbug* and *The Legend of Love*.[69] During this period, the paper did full justice to its name—the newspaper's title, which translates to "for Soviet art," implied that one should combat those who were "against Soviet art." The fact that not only Iakobson was targeted, but also Grigorovich, who before long would become the official face of Soviet choreography, shows the hazardous situation of the ballet reformers in the early 1960s. Unlike Iakobson, Grigorovich's language was firmly based in the classical id-

FIGURE 41. Alla Osipenko as Mekhmene Banu and John Markovsky as Ferkhad in *The Legend of Love*, during an evening performance in honor of Tatiana Vecheslova at the Palace of Cultural Workers named after K. S. Stanislavsky, 1969. © St. Petersburg State Museum of Theater and Music

iom, but like Lopukhov in the 1920s and early 1930s, he experimented with expanding this idiom. Some of his experiments with the form and vocabulary of classical dance offended not just the aesthetic sensitivities of Soviet cultural bureaucrats but also members of the drambalet establishment, once again demonstrating the complex relationship between official demands and artistic norms in the Soviet cultural environment. At the pre-premiere review of Grigorovich's *The Legend of Love* held at the Kirov on 22 March 1961, some people looked askance at Grigorovich's choreographic vocabulary, accusing him of sometimes reverting to acrobatics and movements for movement's sake. In particular, several people, including Dudinskaya and Sergeev, complained about Grigorovich's introduction of a lift that required the female dancer to perform a split head first, calling the movement unaesthetic and unjustified by anything that was happening in the ballet.[70] Possibly, there was also a prudish undertone to the objection against the split, which was performed by both lead female dancers dressed in unitards.

"Eroticism" was also one of *The Bedbug's* offenses, albeit in a more literal way than Grigorovich's "unaesthetic acrobatics." Iakobson had created a love duet for Prisypkin and his bride, Elzevira, that looked as if two giant insects were frolicking on an enormous bed right in the center of the Kirov's venerable stage.[71] At the discussion held after *The Bedbug's* dress rehearsal at the Kirov on 23 June 1962, Dudinskaya had stated point-blank that the adagio on the bed had to be cut,[72] but it doesn't look like Iakobson fulfilled this demand. At the discussion held by the VTO and the Soviet Composers' Union in Leningrad on 22 February 1963, several people had argued about the scene. Gukovsky stated that, in principle, it was good that Iakobson had many erotic colors in his palette, but that this scene was completely out of place in a ballet based on Mayakovsky because Mayakovsky had been "a remarkably bashful person." Gukovsky even announced that "if there is something that didn't exist in either Mayakovsky's creativity or his life, then that's sensuality." Once again, Glikman came to both Iakobson's and Mayakovsky's defense: "I listened to comments about sensuality with amazement. Age fences me off from this delicate topic, but I didn't notice anything like this. It is given in the proportion in which Mayakovsky wanted to show it." One comment indicated that the party's and government's fear that eroticism might corrupt the "pure minds" of Soviet audiences was maybe not totally unjustified: "The moment on the bed is really terrible. I didn't fear sensuality, but Elzevira is too charming and many would like to get under this blanket."[73] This was certainly not what the authorities had in mind when they called on the theaters to contribute to the ideological education of the Soviet people.

The charge of eroticism was not the only one leveled at *The Bedbug*. At

FIGURE 42. Olga Moiseeva as Elzevira and Konstantin Rassadin as Prisypkin in *The Bedbug* at the Kirov Ballet, 1968. © Mariinsky Theater

a party meeting held at the Kirov in April 1963, Strizhova, the secretary of the theater's party bureau, remarked that *The Bedbug* had not developed the theme of labor enough; the secretary of the party bureau of the ballet company added that the ballet lacked the necessary development of positive heroes.[74] Principal conductor A. Klimov expressed the antiexperimental tenor of the entire ideological debate surrounding *The Bedbug* and *The Legend of Love* in an article published in *Za sovetskoe iskusstvo* on 5 July 1963. It shows how quickly anything unusual could be accused of imitating bourgeois influences: "We have to draw the right conclusions from the criticisms addressed to a number of our ballet productions, and above all to the ballets *The Bedbug* and *The Legend of Love*, which distinctly exhibited a tendency to the imitation of models of bourgeois art, the striving for 'novelty' that has nothing in common with genuine innovation."[75]

Even within this climate, there was resistance within the ballet company to the reactionary demands, demonstrating that, despite the rhetoric, the scope for artistic autonomy had indeed increased since Stalin's days: during the antiformalism campaign of 1936, Lopukhov's *The Bright Stream* was simply removed from the repertoire and branded as example of everything socialist realism was not. In contrast, Grigorovich's *The Legend of Love* was staged at the Bolshoi, the Soviet Union's premier opera house, in 1965, the year after Grigorovich had been appointed the company's chief choreographer, a position he held until 1995. As a ballet, it has survived until the present day. Despite the attacks on *The Bedbug*, the ballet was supposed to be kept in the Kirov's repertoire after the necessary changes had been made and to be shown in a double bill with Iakobson's new ballet *The Twelve*, based on Blok's poem (which was to spark even greater controversy than *The Bedbug*), offering the Kirov at least in theory the opportunity to present a "revolutionary-heroic" choreographic evening. Reporting on the progress made on the elimination of "flaws" in Iakobson's and Grigorovich's ballets, Sergeev stated that this work was dragging out unjustifiably. Discussing the reasons for this delay, Sergeev emphasized that there were dancers who tried to pass off as innovation formalist and erotic devices borrowed from the arsenal of bourgeois art: unfortunately, a number of leading dancers were carried away by this "pseudo-innovation."[76]

The limits ultimately imposed on artistic autonomy and on the potential for artistic repossession reflected the dual pressure of artistic and political-ideological attacks on artists who did not fit into the established system. Iakobson's work was as controversial for many dancers from a purely aesthetic point of view as it was for Soviet cultural bureaucrats from an aesthetic-ideological point of view. He offended both the conservative ballet establishment and the Soviet cultural bureaucracy. The Soviet cultural project's vision of art's social role heavily circumscribed possibilities to create art outside the established, state-sponsored, and supervised system of cultural production, especially in the field of choreography, where creating "for the drawer" was not an option. The combination of artistic and ideological pressures on Iakobson was typical of the complex interplay between the creative intelligentsia and the political machine in setting the parameters for cultural production within the Soviet Union.

    The Bedbug's production history shows Iakobson's position as an aesthetic outsider within the field of Soviet choreography and the Kirov Ballet. While some members of the ballet profession thought that Iakobson was a genius, others thought he was threatening the very foundation of their art, classical dance. When analyzing the opposition of the conservative ballet establishment to Iakobson, it is important not to let one's judgment err to the other extreme by condemning the conservative tastes of large parts of the ballet establishment: while choreographic innovation is important, the maintenance of the classical tradition in ballet is just as important if ballet is to be kept alive. In the Soviet Union, "conservatives" in the ballet world also had to defend their art form against ideological criticisms and were therefore maybe particularly sensitive to any perceived threats to the purity of classical ballet. If Iakobson had been born outside the Soviet Union, given the highly experimental and idiosyncratic nature of his talent, he would probably have thrived more as the director of his own, independent company than within one of the great classical ensembles. Maybe Iakobson's tragedy lay less in his rejection by the conservative ballet establishment than in the fact that establishing your own, high-caliber professional ensemble without state support was virtually impossible in the Soviet Union. He was more a victim of the total absence of cultural pluralism than of the ballet establishment.

The Bedbug also shows the problems associated with "Sovietizing" ballet by pushing for the creation of ballets on Soviet themes. Confronted with official demands to create Soviet ballets, ballet faced a catch-22: unsuccessful ballets on Soviet themes could result in criticisms that ballet was inherently incapable of expressing serious topics, but if the theaters did not stage ballets on Soviet topics, ballet could be reprimanded for being alienated from Soviet society. In the case of The Bedbug, this problem was compounded by the fact that an unorthodox artist was trying to create a genuine work of art based on a literary work dangerously open to interpretation. The public criticism of The Bedbug during the Soviet leadership's confrontation with the intelligentsia demonstrates the political and ideological pressures and constraints imposed on artists like Iakobson.

On a more positive note, given this complex set of obstacles, it is remarkable that Iakobson got to stage The Bedbug at all, revealing that artists could push boundaries to a greater extent than is commonly assumed. Unfortunately, the ballet's controversial reception and its quick disappearance from the Kirov's repertoire also show the limitations of Iakobson's tendency to swim completely against the aesthetic and ideological currents of both the classical ballet establishment and the Soviet cultural bureaucracy. Iakobson's artistic repossession strategy of combining a ballet on a Soviet topic with an outright artistic negation of the official aesthetic vision of Soviet ballet as circumscribed by the ballet establishment and the Soviet cultural bureaucracy resulted in a significant but ultimately limited success: he managed to stage the ballet, but it did not survive the pressures of the Soviet context. Toward the end of his life, Iakobson left the Kirov in frustration and, after overcoming major obstacles, managed to establish his own company, Choreographic Miniatures, in Leningrad in 1969. But each new work meant a new fight, and new productions continued to be forbidden. His battle with the authorities continued until he died of cancer in 1975.

7 $\oslash$ *Choreography as Resistance*

Yuri Grigorovich's *Spartacus*, 1968

Yuri Nikolaevich came to us with doubts: "Guys, let's think
. . . " At that time, in 1968, genuine coauthorship united us:
we began together to think up something, to try something
—and became infected with it.

—EKATERINA MAKSIMOVA ON THE CREATION OF
GRIGOROVICH'S *SPARTACUS*

BY THE 1960s, the Kirov and Bolshoi Ballet companies were nationally and internationally celebrated as major Soviet cultural achievements, but the glory of the Soviet ballet continued to rest primarily on the prerevolutionary classical repertoire. Within the Soviet cultural project, the position of classical ballet continued to be defined by a paradox. As the fiftieth anniversary of the October Revolution was drawing near, there was still a glaring discrepancy between the regime's perpetual calls for ballets on contemporary or revolutionary historical themes and the Bolshoi's and Kirov's apparent inability to "Sovietize" and create popular, propagandistic ballet blockbusters shaping audiences' Socialist consciousnesses.

The paradox of declaring a Soviet victory in art based on presenting ballets far removed from Soviet reality to audiences abroad was not lost on the leadership of the Bolshoi Theater. At an all-union meeting of Soviet ballet professionals on the problems of Soviet choreography held in June 1963, the director of the Bolshoi Theater, Mikhail Chulaki, emphasized:

> There springs up a contradiction: What do we take abroad in our
> art? Why am I talking about tours abroad? Our ideology has to carry
> aggressive propagandistic character in all fields. "What new things are

they bringing? Where do we find the new world with which they have arrived?" We have to be aware that so far, we demonstrate very well how we are preserving the classical ballet, but when we turn toward showing our new things, disguised in the element of folk dance, there are the same ingrained princes, fairies—the essence of classical ballet and we haven't set ourselves into forward motion, we haven't created a new alloy from new productions, but we have renovated ballet, we have dressed it up with the help of a routine attitude toward décor, with a humiliating, petty cutesy truth, and we have destroyed the great truth of Soviet realist art.[1]

The upcoming fiftieth anniversary of the revolution in 1967 gave a special urgency to this lack of ballets on Soviet themes. In preparation for the anniversary, the Bolshoi decided to stage Aram Khachaturian's *Spartacus* for a third time in the hope that, this time, the theater would finally manage to create the kind of heroic revolutionary production the authorities were calling for. Of all the ballets created during the Soviet period, Yuri Grigorovich's *Spartacus*, premiered at the Bolshoi in 1968, came closest to providing the regime with a popular ballet on an ideologically sound, educational topic that was also successful with audiences at home and abroad. In many ways, Grigorovich's *Spartacus* managed to square the circle by providing the regime and audiences with a popular Soviet ballet while offering artistically challenging leading roles for generations of dancers.

But far from being just a propagandistic Soviet ballet blockbuster, Grigorovich's *Spartacus* illustrates art's potential to resist ideological straitjackets. The ballet, with its hordes of jumping soldiers and rebels, undoubtedly has ideological overtones, but the choreography in general and the dramatic portrayal of the main characters as expressed in Grigorovich's intense and virtuoso choreography have a potential to pull the spectator into the power of the performance, making the viewer forget about the ballet's propagandistic subtext. In *Spartacus*, choreography becomes larger than politics.

The power of *Spartacus* as a theatrical production points toward a crucial aspect of choreography and its capacity for maintaining its autonomy—it is impossible to completely control either the interpretation of a piece by its performers or its reception by its audience. In ballet, the power of the choreography and the performers often take over and the plot becomes secondary, whether we talk about *Spartacus* or a nineteenth-century ballet with a nonsensical plot like Petipa's *The Pharaoh's Daughter*.[2] The fact that *Spartacus* survived the collapse of the Soviet Union indicates that the choreography trumped the message. Today, the ideological subtext of the ballet has faded into history, but the power of the performance remains. Seventeen years after the collapse of the Soviet Union, Grigorovich's *Spartacus* continues to take its rightful place in the Bolshoi's repertoire, last but not least in its tours abroad: the Bolshoi Ballet once again brought the ballet to London in the summer of 2010, as part of a repertoire ranging from Petipa's *Don Quixote* to Balanchine's *Serenade* and Alexei Ratmansky's *Russian Seasons*.

The problems that had emerged during the Kirov's first *Spartacus* production in 1956, the serial failure of the two *Spartacus* productions at the Bolshoi that preceded Grigorovich's version, and the range of political, ideological, pragmatic, and personal reasons that prompted the Bolshoi to return to the ballet again and again made the artistic success of Grigorovich's *Spartacus* unlikely. The fact that Grigorovich and his team of dancers overcame this cursed legacy and rose above the political-ideological pressures to stage the ballet, achieving a unique level of artistic cooperation, demonstrates that true artistic collaboration was possible under political and ideological pressure. Astounding artistic results could be achieved against all odds of political-ideological intrusion into the creative process. Sometimes, constraints could acquire enabling power, inspiring enormous creativity to overcome the pressure of circumstances.

Aram Khachaturian's *Spartacus*

The history of previous *Spartacus* productions offered little to make the popular and artistic success of Grigorovich's production likely. Grigorovich's *Spartacus* was the fourth production of the ballet by either the Kirov or Bolshoi Ballet in as little as twelve years. The Bolshoi Ballet in particular seemed obsessed with getting *Spartacus* "right." While the Kirov continued to perform Iakobson's 1956 production, the Bolshoi dedicated three attempts to the ballet: Igor' Moiseev created the first production for the Bolshoi in 1958, Iakobson the second in 1962, and Grigorovich the third in 1968.

The Bolshoi's obsession with *Spartacus* was intimately linked to the theater's need to create ballets on Soviet themes and its persistent failure to do so. The immediate context of the Bolshoi's decision to stage the ballet for a third time was highly political: the Kremlin's "court theater" was preparing for the fiftieth anniversary of the October Revolution during the 1967–1968 theatrical season and was supposed to respond to renewed calls by the USSR Ministry of Culture for the creation of ballets on contemporary Soviet or historical revolutionary themes. Complete musical scores by well-respected Soviet composers for full-length ballets on such themes were rare, so the Bolshoi once again returned to Khachaturian's score. By the time the Bolshoi contemplated its third attempt to stage *Spartacus*, it seemed as if the theater's attempts to stage the ballet had been cursed, dooming any

Spartacus production to failure. Certain elements of the production history of Iakobson's first production of the ballet for the Kirov in 1956 highlight several general problems that confronted choreographers intending to stage the ballet.

Nikolai Volkov's original libretto and Khachaturian's score posed significant obstacles to a successful staging of *Spartacus*. The choreographers who turned to the ballet in the 1950s and 1960s faced a libretto from the 1930s that resembled more a historical chronicle than a ballet libretto. Volkov recalled that the idea to stage a ballet on Spartacus, the legendary leader of a slave revolt in ancient Rome, arose at the Bolshoi in the 1930s when Soviet ballet began to look actively for heroic themes. He began working on the libretto in 1933, finishing it a year later. Volkov looked at Raffaello Giovagnoli's popular 1874 novel *Spartacus* but was particularly inspired by Plutarch's historical account and Appianos's *Civil Wars in Rome*.[3]

The ballet's stage existence got off to a very slow start. For almost twenty years, Volkov's libretto collected dust, until Khachaturian began to work on the ballet in 1951, finishing the score in February 1954.[4] The Kirov proposed the work to Moiseev in 1952–1953, but the Ministry of Culture sent Moiseev's Folk Dance Ensemble on so many tours that work on the ballet did not progress.[5] The Kirov then turned toward Vakhtang Chabukiani, who rejected the proposal. Lopukhov, who had replaced Sergeev as director of the Kirov Ballet, now pushed for the controversial Iakobson to be entrusted with the production, a suggestion that was not met with much enthusiasm by the artistic board of the Kirov Ballet.[6]

When Iakobson was commissioned with the ballet, he began to imagine a grandiose, monumental, sculptural ballet, but his excitement received a serious blow when he familiarized himself with Volkov's minutely developed libretto and Khachaturian's music. Iakobson panicked.[7] He thought the libretto had been written without consideration of the specific laws of choreographic action: in his opinion, the scenes didn't develop out of each other, and the plot unfolded without taking into account the requirements of the stage. Iakobson felt that there were no personal characteristics and the main heroes were not given any concrete action. The scene "Feast at Crassus's" was the libretto's largest, most central, and most musically developed scene, creating the impression that Rome's degeneration was the ballet's central subject, relegating the themes of heroism and the uprising to a secondary role.

The libretto prescribed occasions for dances that were purely divertissemental and described situations that were not theatrical, resulting in many incomprehensible pantomimic scenes. For example, Volkov had created a scene in Spartacus's camp showing an argument between some of his followers who, drunk with the apparent success of the uprising, wanted to march on Rome, while Spartacus and others wanted to return home via the sea.[8] How could one express such a scene in dance or even in pantomime? From the choreographer's point of view, basic difficulties in staging *Spartacus* arose from the existence of a detailed, nonchoreographic libretto that had served as a model for a long score that, also according to Lopukhov, suffered from numerous repetitions.[9]

Iakobson embarked on a battle with the librettist and composer who did not allow the choreographer to introduce any changes. Iakobson recalled that Volkov and Khachaturian even requested that he be taken off this project because he was unable to understand their concept.[10] In his memoirs, Lopukhov emphasized that Khachaturian categorically refused to make concessions, insisting that his music had to be respected.[11] Iakobson thought that there was too much music, robbing the ballet of its dynamics, and planned to reduce the score from four to three acts. He began to cut and rearrange the music without the composer's knowledge, but the inevitable clash with the composer could not be avoided. As Iakobson's widow remembers: "Thankfully, Khachaturian lived in Moscow. But then he finally arrived. And after work, the three of us—Khachaturian, Leonid Veniaminovich, and I—were walking on Nevsky Prospekt past the Catherine Garden toward our flat for dinner. Khachaturian is running. He is angered. They are hacking his music to pieces—who had dared to do this, what right had Iakobson to rearrange pieces, to correct Khachaturian! With eastern temperament he gesticulates and accidentally hits Leonid Veniaminovich in the face. Leonid Veniaminovich thought that he had been hit deliberately and quickly gives as good as he got." Iakobson's wife tried to calm down the two men, urging them to talk about everything in their flat as opposed to fist fight in the middle of Leningrad's central thoroughfare, but Khachaturian only asked full of anger: "To this lout? My legs won't carry me." He walked away, turned around, walked away, and Iakobson shouted after him: "I won't let your feet pass the threshold. And not just at home. I will still think about whether or not to let you come to rehearsal!" The composer and choreographer did not talk for many years, even after the ballet had been successfully staged.[12]

Iakobson's *Spartacus* premiered at the Kirov on 27 December 1956. The production was highly controversial for its complete rejection of classical ballet technique: the women did not dance on pointe and the ballet's choreographic language was inspired by antique sculptures and vases. Each scene received a "sculptural headpiece" in form of monumental bas-reliefs, using scores of dancers.[13] Despite the controversy surrounding the ballet—not least among ballet professionals—and in marked contrast to the Bolshoi,

FIGURE 43. Leonid Iakobson's *Spartacus*, third act, at the Kirov Ballet, 1960.
© Mariinsky Theater

which quickly discarded both Moiseev's 1958 and Iakobson's 1962 *Spartacus*, the Kirov kept Iakobson's unconventional *Spartacus* in its repertoire for
a long time after its premiere. It was revived by the Kirov in 1976, 1985, and
2010. According to performance statistics up to 1987, it had received 197
performances.[14] Apparently, the ballet was a success at the box office. At a
meeting of the Kirov's artistic council held on 25 May 1960, the conductor
B. I. Anisimov complained that, in contrast to the Kirov Opera, the Kirov
Ballet had ballets in its repertoire that were box-office successes, giving both
Iakobson's *Spartacus* and his *Choreographic Miniatures* as examples.[15]

Cursed to Failure? *Spartacus* at the Bolshoi, 1958 and 1962

The Bolshoi had entrusted Moiseev with its first production of *Spartacus*.
The ballet's premiere took place on 11 March 1958 but the production was
not a success and received only nine performances.[16] At the Bolshoi Theater's artistic council's discussion following the dress rehearsal on 7 March
1958, the production was openly called an artistic failure. Strictly following
Volkov's libretto, the ballet lacked a dramatic outline and a well-developed
dramatic plot expressed in interesting choreography. Lavrovsky, the Bol-

FIGURE 44. Dmitry Begak as Spartacus in Igor' Moiseev's *Spartacus*, third act, at the Bolshoi Ballet, 1958. © St. Petersburg State Museum of Theater and Music

shoi's principal choreographer, lamented: "The feeling I experienced, having watched the ballet, is a feeling of extreme disappointment. . . . For me, this is not a production—it is a piece with no developed figures, with no build-up of the action."[17] Because of problems in the ballet's dramatic development and the lack of imagination in Moiseev's choreography, the ballet lacked a hero. Unlike Iakobson, Moiseev relied on classical dance vocabulary,[18] but at the discussion of the ballet's dress rehearsal, his work was repeatedly criticized as primitive, naïve, and illustrative, incapable of characterizing the ballet's main figures choreographically. Mikhail Gabovich condemned the production as artistic failure: "This is a 'living pictures' production, not a danced one. *Spartacus* is altogether devoid of any choreography. He is deter-mined illustratively, and this sensation of illustration dominates the production. All characters are determined insufficiently deeply. . . . In our production its hero—Spartacus—doesn't exist. He's just charming in a youthful way. The reason for this is the lack of dance in his image."[19]

After the failure of Moiseev's production, the Bolshoi Theater seemed to become obsessed with *Spartacus*, staging three different productions over the span of approximately ten years. There were certainly some practical considerations fuelling this obsession, which at first glance made little sense. Khachaturian's status and clout as a great Soviet composer played a role in the theater's decision to return to his score time and again: despite some problems associated with Khachaturian's score, notably its length and the composer's refusal to rework it, adequate ballet scores by great Soviet composers were not easy to come by. Moreover, Khachaturian was not just a great Soviet composer but a great Soviet composer willing to write full-length ballets, making him a valuable, potential future collaborator who should not be alienated. At a general meeting held by the ballet company on 3 March 1959 Lavrovsky expressed these considerations: "I now want to talk about the heavy feeling Khachaturian has in connection with the facts that his ballets *Gayané* and *Spartacus*, on which the theater had worked, are not in its repertoire. The music of *Spartacus* is excellent. Everyone attached enormous importance to this production and waited for it. . . . And now, of course, one mustn't talk to him about a new work. He says: 'What is the purpose of me writing ballets, when two of them are not running in your theater, and you are asking for a third ballet?'"[20]

Costs were another concern. According to Lavrovsky, more than a million rubles had been spent on Moiseev's *Spartacus*: at a time when there was a struggle for every ruble and artists had to be laid off, the theater couldn't waste so much money on a production that was not running. Lavrovsky proposed to revise the ballet in the next season, but this plan came to nothing.[21] The Bolshoi then sent Lavrovsky, Galina Ulanova, and Marina Semenova to Leningrad to evaluate Iakobson's *Spartacus*. Iakobson was invited to stage *Spartacus* for the Bolshoi, provided that he would create a new version.[22] The majority of costumes of Moiseev's production would be reused, much to Iakobson's chagrin, who thought that they did not allow for the full view of the human body his choreography required.[23]

Even though practical considerations had an impact on the Bolshoi leadership's decision to persistently return to Khachaturian's score, at the heart of the supposed *Spartacus* curse lay the ballet's unfulfilled heroic promise and potential to answer the regime's call for ideologically uplifting productions. Both Iakobson's production for the Kirov and Moiseev's production for the Bolshoi had failed to create the heroic epic everyone was expecting. As was pointed out with respect to Moiseev's production, "the production is grandiose, but it doesn't respond to the heroic theme of *Spartacus*. But the musical material gives the possibility for the realization of such a production."[24] Year after year, the Soviet regime asked for ballets on contemporary or historical revolutionary topics, but no choreographer seemed able to realize *Spartacus*'s potential as a celebration of revolutionary heroism.

A rethinking of Volkov's original libretto along more heroic and epic lines formed the core of Iakobson's proposal for a new *Spartacus* production for the Bolshoi. In the early afternoon of Monday 23 October 1961, Iakobson met with the party bureau of the Bolshoi Ballet, its section committee, Komsomol organization, and members of the board. Iakobson outlined the main differences between his Leningrad production and his plans for his Moscow production, emphasizing his reconception of the ballet's dramatic outline. In Leningrad, Iakobson had felt that creating an epic about Spartacus was impossible because Volkov's libretto included a distracting palace intrigue: Crassus's lover, the courtesan Aegina, entices one of Spartacus's associates, Garmody, with her seductive beauty and uses him to cause a rift in Spartacus's camp, leading to the movement's defeat.[25]

For the Bolshoi, Iakobson proposed to create a genuinely heroic production that would not include the Aegina-Garmody intrigue, even though the two characters and their dances would be preserved. In contrast to the Leningrad production, Iakobson proposed that "the new version will talk about Spartacus and his companion Phrygia, about Spartacus's heroic deeds. It will be a completely heroic production. It is an antique, heroic fresco about Spartacus and Phrygia, passing through their course of life in heroic spirit." In his new dramatic outline, Spartacus's movement would fail not because of Aegina's seductiveness but because Rome's professional army was stronger. The main defect of the Leningrad production would thus be removed. Iakobson also proposed to give Phrygia a greater role in the scene "Feast at Crassus's," juxtaposing slavery and degeneration and thereby integrating the scene with the ballet's heroic theme. The scene was very long, lasting fifty minutes. People had criticized the imbalance between the ballet's heroic theme and the theme of Rome's degeneration in the Leningrad production, but Iakobson argued that the ballet's new dramatic outline would reestablish the necessary balance, making the production ideologically and artistically significant.[26]

Given its ideological importance, Iakobson's interpretation and representation of Spartacus's heroism would be crucial for the production's fate.[27] V. I. Pakhomov, the director of the Bolshoi Theater, concentrated on the work's ideological aspects, stating that work on the ballet had to be put on "deeper foundations." To think that reading the novel *Spartacus* was enough was wrong. Instead, a study of the history of the movement should be organized, because different evaluations of it existed: it was too simplistic to say that Spartacus's movement had been defeated because his troops were weaker than the Roman troops:

> It's not completely like that. Or rather, it is not at all like that. . . . The Spartacus movement shook the ancient world in its deepest foundations. . . . It made the ancient world waver and showed that despite the greatness of this world, despite its pomposity, its richness, all the same, this world isn't eternal. And Spartacus had to suffer defeat not because the Romans were very strong because of numbers but because Spartacus didn't find a solid social basis in the ancient world. And it is known that the ancient world had such a social basis. And, if the slaves, rising up against the oppressors, wanted to gain victory—they should have drawn to their side all oppressed. But this didn't happen. Now this is why Spartacus suffered defeat. Now this is why it is necessary to deeply study the Spartacus movement, to penetrate the meaning, the character of the social significance, of the revolutionary essence.
>
> For the present this movement is of great interest, because we know that on our planet, an exploitative system exists not just in one state.
>
> Now, if we approach this production from this point of view, we will be able to create a great production, great impressive forces, great political and artistic reverberations.[28]

If Pakhomov had hoped that Iakobson would create an ideologically penetrating study of the Spartacus movement, his expectations were disappointed. Despite the changes in the ballet's dramatic outline, the production still failed to establish the desired balance between heroism and entertainment. At discussions by the artistic council of a run-through on 16 March 1962 and of the dress rehearsal on 2 April 1962, several voices complained that the ballet, with its powerful music, grandiose sets, and Iakobson's monumental bas-reliefs, was a beautiful spectacle for the eyes but not the inspiring tale of revolutionary heroism that the theater's leadership and the representatives of the USSR Ministry of Culture were expecting.[29] At the discussion of the dress rehearsal on 2 April 1962, S. A. Mironov from the USSR Ministry of Culture emphasized that until the premiere planned for two days later, "it is essential to draw out the heroic basis of the production and not the entertaining spectacular one about which so much has been said. One would want the audience to pay not so much attention to the astonishing beauty of the production, than to the idea of this ballet, so that the audience walks out after the performance with a profound understanding of the figure of Spartacus."[30] To a large extent, the perceived lack of heroism resulted from the characterization of the ballet's main figures. Spartacus's image as heroic leader of the suppressed left something to be desired. Vladimir Vasil'ev—who danced the part of the slave in Iakobson's production but who would famously create Spartacus in Grigorovich's *Spartacus*—remarked: "Spartacus—is the central image of this production. I think that the matter here is with the choreographer and the performer himself. The point is that Spartacus's two monologues create the impression of replay. And Spartacus screams all the time. The result is a hysterical Spartacus: 'We will destroy, we will tear down the fetters of slavery.' And all this in one word. . . . And the deep internal strength of Spartacus is lost. The result is a pulverized, hysterical image."[31] Volkov thought that Spartacus was suffering too much for a hero: "I think that at the moment, Spartacus turns out somewhat suffering, and not the leader of an uprising. But Spartacus needs to be the embodiment of courage even in the most difficult conditions; this courage mustn't leave him: 'Why does he suffer from the very beginning?' I asked him. 'After all, I'm in captivity,' he answered. 'But in captivity, you can be a lion or a hare.'" Phrygia—created by Maya Plisetskaya—was also reprimanded for suffering too much and for creating a tragic figure lacking monumental heroism.[32]

If the characters of Spartacus and Phrygia were criticized for suffering too much, Crassus seemed to lack personality altogether. Pakhomov complained that Crassus was undefined and did not provide a strongly characterized opponent: Crassus did not come across as Spartacus's enemy; he did not enter the fight but avoided it. Volkov announced that Crassus reminded him of Oblomov, the proverbial nobleman from Goncharov's nineteenth-century novel who cannot bring himself to action, spending his days instead reclining on his divan in a dressing gown.[33] Instead of creating a mighty adversary providing a potent foil for Spartacus's heroism, the image of Rome revolved not so much around Crassus as around the depiction of Rome's degeneration in the scene "Feast at Crassus's."

Even though Iakobson had stated that his production would be a heroic epic about Spartacus, in the eyes of his critics, he had not met this goal. At the discussion of the dress rehearsal on 2 April 1962, I. E. Shekhonina, a representative from the USSR Ministry of Culture, Department for Musical Establishments, argued that "Feast at Crassus's" was the most vivid, memorable scene of the entire ballet: "But this is after all incorrectly done because the production is dedicated to the figure of Spartacus, this heroic figure. And this needs to give the production great emotional heat." Soviet prudery led the officials to criticize those scenes visualizing Rome's decadence as repulsively erotic. Implicit here was the fear that Soviet audiences would be tempted to sympathize more with the seductive enemy than with the steadfast heroism of the revolutionary, a point that came up repeatedly in discussions of ballets meant to juxtapose an evil, morally corrupt *other* with a pure *us*, for example, Bel'sky's *Coast of Hope*. The ministerial concerns about the eroticism of Iakobson's production reflected the absurdities of Soviet cultural life, where artists had to defend their work against the petty criticisms of narrow-minded bureaucrats, prompting an exasperated Plisetskaya to exclaim sarcastically that they should open a monastery at Crassus's feast.[34] Iakobson's *Spartacus* did not enter the repertoire of the Bolshoi. After a number of performances in Moscow, the ballet was taken on tour to the United States, where it was ripped apart by the critics.[35]

Spartacus and the Fiftieth Anniversary of the Revolution

After two unsuccessful attempts to stage Khachaturian's *Spartacus* in four years, common sense made it unlikely that the Bolshoi would return to the ballet any time soon, but by February 1965, the theater's artistic council was once again discussing plans to stage the ballet. Why would any theater leadership return to a production that had already failed twice within the span of only a few years, willing to spend precious funds and time on a production that at this point seemed more likely to fail than to succeed?

Given the circumstances, the theater's decision probably reflected not so much a stubborn artistic obsession with *Spartacus* as being politically calculated: the Kremlin's "court theater" needed more "Soviet" productions, especially as preparations for the fiftieth anniversary of the revolution were beginning. At the all-union conference of ballet figures on problems of Soviet choreography held in June 1963, several participants already wondered how this important political date should be celebrated on the ballet stage.[36] Apparently, A. N. Kuznetsov, deputy minister of culture and the meeting's chairman, asked the meeting's participants to think what they were doing and could be doing for this important date.[37] In his remarks at the conference, Mikhail Chulaki, director and artistic director of the Bolshoi Theater, also discussed the upcoming anniversary. He argued that it was less important that each theater in the union showed a new ballet that might not hold its ground very long than to accumulate a definite, rich Soviet repertoire by that date: all efforts had to be directed to creating new productions about contemporary life.[38]

Even though *Spartacus* was not about contemporary Soviet life, it qualified as a Soviet ballet because of its score by a Soviet composer and its revolutionary historical plot that could be given contemporary significance by drawing parallels between the oppression of slaves in ancient Rome and the oppression in contemporary—capitalist—countries. Importantly, *Spartacus* existed not just as a hypothetical title in a provisional repertoire plan intended to keep the Ministry of Culture happy, but, notwithstanding serious shortcomings, its musical score and libretto were finished.

On 25 February 1965, the Bolshoi's artistic council and all conductors and secretaries of the party committees of the theater's artistic ensembles met to discuss the theater's repertoire plan until the fiftieth anniversary of Soviet power. A new production of *Spartacus* was planned for March or April 1966 at the Kremlin Palace of Congresses (KDS). The big question was, who would be responsible for the theater's third attempt? Amazingly, the theater initially turned again to Moiseev, whose production had arguably been even less successful than Iakobson's production for the Bolshoi. Chulaki announced that the theater leadership had negotiated with Moiseev, discussing the serious shortcomings of his first production. In other respects, however, the theater was trying to learn from past mistakes: Chulaki added that they had also talked to Khachaturian, "who works with choreographers with difficulty, trying to preserve all symphonic music, and he agreed that the production will be realized and the basic plan be worked out without his usual declarations." The second new ballet planned for that season also reflected the theater's aspiration to add Soviet productions to its repertoire. The choreographer Oleg Vinogradov was supposed to stage a ballet called *Asel'* to music by Vladimir Vlasov based on Chingiz Aitmatov's *My Little Poplar in a Red Scarf*, transformed from an Eastern tale into a Russian psychological drama about a girl's unhappy love for a driver in a motor-transport depot and her true love for a former soldier.[39]

Not everybody thought it wise to once again return to *Spartacus*. Asaf Messerer pointed out that *Spartacus* had been staged twice and failed twice: if it was to be staged for a third time, it was necessary to know in advance what changes needed to be made. Mikhail Gabovich, on the other hand, emphasized that even though the Bolshoi's two previous productions of *Spartacus* had not been up to par, this type of work needed to be shown at the Bolshoi and the KDS, where the Bolshoi was also obliged to perform. Even if this meant trying again and again to produce a successful version of the ballet, the Bolshoi was obliged to show this work to the audience. Others disagreed. Varlamov, for example, referred to *Spartacus*'s sad fate, reminded those present that Moiseev had already tried and failed to stage the ballet successfully, and concluded that it was not right to include the ballet once again in the plan: nobody knew what alterations were planned, and the ballet had simply no dramaturgy.[40]

Given the limited time available to the theater to work on new productions, returning to *Spartacus* would come at a cost, but the political necessity of creating a Soviet repertoire by the fiftieth anniversary apparently overrode all artistic concerns. At the meeting, I. M. Tumanov, the principal (stage) director of the theater, showed that the theater had only 100 to 120 rehearsal days per year; there were about 100 rehearsals for all new opera and ballet productions. Tumanov pointed out that until the anniversary of the revolution, absolute priority must be given not to artistic wishes but to the political necessity of building the theater's Soviet repertoire: "The first thing, to which one has to direct one's attention, is to secure the creation of new, large-scale Soviet works by 1967 and on this one must concentrate the general attention. No matter how interesting *La Fille mal gardée* is, how important it would be to revive *Coppélia* or any opera production, it doesn't matter, it isn't of decisive significance at present. The first matter of business is the Soviet production." Interestingly, at the same discussion, Chulaki had proposed to ask the English choreographer Frederick Ashton whether he could stage his *La Fille mal gardée* for the Bolshoi. Chulaki's suggestion was met enthusiastically, and it was proposed that maybe the theater could even invite Balanchine. During the discussion, there therefore arose an involuntary contrast between Soviet productions the theater should stage for political reasons and dream productions it would like to stage from an artistic point of view.[41] The Bolshoi Ballet had to wait almost thirty years until it danced its first Balanchine ballet, *The Prodigal Son*, in 1991. Ashton's *La Fille mal gardée* entered the company's repertoire almost forty years later in 2002.

A new *Spartacus* production also offered a possible answer to another problem tied to the Bolshoi's status as the Kremlin's quasi "court theater." Since 1962, the Bolshoi Theater had to serve not only its main stage but also the KDS, which had been built for meetings of the Communist Party.[42] The theater's obligation symbolized the Bolshoi's closeness to political power and the problems that came with this closeness. The theater's official obligation to service both the Bolshoi's large stage and the monumental KDS created serious problems for the theater's day-to-day functioning. At the end of the 1965–1966 theatrical season, Chulaki reported to the board of the USSR Ministry of Culture on the past season of the Bolshoi and KDS, emphasizing a series of problems arising from this double obligation.[43] The Bolshoi Theater simply had not enough artists to serve two major stages. Combined with its massive touring commitments, the theater had become totally overextended and was in desperate need for more funds to expand its artistic staff. If formerly the Bolshoi had performed on the Bolshoi's main stage and on the theater's additional, small stage known as the Filial, it now had to fill two large stages that both called for monumental productions. The Bolshoi's obligation increased over time: in 1962, the Bolshoi gave eight performances per month at the KDS, including two to three concerts. In contrast, in 1965, it gave twenty performances per month at the KDS (and

no concerts).[44] The dual demand on the same large productions made repertoire and rehearsal planning almost impossible. Important smaller productions formerly performed on the smaller stage of the Filial had fallen out of
the Bolshoi's repertoire, creating artistic problems beyond an impoverished
repertoire. For example, the Bolshoi no longer offered its singers the kind of
lyrical repertoire essential for training their voices, leading to deterioration
in the quality of singing.

The obligation to serve two stages with large productions, including
operas that often required a large number of ballet dancers, also impoverished the ballet repertoire. For example, operas such as *Ruslan and Ludmilla*, *Ivan Susanin*, and *Prince Igor* required sixty to one hundred dancers.[45]
If the Bolshoi was performing the opera *Prince Igor* at the KDS, the ballet
company only had the capacity to perform smaller ballets such as *Giselle* or
Chopiniana on the main stage. The necessity of serving two stages imposed
more and more restrictions on repertoire planning, and several ballets had
disappeared from the Bolshoi's repertoire.[46] Moreover, while the Bolshoi
Filial had also served as a forum for more risky experimental productions,
the scale and nature of the gigantic KDS was no more appropriate to artistic experiments than the Bolshoi's main stage, leading to artistic stagnation
and making it difficult for the artists of the theater to master more contemporary material.[47]

There were also technical problems with the KDS that influenced the
decision to stage *Spartacus* for a third time. The KDS was used for performances, but it had not been built as a theater and did not have the facilities
of a normal theater: there was no storage space for sets and costumes, no
rehearsal space, there was a completely inadequate number of rooms to accommodate the number of artists needed for the monumental productions
shown at the KDS, and the technical possibilities of the stage left much to
be desired. As a consequence, the repertoire shown at the KDS was limited to a continuous repetition of the same handful of productions from
the Bolshoi's main stage, which meant that operas such as *Boris Godunov*,
Khovanshchina, and *Ivan Susanin* were more rarely shown at the Bolshoi itself.[48] Chulaki concluded that it was necessary to gradually create a special
repertoire for the KDS that reflected not only the monumental scale necessary for the stage of the KDS but also the stage's technical possibilities.[49]

Within the context of the theater's preparation for the fiftieth anniversary of the October Revolution, the Bolshoi's third production of *Spartacus*
was initially intended specifically for the KDS.[50] The Bolshoi planned to
complete and show to the public almost all their new works dedicated to
the anniversary in the 1966–1967 theatrical season. In addition to *Spartacus*,
A. Kholminov's opera *An Optimistic Tragedy* was planned for the KDS, while

the ballet *Asel'* and K. Molchanov's opera *The Fortress* would be shown at the Bolshoi.[51] At the assembly of the Bolshoi Theater after the summer vacation on 13 September 1966, Chulaki emphasized that the production teams of both *Spartacus* and *An Optimistic Tragedy* should use the distinctive features of the KDS to a maximum, making them "productions of a new type" precisely for the KDS. Chulaki also referred to the ideological kinship between these two "productions of a new type": the new *Spartacus* would not be a historical chronicle but a romantic legend based on one of the most brilliant episodes of the liberation struggle of the oppressed against the oppressors; "romantic zeal and legendariness, though of a different kind," ought to distinguish both *Spartacus* and *An Optimistic Tragedy.*[52]

Grigorovich's *Spartacus*: A Danced Conflict between Two Heroes

The failure of the Bolshoi's previous *Spartacus* productions and the pressure to create an ideologically uplifting ballet for the anniversary of the revolution did not augur well for the new *Spartacus*. According to Ekaterina Maksimova, who created the part of Phrygia in Grigorovich's production,[53] *Spartacus* was "the only production by Grigorovich 'made to order,' which they ordered him to do and which he himself did not want to stage."[54] It is not clear when—and by whom—it was decided that Grigorovich would choreograph the new *Spartacus* instead of Moiseev, but at a meeting of the Bolshoi's artistic council on 13 January 1967, Chulaki stated that Grigorovich had begun to work on the ballet. Once again, Chulaki enumerated the flaws of the Bolshoi's previous productions: the ballet's illustrative dramatic outline and the pale characterization of Spartacus. According to Chulaki, the theater had decided to stage the ballet a third time because Grigorovich's creative concept would be absolutely different.[55]

On 27 June 1967, the Bolshoi's artistic council met to discuss two of its productions for the anniversary, *Spartacus* and the opera *An Optimistic Tragedy*. Chulaki emphasized that the decision to stage the ballet for a third time imposed a great responsibility on the theater. It would not have risked such a large-scale production unless the reasons for previous failures had been identified, namely the ballet's faulty musical and literary dramatic composition. Three aspects of Grigorovich's concept discussed fundamentally differentiated his vision of *Spartacus* from previous productions. First, Grigorovich put the contrast and conflict between two heroes—Spartacus and Crassus—at the heart of his production. Grigorovich envisioned Crassus as "the personification of the strength and power of the colonial slavery of Rome's politics" and Spartacus as the "bright type of a man who has begun to answer questions, which weren't asked at that time." He conceived the production as the tragedy of an individual and built the ballet's entire dra-

FIGURE 45. Vladimir Vasil'ev as Spartacus and Ekaterina Maksimova as Phrygia in Yuri Grigorovich's *Spartacus* at the Bolshoi Ballet, circa 1968–1975. © St. Petersburg State Museum of Theater and Music

matic conception on the conflict between the forces of Crassus and Sparta-cus. The two central female characters, Phrygia and Aegina, echoed this conflict between the ballet's two heroes.[56]

Second, Grigorovich proposed a strict structure for the ballet, imposing a sense of logical development on the ballet's dramatic plot. The choreographer divided each of the three acts into four scenes. In each act, there would be three choreographic monologues to be danced by the ballet's main characters.[57] A large canopy that could be lowered and lifted on a rope would

FIGURE 46. Maris Liepa as Crassus and Svetlana Adyrkhaeva as Aegina in Grigorovich's *Spartacus* at the Bolshoi Ballet, about 1968–1975. © St. Petersburg State Museum of Theater and Music

be used to visually separate danced monologues interpolated into the ballet's narrative to offer more psychological insights into a character's internal world. As the implementation of this idea would show, Grigorovich's idea of interpolated monologues for the ballet's main characters enabled the choreographer and the dancers to turn the ballet's characters into strongly painted personalities, notably in the case of Spartacus and Crassus. One of the main points of criticisms aired by the Bolshoi's artistic council at discussions of both Moiseev's and Iakobson's previous productions had been that both failed to create strong characters in general and a strong hero in particular.

Third, Grigorovich's production would be a danced production essentially without any mime scenes, relying on Grigorovich's classically based choreographic idiom.[58] Most importantly, both Spartacus and Crassus would be danced parts—in previous productions, the role of Spartacus had been criticized as too static, while the part of Crassus had been a mime role. In Grigorovich's new production, Vladimir Vasil'ev and Maris Liepa, two extraordinarily charismatic, virtuoso young principal dancers, were creating the parts of Spartacus and Crassus. If Iakobson's Crassus had been compared to Oblomov, Liepa's Crassus offered a physically explosive challenge to Vasil'ev's heroic Spartacus.[59] By juxtaposing two strong, heroic dancers whose parts were developed in dance, Grigorovich would create a choreographically driven dramatic tension at the center of the ballet.

Grigorivich's production has the following dramatic outline: Crassus has led a victorious campaign in Thrace. He has made prisoners, including Spartacus and his beloved Phrygia. In the slave market, Spartacus and Phrygia are separated. At an orgy at Crassus's palace, mimes and courtesans entertain the guests, mocking Phrygia, Crassus's new slave. He is attracted to her, incurring the jealousy of his courtesan Aegina. Crassus orders two gladiators to fight to death: one of them is Spartacus. He wins but is upset at having been forced to kill. He will no longer tolerate captivity and decides to act to win back his freedom. He incites the gladiators to revolt. The gladiators are joined by the populace and the shepherds, and Spartacus is proclaimed the leader of the uprising. Spartacus is haunted by thoughts of Phrygia as slave. He finds her in Crassus's villa, where they express their love for each other. They hide as the guests arrive. A feast at Crassus's villa celebrates his victories as Spartacus's army surrounds the place. The guests disperse, Crassus and Aegina flee. Spartacus breaks into the villa. Crassus is taken prisoner, and Spartacus challenges him to single-hand combat. Crassus is no match for Spartacus, but as he prepares for death, Spartacus releases him, convinced that the gladiators will be victorious. Crassus is tormented by his disgrace, and Aegina calls on him to take revenge. Crassus's defeat thwarts Aegina's ambition, and she decides to sow dissension in Spartacus's camp. Crassus's army is advancing. Spartacus wants to fight but many of his captains desert him. Aegina seduces gladiators still loyal to Spartacus with wine, erotic dances, and prostitutes. She delivers them to Crassus. Crassus wants revenge: victory is not enough; he wants Spartacus. Spartacus's forces are surrounded by the Roman legions, the gladiators are killed. Spartacus fights until the end and dies a hero's death, crucified on Roman spears. Phrygia retrieves his body, her grief is inconsolable.

Previous productions had given an ideologically unsatisfactory explanation for the defeat of Spartacus's movement. If previously the fatal split in his movement was caused by Aegina's corruption of some of his comrades with courtesans and wine, Grigorovich proposed to turn the argument on its head: in his production, a split among Spartacus's followers makes their subsequent corruption with wine and women possible. While Phrygia's lament over Spartacus's body in Iakobson's production for the Bolshoi had been considered unsuccessful, Grigorovich envisioned a big requiem for Spartacus as the ballet's finale, danced by Phrygia, soloists, and the corps de ballet in a major dance scene inspired by the Georgian dance Khorumii.[60]

If Khachaturian's vociferous objections to any changes to his score had been a major impediment in the past, the Bolshoi this time refused to consider the composer's feelings. In Chulaki's laconic words, an "agreement" had been reached with Khachaturian: "He understood that we will do it only *this* way, and not in any other way, proceeding from the demands of the musical, theatrical, and choreographic dramaturgy." Grigorovich added that Khachaturian's score included a great number of divertissement numbers that had now been given a dramatic meaning. For example, Khachaturian had composed a dance for jesters in the scene "Feast at Crassus's," but this number was now used for a powerful dance showing how Phrygia was mocked. A whole series of numbers had been cut.[61]

Chulaki's concluding remarks at this discussion illustrate the theater director's hopes that the Bolshoi would finally get an ideologically uplifting, truly heroic *Spartacus* production. He reiterated that previous productions had failed because of their depiction of Spartacus, leading the audience to see Spartacus as a hooligan bursting into the entertaining scene of Crassus's banquet to rob the audience of its enjoyment of this scene, while Spartacus's struggle had been shown only in weak scenes of a divertissement character. In this new production, Chulaki stated, everything superfluous had been cut in order to show the struggle between the camps of Spartacus and Crassus. Chulaki argued that this struggle would be shown in a completely contemporary way: "And here, everything is treated in a contemporary way. It is shown in the militaristic spirit of our days. . . . Here is the exchange with the present." Chulaki reiterated that the theater was taking a conscious risk in staging Spartacus again, but he believed that the enterprise could succeed because of Grigorovich's new concept.[62]

Choreography Trumps Ideology

But would the artistic implementation of Grigorovich's concept lead to the expected ideological success, and could the production be artistically interesting if, to use Chulaki's words, it reflected "the militaristic spirit of our days"? As Grigorovich began to create the ballet with his four leading dancers, the meeting of these unique artistic talents led to an extraordinary process of mutual inspiration. Judging from the memoirs of two of the dancers who created leading parts, Ekaterina Maksimova (Phrygia) and Maris Liepa (Crassus), their creative collaboration developed a dynamic that apparently transcended any considerations of the work's political significance. True artistic collaboration and mutual inspiration was possible despite the produc-

FIGURE 47. Vladimir Vasil'ev as Spartacus at the Bolshoi Ballet, circa 1968–1975.
© St. Petersburg State Museum of Theater and Music

tion's political-ideological context. Artistic talent and imagination proved stronger than ideological constraints, but it probably helped that the subject of *Spartacus* was ideologically sound without being too stifling. Instead of celebrating some tedious aspect of contemporary Soviet political life, it focused on the universal theme of a heroic struggle against oppression, a topic vague enough to allow room for artistic interpretation.

This successful outcome, however, was not necessarily what the participants expected at the outset. Given that Grigorovich had basically been told to try his luck with a ballet that had already failed twice at the Bolshoi, there were certainly concerns. According to Maksimova: "Yuri Nikolaevich came to us with doubts: 'Guys, let's think . . . ' At that time, in 1968, genuine coauthorship united us: we began together to think up something, to try something—and became infected with it."[63] If most dancers dream of having a part specifically choreographed for them, the four dancers creating the leading parts in Grigorovich's *Spartacus*—Vladimir Vasil'ev (Spartacus), Maksimova, Liepa, and Nina Timofeeva (Aegina)—saw their dream fulfilled. Liepa, whose Crassus would become one of the most famous creations of Soviet ballet and a crowning achievement of the dancer's career, believes that in none of Grigorovich's previous ballets had there been such a precise correspondence between the choreographer's intention and the

FIGURE 48. Maris Liepa as Crassus and Svetlana Adyrkhaeva as Aegina in Grigorovich's *Spartacus* at the Bolshoi Ballet, circa 1968–1975. © St. Petersburg State Museum of Theater and Music

dancer's individuality and dramatic talent. Despite his subsequent fallout with Grigorovich, Liepa continued to remember his collaboration with the choreographer on Crassus as work that was "incomparable to anything in its fascination and novelty!"[64]

Far from merely fulfilling a professional duty by once again producing *Spartacus* within the political context of the revolution's fiftieth anniversary, the choreographer and his four dancers embarked on a creative journey whose artistic significance must have dwarfed most considerations of the Spartacus revolt's potential ideological significance for contemporary politics. Liepa recalls the "creative torment" that plagued him and Grigorovich while they were creating Crassus: they spent whole nights inventing, checking, polishing each movement, each turn of the head.[65] The decision to turn Crassus from a mimed part into a danced part was in many ways the key to Grigorovich's production: by doing so, he gave Spartacus an opponent who was his equal, who could compete with him on the ballet stage in the same language. By presenting the struggle between Spartacus and Crassus as a fight among equals, the heroic image of Spartacus would become more clearly delineated.

Initially, both Liepa, who had danced Spartacus in Iakobson's *Spartacus*, and Vladimir Vasil'ev were rehearsing the part of Spartacus, while Vladimir Levashov, a dancer who was a great actor but who no longer performed danced roles, was cast as Crassus. According to Liepa, the part of Crassus was initially of no interest to him because in all the previous productions Crassus had been a mimed part, but one day, Grigorovich asked Liepa to try to dance Crassus, arguing that world literature demonstrated that the hero's antagonist could be a great figure in his own right: the part of Iago was no less interesting than Othello.[66] Maksimova, the onstage partner and wife of Vasil'ev, remembers this moment slightly differently. According to Maksimova, Liepa and Vasil'ev proposed to Grigorovich that the parts of Spartacus and Crassus should be equally expressed in dance and initially suggested that they would both rehearse both parts.[67] Vladimir Vasil'ev, on the other hand, remembers that Liepa had the idea of a "peculiar experiment" once the idea had arisen to make Crassus a danced part, suggesting that he would prepare Crassus while Vasil'ev would rehearse Spartacus. According to Vasil'ev, initially they wanted to exchange the parts at some point, but this never happened.[68] Just as Crassus came to be identified with Liepa, Vasil'ev's Spartacus became legendary, proving right Grigorovich's decision to cast the dancer in this part, a decision that, according to Maksimova, many had initially doubted. In the past, heroic six-foot-plus giants of monumental exterior had been cast as Spartacus, while Vasil'ev was certainly not among the company's tallest dancers.[69]

The creative fulfillment described by the dancers indicates the multiple layers of meaning of good creative works. The ballet's creation took place primarily at the personal level of choreographer and dancer, irrespective of the ideological tasks the ballet was supposed to fulfill. From an ideological point of view, the jumping hordes of soldiers and insurgents in Grigorovich's *Spartacus* certainly reflected what Chulaki had called "the militaristic

FIGURE 49. Vladimir Vasil'ev as Spartacus at the Bolshoi Ballet, circa 1968–1975.
© St. Petersburg State Museum of Theater and Music

spirit of our days." Similarly, Spartacus's choreographic image is unequivocally heroic, and his impalement on the lances of Crassus's troops creates a
Christlike vision of heroic martyrdom in the name of freedom from oppression. If this was all there was to Grigorovich's *Spartacus*, however, the ballet
would probably not have remained so popular with audiences all over the
world even beyond the collapse of the system that provided the ideological
context for the ballet's creation.

Grigorovich's choreography offered his dancers a text of resistance by
allowing them to add their own shades of meaning and interpretation to
what could have been little more than an ideologically informed struggle
between good and evil. Liepa's analysis of how his interpretation of the anti-
hero evolved explains why the very nature of artistic creation made art such
a threat for a regime seeking to control the minds and hearts of its subjects:
the meaning of works of art is eternally fluid and open to interpretation by
the individual. Liepa's thinking also demonstrates that the restrictive Soviet
political-ideological context could sometimes inspire extraordinary creativity, increasing artists' capacity of suggestive thinking and prompting them
to explore any ambiguities available to them. Paradoxically, constraints

FIGURE 50. Vladimir Vasil'ev as Spartacus and Ekaterina Maksimova as Phrygia in Grigorovich's *Spartacus* at the Bolshoi Ballet, circa 1968–1975. © St. Petersburg State Museum of Theater and Music

could acquire enabling power: the more pressure there was on artists, the more creative they had to become to overcome the constraints of the system.

If *Spartacus* was to show the confrontation between tyrannical Rome and the oppressed as personified by Spartacus, a hero who begins to ask questions ahead of his time, the representation of "evil" would be indicative of the extent to which the ballet was painting an ideologically pure, black-and-white picture of the struggle between oppressors and oppressed. By about 1980, Liepa had danced Crassus in more than 100 performances of the Bolshoi's 130 performances of the ballet, but he still kept on discovering new aspects of the part: "What a large-scale character our Crassus turned out to be! At each of the hundred performances he without fail discloses something new, unexplored to me! It turns out that I myself don't yet know him to the end. He is also for me—a riddle of today's evening, let alone the dreams of tomorrow's Crassus!"[70] Grigorovich's choreography for Crassus includes goose steps that in no uncertain terms evoke Nazism, but Liepa's preparation for his part went far beyond such political allusions. Liepa contrasts his approach to Crassus with his interpretation of Spartacus in Iakobson's production:

> What was the patrician Crassus like? . . . What were ancient Rome, its famous military leaders, commanders, victors like? What were the culture, art, ways of life of this era?
>
> I have to confess that these questions troubled me already in 1962, when in the same Bolshoi Theater I performed the role of Spartacus in Leonid Iakobson's production. But then I was younger, and I didn't dance in the first cast. I obediently followed the traditional line: everything Spartacus does is right, wise, and fair. And the Roman empire is an evil that has to be destroyed.
>
> But now my hero had to live in this Rome, defend it, be flesh of its flesh.[71]

Instead of sticking to an ideologically deterministic interpretation of Crassus, Liepa's characterization of Crassus evolved over time. He immersed himself into studying ancient Rome. His interpretation grew in complexity, and he introduced different colors to his reading. For example, the first scene of the ballet—"Invasion"—shows Crassus as the embodiment of power. The curtain opens to show Crassus in his chariot. "The mighty victor" explodes into a physically grueling cascade of jumps. According to Liepa, initially, his "Crassus the Triumphant" was excessively evil, painted in only one, black color. Gradually, Liepa reached the conclusions that his hero was young, talented, intoxicated by victory, and the beginning of the performance stopped being so awesome: Crassus, who had not yet tasted the bitter cup of humiliation and fear, became a young genius of war, Crassus the Lucky, Crassus the Rich.[72]

Liepa's analysis of Crassus offers a sophisticated example how even within the confines of an overtly unambiguous ideological framework, there could be room left for artistic interpretation. In a 1996 version of *Ia khochu tantsevat' sto let* (I want to dance one hundred years), which restored sections cut by the censors when the book was first published in Riga in 1981,[73] Liepa turned the ballet's ideological message on its head by offering a vision of Crassus as defender of an ancient civilization against barbarism. It does not require a large stretch of imagination to draw parallels between Liepa's description of the barbarians' burning desire to destroy Rome and its civilization and the Russian revolution. Liepa's analysis could be read as a rejection of the official Soviet line, which used ancient Rome as a not-so-veiled metaphor for the oppressive, decadent West of the present. Instead, the Latvian Liepa offers an alternative view in which *Spartacus*'s ancient Rome could be seen as a metaphor for Russia's prerevolutionary civilization threatened by the barbarism of the Soviet utopia's relentless Communist zeal:

> If Crassus and I were to sit opposite each other now . . . and Crassus would ask me, whether he had been right. . . . I would answer: "You acted correctly, my Marc Crassus! You want to get over insulted self-esteem. . . . So get over it! Remember one thing—the barbarians are striving to destroy your Rome. To destroy everything that Rome created over several centuries—palaces and villas, forums and coliseums, aqueducts and marble sculptures. . . . From the past greatness, a naked wilderness will remain, grass will overgrow the squares, and around solitary campfires, the destitute will warm themselves. . . . Don't let Rome perish! Fight for it!" . . . What did you want—that in premonition of the bright Communist future, Crassus would prostrate himself before a slave? A man of high culture would beg alms from an uneducated Thracian gladiator?
>
> This could not be! And Crassus even becomes noble in his struggle, because he fights for the eternal greatness of Rome. Alas, soon, the barbarians will play the master here and the dark shadow of the Middle Ages will lower itself over radiant ancient Rome. . . .
>
> And we have gotten so used to dividing everyone into good and bad, progressive and reactionary.[74]

Creating room for interpretation for the ballet's performers was not the only area of resistance offered by Grigorovich's *Spartacus*. If different dancers were able to develop different interpretations of the ballet's leading parts, each member of the audience could interpret the action on stage in their own way. It is hard to imagine that *Spartacus* would have been so successful in the West if it had been nothing but Soviet propaganda. The fact that *Spartacus* was not about "Soviet contemporary life" but based on a revolutionary historical topic that left much more room for non-Soviet ideological interpretations certainly helped. Capitalist audiences would be perfectly able to sympathize with an uprising of the oppressed against oppressors. After all, the definition of who is the oppressor and who is the oppressed depends on the ideological vantage point of the observer. The inherent vagueness of *Spartacus* and the ultimate universality of its main theme—a struggle for freedom—ensured that the ballet could adapt to changing political circumstances, whether this meant the success of the ballet in the capitalist West or its survival at home after the collapse of communism.

The ballet was first performed in the West in London in July 1969 and conquered audiences by the sheer power of its theatrical performance. A ballet fan reminiscing about this first performance described the experience with the following words: "I must say that the first night of *Spartacus* at the Royal Opera House in 1969 was a night anyone present will never forget. After the first act, the roar of the audience was so extraordinary that I have never heard similar at any ballet or opera performance in the house since. The audience was packed with regulars and critics and though no one I remember thought it a great work, it did create a great performance."[75] In his review of the same performance of *Spartacus* for the *Times*, the well-known ballet critic John Percival focused on the power of Grigorovich's choreographic images and did not even allude to the connection between contemporary Soviet ideology and the ballet's plot. Instead, he enthusiastically wrote: "Right from its first moment, Yuri Grigorovich's *Spartacus* . . . grips with the power of its drama and the vividness of its imagery." With respect to ideology, he merely noted that "with its mixture of ideological implications (liberty versus tyranny) and the clash of strongly characterized individuals, the subject is a splendid one for a ballet." The rest of the review lauds "spectacular group dances" that "are separated by dramatic solos—or soliloquies, as Grigorovich justifiably calls them—for the principals," raves that "Grigorovich's choreography burns with a consuming energy," points out that the "fiercely heroic movement, tremendous leaps" of the two "marvelously contrasted" leading men sometimes looked like "almost suicidal bravado," commends the "breathtakingly effective groups dances," and states that the "ferocious dance of the revolting slaves" brought down the curtain on act one "amid such cheers . . . not heard for a long time." Percival's only serious criticism concerned Khachaturian's music, which he called "simply dreary," noting that "Grigorovich ought not to have to overcome such a disadvantage; that he does makes his achievement doubly impressive."[76] The ballet has remained a staple of the Bolshoi's touring repertoire ever since its first successful performance in London and was again shown during the company's visit to London in summer 2010.

Just like Lavrovsky's *Romeo and Juliet* during its first performance in the West in London in 1956, Grigorovich's *Spartacus* touched the imagination of its professional Western audience. Kenneth MacMillan was scheduled to take over from Frederick Ashton as director of the Royal Ballet in 1970. In an interview about his intentions as director given to the *Times* in September 1969, a few months after the Bolshoi's first performance of *Spartacus* at Covent Garden, MacMillan made a remark about his own future choreography, stating: "I want to get people more involved, so that they really care instead of just sitting and watching."

According to his interviewer, John Percival, MacMillan gave the audiences' excitement about the Bolshoi's *Spartacus* as an example of what can be achieved and said that in his own, different way, he would like to aim for a similar result.[77]

If the Bolshoi's attempts to stage *Spartacus* had at first seemed doomed to failure, the theater's third production of the ballet triumphed. It was not an artistic obsession that prompted the theater to stage the ballet three times over a short time span but political necessity paired with practical considerations. Grigorovich's *Spartacus* showed that ballet could become larger than politics even under these circumstances. *Spartacus* successfully answered the Soviet Ministry of Culture's fantasy of a heroic Soviet ballet delivering a universal revolutionary message—freedom for the oppressed against their oppressors—that could be made more contemporary by alluding to oppression outside the Soviet bloc. At the same time, however, the government could control neither the dancers' interpretation nor the audiences' reception of Grigorovich's choreography. Reflecting the fluidity of works of art whose interpretation and reception is ultimately beyond political control, Grigorovich's *Spartacus* demonstrated that choreography could be resistance, leading to the artistic repossession of a ballet that was largely staged in response to political needs. Maybe the pressure of previous failures and the demand to create a revolutionary ballet in time for the fiftieth anniversary of the revolution even turned into an enabling factor, inspiring extraordinary creativity in the choreographer and dancers to overcome constraints.

In the final analysis, ideological demands never managed to completely stifle the power of artistic autonomy. After the collapse of communism, *Spartacus* has survived the death of the political system that had provided the context of its creation. Today, the ballet stands as a reminder that despite the political-ideological demands and controls the Soviet regime imposed on artistic creativity, artistic imagination proved to be remarkably resilient, creative, and enduring. As the post-Soviet era program in commemoration of the ballet's twenty-fifth anniversary in 1993 pointed out:

> Today, we can talk about *Spartacus* in its absolute values. No one is forced to remember the liberation struggle of the slaves against slave owners; to look for a movement analogy with arms thrown up in Fascist greetings. About all of this, the newspapers of that era wrote seriously, trying to explain the meaning and essence of the masterpiece so elementary, and most importantly, to inscribe it into the political, topical context of the epoch. But the epochs changed, disappeared, and new governments appeared, more than once the map of the world was remade. . . . But *Spartacus* remained untouched. It doesn't require renovation and editing. The theatrical performance—a fleeting illusion—turns out to be more durable, more primary in relation to global evolutions.[78]

Thirteen years later, in 2006, an exchange on a forum of a major British webpage dedicated to ballet, Balletco (ballet.co.uk),[79] illustrated the strong emotions Grigorovich's *Spartacus* continued to evoke among Western audiences almost forty years after its creation. In response to a posting whose author stated that he did not understand why any version of *Spartacus* had managed to remain popular since the collapse of Soviet communism, several participants of the forum sprang to the defense of *Spartacus*, which had recently been shown by the Bolshoi during a regional tour of the United Kingdom.[80] While it would certainly be wrong to argue that Grigorovich's *Spartacus* is—or should be—to everyone's taste, one of the impassioned defenses of the ballet reflects the view of all those audiences who continue to flock to see *Spartacus*:

> Why should genuine works of art be thrown out after the collapse of a political system? David, Delacroix, and others "managed" to remain in the Musée du Louvre. *Spartacus* remains popular because it is great theater! And the ordinary public, unlike the critics, don't care very much about socialist realism (I doubt that critics understand what it is about too) but just respond to the skilful dramatic composition of this ballet so well supported by the restrained but expressive design, to the power of human emotions, and to enthusiasm of the performers who can not stop loving this ballet—because it is a great theatrical production. . . . When seeing *Spartacus* I personally never think about "revolution-

ary totalitarian governments" and "political works . . . produced for political reasons." As far as I know the Russian critics also are not worried unnecessarily about the political aspect of this ballet. One does not have to be a Socialist to understand that oppression, debauchery, cruelty, and betrayal are bad while freedom, love, and personal sacrifice are good. Why cannot the Western critics have the same ingenious perception of obvious things? Where does their obsession with socialist realism come from?[81]

Conclusion

IN 1917, THE violence of the Russian Revolution shook Russian civilization to its core. Standing seemingly triumphant on the rubble of Russia's old political, social, economic, and cultural order, the Bolsheviks claimed they were setting the country on a path toward socialism and sought to enroll art as a potent weapon in their utopian drive toward a new civilization. More than any other art form, Russian classical ballet had been a part of aristocratic court culture, but before long, it too was assigned a part in the Soviet cultural project. Paradoxically, Russia's former imperial ballet metamorphosed into one of the most celebrated cultural achievements of the Soviet Union.

In the final analysis, during the first fifty years of Soviet power, ballet proved stronger than politics and ideology. This was not a straightforward or easy process, but artists of the ballet companies continued to push the boundaries of their art form as choreographers and performers and found ways to renegotiate the restrictive and intrusive framework set for artistic creation by the Soviet regime. Even though the regime's supervision of the companies' work made complete artistic autonomy impossible, the potential for creative freedom was greater than a superficial glance might at first suggest.

Constraints could acquire enabling power: the more pressure there was on artists, the more creative they had to become to overcome the constraints of the system. No matter how unequal the power relationship between artists and politics might have looked from the outside, it was in fact a complex relationship of mutual influence that included the potential for artistic subversion of political-ideological power. Again, we should be reminded of Michel Foucault's words, that "there is no relationship of power without the means of escape or possible flight."[1] However hard the regime tried to control artistic life, artists at the Kirov and Bolshoi Ballet developed strategies of artistic repossession to cope with the political-ideological realities of life in the Soviet Union and to reclaim autonomy from the system they had no choice but to accept. By reclaiming autonomy, incremental adaptation could thus become a form of resistance, leading to a subversion of the system without necessarily presupposing its conscious rejection.

According to conventional wisdom, the choreographic development of ballet was stifled in the Soviet Union, but—at least until 1968—the reality was more complex. In 1956, the reaction to the Bolshoi Ballet's first international tour demonstrated that even during the restrictive climate of Stalinism, Soviet ballet had managed to push some artistic boundaries. The dramatic coherence and theatricality of Lavrovsky's *Romeo and Juliet* had a major impact on the development of modern narrative ballet in the West. Similarly, in the late 1960s, Grigorovich's *Spartacus* was admired for its ability to stir audiences. The amazing collaboration of the *Spartacus* team during the creation of the ballet demonstrated that true artistic collaboration was possible under ideological constraints. Astounding artistic results were achieved against all odds of ideological and political intrusion. The pressure of previous failures and the demand to create a revolutionary ballet in time for the fiftieth anniversary of the revolution seemingly turned into an enabling factor of artistic imagination. As Grigorovich and his dancers repossessed the field of choreography from the intrusion of ideology and politics during the creation of *Spartacus*, choreography proved that it was larger than ideology and politics.

Challenging established norms of choreographic expression within the world of Soviet ballet often required artists to play the system. During the cultural Thaw, choreographers like Yuri Grigorovich exploited the regime's policy of promoting cultural invigoration and its support for youth initiatives in their struggle to stage choreographically innovative ballets that challenged the main creative principles of the genre of *drambalet*. The involvement of the Komsomol in ensuring the successful staging of Grigorovich's *The Stone Flower* shows how artists could take advantage of the ambiguity inherent in any social structure or organization: they could use the system for achieving goals foreign to the system, thus reclaiming autonomy from all-pervasive political and ideological forces, ultimately undermining the regime's ideological mission.

Even though the scope for artistic autonomy in choreography was greater than conventional wisdom on Soviet choreography might suggest, there were limits. Most importantly, the Soviet cultural project presupposed that in art, there were clear "rights" and "wrongs," just as there were clear "rights" and "wrongs" in politics. Also, the context of the cultural Cold War reinforced a natural tendency to define one's identity in terms of "Us" against "the Other": Soviet ballet had to be different from Western ballet by definition, because "Soviet" culture was supposed to embody not just different national traditions but an ideological struggle between two camps. Cold War cultural competition could be an additional constraint on a key area of artistic autonomy, the evolution of Soviet ballet's artistic identity, by reinforcing a definition of identity as antithesis of the Other. In the case of Soviet ballet, the ultimate other was George Balanchine, the "lost son" of Soviet ballet. At the same time, the cultural Cold War could also become an enabling factor: fear of Western competition promoted choreographic reforms at home, while admiration of the Other's achievements inspired artists on both sides of the Iron Curtain.

The Soviet regime promoted an antipluralist, black-and-white mindset, making paradigm shifts in choreographic aesthetics difficult, as demonstrated by the ideologically framed confrontation between defenders of drambalet and their challengers in the late 1950s and early 1960s. Leonid Iakobson's artistic fate shows that within the world of Soviet choreography, there were both artistic and political-ideological pressures on choreographic experimentation. Artistic repossession was a response to these pressures, but they also imposed limits on the scope of choreographic innovation. Nonconformists like Iakobson had to fight a two-front battle both against the artistic preferences of the establishment within their own profession and against the aesthetic and ideological restrictions on artistic creation set by the regime. At the same time, the fact that a choreographer like Iakobson got to stage anything at all shows that artists could force remarkable concession from the system.

Despite the potential for reclaiming artistic autonomy, artistic repossession in ballet was circumscribed by the particularities of the Soviet cultural project. Within the parameters of the Soviet cultural project, "pure art" was condemned, and artistic creation in the Soviet Union was supposed to fulfill a social function. Given the nature of classical dance as a nonrepresentational artistic medium, ballet faced particularly acute problems in an ideological system that, reflecting both the regime's social requirements of art and its desire for control, demanded realism in art.

The verbal requirements made of ballet reflected both the regime's adoption of the demand made by Russia's nineteenth-century intelligentsia that art provide an explicit commentary on life and the regime's desire to control artistic output. Socialist realism was supposed to be a tool for implementing the Soviet cultural project, and it reflected the regime's conception of reality as a construct to be used to control the population from the top. Verbalization is only one way of creating meaning in art, and the regime's rejection of abstraction, modernism, and formalism reflected its fear of ambiguity and its desire for control: narrative content that can be verbalized is more easily controllable than vaguer artistic messages that elude verbalization, offering a dangerous scope for interpretation beyond the regime's control.

Classical dance is by its very nature an allusive language difficult to control by the censor's hand. As an intrinsic part of aristocratic court culture, it was also far from clear how the Soviet regime could recast this symbol of Romanov culture in its own image. In the immediate aftermath of the revolution, ballet was accused of being nothing but a celebration of meaningless prettiness. Before long, ballet was at least in theory elevated to a "serious" art form equal to other artistic mediums, but the prejudice that it was beyond classical dance to express certain topics persisted.

Nonetheless, ballet was celebrated as a major Soviet cultural achievement. Ballet's evolving position within the Soviet cultural project illustrates the complex ways in which the revolution related to the cultural symbols of the old order. It shows both the power of tradition—the survival of classical ballet—and the reinvention of tradition under the new regime. In the Soviet Union, the meaning of tradition was complex and fluid: invented tradition could exist side by side with continuous tradition, and the alleged "transformation" of cultural symbols of the old order often merely provided a rhetorical mask for the persistence of tradition.[2] Even though the prerevolutionary classics continued to provide the backbone of Russian ballet, on a rhetorical level, ballet's continued existence was at times justified by an ideologically informed claim that the revolution had transformed the very nature of Russian ballet. In 1928, for example, the Bolshoi ballerina Viktorina Kriger tried to address the prejudice that ballet was frivolous by publicly arguing that after the revolution the ballerina had successfully metamorphosed from a mindless doll into a socially conscious citizen.[3] In an article tellingly titled "Balerina zagovorila" (The ballerina has begun to talk), Kriger wrote that before the revolution the ballerina was seen as:

> dolly, as frisky butterfly, as chic femme fatal, as grand-ducal amusement, or as concubine of moneybags. The ballerina is not a human being. She is a toy, a bagatelle, a creature, woven from short tarlatan skirts and Brussels lace. She must not eat. She can drink only champagne, which is just as sparkling and reproachful as her art. If it happens that she eats, the table has to consist of "airy relishes," "otherworldly" little pies. She—the ballerina—is a light dandelion, which

now flies away in the breath of the breeze. But what about intellect? Well, to be intelligent in ballet is even inconvenient.[4]

In official Soviet ballet hagiography, the revolution gave the decadent imperial ballet a brain and a social conscience, bestowing on the formerly frivolous art form the right to take its place within Soviet culture. In Kriger's metamorphic story, the dolly ballerina's world is hit by the revolution: the dandelion has to put coarse felt boots on its finely chiseled legs and entertain the proletariat at district concerts. The organizer of the concert would ask the ballerina: "Citizen, do you want herring or horsemeat for the performance?" and the ballerina would be shocked: horsemeat instead of "otherworldly" little pies? But as years go by, the ballerina, having shifted from "airy" prerevolutionary to hearty Soviet food, becomes more "earthy." She now performs for the simple proletarian audience with the same trepidation as hitherto for the bourgeois audience. In the Soviet cultural project, art is for the masses, and "the ballerina has begun to talk—and not in the language of ballet but in the language common to all mankind. . . . The place of the 'hothouse' plant, of the light dandelion has been taken by a new, healthier, real ballerina–human being, a ballerina–social activist."[5]

In reality, however, the Soviet ballerina continued to be less a "real ballerina–human being, a ballerina–social activist," than an emblem of grace and female beauty, enchanting audiences not "in the language common to all mankind" and in ballets depicting Soviet "reality" but, above all, in the masterworks of the classical repertoire. The persistent failure of the Kirov and Bolshoi Ballet companies to create enduringly successful ballets on contemporary Soviet themes was ultimately a proof of the victory of art over politics because it reflected the integrity of art: much of the art created under political pressure was—intentionally or unintentionally—doomed to failure. Ballet continued to celebrate beauty and glamour, not Socialist construction, and the audiences loved it. On a superficial level, images of the ballerina Maya Plisetskaya dressed in elegant dresses by the French couturier Pierre Cardin offered a subversive respite from Socialist austerity and the gray reality of Soviet consumer goods. On a much more profound level, the prerevolutionary classical heritage of Soviet ballet provided a direct link to a world that was supposed to be irrevocably lost. Ballet offered audiences a window into this world, and Soviet ballet dancers lived in a double reality of Soviet life and independent professional values and traditions.

Even though Soviet cultural ideology superimposed its rhetoric on the field of culture, under the veneer of Soviet rhetoric the continuity of artistic thought and of artistic debates in the world of Russian ballet across the historical break of the revolution was remarkable. At the risk of oversimpli-

fication, Soviet ballet debates to a large extent continued two prerevolutionary artistic debates: the tension in ballet between its narrative potential and
the nonrepresentational nature of classical dance and the tension in Russian
nineteenth-century art between pure and social art.

While the intellectual origins of many Soviet ballet debates were therefore entirely non-Soviet, the context of the Soviet cultural project superimposed a Manichaean ideology on art that looked for clear "rights" and
"wrongs." In this climate, artistic repossession could also take on a form that
actually stifled artistic autonomy and pluralism: artists could use ideological
rhetoric not because they wanted to defend the Soviet system but because
they wanted to ensure their own, personal position by branding their competitors as dangerous enemies of Soviet art. The interplay between ideology and artistic thought could thus be complex—and not necessarily what
it appeared to be on the surface. Seemingly orthodox artists were not necessarily true believers or opportunists but could be astute actors practicing
Orwellian doublethink and doublespeak and trying to use the system for
their own purposes that had little, if anything, to do with staunch ideological goals they claimed to defend.

Similarly, a superficial look at Soviet ballet could lead outsiders to argue
that the conservatism of Soviet ballet was nothing but a reflection of the regime's opposition to artistic innovation and its conservative tastes, of Soviet
"middlebrow culture."[6] Moreover, over time, the Kremlin arguably adopted
certain elements of monarchism's visual culture that made "aristocratic" classical ballet maybe particularly suitable for its purposes: while democracies
encourage a more critical culture that exposes the follies of the elites like
the fairy tale "The Emperor's New Clothes," monarchism endorses a culture
of celebratory visual orientations and expects the public to admire and wor-
ship those at the top.[7] The image of Kremlin leaders taking foreign leaders
to watch *Swan Lake* at the Bolshoi could be seen as powerful expression of
the continuation of certain elements of monarchist culture under the Communist dictatorship.

While these factors certainly contributed to the Soviet Union's ultimate
endorsement of ballet classicism, the opposite argument could also be made.
Given the pressures of the Soviet cultural project on ballet and the regime's
persistent calls for ballets on Soviet topics, nurturing Russia's classical ballet
tradition could also be an act of resistance against Sovietization. In the early
years of Soviet power, when the survival of Russia's classical ballet heritage was still far from assured, this was obviously the case, but the power
of tradition arguably continued to be one of Russian ballet's strongest acts
of resistance to the Soviet system. The meaning of tradition in Soviet ballet

proved at times a fluid concept open to reinvention, but Dudinskaya's resistance to expose the Kirov's *La Bayadère* to Moscow's gaze in 1959 exemplifies a desire to shield prerevolutionary ballet traditions from the authorities' gaze, a desire that operated at a very fundament level.

Within this context, there has been a lot of debate about the authenticity of the choreographic texts used for Soviet productions of the classics. This is a very important question of great historical interest, but given the fact that Petipa himself would routinely recompose variations for different ballerinas and restage his ballets, if taken to the extreme, this focus on the authenticity of steps can become somewhat academic in light of the continuity and organic evolution of performance tradition and the unity of style that continues to be a hallmark of the Mariinsky and Bolshoi's performances of the classics. Ballet is an art form that lives in space and not on paper. Arguably, Russia's prerevolutionary ballet tradition was saved not because of a faithful preservation of old ballet productions but because ballet was remembered in bodies and souls, and this physical and spiritual memory was reverentially passed on from one generation to the next.

Whether in the classics or in new ballets, on a very basic level the joy of the individual performer and the physical freedom of dance embodied the invincibility of individualism, even in a system that wanted to suppress the individual and their aspirations. Maris Liepa's musings on his interpretation of Crassus in *Spartacus* offer one of the most powerful examples of artistic repossession in this book and shows that there is a reason why dictatorships take the subversive potential of art so seriously: interpretation cannot be controlled, and even supposedly simple messages leave leftovers of meaning that are open to interpretation. According to official ideology, Crassus was supposed to be Spartacus's evil opponent, but Liepa's interpretation of the Roman leader as a defender of Roman civilization against barbarism in a thinly veiled analogy to the Russian revolution demonstrates how the ideological constraints imposed on Soviet artists could increase their capacity for creative thinking.

Totalitarian regimes and dictatorships fear art precisely because of this impossibility to control human thought and individuality. If artists could develop their own interpretation of the parts they danced, audiences could interpret what they saw in their own way as well. But even though their art could offer an escape, many artists were driven to despair by the inhumane system they had to combat and their constant exposure to humiliation by the authorities. The frustration and internal conflict that many artists experienced under the Soviet regime is eloquently expressed in the words of the Kirov ballerina Alla Osipenko, who worked closely with Iakobson: "What sort of fatherland is this when we all think that one must leave it in order to become a human being? . . . I love it madly. . . . I can't imagine life without it."[8]

Despite the human costs the Soviet system imposed on its artists, ballet undoubtedly benefited from strong state support and a state-sponsored mindset that promoted a high regard for cultural achievements and a popularization of high culture as core value of Soviet civilization. In prerevolutionary Russia, the Mariinsky and the Bolshoi and their schools were the only state-funded public ballet theaters and schools, but by 1947, there were thirty-one state opera and ballet theaters and fifteen state choreographic institutes across the Soviet Union. Eleven of the opera and ballet theaters were located in the Russian Soviet Federative Socialist Republic.[9] With the expansion of Soviet power, ballet made forays into remote parts of the Soviet Union, and the Vaganova system of ballet training and artistic exchanges linked ballet in the Central and Eastern European satellites to Russia.

Swans of the Kremlin ends with the premiere of *Spartacus* in 1968. The 1970s and 1980s were decades beset by different problems that would warrant a separate study. For the Kirov Ballet, the years of stagnation under Brezhnev were a period of crisis overshadowed by the defections of Natalia Makarova in 1970 and of Mikhail Baryshnikov in 1974, by the negative international attention created by Valery Panov's and his wife Galina Ragozina's request to emigrate to Israel in 1974, and by Yuri Solov'ev's suicide in 1977. But even during these years of crisis, great artists continued to emerge, enchanting their audiences. In 1977, Oleg Vinogradov became the company's choreographer in chief. Slowly, works by foreign choreographers began to enter the ensemble's repertoire. At the Bolshoi, the 1970s continued to be defined by Yuri Grigorovich. In the late 1970s and 1980s, Grigorovich began to be criticized for an increasingly dictatorial leadership style, and some of the company's biggest stars, such as Maya Plisetskaya, Maris Liepa, Ekaterina Maksimova, and Vladimir Vasil'ev, began to revolt against the monopoly of one choreographer, putting them on collision course with Grigorovich. In the final years of the Soviet Union, artists of both companies began to explore new artistic opportunities that presented themselves as a result of greater openness to the West during the heady days of Gorbachev's perestroika and glasnost.

In the chaos of the immediate post-Soviet era, it could only be hoped that Russia would manage to maintain its rich ballet tradition. Ironically, if the ballet dancer had once been the symbol of prerevolutionary aristocratic culture after the October Revolution, ballet's successful incorporation into the Soviet cultural project could now turn the ballet dancer into a symbol of the human costs of the collapse of communism and the Soviet Union. In 1998, the contemporary Ukrainian artist Arsen Savadov created the Donbass Chocolate project that comprises photographs showing grimy Donbass miners in tutus. The project was auctioned off by Sotheby's. According to the auction catalogue, Soviet propaganda equated miners to heroes and ballet was considered the leading example of classical Russian culture, but after the collapse of the Soviet Union, miners descended into great poverty and the neglect of ballet forced dancers to emigrate. Savadov, on the other hand, sees an additional dimension to his photos of miners in tutus: miners symbolize a huge tragedy, but "this is the only social group whose power was equal to that of artists." The tutus in Savadov's picture therefore reflect the ballet dancer's status as the most recognizable personification of the "Soviet" artist.[10]

Despite initial turmoil after the collapse of the Soviet Union, the Kirov —which has reverted back to its prerevolutionary name, the Mariinsky— and the Bolshoi Ballet companies have successfully defended their place of honor among the best ballet companies in the world. For many, they continue to be the standard bearers of classical ballet. With the passage of time, the Bolshoi and the Mariinsky now seem increasingly interested in both reconstructing treasures of the prerevolutionary repertoire and in taking a fresh look at their Soviet heritage as an opportunity to maintain a unique identity in an increasingly globalized world where the repertoire of the major international ballet companies is looking remarkably similar across geographic boundaries. Ballet continues to flourish in Russia, and now that the political-ideological restrictions on artistic autonomy in the world of Russian ballet have been confined to the dustbin of history, we may even allow ourselves to sum up the Soviet experience in ballet with the following words: "The people who were reading the most were also dancing the most. The general collectivization was nothing in comparison to the general balletization of the country."[11]

Appendix 1

A WHO'S WHO

The following biographical entries focus on those aspects of each individual's life that are most relevant for this book. Unless noted otherwise, entries are based on *Russkii balet entsiklopediia* (Moscow: Bol'shaia rosiiskaia entsiklopediia, "Soglasie," 1997); Arsen Degen and Igor' Stupnikov, *Peterburgskii balet, 1903–2003* (St. Petersburg: Baltiiskie Sezony, 2003); and Debra Craine and Judith Mackrell, *The Oxford Dictionary of Dance* (Oxford: Oxford University Press, 2000). Until February 1918, Russia used the Julian calendar, which ran thirteen days behind the Gregorian calendar used in Western Europe. Where applicable, dates are given in both the Julian and Gregorian calendar.

GEORGE BALANCHINE (orginally Georgii Balanchivadze; 9 [22] January 1904, St. Petersburg–30 April 1983, New York) was a dancer, arguably the most influential choreographer for twentieth-century ballet, and the chief architect of ballet in the United States. He graduated from the Petrograd Theatrical Institute in 1921 and danced with the former Mariinsky until 1924.[1] Balanchine began to choreograph while still in Russia and danced in Lopukhov's *Dance Symphony*. He left Russia and joined Diaghilev in 1924 and became the chief choreographer of the Ballets Russes within a year. He went to the United States on Lincoln Kirstein's invitation and founded the School of American Ballet in 1934. Subsequently, he and Kirstein founded the New York City Ballet (for two years known as the Ballet Society) in 1946. Balanchine's musically driven choreographic vision of neoclassical ballet became the most influential choreographic movement in twentieth-century ballet in the West: Balanchine believed that dance was visualized music. His choreography was firmly based on classical ballet technique but filtered through his own, innovative personal style. He stripped ballet of narrative and theatrical settings. During the Cold War, Balanchine's nonnarrative ballets were seen as the antithesis to Soviet ballet's full-length, narrative ballets. Major works include *Apollon Musagète* (1928), *Prodigal Son* (1929), *Serenade* (1934), *Le Baiser de la Fée* (1937), *Card Game* (1937), *Concerto Barocco* (1941), *Ballet Imperial* (1941, later renamed *Tschaikovsky Piano Concerto No. 2*), *The Four Temperaments* (1946), *Orpheus* (1948), *Le Palais de Cristal* (1947), *La Valse* (1951), *Scotch Symphony* (1952), *The Nutcracker, Western Symphony*, and *Ivesiana* (1954), *Allegro Brillante* (1956), *Agon* (1957), *Stars and Stripes* and *The Seven Deadly Sins* (1958), *Tschaikovsky Pas de Deux* and *Liebeslieder Walzer* (1960), *A Midsummer Night's Dream* (1962), *Jewels* (called the first full-length plotless ballet, 1967), *Who Cares?* (1970), *Ballo della Regina* (1978), *Robert Schumann's "Davidsbündlertänze"* and *Walpurgisnacht Ballet* (1980), and *Mozartiana* (re-created for the Tschaikovsky Festival of 1981).

IGOR' BEL'SKY (28 March 1925, Leningrad–3 July 1999, St. Petersburg) was a dancer, choreographer, and pedagogue. Bel'sky graduated from the Leningrad Choreographic Institute in 1943, danced with the Kirov, 1943–1963, and developed into one of the company's leading character dancers. Artistic director (*glavnyi baletmeister*) of the ballet of the Leningrad Maly Theater, 1962–1973, and of the Kirov Ballet, 1973–1977, he taught the course Art of the Choreographer at the Leningrad Conservatory, 1962–1964 and from 1966 onward; from 1992 until his death, he was artistic director of the Academy of Russian Ballet named after A. Ia. Vaganova. One of the most important innovative choreographers of the late 1950s and 1960s, Bel'sky was a "symphonic" choreographer and a central figure in the choreographic battle between choreographic symphonism and *drambalet*. He produced works on contemporary, Soviet topics, abstracting the action and setting his ballets in pure dance, using minimalist sets and costumes. Major works include *Coast of Hope* (1959) and *Leningrad Symphony* (1961).

VAKHTANG CHABUKIANI (27 February [12 March] 1910, Tiflis–6 April 1992, Tbilisi) was a dancer, choreographer, and pedagogue. He trained locally and enrolled at the Leningrad Choreographic Institute in 1926. He danced with the Kirov from 1929 until 1941. A dancer of the heroic type, he was one of the leading stars of the drambalet generation, combining virtuosity with expressive acting. Fearlessly virtuosic, he took male dancing to a new level. From 1941 until 1973, he was the director of the ballet ensemble of the Paliashvili Theater in Tbilisi. He headed the Tbilisi Choreographic Institute from 1950 until 1973. Major roles include Siegfrid (*Swan Lake*), Solor (*La Bayadère*), Slave (*Le Corsaire*), Basil (*Don Quixote*), Albert (*Giselle*), Jerome (*Flames of Paris*), Kerim (*Partisan Days*), Andrei (*Taras Bulba*), Dzhardzhi (*Heart of the Mountain*), and Frondoso (*Laurenzia*). Major works include *Heart of the Mountain* (1938), *Laurenzia* (1939), and *Othello* (1957).

MIKHAIL CHULAKI (6 [19] November 1908, Simferopol'–29 January 1989, Moscow) was a composer and pedagogue. Chulaki served as the Bolshoi Theater's director from 1955 until 1959 and as its director and artistic director from 1963 until 1970. He graduated from the Leningrad Conservatory in 1931, was chairman of the artistic council on choreography under the auspices of the USSR Ministry of Culture, composed several ballets, and taught at the Leningrad (1933–1934, 1944–1948) and Moscow conservatories (from 1948, from 1962 as professor).

CHARLES-LOUIS DIDELOT (1767, Stockholm–7 [19] November 1837, Kiev) was a French dancer, choreographer, and teacher. Didelot studied in Stockholm and in Paris with Dauberval, Noverre, and others. He was appointed leading dancer under Noverre at the Paris Opera in 1791. One of the most influential choreographers of his time, he was influenced by Noverre's and Dauberval's ballet d'action. He staged his most famous ballet, *Zephir and Flora*, in London in 1796. He was the most important figure in Russian ballet during the early nineteenth century, transforming St. Petersburg into one of the leading ballet centers. In 1801, he headed the ballet department of the Petersburg Theatrical Institute and achieved fame for the ballets he staged. In 1811, he had to leave Russia because of the war with France but returned in 1816 and staged more than forty ballets and divertissements in St. Petersburg. He retired in 1829 from the St. Petersburg company following a conflict with the directorate of the Imperial Theaters. Major works include *Apollo and Daphne* (1802), *Cupid and Psyche* (1810), and *The Prisoner of the Caucasus* (1823).

NATALIA DUDINSKAYA (8 [21] August 1912, Kharkov–29 January 2003, St. Petersburg) was a dancer and teacher. Dudinskaya graduated from the Leningrad Choreographic Institute as Vaganova's student in 1931; she danced with the Kirov, 1931–1962, and was a brilliant virtuoso with a sparkling temperament. She was the leading female heroic dancer at the Kirov during the drambalet era, and she dominated the Kirov Ballet for much of her career, especially after Galina Ulanova's departure for the Bolshoi. She was married to Konstantin Sergeev, taught the Class of Perfection at the Kirov from 1951, was the leading teacher at the Leningrad Choreographic Institute from 1964 onward, and served as repetiteur at the Kirov, 1963–1978. Major roles include Odette-Odile (*Swan Lake*), Aurora (*The Sleeping Beauty*), Masha (*Nutcracker*), Kitri (*Don Quixote*), Giselle (*Giselle*), Raymonda (*Raymonda*),

Mireille de Poitiers (*Flames of Paris*), Coralli (*Lost Illusions*), Laurencia (*Laurencia*), Cinderella (*Cinderella*), and Sari (*Paths of Thunder*)

MIKHAIL FOKINE (23 April [5 May] 1880, St. Petersburg–22 August 1942, New York) was a dancer, choreographer, and teacher. Fokine graduated from the Petersburg Theatrical Institute in 1898 and joined the Mariinsky, where he worked—with interruption—from 1898 until 1918. Fokine wrote ballet history as an innovative choreographer, but he was also an excellent dancer. As a choreographer, he was a pioneering influence on twentieth-century ballet: wanting to turn ballet into a more serious, integrated art form, he rejected the traditional division in nineteenth-century ballets between dance and pantomime expressed in a conventionalized system of gestures. He argued that instead of creating dances out of readymade dance movements, each ballet needed to be expressed in its own, new form, corresponding to the ballet's subject. The Mariinsky's conservative directorate looked at his ideas with hostility, and he accepted Diaghilev's invitation to join the Ballets Russes, where he put his ideas into practice (1909–1914), while continuing to work for the Imperial Theaters on occasion, returning to St. Petersburg in 1914 after falling out with Diaghilev. He left Russia in 1918. His most famous ballets were created for the Ballets Russes in a creative collaboration with composers like Stravinsky and artists like Léon Bakst. Major works include *Le Pavillon d'Armide* (1907), *The Dying Swan* (1907), *Les Sylphides* (1907; also known as *Chopiniana*), the Polovtsian dances from *Prince Igor* (1909), *Firebird* (1910), *Scheherazade* (1910), *Le Spectre de la Rose* (1911), and *Petrushka* (1911).

MIKHAIL GABOVICH (24 November [7 December] 1905, Velikie Guliaki–12 July 1965, Moscow) was a dancer and teacher. Gabovich graduated from the Moscow Choreographic Institute in 1924 and danced with the Bolshoi from 1924 to 1952. He was one of the company's leading principal dancers. From 1951, he taught at the Moscow Choreographic Institute. He also published articles on ballet. Major roles include Solor (*La Bayadère*), Désiré (*Sleeping Beauty*), Basil (*Don Quixote*), Siegfried (*Swan Lake*), Albert (*Giselle*), Jean de Brienne (*Raymonda*), Vazlav (*The Fountain of Bakhchisarai*), Evgeny (*The Bronze Horseman*), and Romeo (*Romeo and Juliet*).

ALEKSANDR GORSKY (6 [18] August 1871, St. Petersburg–20 October 1924, Moscow) was a dancer, choreographer, and teacher. Gorsky graduated from the Petersburg Theatrical Institute in 1889, danced with the Mariinsky, 1889–1900, and was the ballet regisseur (from 1901) and chief choreographer (1902–1924) of the Bolshoi Ballet, leading the company until his death in 1924. As a reformer of Russian ballet in the early twentieth century, he tried to overcome conventions of nineteenth-century ballet, most notably the division between dance and pantomime in ballet productions, and sought to give ballets greater dramatic relevance. The Moscow Art Theater under Stanislavsky exerted great influence on him. His production of *Don Quixote* (1900) for the Bolshoi remains one of his most lasting legacies. Major works include *Gudule's Daughter* (1902, based on *The Hunchback of Notre Dame*) and *Salambo* (1910).

YURI GRIGOROVICH (2 January 1927, Leningrad–) was a dancer and choreographer. Grigorovich graduated from the Leningrad Choreographic Institute in 1946 and danced with the Kirov, 1946–1961. He was a choreographer at the Kirov, 1961–1964, and served as chief choreographer of the Bolshoi Ballet, 1964–1995, and the company's artistic director, 1988–1995. Since 2008, he has been ballet master at the Bolshoi. Grigorovich is the choreographer most closely associated with the rise of choreographic symphonism in the 1950s and 1960s and is arguably the most important Soviet choreographer of the second half of the twentieth century, creating full-length, narrative ballets expressed in dance, not pantomime, that focused on the psychology of their main characters. He was instrumental in shaping the worldwide perception of Soviet ballet as the Bolshoi's long-standing principal choreographer. He was criticized for pushing the Bolshoi into artistic stagnation during the later years of his long tenure at the company's helm. In addition to his productions of the major classics, major works include *The Stone Flower* (1957), *The Legend of Love* (1961), *Spartacus* (1968), *Ivan the Terrible* (1975), *Angara* (1976), and *The Golden Age* (1982).

ALEKSEI GVOZDEV (9 [21] March 1887, St. Petersburg–10 April 1939, Leningrad) was a theater and literature specialist, critic, and teacher. Gvozdev graduated from St. Petersburg University and taught at the Leningrad Pedagogical Institute from 1920 onward, heading the Institute of Art History. His views on ballet were expressed in a series of articles in *Zhizn' iskusstva* in 1928. His theoretical views on ballet, advocating its dramatization, influenced the development of Soviet ballet in the 1930s. His students included Yuri Slonimsky and Ivan Sollertinsky. He dismissed the significance of classical dance for ballet, considering it formal and purely decorative, ascribing instead great significance to pantomime, pantomimic and character dance, and calling for a dramatization of the ballet theater.

LEONID IAKOBSON (2 [15] January 1904, St. Petersburg–17 October 1975) was a dancer and choreographer. Iakobson graduated from the Leningrad

Choreographic Institute, danced with the Kirov, 1926–1933, was a dancer and choreographer at the Bolshoi, 1933–1942, and was choreographer at the Kirov, 1942–1950 and 1955–1975; in 1969, he founded his own ensemble in Leningrad, Choreographic Miniatures. A follower of Fokine, Iakobson always swam against the current. His life in ballet spanned most of the Soviet period. Iakobson's vision of ballet centered on a radical break with its classical past through the creation of uniquely new, nonclassical dance steps, putting him on a collision course with the defenders of Russia's classical ballet tradition. While most of ballet's iconoclastic critics in the 1920s were from outside the ballet profession, Iakobson became one of the rare voices calling for a radical break with ballet's classical base from within. In 1930, he created his first major choreographic work when he staged the second act of Shostakovich's ballet *The Golden Age*, relying heavily on athletic-acrobatic movements.[2] A master of the choreographic miniature, his major longer ballets include *Shurale* (1950), *Solveig* (1952), *Spartacus* (1956), *The Bedbug* (1962), *The Twelve* (1964), and *Land of Miracles* (1967).

IRINA KOLPAKOVA (22 May 1933, Leningrad–) was a leading ballerina of the Kirov, renowned for the purity of her classical style and considered one of the greatest representatives of the academic St. Petersburg style. She graduated from the Leningrad Choreographic Institute from Vaganova's class in 1951 and was the last ballerina trained by the great pedagogue. She danced with the Kirov, 1951–1995. Her most celebrated roles of the classical repertoire included Aurora (*The Sleeping Beauty*) and Raymonda (*Raymonda*). Her work with the choreographic reformers of the 1950s and 1960s, Yuri Grigorovich and Igor' Bel'sky, opened new, more contemporary artistic horizons for her. She created the roles of Katerina (Grigorovich, *The Stone Flower*), Shirin (Grigorovich, *The Legend of Love*), and His Beloved (Bel'sky, *Shores of Hope*). From 1971, she worked as pedagogue-repetiteur at the Kirov. Since 1989, she has worked as a ballet master for American Ballet Theater.

GEORGY KORKIN (1904, St. Petersburg–?) was a director of the Kirov Theater (1959–1962). His biography clearly showed the hallmarks of a Soviet cultural bureaucrat: he finished middle school and worked as a worker in the First May Factory and, after serving in the Red Army, in the Elektrik factory. In 1929, he became a member of the CPSU. One year later, he graduated from the vocal department of the Musical Technikum and embarked on the career of a Soviet cultural bureaucrat. He occupied the post of director in major dramatic and musical theaters in Leningrad, including the Pushkin Theater, the Leningrad Dramatic Theater, the theater named after Lenin's Komsomol, the Maly Opera Theater, and the Bolshoi Dramatic

Theater named after Gorky. He was repeatedly elected member of the Rai-kom of the CPSU and deputy of Leningrad rayon soviets.[3]

VERA KRASOVSKAYA (29 August [11 September] 1915, Petrograd–15 August 1999, St. Petersburg) was a dancer, ballet historian, and critic. She graduated from the Leningrad Choreographic Institute from Vaganova's class into the Kirov Ballet in 1933. In 1941, she began to publish articles on ballet. One of the most respected and influential ballet historians and critics of the postwar Soviet period, Krasovskaya emerged as one of the most vocal advocates of dance symphonism in the choreographic polemics of the 1950s. Her major publications include *Russkii baletnyi teatr ot vozniknoveniia do serediny XIX veka* (Russian ballet theater from its beginnings until the mid-nineteenth century) (1958); *Russkii baletnyi teatr vtoroi poloviny XIX veka* (Russian ballet theater of the second half of the nineteenth century) (1963); *Russkii baletnyi teatr nachala XX veka. 1. Khoreografy, 2. Tantsovshchiki* (Russian ballet theater of the early twentieth century, vol. 1: Choreographers; vol. 2: Dancers) (1971–1972); *Stati o balete* (Articles about ballet) (1967); and *Zapad-noevropeiskii baletnyi teatr: Ocherki istorii ot istokov do serediny XVIII veka* (West-European ballet theater: From its origins until the mid-eighteenth century) (1979).

VIKTORINA KRIGER (28 March [9 April] 1893, St. Petersburg–23 December 1978, Moscow) was a dancer and ballet critic. Kriger graduated from the Moscow Choreographic Institute and danced with the Bolshoi from 1910 until 1949, reaching ballerina status. In 1929, together with I. Shlugleit, she founded the Moscow Art Ballet, becoming its artistic director and leading ballerina. The company evolved into today's second most important ballet company in Moscow, the ballet company of the musical theater named after Stanislavsky-Nemirovich-Danchenko. She was the director of the Bolshoi Theater's museum from 1955 until 1963. Major roles include Kitri (*Don Quixote*), Odette-Odile (*Swan Lake*), Tsar-Maiden (*The Little Hump-backed Horse*), and Tao Khoa (*The Red Poppy*).

MATHILDA KSCHESSINSKAYA (19 [31] August 1872, Ligovo–6 December 1971, Paris) was a dancer and teacher. She graduated into the Mariinsky Ballet from the St. Petersburg Theatrical Institute in 1890 and performed with the company until 1917, reducing her performances at the Mariinsky to guest performances after 1904. She was appointed prima ballerina assoluta in 1895, the only ballerina other than the Italian ballerina Pierina Legnani to be officially awarded this title. She left Russia for France in 1920 and died in Paris in 1971. A glamorous dancer of great virtuosity and spirit, her career greatly benefited from her ties to the Romanovs, a connection empowering her as the de facto ruler of the Mariinsky Ballet: she was mistress of Nicholas II before he became tsar and then of Grand Duke Andrei, whom she married in 1921. Major roles include Paquita (*Paquita*), Odette-Odile (*Swan Lake*), Nikiya (*La Bayadère*), Sugar Plum Fairy (*Nutcracker*), Aspicia (*The Pharaoh's Daughter*), Aurora (*The Sleeping Beauty*), and Esmeralda (*Esmeralda*).

MARIS LIEPA (27 July 1936, Riga–26 March 1989, Moscow) was a dancer, choreographer, and teacher. Liepa graduated from the Moscow Choreographic Institute in 1955, danced with the Stanislavsky Ballet, 1956–1960, and then danced with the Bolshoi, 1960–1984. A masculine, strong, and precise dancer of assured and generous movements, he was one of the most interesting "dancing actors" of his generation, being most well known for creating Crassus in Grigorovich's *Spartacus*. Major roles include Basil (*Don Quixote*), Albert (*Giselle*), Siegfried (*Swan Lake*), Jean de Brienne (*Raymonda*), Ferkhad (*Legend of Love*), Désiré (*The Sleeping Beauty*), and Romeo (*Romeo and Juliet*).

FEDOR LOPUKHOV (8 [20] October 1886, St. Petersburg–28 January 1973, Leningrad) was a dancer, choreographer, and teacher. He graduated from the St. Petersburg Theatrical Institute in 1905, danced with the Mariinsky Ballet, 1905–1909 and 1911–1922, danced with the Bolshoi in 1909–1910, and toured the United States in 1910. He was the artistic director of the former Mariinsky/Kirov Ballet, 1922–1930, 1944–1945, and 1955–1956; he founded and directed the ballet company at Leningrad's Maly Theater, 1931–1935; and he served as director of the choreography department of the Leningrad Conservatory, 1962–1967. Lopukhov was one of the most important figures in Soviet ballet in the 1920s and 1930s, both as an innovative choreographer and as a guardian of the Mariinsky's prerevolutionary classical heritage, even though his restorations of old ballets caused some controversy. Lopukhov is of seminal importance for theorizing the kind of abstract, musically driven choreography that became the key feature of ballet modernism in the twentieth century. He tried to implement his program in the ballet *Dance Symphony: The Magnificence of the Universe* (1923). In his book *Puti baletmeistera*, published in 1925, Lopukhov developed several, at times somewhat dogmatic, rules for integrating dance and music. After *Pravda*'s attack against Lopukhov's ballet *The Bright Stream* during the antiformalism campaign in 1936, he was pushed to the sidelines of Soviet ballet. For the next ten years, he staged only very few new ballets. From 1937 until 1941, he organized choreographers' courses at the Leningrad Choreographic Institute. In 1944–1945, Lopukhov was again briefly the artistic director of the Kirov Ballet. After the war, he restored the classical repertoire, and in 1947, he staged Boris Asafiev's ballet *A Spring Fairy Tale*.[4] Lopukhov played an instrumental role in the return of choreographic symphonism in the 1950s. Major works include *Dance Symphony* (1923), *Pulcinella* (1926), *The Ice Maiden* (1927), *The Bolt* (1931), *The Bright Stream* (1935), and *A Spring Fairy Tale* (1947).

ASKOL'D MAKAROV (3 May 1925, Novo-Masal'skoe Zubtsovskoe–24 December 2000, St. Petersburg) was a dancer. Makarov graduated from the Leningrad Choreographic Institute and danced with the Kirov, 1943–1970. He was a heroic dancer with a special gift for psychological mime and sculptural gesture. Makarov worked closely with Leonid Iakobson, creating—and remaining unsurpassed in—leading roles in many of his ballets. He also was the artistic director of Iakobson's ensemble Choreographic Miniatures, 1976–2000, after the choreographer's death. Major roles include Ali Batyr (*Shurale*), Spartacus (*Spartacus*), Prometheus (*Choreographic Miniatures*), Poet (*The Bedbug*), the Fisherman (*Shores of Hope*), Siegfried (*Swan Lake*), Solor (*La Bayadère*), Basil (*Don Quixote*), and Jean de Brienne (*Raymonda*).

NATALIA MAKAROVA (21 November 1940, Leningrad–) ranks among the most famous ballerinas of the twentieth century. She graduated from the Leningrad Choreographic Institute in 1959. A leading dancer with the Kirov, she danced with the company until her defection while on tour in London in 1970. In the West, she built a highly successful freelance career, dancing as a principal dancer with American Ballet Theater and as principal guest artist with the Royal Ballet. Makarova combined a unique lyrical gift with an ability to imbue her heroines with a passionate emotionality. In the West, her dancing greatly influenced other dancers, and by staging her own productions of the classics reflecting her Kirov upbringing, she has had a great impact on classical dance in the West. She has danced all major roles of the classical repertoire and many works by contemporary choreographers. Her most famous roles in the classical repertoire included Odette (*Swan Lake*) and Giselle (*Giselle*).

EKATERINA MAKSIMOVA (1 February 1939, Moscow–28 April 2009, Moscow) was a dancer and repetiteur. She graduated from the Moscow Choreographic Institute in 1958 and danced with the Bolshoi, 1958–1989. She was a delicate, graceful, and feminine dancer of great charm with an elegant, academic technique; she was one of the best-loved dancers of her generation. She married Vladimir Vasil'ev, with whom she formed one of the most popular partnerships on the Bolshoi stage. She performed more and more abroad with Vasil'ev as they began to openly criticize Grigorov-ich in the 1980s. Major roles include Masha (*Nutcracker*), Odette-Odile (*Swan Lake*), Aurora (*Sleeping Beauty*), Kitri (*Don Quixote*), Giselle (*Giselle*), Phrygia (*Spartacus*), Anyuta (*Anyuta*), Katerina (*The Stone Flower*), Sylph (*Chopiniana*), and Juliet (*Romeo and Juliet*).

ASAF MESSERER (6 [19] November 1903, Vilnius–7 March 1992, Moscow) was a dancer, choreographer, and teacher. He graduated from the Moscow Choreographic Institute in 1921, joined the Bolshoi upon graduation, and was a principal dancer until 1954. A virtuoso dancer, Messerer became one of the most important teachers at the Bolshoi, where he began instructing in 1923, teaching the class for the Bolshoi's leading ballerinas and dancers from 1946 onward. He was also Maya Plisetskaya's uncle.

IGOR' MOISEEV (8 [21] January 1906, Kiev–2 November 2007, Moscow) was a dancer and choreographer. Moiseev graduated from the Moscow Choreographic Institute in 1924, danced with the Bolshoi, 1924–1939, and founded and directed the USSR Folk Dance Ensemble (known abroad as the Moiseyev Dance Company) in 1937, the first professional folk dance ensem-ble, which he led until his death in 2007. Moiseev started his choreographic career while still a dancer with the Bolshoi. He turned to folk dance after he felt that all choreographic possibilities at the Bolshoi had been closed to him in the aftermath of the antiformalism campaign of 1936.[5]

GEORGY NIKOFORIVICH ORLOV (1900–1961) was born the son of peasants. He finished middle school, worked in a local branch of the teach-ers' union, at the military registration and enlistment office, and as tax in-spector of the finance department. His voice attracted attention at amateur performances, and he was sent to Leningrad to study at a music school. While studying, he performed at agit-studios, agit-theaters, and the State Varieté. In 1926, he joined the Leningrad Conservatory, in 1931 the Maly Opera Theater, and in 1937 he started to sing at the Kirov. He joined the company in 1941 and performed as a soloist. In 1949, he became direc-tor of the Maly Opera Theater. In 1951, he was appointed director of the Kirov Theater and became a deputy of Leningrad City Soviet of Workers' Deputies.[6]

ALLA OSIPENKO (16 June 1932, Leningrad–) graduated from Vaganova's class at the Leningrad Choreographic Institute in 1950 and danced with the Kirov until 1970. She was a great classical ballerina with a beautifully pro-portioned body with elongated limbs, but her work with Yuri Grigorovich and Igor' Bel'sky demonstrated her unique affinity for the more angular graphics of contemporary choreography. Her most famous role became the Mistress of the Copper Mountain, the part she created as a young dancer in Grigorovich's *The Stone Flower* (1957). In 1971, she caused a scandal by demonstratively leaving the Kirov in search for greater artistic freedom, joining Leonid Iakobson's ensemble Choreographic Miniatures until 1973. Subsequently, she danced with Lenkontsert and from 1977 until 1982 with Boris Eifman's company. From the late 1980s, she taught classical dance in the West, and since 2007, she has been a repetiteur at the ballet company of the Mikhailovsky Theater in St. Petersburg.

MARIUS PETIPA (11 March 1818, Marseilles–14 July 1910, Gurzuf/Crimea) was a dancer, choreographer, and teacher. He trained with his father and August Vestris, but his career took off in earnest after his arrival in St. Petersburg in 1847, first as dancer with the Mariinsky Ballet. He was appointed choreographer for the Mariinsky in 1862, the year of his first major choreographic success, *The Pharaoh's Daughter*. From 1869 to 1903, he was the company's chief choreographer, defining St. Petersburg's golden age as the international capital of classical ballet. He choreographed about fifty ballets for the imperial theaters in St. Petersburg and Moscow, including *The Pharaoh's Daughter* (1862), *Don Quixote* (1869), *La Bayadère* (1877), *The Sleeping Beauty* (1890), *Swan Lake* (1895), *Raymonda* (1898), and restagings of French classics in productions that still form the basis for productions all over the world today, including *Paquita* (1881), *Coppélia* (1884), *Giselle* (1884), *Esmeralda* (1886), and *Le Corsaire* (1858, 1868, and 1899). Petipa remains the defining choreographer of classical ballet.

ANDREI PETROV (2 September 1930, Leningrad–) is a composer. He graduated from the Leningrad Conservatory in composition in 1954. From 1954, he headed the Leningrad organization of the RSFSR Composers' Union. Petrov tried to create an atmosphere beneficial to moderately modernist Leningrad composers at a time when even the concept of a distinctive Petersburg school of composition was rejected in Moscow.[7] He composed several ballets, including *Coast of Hope*. Igor' Bel'sky's production of this ballet was pivotal for the rise of choreographic symphonism.

MAYA PLISETSKAYA (20 November 1925, Moscow–) is a dancer. She graduated from the Moscow Choreographic Institute in 1943 and danced with the Bolshoi, 1943–1990. Plisetskaya is one of the greatest dancers of the second half of the twentieth century. She combines a strong character with a unique style, expressing intense emotions with a graphic style, great fluidity of movement, and clear forms; a free spirit eternally thirsty for the new, she famously protested against the Bolshoi management. Plisetskaya began to stage her own ballets, including *Anna Karenina* (1972), *The Seagull* (1980), and *Lady with a Lapdog* (1985), and worked abroad with foreign choreographers, most notably Maurice Béjart and Roland Petit; she had a dancing career of rare longevity, performing into her seventies. Major roles include Odette-Odile (*Swan Lake*), Kitri (*Don Quixote*), Raymonda (*Raymonda*), Aurora (*The Sleeping Beauty*), Myrtha (*Giselle*), Carmen (*Carmen Suite*), Laurencia (*Laurencia*), Mistress of the Copper Mountain (*The Stone Flower*), Mekhmene Banu (*Legend of Love*), Rose (*La Rose Malade*), Isadora (*Isadora*), and Leda (*Leda*).

PETR IVANOVICH RACHINSKY (1912–1994) was director of the Kirov Theater, 1962–1973. He graduated from middle school and a musical school, was a member of the CPSU since 1939, and studied at the Pedagogical Institute and at the High Party School of the CPSU in Moscow. In 1937, he became involved in the administration of cultural and artistic institutions as deputy director of the Institute for Theater and Music. For more than six years, he was deputy head of the Department for Cultural Affairs and also headed the city department of cultural educational work of the Lengorispolkom. Before his appointment as director of the Kirov, he was deputy director of the Leningrad Varieté (Estrada), deputy director and director of the Leningrad Comedy Theater, director of Lenknigi, and director of the Leningrad Television Studio.[8] Rachinsky was a career cultural bureaucrat whom Makarova characterized as "an ex-fireman, whose all-powerful party card blanketed the directorate at the theater."[9]

KONSTANTIN SERGEEV (20 February [5 March] 1910, St. Petersburg–1 April 1992, St. Petersburg) was a dancer, choreographer, and teacher. Sergeev graduated from the Leningrad Choreographic Institute in 1930 and was a leading dancer at the Kirov, 1930–1961. A dancer of natural nobility and strict academic forms who was also a devoted actor, his psychological interpretation of the classical repertoire influenced future generations; he was one of the most celebrated dancers of the drambalet generation, excelling in the lyrical-romantic repertoire. His onstage partnership with Galina Ulanova in the 1930s and early 1940s has entered Russian ballet history. In the postwar period, his stage life was most closely connected to his second wife, the ballerina Natalia Dudinskaya. Both occupied a central role in the life of the Kirov Ballet and its school until their deaths. Conservative in his artistic tastes, Sergeev shaped the Kirov Ballet as its artistic director, 1951–1955 and 1960–1970. He also staged Petipa's classics for the Kirov:

Raymonda (1948), *Swan Lake* (1950), and *The Sleeping Beauty* (1952). His own ballets as choreographer include *Cinderella* (1946), *Path of Thunder* (1958), and *Far Planet* (1963). He taught classical dance at the Leningrad Choreographic Institute from 1931, serving as the school's artistic director, 1938–1940 and 1973–1992. Major roles include Siegfried (*Swan Lake*), Albert (*Giselle*), Désiré (*The Sleeping Beauty*), Jean de Brienne (*Raymonda*), Actor (*Flames of Paris*), Vazlav (*The Fountain of Bakhchisarai*), Lucien (*Lost Illusions*), Romeo (*Romeo and Juliet*), Prince (*Cinderella*), Evgeny (*The Bronze Horseman*), and Lenni (*Path of Thunder*).

IVAN SOLLERTINSKY (20 November [3 December] 1902, Vitebsk–11 February 1944, Novosibirsk) was a musicologist and ballet specialist (*baletoved*). Sollertinsky graduated from the Petrograd Institute for Art History in 1923 and from the Romance and Germanic Languages Department of Leningrad University in 1924. He taught at the Leningrad Choreographic Institute and the Leningrad and Moscow Conservatories. He joined the former Mariinsky's artistic council in 1928 and, from 1939, was a professor at the Leningrad Conservatory and artistic director of the Leningrad Philharmonic Orchestra. He was primarily known as one of the most important musicologists of the era, as a promoter of modernism in music, and as a steadfast supporter of Shostakovich. In fact, especially at the beginning of his career, Sollertinsky was just as involved in the critical discussion of ballet as in the discussion of music. Emphasizing the importance of "content" in ballet, Sollertinsky was an eloquent advocate of dramatizing dance, radically rejecting classical dance, even though he later somewhat adjusted his position, recognizing the importance of Marius Petipa for contemporary ballet. His views exerted a great influence on the development of Soviet ballet in the 1930s and 1940s.

GALINA ULANOVA (26 December 1909 [8 January 1910], St. Petersburg–21 March 1998, Moscow) was a dancer and teacher. She graduated from the Leningrad Choreographic Institute in 1928 from Vaganova's class and danced with the former Mariinsky/Kirov, 1928–1944, and the Bolshoi, 1944–1960. From 1960, she was repetiteur at the Bolshoi. One of the most legendary dancers of the twentieth century, Ulanova had the rare gift of being able to completely fuse her technique with the dramatic aspect of a role: she didn't dance a character; she became that character. Her movements seemed without physical limit, extending endlessly into space. In her artistic development as a dancer, she moved from lyricism to tragedy. An icon of the drambalet era and of Soviet ballet, she was a public figure but at the same time managed to maintain an impenetrable wall between her public and private personas. Major roles include Odette-Odile (*Swan Lake*), Aurora (*The Sleeping Beauty*), Raymonda (*Raymonda*), Masha (*The Nutcracker*), Giselle (*Giselle*), waltz/nocturne/mazurka (*Chopiniana*), Maria (*The Fountain of Bakhchisarai*), Coralli (*Lost Illusions*), Juliet (*Romeo and Juliet*), and Parasha (*The Bronze Horseman*).

AGRIPPINA VAGANOVA (14 [27] June 1879, St. Petersburg–5 November 1951, Leningrad) was a dancer, teacher, and choreographer. She graduated from the Petersburg Theatrical Institute in 1897 and danced with the Mariinsky Ballet, 1897–1916. Even though she had a very good technique, she was not promoted to ballerina until 1915 but was known as "tsarina of variations." She began to teach at Akim Volynsky's ballet school in St. Petersburg in 1917 and then taught at the Petrograd Choreographic Institute from 1917, teaching the graduating class from 1921 until 1951.[10] She had a great analytical mind, setting out a methodology of classical ballet training that became the basis for professional training across the Soviet Union and influenced professional ballet training in many other countries. Since 1957, the school in St. Petersburg carries her name. She is one of the most important teachers in the history of ballet.

NINETTE DE VALOIS (orig. Edris Stannus; 6 June 1898, Baltiboys, Ireland–8 March 2001) was a dancer, choreographer, teacher, and the founder of the Royal Ballet. She studied locally and with Edouard Espinosa, Cecchetti, and later with Nikolai Legat in London, and she danced in revues and pantomimes before joining Diaghilev's Ballets Russes in 1923, staying with the company until 1925. She opened her own school in 1926 in London, and in 1931 she moved to the school linked to the newly opened Sadler's Wells Theater, which eventually became the Royal Ballet School. Her company, the Vic-Wells Ballet, was renamed the Royal Ballet in 1956.

VLADIMIR VASIL'EV (18 April 1940, Moscow–) is a dancer, choreographer, and teacher. Upon graduation from the Moscow Choreographic Institute in 1958, he danced with the Bolshoi until 1988; a heroic, dynamic virtuoso dancer, he was one of the most loved dancers of his generation, forming one of the Bolshoi's most celebrated partnerships with his wife, Ekaterina Maksimova. He is most famous for creating Spartacus in Grigorovich's *Spartacus*; for many, he embodied the strong male of Grigorovich's Bolshoi. In the 1970s, he started to choreograph his own ballets, and he and Maksimova performed more and more abroad as they began to openly criticize Grigorovich in the 1980s. Vasil'ev served as general and artistic director of the Bolshoi Theater, 1995–2000. Major roles include Basil (*Don*

Quixote), Désiré (*The Sleeping Beauty*), Albert (*Giselle*), Nutracker Prince (*The Nutcracker*), Danila (*The Stone Flower*), Spartacus (*Spartacus*), Ivanushka (*The Little Humpbacked Horse*), and Romeo (*Romeo and Juliet*). Major works include *Ikar* (1971), *Anyuta* (1986), and *Macbeth* (1980).

TATIANA VECHESLOVA (12 [25] February 1910, St. Petersburg–11 July 1991, Leningrad) was one of the Kirov Ballet's great stars during the Stalinist era. She graduated from the Leningrad Choreographic Institute in 1928 and danced with the former Mariinsky/Kirov Ballet, 1928–1953. She taught at the school and was its artistic director, 1952–1954. From 1954 until 1971, she was a repetiteur for the Kirov Ballet. A great ballerina and a great actress, her wide repertoire included dramatic, comic, lyrical, and bravura-virtuoso roles. She participated in the searches and experiments by choreographers such as Lopukhov, Zakharov, Lavrovsky, and Chabukiani. One of her greatest roles was Zarema (*The Fountain of Bakhchisarai*). As repetiteur of the Kirov, she supported the young generation of choreographers and artists.

SIMON VIRSALADZE (31 December 1908 [13 January 1909], Tiflis–7 February 1989, Tbilisi) was a major stage designer. He studied in Tbilisi, Leningrad, and Moscow and was the principal stage designer at the Paliashvili Theater in Tbilisi, 1932–1936, designing both operas and ballets. From 1937, he was an artist and then the principal stage designer at the Kirov Theater, 1945–1962. From 1957, he worked closely with Yuri Grigorovich, collaborating with him on all his major ballets until his death. From 1964 until his death, he was the principal designer of the Bolshoi Ballet. In his work with Grigorovich, Virsaladze defined a new aesthetic for set and costume designs for Soviet ballet, moving away from the painstakingly realist designs of the drambalet era.

NIKOLAI VOLKOV (10 [22] December 1894, Penza–3 April 1965, Moscow) was a critic, theater specialist, and playwright. Volkov wrote—or co-authored—the libretto of many major drambalet productions of the 1930s and 1940s, including *Flames of Paris* (1932), *The Fountain of Bakhchisarai* (1934), *Heart of the Mountain* (under the name *Mzechabuki* at the Teatr Paliashchvili/Tbilisi, 1936; Kirov, 1938), *The Caucasian Prisoner* (Leningrad Maly Theater, 1938), *Mistress into Maid* (Bolshoi Filial, 1946; Leningrad Maly Theater, 1951), and *Cinderella* (Bolshoi, 1945; Kirov, 1946). He also wrote the original *Spartacus* libretto on which Khachaturian based his score.

ROSTISLAV ZAKHAROV (25 August [7 September] 1907, Astrakhan–15 January 1984, Moscow) was a choreographer, director, and teacher. He graduated from the Leningrad Choreographic Institute in 1926 and from the director's department of the Leningrad Theatrical Technikum in 1932. Zakharov danced with the Kiev Theater, 1926–1929, and was a choreographer at the Kirov Theater, 1934–1936, choreographer and opera director at the Bolshoi Theater, 1936–1956, and director of the Bolshoi Ballet, 1936–1939. His first major ballet, *The Fountain of Bakhchisarai* (Kirov Theater, 1934), turned out to be his most important one. It was seen as the birth of drambalet and one of its crowning achievements. The ballet is still in the repertoire of the Mariinsky Ballet. During the preparation of the ballet, Zakharov introduced Stanislavsky's method of character development to the dancers' preparation, asking them to do "table work" and to study Pushkin's poem and materials on the period.[11] Trained originally as a dancer, Zakharov studied directing with Sergei Radlov at the Leningrad Theatrical Technikum. He tried to apply his training as dramatic theater director to the conception of his ballets, but the scope of his choreographic language, the most important tool of a choreographer, was rather limited. From 1946 until his death, he headed the choreography department at the Gosudarstvennyi Institut Teatral'nogo Iskusstva im. A. V. Lunacharskogo (GITIS; Lunacharsky State Institute for Theatre Arts) in Moscow. In the 1950s, Zakharov became a belligerent polemicist who negated the right of any tendency in ballet other than drambalet. In his writings, he outlined a theoretical basis for the position that drambalet was the only form of ballet conforming to socialist realism. Major works include *The Fountain of Bakhchisarai* (1934), *Lost Illusions* (1936), *The Caucasian Prisoner* (1938), *Taras Bulba* (1941), *Cinderella* (1945), *Mistress into Maid* (1946), and *The Bronze Horseman* (1949). Major publications include *Iskusstvo baletmeistera* (1954).

Appendix 2

BALLETS

This appendix provides information on the production of ballets mentioned in the text. It therefore does not provide information on other productions of these ballets unless relevant for this book. I will give production details but no libretto descriptions for those ballets mentioned for repertoire statistics purposes only. If applicable, the original Russian titles are given in parentheses. Please note that several plot summaries (primarily of those ballets regularly performed in the West, such as *Giselle* and Petipa's classics) are derived from Debra Craine and Judith Mackrell, *The Oxford Dictionary of Dance* (Oxford: Oxford University Press, 2000).

Abbreviations

a. acts

c. choreography

m. music

l. libretto

d. designs (sets and costumes)

p. premiere

B. Bolshoi Theater

K. Kirov Theater (name of the Mariinsky Theater, 1935–1992)

M. Mariinsky Theater (to avoid confusion, I will also use this abbreviation when referring to nineteenth-century premieres taking place when the St. Petersburg company still performed in the Bolshoi Theater in St. Petersburg, and for the years 1920–1935, when the former Mariinsky Theater was called the State Academic Theater of Opera and Ballet, GATOB)

Asel'

3 a.; m. V. Vlasov; l. B. Khaliulov, N. Kharitonov, after the story by
C. Aitmatov, *My Little Poplar in a Red Scarf*; c. O. Vinogradov;
d. V. Levental'; p. B., 7 February 1967

The ballet *Asel'* tells the story of the girl Asel', who falls in love with Il'ias, a driver at a motor-transport depot. Il'ias betrays her with Kadicha, the dispatcher of the depot. Asel' leaves and finds a new love in Baitemir, who has fought in the war. When Il'ias suddenly appears at their home, she chooses Baitemir. The ballet was created for the theater season celebrating the fiftieth anniversary of the revolution.

La Bayadère (Baiaderka)

4 a.; m. L. Minkus; l. M. Petipa and S. Khudekov; c. M. Petipa;
d. M. Bocharov, G. Vagner, I. Andreev, and A. Roller; p. M., 23 January
1877

The ballet is set in India. The bayadère (temple dancer) Nikiya loves the warrior Solor. Solor loves her, too, but becomes engaged to the Rajah's daughter Gamzatti. Gamzatti has her rival bitten by a snake; Nikiya dies. In the famous "Kingdom of the Shades" act, which is considered one of Petipa's masterpieces, a remorseful, opium-smoking Solor dreams of meeting his beloved (surrounded by a large female corps de ballet, the shades). In the final act, Gamzatti and Solor's wedding ceremony is interrupted by a vision of Nikiya, visible only to him. As the wedding ceremony is taking place, the gods take vengeance for Nikiya's death: the temple collapses, burying everyone. In an apotheosis, Nikiya and Solor are united in eternal love.

The Bedbug (Klop)

2 a.; m. O. Karavaichuk, F. Otkazov, and G. Firtich; c. and
l. L. Iakobson; d. A. Goncharov, F. Zbarskii, B. Messerer, and
T. Sel'vinskaya; p. K., 24 June 1962

Based on Vladimir Mayakovsky's play of the same name, *The Bedbug* was one of two ballets staged by the Kirov singled out for attack during Khrushchev's showdown with the creative intelligentsia in 1962–1963. The ballet received only fifteen performances. The ballet's music was originally composed by O. Karavaichuk, but the composer and choreographer broke with each other during the production of the ballet, and F. Otkazov was named as composer on the playbill. In 1974, Iakobson's company Choreographic Miniatures showed a new, one-act version of the ballet to the public, using music by Shostakovich.

Ivan Prisypkin, a former party member and a former worker of immaculate proletarian background, fulfills his dream of bourgeois comforts by marrying Elzevira Renaissance, manicurist and cashier of a beauty parlor. The ballet culminates in the wedding cortege deriding the petty-bourgeois philistinism of Prisypkin's world. After the wedding, Prisypkin and his bride are frolicking like two insects on a giant bed with pink satin covers. The ballet ends with Mayakovsky setting his heroes on fire.

Iakobson wanted to make Mayakovsky the real hero of the ballet. Transposing the poet's creative writing process into the realm of the ballet theater, Mayakovsky was shown creating the ballet's different characters by showing them how to move, making the ballet a product of the poet's fantasy. Iakobson fused the first half of Mayakovsky's play of the same name with episodes from the First World War, the revolution, the civil war, and the construction of socialism. He did not manage to include the second part of the play in his ballet.

The Bright Stream (Svetlyi ruchei)

3 a.; m. D. Shostakovich; l. A. Piotrovsky and F. Lopukhov; c. F. Lopukhov; d. M. Bobyshov; p. Leningrad Maly Theater, 4 April 1935; d. V. Dmitriev; p. B., 30 November 1935

2 a.; m. D. Shostakovich; l. A. Piotrovsky and F. Lopukhov; c. A. Ratmansky; d. B. Messerer; p. B., 18 April 2003

The ballet was attacked during the antiformalism campaign of 1936. The accusations hurled against the ballet in the Pravda editorial "Baletnaia fal'sh'" had an important impact on the development of Soviet ballet.

A brigade of artists arrives from the capital to participate in celebrations of a kolkhoz's production success but finds itself entangled in amorous intrigues. The kolkhoz is called "The Bright Stream" and is located in the Kuban. The artists quickly befriend the kolkhozniks. It turns out that Zina, the wife of the agronomist Petr, knows the ballerina of the group well because she also used to study at the ballet school. Petr is fascinated by the ballerina, a fascination shared by an old-fashioned dacha dweller who spends his summers in the kolkhoz. The wife of the dacha dweller in turn falls in love with the ballerina's male dancing partner. The kolkhozniks decide to play a trick on the dacha dweller and the agronomist: Zina dresses up as the ballerina and goes to a rendezvous with her husband, and the male dancer dressed up as the ballerina meets the dacha dweller, while the ballerina disguised as the male dancer meets the dacha dweller's wife. The buffoonery culminates in a mock duel between the ballerina, dressed up as her male partner, and the dacha dweller, in which the ballerina "dies." The next morning, the misunderstandings of the previous night disentangle themselves. The dacha dwellers are being ridiculed, and the agronomist asks his wife for forgiveness. The friendship of the artists and the kolkhozniks is celebrated in a holiday in honor of the successful completion of the fieldwork.[1]

In 2003, Aleksei Ratmansky staged a new production of the ballet for the Bolshoi.

The Bronze Horseman (Mednyi vsadnik)

4 a.; m. R. Glière; l. P. Abolimov; c. Rostislav Zakharov; d. M. Bobyshev; p. K., 14 March 1949

A popular ballet of the *drambalet* genre and based on Pushkin's poem.

Carneval

1 a.; m. R. Schumann; l. and c. M. Fokine; d. L. Bakst; p. M., 6 February 1911; revived 1962

Chopiniana

1 a.; m. F. Chopin, orchestrated by A. Glazunov; c. M. Fokine; p. M., 10 February 1907

The ballet is known as *Les Sylphides* in the West.

Choreographic Miniatures (Khoreograficheskie miniatury)

3 a.; m. various; c. L. Iakobson; costumes by S. Virsaladze and T. Bruni; p. K., 6 January 1959

A collection of different choreographic miniatures.

Cinderella (Zolushka)

3 a.; m. S. Prokofiev; l. N. Volkov; c. R. Zakharov; d. P. Wiliams; p. B., 21 November 1945

3 a.; m. S. Prokofiev; l. N. Volkov; c. K. Sergeev; d. B. Erdman; p. K., 8 April 1946

3 a.; m. S. Prokofiev; l. N. Volkov; c. A. Ratmansky; d. I. Utkin, E. Monakhov, and E. Markovskaya; p. M., 5 March 2002

Coast of Hope (Bereg nadezhdy)

3 a.; m. A. Petrov; l. Y. Slonimsky; c. I. Bel'sky; d. V. Dorrer; p. K., 16 April 1959

An important production marking the rise of choreographic symphonism in the 1950s and 1960s. A choreographic allegory to patriotism and loyalty: a fisherman is stranded on an alien shore and thrown into prison, but neither threats nor temptations can weaken his loyalty to "his shore." The prison walls give way to the power of his loyalty to "his shore" and his friends. The fisherman returns home.

Dance Symphony: The Magnificence of the Universe (also, The Greatness of Creation) (Velichie mirozdaniia, Tants simfoniia)

m. L. Beethoven, Fourth Symphony; scenario and c. F. Lopukhov;
d. costumes by P. Goncharov; p. M., 7 March 1923

The first major attempt at creating a nonnarrative, symphonic ballet. The piece's four themes were titled "Birth of Light," "Triumph of Life over Death," "Awakening of Nature in the Sun of Spring," and "The Cosmogonic Spiral." The eighteen dancers included George Balanchine, Alexandra Danilova, and Leonid Lavrovsky.

Distant Planet (Dalekaia planeta)

3 a.; m. B. Maizel'; l. B. Maizel' and K. Sergeev; c. K. Sergeev;
d. V. Dorrer; p. K., 12 April 1964

A ballet about space, a theme that became popular after Yuri Gagarin's flight.

Don Quixote

4 a.; m. L. Minkus; l. M. Petipa; c. M. Petipa; d. P. Isakov, I. Shangin,
and F. Shen'ian; p. B., 14 December 1869

One of the most famous comedy ballets, a staple of the classical repertoire. The plot centers on the love affair between Kitri and Basil and their successful ploy to escape Kitri's betrothal to the wealthy fop Gamache, a match that has been arranged by her money-loving father, an innkeeper. Don Quixote and his Sancho Panza link the plot together, providing a pretext for the ballet's lyrical vision scene in which Don Quixote dreams of his ideal woman, Dulcinea, danced by the same dancer who dances Kitri. The ballet culminates in Kitri and Basil's wedding.

Egyptian Nights

1 a.; m. A. Arensky; l. M. Fokine, after T. Gautier; c. M. Fokine; p. M.,
8 March 1908; revived 1923 and 1962

Esmeralda

4 a.; m. C. Pugni; l. and c. J. Perrot; p. of a new version by M. Petipa;
M., 1886; new versions by A. Vaganova, in 3 a., K., 23 April 1935 and
15 November 1948; d. for both, V. Khodasevich

Based on Victor Hugo's novel Notre-Dame de Paris.

La Fille mal gardée

2 a.; l. and c. J. Dauberval; m. various popular French songs;
p. Bourdeux Grand Theater, 1 July 1789

In the year of the French Revolution, Jean Dauberval, a student of Noverre, staged the ballet *La Fille mal gardée* in Bourdeaux, a light-hearted comedy and the first ballet that has everyday characters—farmers and peasants— as its heroes. The ballet tells the story of Lise, a farmer's daughter, and her sweetheart Colas, a poor farmer, who try to outwit Lise's mother, who wants her daughter to marry the dim-witted son of a prosperous landowner. Like Noverre, Dauberval believed in the expressiveness of pantomime and gesture and in the power of ballet to tell a story: "I do not want just to please the eyes, I must interest the heart."[2] Various choreographers have created their versions of the ballet since then, for example, Aumer for the Paris Opéra (1828), Didelot for the Mariinsky (1818), and Petipa and Ivanov for the Mariinsky (1885); the most popular version today is Frederick Ashton's version (m. John Lanchbery's arrangement of Hérold's score created in 1828; d. Osbert Lancaster; p. Royal Ballet, 28 January 1960).

Flames of Paris (Plamia Parizha)

4 a.; m. B. Asaf'ev; l. V. Dmitriev and N. Volkov, after F. Gras's novel *Le Marceliers*; c. V. Vainonen; director, S. Radlov; d. V. Dmitriev;
p. M., 7 November 1932

2 a.; m. B. Asaf'ev, l. A. Belinsky and A. Ratmansky on the basis of the original libretto by N. Volkov and V. Dmitriev; c. A. Ratmansky with use of the original choreography by V. Vainonen; d. I. Utkin, E. Monakhov, and Y. Markovskaya; p. B., 3 July 2008

One of the first and most famous ballets of the drambalet genre. Set during the time of the French Revolution, it contrasts the political fervor of the people of Marseilles with the treacherous, decadent evilness of the aristocracy. It tells the story of Jeanne and Pierre, the children of a peasant living not far from Marseilles. One day, Count Geoffrey, son of the local lord of the manor, Marquis de Beauregard, tries to force himself on Jeanne in the forest but is pushed back by her. When her father tries to defend his daughter, he is arrested. Jeanne and her brother Pierre call upon the peasants to march on the marquis's castle. The angry peasants free the marquis's captives from a prison in Marseilles and unite with an attachment of citizens in the name of the revolution. Jeanne and Pierre are among them. The second act is set in Versailles: the dancers Mireille de Poitiers and Antoine Mistral are performing a ballet. A banquet follows; the Marquis de Beauregard and his son Geoffrey are among the guests and recount the peasant uprising and the march on Marseilles. The king and the queen appear, and the officers pay their homage and write a letter to royalist émigrés in Koblenz about plans to crush the revolution. Count Geoffrey is supposed to deliver the letter. When Mistral reads the letter while the count dances with Mireille, he wants to go into hiding, but the count kills him, fearing that the secret plans might be revealed. In the meantime, the volunteers from Marseilles have arrived in Paris and join forces with other volunteers on a central square. Workers begin to fill the square, and young people parade puppets of the royal couple, when Mireille runs into the square, exposing the plans to crush the revolution. Courtiers and officers cross the square, Count Geoffrey among them, but Mireille demands his arrest. He is surrounded by the revolutionary crowd and led away. The crowd sets out to storm the Tuileries to the revolutionary song "Ça ira." A battle ensues inside the castle, and the marquis once again attacks Jeanne, but her brother kills him. The people are victorious and celebrate on the Mars Field, culminating in an impassioned, wild revolutionary dance, the carmagnole.

The Fountain of Bakhchisarai (Bakhchisaraiskii fontan)

4 a.; m. B. Asafiev; l. N. Volkov, after Pushkin's poem; c. R. Zakharov;
d. V. Khodasevich; p. M., 28 September 1934

With *Romeo and Juliet*, *The Fountain of Bakhchisarai* is one of the two most successful and long-lived ballets of the drambalet era. It is based on Pushkin's poem and still performed by the Mariinsky today.

Maria, a Polish princess, is abducted by the Crimean Khan Girei. Though she does not return his love, she arouses the jealousy of his chief wife, Zarema, who stabs her. The Khan builds a fountain of tears to Maria's memory. Maria was one of Galina Ulanova's most famous roles.

Gayané

4 a.; m. A. Khachaturian; l. K. Derzhavin; c. N. Anisimova;
d. N. Alt'man; p. Kirov Ballet, in Perm, 9 December 1942; restaged for
the Kirov in Leningrad, 1945 and 1952; c. V. Vainonen; d. V. Ryndin;
p. B., 22 May 1957

Set in an Armenian cotton collective, the ballet tells the story of the cotton picker Gayané and her lover, Armen.

Giselle

2 a.; m. A. Adam; l. V. Saint-Georges, T. Gautier, and J. Coralli;
c. J. Coralli and J. Perrot; d. P. Ciceri and P. Lormier; p. Paris Opera,
28 June 1841

One of the most famous romantic ballets. The peasant girl Giselle is in love with Count Albrecht, who is engaged to Bathilde, the daughter of a duke. Giselle is not aware of Albrecht's true identity, but the jealous gamekeeper Hilarion exposes him. Giselle goes mad and dies. The second act is set in the moonlit realm of the Wilis, spirits of brides who died before their wedding and who now drive any man to death who finds himself in their realm during the ghostly hours. Visiting Giselle's grave, Hilarion thus finds his death, but Giselle's love for Albrecht saves him from the same fate. When dawns breaks, the Wilis return to their graves. Albrecht is left alive but alone and full of grief. The original Paris version survived until 1868. Most subsequent productions have been based on Petipa's 1884 St. Petersburg production of the ballet.

The Golden Age (Zolotoi vek)

3 a.; m. D. Shostakovich; l. A. Ivanovsky; c. V. Vainonen and
L. Iakobson, with some dances by V. Chesnokov; d. V. Khodasevich;
p. Leningrad Maly Theater, 26 or 27 October 1930, with G. Ulanova
and O. Jordan

The ballet was a result of a libretto competition run within the context of the cultural revolution. Set in the West in a capitalist city, the ballet shows a fight between Fascists and a touring Soviet football team. Grigorovich created a completely new version to a new libretto for the Bolshoi in 1982.

Heart of the Mountain (Sertse gor)

3 a.; m. A. Balanchivadze; l. G. Leonidze; c. V. Chabukiani;
d. S. Virsaladze; p. K., 28 June 1938

Set in Georgia, the ballet portrayed a peasant uprising and culminated in the self-sacrifice of the aristocratic heroine for her lover, a leader of the mountain people. Chabukiani, a native Georgian, drew his choreographic inspiration from Caucasian national dances. Unlike many other ballets of this period, the ballet relied primarily on dance to express the action, not on pantomime.

The Little Humpbacked Horse (Konek-Gorbunok)

4 a.; m. C. Pugni; c. A. Saint-Léon; p. M., 1864, new versions by M.
Petipa (1895) and A. Gorsky (1912); revived in 1922, 1945, and 1963

Based on a popular Russian fairy tale about Ivanushka, who overcomes the wicked Khan and wins the tsar maiden with the help of the little Humpbacked Horse.

Laurencia

3 a.; m. A. Krein; l. E. Mandel'berg; director, E. Kaplan;
c. V. Chabukiani; d. S. Virsaladze; p. K., 22 March 1939

Based on the seventeenth-century play *Fuente ovejuna*, by Lope de Vega, about a peasant uprising in a Castilian village.

Legend of Love (*Legenda o liubvi*)

3 a.; m. A. Melikov; l. N. Hikmet; c. Y. Grigorovich; d. S. Virsaladze;
p. K., 23 March 1961

This production is based on Hikmet's play. Queen Mekhmene Banu sacrifices her beauty to save the life of her sick sister Shirin, but she is filled with jealousy when Shirin falls in love with Ferkhad, the man she loves. Mekhmene Banu orders him to sacrifice his love for Shirin and to go and build a waterway through the Iron Mountain to bring water to his people. The ballet's innovative choreography was singled out for criticism during the regime's 1962–1963 showdown with the creative intelligentsia.

Leningrad Symphony (*Leningradskaia simfoniia*)

1 a.; m. first part of D. Shostakovich's Seventh Symphony; scenario and
c. I. Bel'sky; d. M. Gordon; p. K., 14 April 1961

An important production associated with the rise of choreographic symphonism in the late 1950s and early 1960s. It is dedicated to Leningrad's heroic resistance to the German siege during the Second World War.

Masquerade (*Maskarad*)

4 a., m. L. Laputin; l. O. Dadishkiliani; c. B. Fenster; d. T. Bruni; p. K.,
29 December 1960

This production is based on Mikhail Lermontov's play.

Native Fields (*Rodnye polia*)

4 a.; m. P. Chervinsky; l. N. Korin; c. A. Andreev; d. I. Veselkina; p. K.,
4 June 1953

Native Fields was an outright failure from the beginning and became synonymous with the shortcomings of drambalet, inspiring a parody soon after its unsuccessful premiere. The action starts in a southern village in 1945. Andrei, nephew of the kolkhoz director, loves Galia, a Komsomol girl. He declares his love but has to leave for Moscow to study. A scene follows depicting the struggle of the kolkhoz against heat and drought, accompanied by dreams that Andrei will return from Moscow to help his kolkhoz erect an electric power station. Four years have passed. Andrei awaits the results of the defense of his diploma project. He passes with excellent marks and writes to Galia to ask her to join him in Moscow. In the meantime, life in the kolhoz has become better and more joyful. Galia is now the leader of the Komsomol brigade, and their harvest gives her the right to receive the title Hero of Socialist Labor. She receives Andrei's letter but decides to stay in her kolkhoz. Galia and other members of the kolkhoz travel to Moscow to receive decorations, she meets with Andrei, he paints an enthusiastic picture of their future life in Moscow, but she does not want to leave their kolkhoz. They argue. The other decorated members of the kolkhoz arrive, they all celebrate because they think that Andrei will now return to the kolkhoz to build a hydroelectric power station, but he insists on staying in the capital. Galia leaves. Andrei comes to the kolkhoz: he has decided to return. A hot wind rises and turns into a sandstorm, destroying the wheat. Andrei decides to put all his knowledge and efforts toward speeding up the construction of the hydroelectric power station. In the ballet's epilogue, a powerful dam can be seen: the kolkhoz no longer has to fear wind and sand. The director of the kolkhoz reads from the governmental decree and paints a grandiose picture of the future canal for the kolkhozniks.

The Nutcracker (*Shchelkunchik*)

2 a.; m. P. Tchaikovsky; c. L. Ivanov; p. M., 1892

2 a.; m. P. Tchaikovsky; l. and c. V. Vainonen, d. N. Seleznev; p. K., 18 February 1934

Othello

4 a.; m. A. Machavariani; l. and c. V. Chabukiani; d. S. Virsaladze; p. K., 24 March 1960

Path of Thunder (*Tropoiu groma*)

3 a.; m. K. Karayev; l. Y. Slonismky; c. K. Sergeev; d. V. Dorrer; p. K., 4 January 1958

This production was inspired by a novel by the South African writer Peter Abrahams. A black teacher and a white girl have a love affair and are killed by the girl's landowning father.

The Pharaoh's Daughter (*Doch' faraona*)

3 a.; m. C. Pugni; l. V. Saint-Georges and M. Petipa, after a novel by T. Gautier; c. M. Petipa; d. A. Roller, G. Wagner, Kel'ver, and Stoliarov; p. M., 18 January 1862

3 a.; m. C. Pugni; l. V. Saint-Georges and M. Petipa, after a novel by
T. Gautier; c. P. Lacotte; d. P. Lacotte; p. B., 5 May 2000

The Pharaoh's Daughter was Marius Petipa's first major success, leading to his appointment as second ballet master in St. Petersburg. A sumptuous spectacle lasting four hours, its cast of around four hundred spun an unlikely, exotic tale. Traveling through Egypt, the English Lord Wilson seeks refuge from a storm in a pyramid and falls into an opium dream. In his dream, he metamorphoses into an Egyptian man, Taor, and falls in love with Aspicia, the pharaoh's daughter who is supposed to marry the king of Nubia. After several twists and turns in the plot, threatened by the king of Nubia, Aspicia throws herself into the Nile and encounters the ruler of the Nile. A divertissement of dances involving major rivers follows. Fishermen find Aspicia and return her to the palace. The pharaoh gives his blessing to the union of Taor and Aspicia. Lord Wilson wakes up and smiles at the remembrance of his dream.

Raymonda

3 a.; m. A. Glazunov; l. L. Pashkova and M. Petipa; c. M. Petipa;

p. M., 19 January 1898

revived at M./K. 1922, c. F. Lopukhov, after Petipa; 1931,

c. A. Vaganova, after Petipa; 1938, c. V. Vainonen, after Petipa; 1948,

c. K. Sergeev, after Petipa

The Red Poppy (*Krasnyi mak*)

3 a.; m. R. Glière; l. M. Kurilko; c. first and third act, L. Lashilin;
c. second act, V. Tikhomirov; d. Kurilko; p. B., 14 June 1927

(production details for the Kirov production referred to in
chapter 3 are same as above, except c. R. Zakharov; d. Ia. Shtoffer;

p. K., 21 December 1949)

For the radical artistic avant-garde of the 1920s, the ballet *The Red Poppy* by the composer Reinhold Glière exemplified the contradictions between the revolutionary art they were advocating and the old-fashioned, bourgeois art still shown at the academic theaters. Premiered at the Bolshoi on June 1927, *The Red Poppy* was the first evening-filling, narrative ballet on a contemporary revolutionary topic. The premiere of the ballet coincided with a raid on the Soviet consulate in Canton, during which the consul himself and some employees were killed. Set in a Chinese port in the 1920s, the ballet tells the story of the suppressed Chinese people, their imperialist British and rich Chinese oppressors, their Soviet brothers, and the dancer Tao Khoa. Even though the ballet's plot was overtly a contemporary propaganda plot, the libretto was in essence little more than a Sovietized version of the tragic love story central to nineteenth-century ballet. It even included a narrative device typical of nineteenth-century ballet, namely the inclusion of a fantastic act to provide a dramatic excuse for a cascade of dances unrelated to the narrative plot of the ballet. Choreographed by the traditionalist Vasily Tikhomirov, this act mirrored dream scenes of ballets such as Petipa's *The Pharaoh's Daughter* and *La Bayadère*: the heroine of *The Red Poppy* falls into an opium-induced dream peopled by golden fish, phoenixes, living flowers, and butterflies performing a fantastic panorama of divertissement dances.

Romeo and Juliet

3 a.; m. S. Prokofiev; l. A. Piotrovsky, S. Prokofiev, and S. Radlov, after Shakespeare; c. L. Lavrovsky; d. P. Williams; p. K., 11 January 1940

The most important ballet of the drambalet era. Lavrovsky's production influenced choreographers worldwide. Juliet was one of Galina Ulanova's most famous roles.

"Russia" Has Come into Port (V port voshla "Rossiia")

3 a.; m. V. Solov'ev-Sedoi; l. Solov'ev-Sedoi and Rostislav Zakharov; c. R. Zakharov; d. I. Sevast'ianov and L. Korotkovoi; p. K., 14 February 1964

In a square in an Italian port, a group of young Italians, including the street-dancer Pepelina and the fisherman Peppo, collects money for traveling to a festival in Moscow. There are sailors from a Soviet motor ship. Money flies into Pepelina's tambourine. Some Fascist thugs don't like this. Pepelina and Peppo attach the festival's emblem to the back of a policeman without his noticing it. Pepelina dances for the Soviet sailors, including Andrei, who saved her as a little baby when he participated in the Italian resistance. Pepelina and Peppo run from the angry policeman. They hide in a circus-vaudeville theater, and Pepelina joins the dancers who are rehearsing at that moment to go unnoticed. The art patron Marcio takes an interest in her and tells the policeman that she is a dancer with the company. His lover, the prima ballerina Carolina, notices his interest. Peppo and Pepelina run to the port to see the departure of the ship *Russia*. Marcio and the director of the circus-vaudeville theater invite Pepelina to join their company. At the theater, Peppo and his friends visit Pepelina in her changing room. She gives them money for the journey to the festival. Soviet sailors and their Italian friends go to a performance of the new star of the theater, Pepelina. Andrei looks with anger and disgust at the central number "The Golden Cascade," where brutal men encircle Pepelina in a solid ring. Pepelina is ashamed when she sees Andrei, and a feeling of protest arises in her: she rips her adornments off and throws them to Marcio. She leaves the theater with her friends. Again in the square at the port, youth delegations from different countries traveling to the festival in Moscow hurry to the *Russia*. Young Fascists try in vain to block the path of the Italian group, which includes Pepelina. *Russia* leaves the port and the festival in Italy. Andrei, Pepelina, and Peppo meet again. The international youth demonstrate their friendship; they celebrate peace and friendship among the nations. The ballet was a resounding failure.

Shurale

3 a.; m. F. Iarullin; l. A. Faizi and L. Iakobson; c. L. Iakobson;
d. A. Ptushko, L. Mil'chin, and I. Vano; p. K., 28 May 1950

In 1950, Leonid Iakobson staged his ballet *Shurale* (which he had originally created in Kazan in 1941) for the Kirov Ballet under the name *Ali-Batyr* (in 1955, he staged the ballet for the Bolshoi under the name *Shurale*). Iakobson's use of classical dance in the ballet and his determination to resolve all images strictly with choreographic language—albeit not necessarily using classical vocabulary—in many ways corresponded to the artistic agenda of the symphonic choreographers of the late 1950s, but as the return of choreographic symphonism in postwar Soviet ballet is primarily associated with choreographers like Grigorovich and Bel'sky, it seems more logical to consider *The Stone Flower* the "proper" rebirth of choreographic symphonism. This ballet is based on a Tartar folk tale. The maiden Suimbike has been turned into a bird. She falls in love with the hunter Ali-Batyr. The malicious wood spirit Shurale tries to keep them apart, but the couple breaks the spell cast on Suimbike.

The Sleeping Beauty (Spiashchaia krasavitsa)

prologue and 3 a.; m. P. Tchaikovsky; l. M. Petipa and I. Vsevolozhsky,
after Perrault's fairy tale; c. M. Petipa; d. Vsevolozhsky (costumes), H.
Levogt, I. Andreev, K. Ivanov, M. Shishkov, and M. Bocharov; p. M., 3
January 1890

revived at M./K. 1914, c. Petipa, staged by N. Sergeev; 1922,
c. F. Lopukhov, after Petipa; 1952, c. K. Sergeev, after Petipa

Arguably, this is the pinnacle of nineteenth-century ballet classicism. The story is based on Perrault's fairy tale. The third act celebrates the wedding of Aurora and Prince Désiré with a divertissement of fairy tale characters.

Spartacus (Spartak)

3 a.; m. A. Khachaturian; l. N. Volkov; c. L. Iakobson;
d. V. Khodasevich; p. K., 27 December 1956; Spartacus: A. Makarov;
Phrygia: I. Zubkovskaya; Aegina: A. Shelest; Crassus: R. Gerbek;
revived: M., 1 July 2010

3 a.; m. A. Khachaturian; l. N. Volkov; c. Igor' Moiseev,
d. A. I. Konstantinovsky; p. B., 11 March 1958; Spartacus: D. Begak;
Phrygia: N. Ryzhenko; Aegina: M. Plisetskaya; Garmody:
N. Fadeechev

3 a.; m. A. Khachaturian; l. N. Volkov; c. L. Iakobson; d. V. Ryndin;
p. B., 4 April 1962; Spartacus: D. Begak; Phrygia: M. Plisetskaya;
Aegina: Ryshenko; Crassus: A. Radunsky

3 a.; m. A. Khachaturian; l. N. Volkov; c. Y. Grigorovich;
d. S. Virsaladze; p. B., 9 April 1968; Spartak: V. Vasil'ev; Phrygia:
E. Maksimova; Aegina: N. Timofeeva; Crassus: M. Liepa

The ballet tells the story of the Thracian slave Spartacus, who leads his fellow gladiators and slaves in a revolt against their Roman oppressors in the first century A.D. The following synopsis refers to Grigorovich's production, which became one of the signature works of the Bolshoi Ballet.

Crassus has led a victorious campaign in Thrace. He has made prisoners, including Spartacus and Phrygia, Spartacus's beloved. In the slave market, Spartacus and Phrygia are separated. At an orgy at Crassus's palace, mimes and courtesans entertain the guests, mocking Phrygia, Crassus's new slave. He is attracted to her, incurring the jealousy of his courtesan Aegina. Crassus orders two gladiators to fight to death: one of them is Spartacus. Spartacus wins but is upset at having been forced to kill. He will no longer tolerate captivity and decides to act to win back his freedom. He incites the gladiators to revolt. The gladiators are joined by the populace and the shepherds; Spartacus is proclaimed the leader of the uprising. Spartacus is haunted by thoughts of Phrygia as a slave. He finds her in Crassus's villa, and they express their love for each other. They hide as guests arrive. Aegina has long hoped to seduce Crassus to rise in social status. A feast at Crassus's villa celebrates his victories as Spartacus's army surrounds the place. The guests disperse, and Crassus and Aegina flee. Spartacus breaks into the villa. Crassus is taken prisoner, and Spartacus challenges him to single-hand combat. Crassus is no match for Spartacus, but as he prepares for death, Spartacus releases him, convinced that the gladiators will be victorious. Crassus is tormented by his disgrace, and Aegina calls on him to take revenge. Crassus's defeat thwarts Aegina's ambition, and she decides to sow dissension in Spartacus's camp. Crassus army is advancing. Spartacus wants to fight, but many of his captains desert him. Aegina seduces gladiators still loyal to Spartacus with wine, erotic dances, and prostitutes. She delivers them to Crassus. Crassus wants revenge: victory is not enough; he wants Spartacus. Spartacus's forces are surrounded by the Roman legions, and the gladiators are killed. Spartacus fights until the end and dies a hero's death, crucified on Roman spears. Phrygia retrieves his body; her grief is inconsolable.

The Stone Flower (Kammenyi tsvetok)

4 a.; m. S. Prokofiev; l. M. A. Mendel'son-Prokof'eva and L. Lavrovsky, based on motives from Ural fairy tales by P. Bazhov; c. L. Lavrovsky; d. T. Starzhenetskaya; p. B., under the title Skaz o kamennom tsvetke, 12 February 1954

3 a.; m. S. Prokofiev; l. M. A. Mendel'son-Prokof'eva and L. Lavrovsky; c. Y. Grigorovich; d. S. Virsaladze, p. K., 22 April 1957

Lavrovsky's production in 1954 proved to be a failure, but Grigorovich's production of the ballet in 1957 marked the rise of choreographic symphonism in Soviet ballet. *The Stone Flower* is an allegory on the problems of artistic creation, on the pursuit of discovering the secret of beauty. Set in the Urals, it tells the story of the stonecutter Danila, who dreams of creating the perfect malachite vase, the semblance of a real flower, but he can't discover the mystery of nature, the secret of its beauty, and the secret of artistic creation. He gets engaged to Katerina, who is threatened by the evil steward Sever'ian. In his pursuit for the secret of art, Danila ends up in the subterranean kingdom of the Mistress of the Copper Mountain. Katerina goes in search of Danila, pursued by Sever'ian, who is swallowed by the earth on command of the Mistress of the Copper Mountain. In the meantime, the mistress has disclosed the creative secret of beauty to Danila. She admits her love for him, but Danila confesses that he loves Katerina, and the mistress turns him into stone. Katerina enters her kingdom. Impressed by her love, the mistress lets Danila and Katerina go.

Swan Lake (Lebedinoe ozero)

4 a.; c. P. Tchaikovsky; l. V. Begichev and V. Gel'tser; c. V. Reisinger; p. B., 20 February 1877; this production was a failure

4 a.; c. first and third acts, M. Petipa; c. second and fourth acts (swan acts), L. Ivanov; d. (sets) I. Andreev, M. Bocharov, and H. Levogt; costumes by E. Ponomarev; p. M., 15 January 1895

revised versions at the Mariinsky/Kirov during the Soviet period: 1933, c. A. Vaganova, after Petipa and Ivanov; 1945, c. F. Lopukhov, after Petipa and Ivanov; 1950, c. K. Sergeev, after Petipa and Ivanov

The canonical version was created by Petipa and Ivanov for the Mariinsky in 1895. Arguably the most famous of all ballets. The evil sorcerer Rothbart has turned Princess Odette into a swan. Only true love can restore her to human form. While hunting by the lake, Prince Siegfried falls in love with her and vows to rescue her. Back at the castle, he attends a ball. Rothbart appears with his daughter Odile in disguise. The prince thinks she is Odette (Odette and Odile are danced by the same dancer). Siegfried is completely taken by Odile and proposes to marry her. Now that his vow to Odette is broken, Rothbart and Odile reveal their identity. Heartbroken, Siegfried runs to the lake to console Odette. Siegfried and Odette plunge into the lake, and a final apotheosis shows their love and happiness after death. In Soviet versions, reflecting ideological requirements, the traditional ending was replaced by a victory of good over evil in this world: Siegfried fights Rothbart and overcomes him, and the spell is then broken.

Talisman

4 a.; m. R. Drigo; l. K. Tarnovsky; c. M. Petipa; p. M., 25 January 1889

Taras Bul'ba

3 a.; m. V. Solov'ev-Sedoi; l. S. Kaplan; c. Fedor Lopukhov and
I. Kovtunov; d. V. Ryndin; p. K., 12 December 1940

Production mentioned in performance statistics, chapter 3: same as above, except 4 a.; c. Boris Fenster; d. A. Konstantinovsky; p. K., 28 June 1955

This ballet is based on Nikolai Gogol's novella of the same name.

The Twelve

1 a.; m. B. Tishchenko; l. L. Iakobson, after A. Blok; c. L. Iakobson;
d. E. Stenberg; 31 December 1964

This was a highly controversial production that received only three performances after a long battle. It was based on Aleksandr Blok's poem.

Notes

Abbreviations Used in Notes

RGALI   Rossiiskii gosudarstvennyi arkhiv literatury i iskusstva, Moscow

TsGALI   Tsentral'nyi gosudarstvennyi arkhiv literatury i iskusstva,
         St. Petersburg

Introduction

1. Matil'da Kshesinskaia, *Vospominaniia* (Moscow: ART, 1992), 179–80, 191.

2. I use Pierre Bourdieu's concept of a "field of cultural production" in broad terms to conceptualize the struggle for artistic autonomy in a state of power relations where the field of cultural production and the field of power were of necessity unusually close (Pierre Bourdieu, *The Field of Cultural Production: Essays on Art and Literature*, ed. and intro. Randal Johnson [Cambridge: Polity Press, 1993]). My concept of artistic repossession describes strategies of resistance or subversion, reflecting Michel de Certeau's work on tactics available to the ordinary person to reclaim autonomy of action from all-pervading forces such as commerce and politics, but applying it not to the everyday life of the average person but to "everyday life" in the realm of high culture (Michel de Certeau, *The Practice of Everyday Life*, trans. Steven Rendall [Berkeley: University of California Press, 1984]).

There are dangers with strictly applying the frames developed by either theorist for analyzing Western culture to the Soviet context, and implicit adjustments have to be made at every step, for example, concerning myths of individual initiative versus myths of collectivism, myths of democracy versus myths of democratic centralism, and so forth. Only a loosely functioning understanding of either theorist can be useful for interpreting Soviet cultural politics, but it is helpful to look at the work of either theorist as they address issues similar to those at the core of this book. My concept of *artistic repossession* offers a way of understanding how these theorists' works can be adapted to take into account the differences in the environment of cultural production in the West and the Soviet Union and the internal politics of their cultural institutions.

3. Sheila Fitzpatrick, *Everyday Stalinism: Ordinary Life in Extraordinary Times: Soviet Russia in the 1930s* (Oxford: Oxford University Press, 1999), 2.

4. Stephen Kotkin, *Magnetic Mountain: Stalinism as a Civilization* (Berkeley: University of California Press, 1995), 21–22.

5. Kotkin, *Magnetic Mountain*, 22.

6. Alena Ledeneva, *Russia's Economy of Favors: Blat, Networking, and Informal Exchange* (Cambridge: Cambridge University Press, 1998), 76, 103.

7. James C. Scott, *Weapons of the Weak: Everyday Forms of Peasant Resistance* (New Haven: Yale University Press, 1985).

8. Michel Foucault, "The Subject and Power," afterword to *Michel Foucault: Beyond Structuralism and Hermeneutics* by Hubert L. Dreyfus and Paul Rabinow (New York: Harvester Press, 1982), 225.

1. Survival: The Mariinsky and Bolshoi after the October Revolution

Epigraph: Iurii Slonimskii, *Sovetskii balet. Materialy k istorii sovetskogo baletnogo teatra* (Moscow, Leningrad: Iskusstvo, 1950), 44.

1. *Novoe Vremia*, 25 October (7 November) 1917, 5.

2. Tamara Karsavina, *Theatre Street* (London: Readers Union Constable, 1950), 205. Karsavina gives 8 November (26 October, O.S.) 1917 as the date, but as she describes political events that took place on 7 November (25 October, O.S.), and as there was a ballet she performed in at the Mariinsky on 7 November but not on 8 November, it can be assumed that she erred in her dating of the events.

3. While I emphasize ballet's roots as a courtly art for the purpose of discussing the fate of ballet in Soviet Russia, I do not wish to deny the important interrelationship between elite and popular forms in dance and its impact on the development of ballet, for example, by the absorption of virtuoso techniques of Italian *grotteschi* dancers in the eighteenth century and by the influence of national dances in the nineteenth century, of modern-dance and avant-garde movements in the twentieth century, and of social dances throughout the history of ballet. Nevertheless, the art form's origins as princely entertainment and royal self-representation had a profound impact on the self-definition of ballet and the outside perception of it, especially in Russia, where it was consciously imported as a Western court art.

4. St. Petersburg's Mariinsky Theater was the most important opera and ballet theater of the imperial period. When talking about the role of ballet in tsarist Russia, it is thus natural to focus on the Mariinsky.

5. Mary Clarke and Clement Crisp, *Ballet: An Illustrated History* (London: Hamish Hamilton, 1992), 76.

6. Marius Petipa arrived in St. Petersburg from his native France in 1847 and became the defining choreographer of classical ballet, creating masterworks such as *Swan Lake, The Sleeping Beauty,* and *La Bayadère* for the Mariinsky.

7. Dmitrij Chwidkowskij, *Sankt Petersburg* (Cologne: Könemann, 1996), 157.

8. In those days, the ballet company rehearsed in the same building.

9. Karsavina, *Theatre Street,* 45.

10. Bernard Taper, *Balanchine: A Biography,* 3rd ed. (Berkeley: University of California Press, 1996), 45, 38.

11. Balanchine emigrated to the West in 1924. He is one of the most important choreographers of the twentieth century.

12. Robert K. Massie, *Nicholas and Alexandra: The Tragic, Compelling Story of the Last Tsar and His Family* (London: Phoenix Press, 2000), 346. Taper, *Balanchine,* 45.

13. For the composition of the ballet audience, see Robert John Wiley, *Tchaikovsky's Ballets: Swan Lake, Sleeping Beauty, Nutcracker* (Oxford: Oxford Univeristy Press, 1985), 10–11.

14. Elizabeth Souritz, *Soviet Choreographers in the 1920s,* trans. Lynn Visson (Durham: Duke University Press, 1990), 42.

15. Souritz, *Soviet Choreographers,* 42–43.

16. In 1920, the Mariinsky was renamed the State Academic Theater for Opera and Ballet, GATOB, and in 1935, the Leningrad Theater for Opera and Ballet named after Kirov. For simplicity's sake, I refer to the Mariinsky Theater as the former Mariinsky Theater for the period 1920–1935 and as the Kirov Theater thereafter. After the collapse of the Soviet Union, the Mariinsky reverted back to its prerevolutionary name.

17. Fedor Lopukhov, *Shest' desiat let v balete. Vospominaniia i zapiski baletmeistera* (Moscow: Iskusstvo, 1966), 187–88.

18. A. S. Poliakov, ed., *Biriuch petrogradskikh gosudarstvennykh teatrov: Sbornik statei* (1921): 381.

19. Slonimskii, *Sovetskii balet,* 26.

20. Lopukhov, *Shest' desiat let v balete,* 188.

21. Slonimskii, *Sovetskii balet,* 28, 30–31.

22. Lopukhov, *Shest' desiat let v balete,* 192.

23. Ibid., 192–93.

24. Wiley, *Tchaikovsky's Ballets,* 10–11.

25. Iurii Slonimskii, *Chudesnoe bylo riadom s nami* (Leningrad: Sovetskii Kompositor, 1984), 69.

26. Konstantin Ostrozhenskii, "Balet (Tshchetnaia predostorozhnost' i Cho-

piniana)," *Vechernie ogni*, 15 April 1918, 4; quoted in Souritz, *Soviet Choreographers*, 43–44.

27. Asaf Messerer, *Tanets. Mysl.' Vremia* (Moscow: Iskusstvo, 1990), 15.

28. A. S. Poliakov, ed., *Biriuch petrogradskikh gosudarstvennikh teatrov*, no. 8 (23–31 December 1918): 60.

29. Poliakov, *Biriuch petrogradskikh gosudarstvennikh teatrov*, no. 8: 60.

30. Anatolii Lunacharskii, "Iz Moskovskikh vpechatlenii," *Zhizn' iskusstva*, 4 January 1919; reprinted in Anatolii Lunacharskii, *V mire muzyka: Stat'i i rechi* (Moscow: Sovetskii Kompozitor, 1971), 263.

31. Quoted in Mary Grace Swift, *The Art of the Dance in the U.S.S.R.* (South Bend: University of Notre Dame Press, 1968), 54.

32. Slonimskii, *Sovetskii balet*, 52.

33. A. S. Poliakov, ed., *Biriuch petrogradskikh gosudarstvennikh teatrov*, no. 10 (9–22 January 1919): 55.

34. A. S. Poliakov, ed., *Biriuch petrogradskikh gosudarstvennikh teatrov: Sbornik statei, 1919* (June–August 1919): 172.

35. A. S. Poliakov, ed., *Biriuch petrogradskikh gosudarstvennikh teatrov*, no. 7 (16–22 December 1918): 57.

36. A. S. Poliakov, ed., *Biriuch petrogradskikh gosudarstvennikh teatrov: Sbornik statei,* (June–August 1919): 175.

37. Poliakov, *Biriuch petrogradskikh gosudarstvennikh teatrov: Sbornik statei* (1921): 370.

38. Messerer, *Tanets. Mysl.' Vremia*, 30–31.

39. Quoted by Patricia Blake, introduction to V. Mayakovsky, *The Bedbug and Selected Poetry*, ed. Patricia Blake, trans. Max Hayward and George Reavey (Bloomington: Indiana University Press, 1975), 17–18.

40. Richard Thorpe, "The Academic Theaters and the Fate of Soviet Artistic Pluralism, 1919–1928," *Slavic Review* 51, no. 3 (1992): 389–410, see esp. 389.

41. Sheila Fitzpatrick, *The Commissariat of Enlightenment: Soviet Organization of Education and the Arts under Lunacharsky, October 1917–1921* (Cambridge: Cambridge University Press, 1970), 11.

42. Thorpe, "Academic Theaters," 389.

43. Quoted in Boris Schwarz, *Music and Musical Life in Soviet Russia, 1917–1970* (London: Barrie and Jenkins, 1972), 12.

44. Thorpe, "Academic Theaters," 391.

45. Souritz, *Soviet Choreographers*, 122.

46. "Khronika," *Izvestiia*, 5 November 1921, 2.

47. "Pis'ma v redaktsiiu. O Bol'shom teatre," *Izvestiia*, 13 November 1921, 2.

48. Souritz, *Soviet Choreographers*, 326n29.

49. For a description of this episode, consult Souritz, *Soviet Choreographers*, 44–46; and Thorpe, "Academic Theaters," 391.

50. Thorpe, "Academic Theaters," 397.

51. Souritz, *Soviet Choreographers*, 48.

52. Quoted in Slonimskii, *Sovetskii balet*, 43.

53. Quoted in ibid.

54. Quoted in Tim Scholl, *"Sleeping Beauty," a Legend in Progress* (New Haven: Yale University Press, 2004), 69–70.

55. Anatolii Lunacharskii, "Dlia chevo my sokhraniaem Bol'shoi teatr?," in Lunacharskii, *V mire muzyka*, 296.

56. Slonimskii, *Sovetskii balet*, 44.

57. Lunacharskii, "Dlia chevo my sokhraniaem Bol'shoi teatr?," 296.

58. Messerer, *Tanets. Mysl'. Vremia*, 71.

59. Timothy O'Connor, *The Politics of Soviet Culture: Anatolii Lunacharskii* (Ann Arbour: University of Michigan Research Press, 1980), 67–68.

60. Sheila Fitzpatrick, *The Cultural Front: Power and Culture in Revolutionary Russia* (Ithaca: Cornell University Press, 1992), 3.

61. O'Connor, *Politics of Soviet Culture*, 72.

62. Anatolii Lunacharskii, "K 100-Letiiu Bol'shogo Teatra," in Lunacharskii, *V mire muzyka*, 291.

63. Lunacharskii, "Dlia chevo my sokhraniaem Bol'shoi teatr?," 301.

64. Lunacharskii, "K 100-Letiiu Bol'shogo Teatra," 294.

65. Richard Stites, *Revolutionary Dreams: Utopian Vision and Experimental Life in the Russian Revolution* (Oxford: Oxford University Press, 1989), 102.

66. Lunacharskii, "Dlia chevo my sokhraniaem Bol'shoi teatr?," 302, 304.

67. Ibid., 303, 304.

68. Ibid., 304.

69. Anatolii Lunacharskii, "Novye puti operi i baleta" (address on 12 May 1930 at the Bolshoi Theater), in Lunacharskii, *V mire muzyka*, 462.

70. This episode is described in Swift, *Art of the Dance*, 70–71.

2. Ideological Pressure: Classical Ballet and Soviet Cultural Politics, 1923–1936

1. The Russian title of the ballet, *Svetlyi ruchei*, is sometimes translated as *The Limpid Stream*. I use the translation *The Bright Stream* because the Bolshoi uses this translation for choreographer Alexei Ratmansky's new version of the ballet, which had its premiere in 2003.

2. The noninterpretative elements of the following general outline of ballet history are based on Mary Clarke and Clement Crisp, *Ballet: An Illustrated History* (London: Hamish Hamilton, 1992); Debra Craine and Judith Mackrell, *The Oxford Dictionary of Dance* (Oxford: Oxford University Press, 2000); and *Russkii balet entsiklopediia* (Moscow: Bol'shaia rosiiskaia entsiklopediia, 1997).

3. Clarke and Crisp, *Ballet*, 37.

4. James Billington, *The Icon and the Axe: An Interpretive History of Russian Culture* (New York: Vintage Books, 1970), 339, 349.

5. Billington, *Icon and the Axe* 349, 386.

6. Charles-Louis Didelot, a French dancer, choreographer, and teacher, was the most important figure in Russian ballet during the early nineteenth century, transforming St. Petersburg into one of the leading ballet centers.

7. Quoted by Oleg Petrov and Tim Scholl, "Russian Ballet and Its Place in Russian Artistic Culture of the Second Half of the Nineteenth Century: The Age of Petipa," *Dance Chronicle* 15, no. 1 (1992): 41.

8. For a fascinating discussion of experimentation at the Bolshoi and former Mariinsky Ballet companies in the 1920s, consult Elizabeth Souritz, *Soviet Choreographers in the 1920s*, trans. Lynn Visson (Durham: Duke University Press, 1990).

9. Stephanie Jordan, introduction to *Writings on Ballet and Music*, by Fedor Lopukhov, ed. Stephanie Jordan (Madison: University of Wisconsin Press, 2002), 3.

10. Fedor Lopukhov, *Shest' desiat let v balete. Vospominaniia i zapiski baletmeistera* (Moscow: Iskusstvo, 1966), 243, 244. Lopukhov notes that Alexander Gorsky had staged Glazunov's Fifth Symphony in Moscow in 1915, but he heard about this production significantly later as he was in military service (243). This seems to have been the first time in Russian ballet that a symphony was used, but the ballet was not abstract, it had a narrative plot; see Elizaveta Suritz, "A. A. Gorskii i moskovskii balet," introduction to *Baletmeister A. A. Gorskii: Materialy. Vospominaniia. Stat'i* (St. Petersburg: Dmitrii Bulanin, 2000), 46–47.

11. Souritz, *Soviet Choreographers in the 1920s*, 275.

12. Jordan, introduction, 4.

13. Lopukhov, *Writings on Ballet and Music*, 146–47.

14. Lopukhov, *Shest' desiat let v balete*, 244.

15. Souritz, *Soviet Choreographers in the 1920s*, 268–73. For a more detailed description of the ballet and analysis of its lasting significance, consult Souritz, *Soviet Choreographers in the 1920s*, 266–77.

16. Lopukhov, *Shest' desiat' let v balete*, 23.

17. Lopukhov, *Writings on Ballet and Music*, 155–56.

18. Sheila Fitzpatrick, *The Cultural Front: Power and Culture in Revolutionary Russia* (Ithaca: Cornell University Press, 1992), 115.

19. According to the Soviet ballet writer Yuri Slonimsky, he and Sollertinsky began to work on this translation together, but when Slonimsky had to leave Leningrad for the Red Army, Sollertinsky became the sole translator. See Slonimskii, *Chudesnoe bylo riadom s nami* (Leningrad: Sovetskii Kompozitor, 1984), 53.

20. Aleksei Gvozdev, "O reforme baleta," *Zhizn' iskusstva*, 3 January 1928, 5–6.

21. Gvozdev, "Reforma baleta: klassicheskii tanets," *Zhizn' iskusstva*, 10 January 1928, 4.

22. Ivan Sollertinskii, "Za novyi khoreograficheskii teatr," *Zhizn' iskusstva*, 17 June 1928, 4.

23. Sollertinskii, "Za novyi khoreograficheskii teatr," 5–6, and 24 June 1928, 4–5.

24. Ernst Krenek's *Leap over the Shadow* and Alban Berg's *Wozzeck* premiered at the end of the 1926–1927 opera season in Leningrad.

25. Katerina Clark, *Petersburg: Crucible of Cultural Revolution* (Cambridge: Harvard University Press, 1995), 227–30.

26. Ivan Sollertinskii, "Blizhaishie puti GATOBA," *Zhizn' iskusstva*, 29 July 1928, 10.

27. Islamei, "Simfoniia tantsa," *Zhizn' iskusstva*, 1 July 1928, 4. According to Tim Scholl, "Islamei" was a pseudonym for N. Malkov (*"Sleeping Beauty," a Legend in Progress* [New Haven: Yale University Press, 2004], 75). Scholl probably means Nikolai Malko.

28. Islamei, "Simfoniia tantsa," 4.

29. Ivan Sollertinskii, "Sporakh o tantseval'nom teatre'," *Zhizn' iskusstva*, 1 July 1928, 5.

30. Mary Grace Swift, *The Art of the Dance in the U.S.S.R.* (South Bend: University of Notre Dame Press, 1968), 80, 301–3.

31. Slonimskii, *Chudesnoe bylo riadom s nami*, 58.

32. Swift, *Art of the Dance in the U.S.S.R.*, 85–86, 86–87.

33. Iurii Slonimskii, *Sovetskii balet. Materialy k istorii sovetskogo baletnogo teatra* (Moscow-Leningrad: Iskusstvo, 1950), 88.

34. Fitzpatrick, *Cultural Front*, 143, 146–47.

35. Ibid., 248.

36. Nicholas S. Timasheff, *The Great Retreat: The Growth and Decline of Communism in Russia* (New York: E. P. Dutton and Co., 1946), 13–19, 268, 395.

37. Sheila Fitzpatrick, *Everyday Stalinism. Ordinary Life in Extraordinary Times: Soviet Russia in the 1930s* (Oxford: Oxford University Press, 1999), 82.

38. Dmitri Volkogonov, *Stalin: Triumph and Tragedy* (London: Weidenfeld and Nicolson, 1991), 148.

39. For a discussion of the production, consult Vera Krasovskaya, *Vaganova: A Dance Journey from Petersburg to Leningrad*, trans. Vera M. Siegel (Gainesville: University Press of Florida, 2005), 169–81.

40. Ivan Sollertinskii, "Muzykal'nyi teatr na poroge otiabria i problema operno-baletnogo naslediia v epokhu voennogo kommunizma," *Istoriia Sovetskogo Teatra. Tom pervyi: Petrogradskie teatry na poroge oktiabria i v epokhu voennogo kommunizma. 1917–1921* (Leningrad: Leningradskoe otdelenie gosudarstvennogo izdatel'stva khudozhestvennoi literatury, 1933).

41. Sollertinskii, "Muzykal'nyi teatr na poroge otkiabria i problema operno-baletnogo naslediia v epokhu voennogo kommunizma," 324.

42. Ibid., 324–25.

43. Vladimir Paperny, *Architecture in the Age of Stalin: Culture Two*, trans. John Hill and Roann Barris (Cambridge: Cambridge University Press, 2002), 173–80.

44. Paperny, *Architecture in the Age of Stalin*, xxiii–xxiv.

45. Boris Groys, "The Birth of Socialist Realism from the Spirit of the Russian Avant-Garde," in *The Culture of the Stalin Period*, ed. Hans Günther (London: Macmillan, 1990), 122–48.

46. Radlov declared war against opera in which music is the only self-valuable element and called for replacing the traditional opera singer with a performer who uses the entire intonational range, from the spoken to the sung word (Clark, *Petersburg*, 229–30).

47. A new production of Petipa's *Swan Lake* by Agrippina Vaganova was the third ballet production Radlov was involved in. Given the existence of Petipa's choreography, the scope for implementing his ideas on the integration of dance and drama was limited.

48. Slonimskii, *Sovetskii balet*, 105–17.

49. An abridged version of the ballet was recorded in 1953 and is available on *Stars of the Russian Ballet* DVD (Video Artists International, 2003).

50. In 2008, Aleksei Ratmansky staged a new version of the ballet for the Bolshoi that included some fragments of the original version, including the famous pas de deux.

51. Vadim Gaevskii, *Dom Petipa* (Moscow: Artist. Rezhisser. Teatr, 2000), 220; see also the DVD recording from 1953, *Stars of the Russian Ballet*.

52. From 1936 until 1939 he was the director of the Bolshoi Ballet and from 1936 until 1956 choreographer and opera director at the Bolshoi.

53. Natalia Roslavleva, *Era of the Russian Ballet* (London: Victor Gollancz, 1966), 230–31.

54. Slonimskii, *Sovetskii balet*, 91.

55. Lopukhov, *Shest' desiat let v balete*, 258–59.

56. Ibid., 270.

57. Slonimskii, *Sovetskii balet*, 160.

58. Lopukhov, *Shest' desiat let v balete*, 272, 273.

59. Faier extensively quotes the program brochure published in conjunction with the premiere of the ballet at the Bolshoi (Iurii Faier, *O sebe, o muzyke, o balete* [Moscow: Sovetskii Kompozitor, 1974], 303–5).

60. Ekaterina Vlasova, "Stalin smotrit 'Svetlyi ruchei,'" *Balet* 6, no. 154 (2008): 34–37.

61. RGALI, f. 648, op. 2, d. 1031, ll. 51–59, 60, 61.

62. RGALI, f. 648, op. 5, d. 5, l. 8.

63. Vlasova, "Stalin smotrit 'Svetlyi ruchei,'" 35.

64. Ibid., 36.

65. Ibid., 36–37.

66. Fitzpatrick, *Cultural Front,* 199–200, 204.

67. For example, Sheila Fitzpatrick writes, "within ten days of the editorial on *Lady Macbeth, Pravda* came out with a second attack on a Shostakovich work, this time his ballet *Limpid Stream,* staged by the Bolshoi Theater" (Fitzpatrick, *Cultural Front,* 198). Katerina Clark writes that Shostakovich was the focus of the article on *The Limpid Stream* but states that the attack focused primarily on the libretto (Clark, *Petersburg,* 291). Neither Fitzpatrick nor Clark mentions the article's criticisms of the choreography. A post-Soviet, Russian study of Stalin's "cultural revolution" in 1936–1938, using fascinating archival materials, discusses the impact of the antiformalism campaign on the Bolshoi Theater, but the name of Fedor Lopukhov does not even appear in the book's index (Leonid Maksimenkov, *Sumbur vmesto muzyki. Stalinskaia kul'turnaia revolutsiia, 1936–1938* [Moscow: Iuridicheskaia Kniga, 1997]).

68. "Baletnaia fal'sh'," *Pravda,* 6 February 1935, as reproduced in *Sovetskaia muzyka* 2, 1 February 1936, 6.

69. "Baletnaia fal'sh'," 6.

70. Ibid., 6, 7.

71. RGALI, f. 648, op. 2, d. 1031, ll. 27-28.

72. Faier, *O sebe, o muzyke, o balete,* 309, 310.

73. "Spravka sekretno-politicheskogo otdela GUGB NKVD SSSR ob otklikakh literatorov i rabotnikov iskusstva na stat'i v gazete 'Pravda' o compositore D. D. Shostakovich" (ne pozdnee 11 fevralia 1936g.), in *Vlast' i khudozhestvennaia intelligentsia: Dokumenty TsK RKP (b)-VKP (b), VChK-OGPU-NKVD o kul'turnoi politike. 1917–1953gg,* ed. Andrei Artizov and Oleg Naumov (Moscow: Mezhdunarodnii fond "Demokratiia," 1999), 294.

74. On Meyerhold as hidden target of the antiformalist campaign, consult Fitzpatrick, *Cultural Front,* 200.

75. On 6 November 1936, a new production of *The Flames of Paris* premiered at the Kirov.

76. Slonimskii, *Sovetskii balet,* 150.

77. There exists a 1954 film version of Lavrovskii's *Romeo and Juliet* with Ulanova and Iurii Zhdanov (*Romeo i Dzhul'etta* [Mosfil'm 1954; Krupnyi Plan, 1999], VHS).

78. Descriptions of the choreography of these ballets can be found in Slonimskii, *Sovetskii balet,* 146–51, 175–79, 185–94, 208–14, 237–41.

79. Asaf Messerer, *Tanets. Mysl'. Vremia* (Moscow: Iskusstvo, 1990), 192; see also Faier, *O sebe, o muzyke, o balete,* 311–12.

3. Art versus Politics: The Kirov's Artistic Council, 1950s–1960s

Epigraph: Maiia Plisetskaia, *Ia, Maiia Plisetskaia* (Moscow: Novosti, 1997), 170.

1. William Taubman, *Khrushchev: The Man and His Era* (London: Free Press, 2003), 51.

2. Plisetskaia, *Ia, Maiia Plisetskaia*, 170.

3. I use the terms *Soviet power* and *Soviet regime* in the wider sense, referring both to the party and government machines trying to translate political-ideological goals into reality.

4. Prikaz Ministra kul'tury SSSR No. 772, 31/12/57, "O merakh po dal'neishemy razvitiiu sovetskogo baletnogo iskusstva," TsGALI, f. 337, op. 1, d. 741, ll. 22–28.

5. Iurii Slonimskii, *Sovetskii balet. Materialy k istorii sovetskogo baletnogo teatra* (Moscow-Leningrad: Iskusstvo, 1950), 310.

6. TsGALI, f. 337, op. 1, d. 741, l. 22.

7. The Russian term *glavnyi baletmeister* is difficult to translate into English. The literal translation "principal ballet master" would be confusing because in English-speaking countries, the term *ballet master* usually refers to a person teaching company class at a ballet company. The Russian term *baletmeister* is closer to the English-term *choreographer*. At the time, the glavnyi baletmeister usually combined the duties of the ballet company's artistic director with those of a choreographer, or even the company's principal choreographer. According to an article by Galina Ulanova published in 1953, the Committee on Artistic Affairs (Komitet po delam iskusstv) prescribed that the artistic director of the ballet also had to be the theater's principal choreographer (Galina Ulanova, "S khudozhnika sprositsia," *Sovetskaia Muzyka* 4 [April 1953]: 39). For simplicity sake, I will translate *glavnyi baletmeister* as artistic director.

8. TsGALI, f. 337, op. 1, d. 741, ll. 23–24.

9. Choreographers did not have their own creative union, but the theaters fulfilled many of the professional purposes of a creative union. It is difficult to gauge why there was no such union. Maybe writers and composers were considered more important and therefore more in need of control. The absence of a specific union for choreographers might reflect the particularity of the ballet profession. At any time, there are probably fewer choreographers than writers and composers. Unlike writers and composers who can create in solitude for the drawer, choreographers generally need trained dancers to work with, making them more dependent on commissions by theaters and thus more easily controllable than writers or composers.

10. TsGALI, f. 337, op. 1, d. 741, ll. 27–28, ll. 26–27.

11. TsGALI, f. 337, op. 1, d. 652, l. 2.

12. TsGALI, f. 337, op. 1, d. 693, ll. 59, 60.

13. TsGALI, f. 337, op. 1, d. 747, ll. 12–13.

14. TsGALI, f. 337, op. 1, d. 858, l. 4.

15. TsGALI, f. 337, op. 1, d. 747, ll. 12–13.

16. Ibid., l. 13.

17. TsGALI, f. 337, op. 1, d. 897, l. 1.

18. TsGALI, f. 337, op. 1, d. 747, l. 4.

19. Ibid.

20. TsGALI, f. 337, op. 1, d. 693, l. 59.

21. In July 1956, the responsibility for several cultural institutions was transferred from the USSR Ministry of Culture to the RSFSR Ministry of Culture, including the Kirov Theater and the Leningrad Choreographic Institute. The Bolshoi and the Moscow Choreographic Institute remained under the auspices of the USSR Ministry of Culture (TsGALI, f. 337, op. 1, d. 693, l. 45).

22. Sergeev was the Kirov Ballet's artistic director between 1951–1955 and 1960–1970.

23. Natalia Makarova, *A Dance Autobiography*, ed. and intro. by Gennady Smakov (London: Adam and Charles Black, 1980), 52–54.

24. TsGALI, f. 337, op. 1, d. 781, l. 30.

25. During the Soviet period, *La Bayadère* was in the Bolshoi's repertoire from 1917 until 1936. During the war, in 1943, the ballet was revived at the Bolshoi Theater Small Stage (Filial). After that, only the "Kingdom of the Shades" act appeared in the repertoire (revived in 1977 and 1988). The full-length ballet only returned to the stage of the Bolshoi in 1991 (Bolshoi Theater, program for *La Bayadère*, 2005).

26. "Classification of Ballets given in Repertoire Index of 1929" is reproduced in Mary Grace Swift, *The Art of the Dance in the U.S.S.R.* (South Bend: University of Notre Dame Press, 1968), 301–3.

27. TsGALI, f. 337, op. 1, d. 781, l. 33. Originally, the ballet had four acts, but at the time of this discussion the Kirov's production of the ballet no longer included the fourth act, turning the third act ("Kingdom of the Shades") into the final act.

28. TsGALI, f. 337, op. 1, d. 781, l. 35.

29. This presence of competing, contradictory value systems at the core of an individual directly contradicts new scholarship on Soviet identity and subjectivity that maintains that it was impossible for individuals living in the Soviet Union to think outside the system of Soviet mentalities. According to scholars such as Jochen Hellbeck, as Soviet citizens had no conceptual alternative to Soviet values, their identity was completely determined by the Soviet system; their self had no autonomy and tried to purge itself of anything that could potentially compete with the official values. The experience of Soviet ballet dancers shows that the reality was much more complex and that a person's identity could be shaped by conflicting, even diametrically opposed, value systems.

30. Makarova, *Dance Autobiography*, 24.

31. Makarova gives Nikolai Ivanovsky's patronymic as "Ivanovich," but this is inaccurate. His patronymic was Pavlovich.

32. Makarova, *Dance Autobiography*, 22–23.

33. Ibid., 22.

34. Barbara Newman, *Grace under Pressure: Passing Dance through Times* (New York: Limelight Editions, 2003), 361–62.

35. *Nataliia Dudinskaia: Dialog so stsenoi* (Lentelefil'm 1988; Kinotsentr "Ocha-kovo," 2003), VHS.

36. For example, TsGALI, f. 337, op. 1, d. 897, l. 28.

37. "I nas eto udovletvorit ne mozhet," *Za sovetskoe iskusstvo*, 27 January 1956, 1.

38. "Za novyi pod'em opernogo i baletnogo iskusstva. Kommunisty obsuzh-daiut reshenie Gorkoma KPSS," *Za sovetskoe iskusstvo*, 17 May 1960, 2.

39. Li Cunxin, *Mao's Last Dancer* (London: Fusion Press, 2003), 132.

40. TsGALI, f. 337, op. 1, d. 897, l. 28. It is not clear whether "Soviet" within this context referred to Soviet themes or Soviet authors working on non-Soviet topics such as Shakespeare's *Romeo and Juliet*. Given the numbers of Soviet pro-ductions cited, it is likely that Soviet within this context meant the former.

41. The performance statistics are based on listings in the weekly publication *Teatral'nyi Leningrad* (called *Leningradskie teatri* before 1957), published by Uprav-lenie kul'tury Ispolkoma Lengorsoveta, Direktsiia Teatral'nykh kass, and (after 1957) Vserossiiskoe Teatral'noe Obshchestvo. Unless noted otherwise, the statis-tics are given by calendar year and not by theatrical season.

42. *Esmeralda* was original a classical ballet of the prerevolutionary period, shown at the Mariinsky in a production by Petipa after Perrot. In 1935, Vagan-ova created a new version for the Kirov, which was revived in 1948.

43. TsGALI, f. 337, op. 1, d. 781, l. 77.

44. TsGALI, f. 337, op. 1, d. 747, l. 4, 5.

45. TsGALI, f. 337, op. 1, d. 897, l. 28.

46. TsGALI, f. 337, op. 1, d. 781, l. 72.

47. Ibid., l. 78.

48. Ibid., ll. 79, 81, 72.

49. Ibid., l. 81.

50. For a detailed description of the plot, consult appendix 2.

51. TsGALI, f. 337, op. 1, d. 937, l. 13.

52. Ibid.

53. Ibid.

54. TsGALI, f. 337, op. 1, d. 1000, l. 4, 5.

55. Ibid., ll. 92–93.

56. Ibid., l. 93.

57. TsGALI, f. 337, op. 1, d. 1051, ll. 9–12, 10.

58. Ibid., ll. 10, 9, 11.

59. Ibid., l. 9.

60. Ibid.

61. For the source of this statistic, see *Teatral'nyi Leningrad* for the years 1964–1965. The issue for 6 June 1965–23 June 1965 was missing.

62. "Zritel' beret slovo," *Za sovetskoe iskusstvo*, 15 May 1963, 4; "Konferentsiia zritelei," *Za sovetskoe iskusstvo*, 16 April 1963, 2.

63. TsGALI, f. 337, op. 1, d. 1001, l. 40.

64. Makarova, *Dance Autobiography*, 52–54.

4. Ballet Battles: The Kirov Ballet during Khrushchev's Thaw

Epigraph: Larisa Abyzova, *Igor' Bel'skii. Simfoniia zhizni* (St. Petersburg: Akademiia Russkogo Baleta imeni A. Ia. Vaganova, 2000), 132.

1. Polly Jones, "Introduction: The Dilemmas of De-Stalinization," in *The Dilemmas of De-Stalinization: Negotiating Cultural and Social Change in the Khrushchev Era*, ed. Polly Jones (London: Routledge, 2006), 10.

2. As de Certeau has argued in *The Practice of Everyday Life* (Berkeley: University of California Press, 1984), there are always strategies available to the ordinary person for reclaiming autonomy from all-pervasive forces such as politics (xiii). By proposing the concept of artistic repossession as analytical tool, I am applying de Certeau's analysis of tactics available to the ordinary person to reclaim autonomy of action from forces like commerce and politics to the field of high culture in the Soviet Union.

3. Michel Foucault, "The Subject and Power," afterword to *Michel Foucault: Beyond Structuralism and Hermeneutics*, by Hubert L. Dreyfus and Paul Rabinow (New York: Harvester Press, 1982), 225.

4. Igor Moiseyev, "The Ballet and Reality," in *Ulanova, Moiseyev, and Zakharov on Soviet Ballet*, ed. Peter Brinson, trans. E. Fox and D. Fry (London: SCR, 1954), 12.

5. Moiseyev, "Ballet and Reality," 13–14.

6. Ibid., 14.

7. Galina Ulanova, "S khudozhnika sprositsia," *Sovetskaia muzyka* 4 (April 1953): 38.

8. Ulanova, "S khudozhnika sprositsia," 39.

9. Asaf Messerer, *Tanets. Mysl'. Vremia* (Moscow: Iskusstvo, 1990), 192.

10. "Zapiska ministra kul'tury SSSR N. A. Mikhailova N. S. Khrushchevy o sostaianii sovetskoi kul'tury," *Apparat TsK KPSS i Kul'tura 1953–1957. Dokumenty*, ed. E. S. Afanas'eva, V. Iu. Afiani, Z. K. Vodop'ianova, et al. (Moscow: Rosspen, 2001), 425–33. The memorandum also touched on issues such as erecting a monument to Lenin in Moscow for 1957, technical questions, and issues concerning cadres.

11. "Zapiska ministra kul'tury SSSR N. A. Mikhailova N. S. Khrushchevy o sostaianii sovetskoi kul'tury," 427–28.

12. Ibid., 428.

13. This emerges from the archival records of the Kirov Theater's artistic council.

14. Sergeev danced with the Kirov from 1930 until 1961, Dudinskaya from 1931 until 1962, and Vecheslova from 1928 until 1953. Sergeev and Dudinskaya were fifty-one and fifty years old respectively when they retired from the stage, which was late for principal dancers even at that time. Similarly, Galina Ulanova retired from dancing in 1960 at the age of fifty. Vecheslova retired at the age of forty-three. Within this context, it is important to distinguish between the human and artistic age of the artists in question: the camp of the "young" challengers of Stalinist ballet orthodoxies included not just members of the younger generation but also experimental choreographers of the 1920s or early 1930s who had been more or less forced into creative silence for the past twenty years, for example, Leonid Iakobson, who was born in 1904.

15. Makarov (1925–2000) danced with the Kirov Ballet from 1943 until 1970, Shatilov (1924–2003) from 1947 until 1965, and Zubkovskii (1911–1971) from 1931 until 1962. Unlike Makarov and Shatilov, Zubkovskii belonged to the same generation as Sergeev.

16. A. Makarov, K. Shatilov, N. Zubkovskii, "Chto meshaet rostu molodykh darovanii. Pis'mo v redaktsiiu," *Pravda*, 23 February 1955, 2.

17. Judging from comments made by artists of the Kirov at the meeting with Deputy Minister Kemenov, such high-level visits from the Ministry of Culture happened rarely (TsGALI, f. 337, op. 4, d. 21).

18. TsGALI, f. 337, op. 4, d. 21, ll. 1–2, 1–8, 6–7, 7–8.

19. Ibid., ll. 2, 3.

20. Ibid., l. 4.

21. Ibid., l. 6.

22. Ibid., ll. 80–81.

23. Ibid., l. 82.

24. Ibid., l. 83.

25. Ibid., l. 84.

26. "Po Materialam 'Pravdy.' 'Chto meshaet rostu molodykh darovanii,'" *Pravda*, 16 March 1955, 2.

27. "Prikaz ministerstva kul'tury SSSR," *Za sovetskoe iskusstvo*, 24 March 1955, 1.

28. TsGALI, f. 337, op. 4, d. 21, l. 79.

29. Pierre Bourdieu, *The Field of Cultural Production: Essays on Art and Literature*, ed. Randal Johnson (Cambridge: Polity Press, 1993), 58.

30. Fedor Lopukhov, *Shest' desiat let v balete. Vospominaniia i zapiski baletmeistera* (Moscow: Iskusstvo, 1966), 342.

31. "Theater Courier: Once More on the New Ballet," *Peterburgsky listok*, 5 January 1890; translated in Tim Scholl, *"Sleeping Beauty," a Legend in Progress* (New Haven: Yale University Press, 2004), 182.

32. Herman Laroche, excerpt from *P. I. Tchaikovsky as a Dramatic Composer* (reprinted from the *Yearbook of the Imperial Theaters,* 1893–1894 season, 1895), translated in Scholl, *"Sleeping Beauty,"* 195–96.

33. Rostislav Zakharov, *Iskusstvo baletmeistera* (Moscow: Iskusstvo, 1954), 32–33, 112–16, 210, 212, 52. Zakharov was the main theoretician of the genre and one of its most vicious defenders in the 1950s.

34. Zakharov, *Iskusstvo baletmeistera,* 218–19.

35. For example, ibid., 21–22.

36. The article was reprinted in Vera Krasovskaia, *Stat'i o balete* (Leningrad: Iskusstvo, 1967), 9.

37. Krasovskaia, *Stat'i o balete,* 13, 14. It is thus misleading to argue that in Soviet writings on ballet that the term *symphonism* "carries no literal or denotative meaning. Instead, it serves as a floating signifier to indicate nothing more than the presence of an absence: the lack of 'bad' ballet music" (Scholl, *"Sleeping Beauty,"* 85).

38. For example, Krasovskaia, *Stat'i o balete,* 30.

39. Ibid., 25, 26.

40. Ibid., 27.

41. Ibid., 15–16. Krasovskaia writes that petite batterie and petit allegro jumps had disappeared, while adagio had been confined to pas de deux, often in form of a dance dialogue where each gesture and movement conveyed one concrete thought.

42. Lopukhov, *Shest' desiat let v balete,* 335.

43. Ibid.

44. Mikhail Meilakh, *Evterpa, ty? Khudozhestvennye zametki. Besedy s artistami russkoi emigratsii. Tom I Balet* (Moscow: Novoe literaturnoe obozrenie, 2008), 535.

45. Lopukhov, *Shest' desiat let v balete,* 336.

46. Alla Osipenko, "Parizh v moei zhizni," *Alla Osipenko* (St. Petersburg: Terpsichore, 2007), 29, 25, 27.

47. Lopukhov, *Shest' desiat let v balete,* 336.

48. "Balet *Kamennyi tsvetok*: Poka postavleno neskol'ko nomerov," *Za sovetskoe iskusstvo,* 4 November 1955, 4.

49. V. Kataev, *"Kamennyi tsvetok—*Nash spektakl'," *Za sovetskoe iskusstvo,* 15 December 1955, 2.

50. "Balet *Kamennyi tsvetok*: Umelo planirovat' repetitsii," *Za sovetskoe iskusstvo,* 22 February 1956, 1.

51. "Balet *Kamennyi tsvetok*: Kontury budushchego spektaklia," *Za sovetskoe iskusstvo*, 14 April 1956, 1.

52. Ekaterina Maksimova, *Madam "Net"* (Moscow: AST-Press Kniga, 2003), 152.

53. "V partorganizatsii baleta: Vospitanie molodezhi—v tsentr vnimaniia," *Za sovetskoe iskusstvo*, 7 July 1956, 2.

54. De Certeau, *Practice of Everyday Life*, xiii.

55. "Komitet VLKSM teatra: 'Nas volnuet zavtra nashego baleta.' Otkrytoe pis'mo Ministry Kul'tury SSSR tov. Mikhailovu N. A.," *Za sovetskoe iskusstvo*, 20 May 1956, 1–2.

56. "Komitet VLKSM teatra," 2.

57. The team lost its supporter Lopukhov, who retired in June 1956. He was succeeded by Boris Fenster.

58. "Iu. Grigorovich, 'Postavlena polovina nomerov,'" *Za sovetskoe iskusstvo*, 19 June 1956, 2.

59. "Balet *Kamennyi Tsvetok*: Repetitsii idut reguliarno," *Za sovetskoe iskusstvo*, 26 October 1956, 1.

60. "Balet *Kamennyi Tsvetok*: Pered vykhodom na stsenu," *Za sovetskoe iskusstvo*, 20 January 1957, 1.

61. "Gotovit'sia k VI Vsemirnomu festivaliu molodozhi," *Za sovetskoe iskusstvo*, 5 February 1957, 1.

62. TsGALI, f. 337, op. 1, d. 442, l. 40.

63. "Prikaz ministra budet vypolnen. Beseda s direktorom teatra G. N. Orlovym," *Za sovetskoe iskusstvo*, 28 February 1957, 4.

64. "Boevoe sodruzhestvo," *Za sovetskoe iskusstvo*, 19 March 1957, 1.

65. "'Navstrechu festivaliu,' B. Gudkov, sekretar' Oktiabr'skogo RK VLKSM," *Za sovetskoe iskusstvo*, 31 March 1957, 1.

66. Gavriela Komleva, *Tanets—schast'e i bol' . . . Zapiski peterburgskoi baleriny* (Moscow: Rosspen, 2000), 128–29.

67. Komleva, *Tanets—schast'e i bol'*, 130–31.

68. Quoted in Abyzova, *Igor' Bel'skii*, 132.

69. L. M. Lavrovskii, "O putakh razvitiia sovetskogo baleta," *Muzykal'nyi teatr i sovremennost'. Voprosy razvitiia sovetskogo baleta* (Moscow: Vserossiiskoe teatral'noe obshchestvo, 1962), 24–26, 105.

70. Lavrovskii, "O putakh razvitiia sovetskogo baleta," 72, 82, 83.

71. Ibid., 86, 107.

72. Ibid., 75–76.

73. Galina Ulanova, "Dolg starshikh," *Izvestiia*, 27 May 1962, 6.

74. Valeriia Chistiakova, "Novye puti, novye resheniia," *Za sovetskoe iskusstvo*, 4 April 1961, 2.

5. Beyond the Iron Curtain: The Bolshoi Ballet in London in 1956

Epigraph: Barbara Newman, *Antoinette Sibley: Reflections of a Ballerina* (London: Hutchinson, 1968), 67.

1. David Caute, *The Dancer Defects: The Struggle for Cultural Supremacy during the Cold War* (Oxford: Oxford University Press, 2003), 3.

2. For example, Caute, *Dancer Defects*; Frances Stonor-Saunders, *Who Paid the Piper? The CIA and the Cultural Cold War* (London: Granta Books, 1999); Scott Lucas, *Freedom's War: The U.S. Crusade against the Soviet Union 1945–56* (Manchester: Manchester University Press, 1999); Walter Hixson, *Parting the Curtain: Propaganda, Culture, and the Cold War, 1945–1961* (New York: St. Martin's Press, 1997); Serge Guilbaut, *How New York Stole the Idea of Modern Art: Abstract Expressionism, Freedom, and the Cold War* (Chicago: University of Chicago Press, 1993).

3. Starting with Nureyev's defection in 1961, international tours provided the background for maybe the most evocative statement on artistic autonomy during the Cold War era, defection. In addition to any private reasons, the defectors contrasted the West's artistic pluralism with the narrow repertoire at home. It is beyond the scope, and purpose, of this chapter to analyze later decisions of artists such as Rudolf Nureyev, Mikhail Baryshnikov, and Natalia Makarova to defect or the defections' impact on Soviet ballet.

4. William Taubman, *Khrushchev: The Man, His Era* (Great Britain: Free Press, 2003), 325, 358, 738n110.

5. Margot Fonteyn, *Autobiography* (London: W. H. Allen, 1975), 165.

6. "Doklad ministra kultury SSSR N. A. Mikhailova o rabote Ministerstva po razvitiiu kul'turnykh sviazei SSSR i Angliei, v sviazi s itogami poezdki sovetskoi pravitel'stvennoi delegatsii v Angliiu," RGALI, f. 2329, op. 9, d. 24, l. 3.

7. "Doklad ministra kultury SSSR N. A. Mikhailova o rabote Ministerstva po razvitiiu kul'turnykh sviazei SSSR i Angliei, v sviazi s itogami poezdki sovetskoi pravitel'stvennoi delegatsii v Angliiu," RGALI, f. 2329, op. 9, d. 24, l. 3.

8. RGALI, f. 648, op. 7, d. 215, l. 16.

9. Ibid., l. 63.

10. Letter by USSR Minister of Culture N. Mikhailov to the Central Committee of the CPSU, 14 August 1956, RGALI, f. 648, op. 7, d. 215, l. 12.

11. Viktorina Kriger, "Khochu v Afriku," *Sovetskii artist*, 28 March 1956, 4.

12. RGALI, f. 648, op. 7, d. 723, l. 17.

13. Ibid., l. 14.

14. Ibid., l. 35.

15. In her autobiography, Plisetskaya discusses her travel problems (Maiia Plisetskaia, *Ia, Maiia Plisetskaia* [Moscow: Novosti, 1997], 170–93, 212–16).

16. Plisetskaia, *Ia, Maiia Plisetskaia*, 21, 26, 25–28.

17. RGALI, f. 2329, op. 8, ed. khr. 234, l. 30.

18. RGALI, f. 648, op. 7, ed. khr. 473, ll. 20–21.

19. RGALI, f. 648, op. 7, ed. khr. 227, l. 46 (original of letter: f. 648, op. 7, ed. khr. 474, l. 75).

20. "Bolshoi Here Next Week. Ulanova Not Coming. Advance Party's Flight Today," *Times*, 29 September 1956, 6.

21. "All-Night Filming at Coven Garden. Record of Ulanova's 'Giselle,'" *Times*, 27 October 1956, 5.

22. "Sostoianie zdorov'ia G. S. Ulanovoi," *Sovetskii artist*, 28 November 1956, 1.

23. RGALI, f. 2930, op. 1, ed. khr. 40, ll. 2–3.

24. For a brief account of the episode, see Caute, *Dancer Defects*, 472–74.

25. "V Redaktsiu gazety 'Izvestiia,'" *Sovetskii artist*, 26 September 1956, 2.

26. "Cancellation of Bolshoi Ballet 'Not Definite.' Visit Possible if Charge against Athlete Dropped," *Times*, 22 September 1956, 6.

27. "A Grievous Misunderstanding," *Times*, 22 September 1956, editorials/leaders, 7.

28. RGALI, f. 2329, op. 8, ed. khr. 234, l. 16.

29. Ibid., l. 19.

30. See, for example, *Times*, 24 September 1956, 9, and 25 September 1956, 11.

31. See, for example, RGALI, f. 648, op. 7, ed. khr. 222, l. 35; ed. khr. 223, ll. 19, 22, 25, 28.

32. RGALI, f. 648, op. 7, ed. khr. 222, l. 29.

33. Ibid., l. 22.

34. Ibid., l. 25.

35. "Bolshoi Ballet May Come After All. Russian Minister's Hint," *Times*, 27 September 1956, 10.

36. "Bolshoi Visit Now Almost Assured. Director's Decision," *Times*, 28 September 1956, 10.

37. "Bolshoi Here Next Week. Ulanova Not Coming. Advance Party's Flight Tonight," *Times*, 29 September 1956, 6; "Good Sense Prevails," *Times*, 29 September 1956, editorials, 7.

38. "Good Sense Prevails," 7.

39. Caute, *Dancer Defects*, 473.

40. "Russian Not at Bow Street. Vain Wait for Nina Ponomareva," *Times*, 4 October 1956, 10.

41. Caute, *Dancer Defects*, 474.

42. "The Russian Ballet Comes West. Paris and London to Receive Two Famous Moscow Companies," *Times*, 11 June 1956, 5.

43. "The Bolshoi Ballet," *Dancing Times*, October 1956, 12, 14.

44. RGALI, f. 2930, op. 1, d. 40, l. 29.

45. Ibid., ll. 6–7.

46. Newman, *Antoinette Sibley*, 67–68.

47. RGALI, f. 2930, op. 1, d. 40, l. 29.

48. Ibid., ll. 31-33.

49. "What the Bolshoi Means to Covent Garden," *Times*, 26 October 1956, 3.

50. This is according to BBC statistics. See Elsa Brunelleschi, "Ulanova and Fonteyn on Television," *Dancing Times*, December 1956, 127.

51. "Full House," *Times*, 22 October 1956, editorials, 9.

52. "Visit to be Extended. Three Evenings at Croydon Theater," *Times*, 13 October 1956, 8.

53. "All-Night Queue for Ballet Tickets," *Times*, 20 October 1956, 6.

54. "The Sitter Out," *Dancing Times*, November 1956, 63.

55. Mary Clarke, "The Four Ballets," *Dancing Times*, November 1956, 69.

56. A. V. Coton, "London Ballet Month. Bolshoi," *Ballet Today*, November 1956, 4.

57. Fonteyn, *Autobiography*, 166.

58. Coton, "London Ballet Month. Bolshoi," 4.

59. Ibid., 4.

60. "Bolshoi Ballet. 'Romeo and Juliet,'" *Times*, 4 October 1956, 3.

61. Clarke, "The Four Ballets," 69. Ashton choreographed *Romeo and Juliet* for the Danish Royal Ballet in 1955.

62. Clarke, "Four Ballets," 70, 72.

63. "Bolshoi Ballet. 'The Fountain of Bakhchisarai,'" *Times*, 10 October 1956, 3.

64. Arnold L. Haskell, "Petersburg to Leningrad. Balletomane's Logbook," *Dancing Times*, November 1956, 74.

65. A. Lapauri, "Razdum'ia posle spektaklei gostei," *Sovetskii artist*, 26 October 1962, 4.

66. "What the Bolshoi Means to Covent Garden," *Times*, 26 October 1956, 3.

67. For example, Julie Kavanagh, *Secret Muses: The Life of Frederick Ashton* (London: Faber and Faber, 1996), 416 (on the Bolshoi's influence on Cranko and MacMillan), 438 (on the potential influence of the underlying ideas of drambalet on Ashton's *Ondine*); John Percival, *Theater in My Blood: A Biography of John Cranko* (London: Herbert Press, 1983), 116–17, 122–23, 155–57; Edward Thorpe, *Kenneth MacMillan: The Man and the Ballets*, foreword by Dame Ninette de Valois (London: Hamish Hamilton, 1985), vii, ix, 79–85.

68. Thorpe, *Kenneth MacMillan*, ix.

69. Ibid., 80.

70. "Sumptuous Spectacle at Covent Garden. Royal Opera House: *Romeo and Juliet*," *Times*, 10 February 1965, 16.

71. V. Pakhomov, "Torzhestvo sovetskogo khoreograficheskogo iskusstva," *Sovetskii artist*, 21 November 1956, 1.

72. Aleksandr Pushkin, *Evgenii Onegin. Proza* (Moscow: Ekmo-Press, 1998), part 1, p. 19, ll. 6–7.

73. Igor' Moiseev, "V dobryi put'!" *Sovetskii artist*, 3 October 1956, 1.

74. RGALI, f. 2930, op. 1, d. 59, l. 42.

75. Pakhomov, "Torzhestvo sovetskogo khoreograficheskogo iskusstva," 1.

76. I. Seleznev, "Zhivoe slovo kritiki," *Sovetskii artist*, 28 November 1956, 1.

77. "Partiinaia Zhizn'. Delovaia Kritika," *Sovetskii artist*, 5 December 1956, 4.

78. L. Lavrovskii, "Akademichnost' narodno-kharakternogo tantsa," *Sovetskii artist*, 21 November 1956, 2.

79. RGALI, f. 2930, op.1, d. 40, l. 36.

80. This is my educated guess, as the ballet was spelled in the protocol as *Kapeliia*.

81. RGALI, f. 2930, op. 1, d. 40, l. 36.

82. Ibid., ll. 36–38, 22.

83. Ibid., ll. 36–38.

84. Probably the meeting held in 1960 discussed in the previous chapter.

85. RGALI, f. 2329, op. 3. d. 1928, ll. 30, 37–44.

6. Enfant Terrible: Leonid Iakobson and *The Bedbug*, 1962

Epigraph: Maiia Plisetskaia, *Ia, Maiia Plisetskaia* (Moscow: Novosti, 1997), 291.

1. Natalia Makarova, *A Dance Autobiography*, ed. Gennady Smakov (London: Adam and Charles Black, 1980), 54, 56–57, 61.

2. Plisetskaia, *Ia, Maiia Plisetskaia*, 289–90, 298; Makarova, *Dance Autobiography*, 57, 68.

3. A. Degen, I. Stupnikov, *Leningradskii balet, 1917–1987. Slovar'-Spravochnik* (Leningrad: Sovetskii kompozitor, 1988), 247.

4. TsGALI, f. 87, op.1, d. 54, l. 82.

5. Patricia Blake, "Introduction: The Two Deaths of Vladimir Mayakovsky," in *The Bedbug and Selected Poetry* by Vladimir Mayakovsky, ed. Patricia Blake, trans. Max Hayward and George Reavey (Bloomington: Indiana University Press, 1975), 37.

6. Mayakovsky, *Bedbug and Selected Poetry*, 299–300.

7. Blake, "Introduction," 37.

8. TsGALI, f. 87, op. 1, d. 54, l. 83.

9. Galina Dobrovol'skaia, *Baletmeister Leonid Iakobson* (Leningrad: Iskusstvo, 1968), 131.

10. Makarova, *Dance Autobiography*, 61. In Mayakovsky's play, Zoya does not commit suicide but reappears in the second half of the play set in 1979.

11. Vadim Gaevsky, "The Phenomenon of the St. Petersburg Ballet," *The Mariinsky Theater, 1783–2003: Theme with Variations* (St. Petersburg: Mariinsky

Theater, St. Petersburg State Museum of Theater and Music, JSC "Art Deco," 2003), 35.

12. Premiered at the Bolshoi on June 1927, *The Red Poppy* was the first full-length, narrative ballet on a contemporary revolutionary topic but, it included an old-fashioned, classical divertissement.

13. Elizabeth Souritz, *Soviet Choreographers of the 1920s*, trans. Lynn Visson (Durham: Duke University Press, 1990), 251.

14. Mayakovsky, *Bedbug and Selected Poetry*, 243.

15. Ibid., 246.

16. Blake, "Introduction," 49–50

17. Marc Slonim, *Russian Theater: From the Empire to the Soviets* (New York: Collier Books, 1962), 368.

18. L. Iakobson, "Assotsiatsiia novogo baleta," *Zhizn' iskusstva*, 23 October 1928, 13.

19. Galina Dobrovol'skaia, *Baletmeister Leonid Iakobson* (Leningrad: Iskusstvo, 1968), 14–15.

20. Dobrovol'skaia, *Baletmeister Leonid Iakobson*, 15–17, 25–26.

21. *Russkii balet entsiklopediia* (Moscow: Bol'shaia rosiiskaia entsiklopediia, "Soglasie," 1997), 538–39.

22. Irina Iakobson and Vladimir Zeidel'son, *Besedy o Leonide Iakobsone ili neobkhodimyi razgovor i pis'mo, poslannoe vsled* (St. Petersburg: Maksima, 1993), 27–28.

23. Plisetskaia, *Ia, Maiia Plisetskaia*, 291.

24. Makarova, *Dance Autobiography*, 56.

25. Irina Kolpakova in conversation with the author, 31 September 2006, New York.

26. Iakobson and Zeidel'son, *Besedy o Leonide Iakobsone*, 6.

27. Makarova, *Dance Autobiography*, 56–57.

28. Iakobson and Zeidel'son, *Besedy o Leonide Iakobsone*, 23–24.

29. Ibid., 18–19, 25, 26.

30. Ibid., 5, 23.

31. Ibid., 22.

32. Ibid., 22, 50.

33. "K. M. Sergeev—glavnyi baletmeister," *Za sovetskoe iskusstvo*, 19 April 1960, 3.

34. TsGALI, f. 87, op. 1, d. 54, l. 75.

35. TsGALI, f. 337, op .1, d. 781, l. 164.

36. TsGALI, f. 87, op. 1, d. 54, l. 82.

37. TsGALI, f. 87, op. 1, d. 52, l. 1. The copy of this letter in the archives is addressed to "Nikolai Aleksandrovich," without giving a family name. It is likely

that the addressee is Nikolai Aleksandrovich Mikhailov, the USSR minister of culture at that time: the letter was addressed to a person in Moscow powerful enough to order the Kirov to allow Iakobson to present his idea to the theater's artistic council. The Soviet minister of culture seems the most likely candidate for this, especially as other well-known dancers would appeal to the person holding the position of Soviet minister of culture for patronage.

38. TsGALI, f. 87, op. 1, d. 54, l. 5.

39. Ibid., ll. 2–4.

40. TsGALI, f. 337, op. 1, d. 781, ll. 164–65.

41. Ibid., l. 68.

42. "Balet Misteriia-buff: Idut repetitsii," *Za sovetskoe iskusstvo*, 23 January 1962, 1; TsGALI, f. 87, op. 1, d. 54, ll. 75–76.

43. TsGALI, f. 87, op. 1, d. 54, l. 83.

44. Ibid., ll. 83–84.

45. "Za novyi pod"em opernogo i baletnogo iskusstvo. Kommunisty obsuzhdaiut reshenie Gorkoma KPSS," *Za sovetskoe iskusstvo*, 17 May 1960, 2.

46. Iakobson and Zaidel'son, *Besedy o Leonide Iakobsone*, 48-49.

47. TsGALI, f. 337, op. 1, d. 897, l. 77, 28.

48. K. Sergeev, "Plany sezona," *Za sovetskoe iskusstvo*, 23 January 1962, 2.

49. TsGALI, f. 87, op. 1, d. 54, ll. 19–20.

50. Ibid., l. 32.

51. Ibid., ll. 32–33.

52. Ibid., l. 35.

53. Ibid., ll. 58–59.

54. Ibid., ll. 60–61.

55. Ibid., ll. 70–71.

56. Ibid., l. 14.

57. Ibid., l. 16, 61, 37.

58. Ibid., l. 33.

59. TsGALI, f. 337, op. 1, d. 1000, ll. 74–75.

60. TsGALI, f. 337, op. 1, d. 1047, l. 22.

61. Ibid., l. 26.

62. TsGALI, f. 87, op. 1, d. 54, l. 79.

63. TsGALI, f. 87, op. 1, d. 52, l. 6.

64. Priscilla Johnson, *Khrushchev and the Arts: The Politics of Soviet Culture, 1962–1964* (Cambridge: MIT Press, 1965), 1–2. The following summary of the confrontation is based on this book (Johnson, *Khrushchev and the Arts*, 7–30) and a document recording Khrushchev's reaction at the Manezh Gallery (101–5).

65. "Resheniia noiabr'skogo plenuma TsK KPSS i zadachi teatra," *Za sovetskoe iskusstvo*, 30 December 1962, 2.

66. "Opravdaem doverie rodnoi partii i naroda," *Za sovetskoe iskusstvo*, 27 March 1963, 1.

67. TsGALI, f. 87, op. 1, d. 54, ll. 80-81. The Moskovskii khudozhestvennyi teatr (Moscow Art Theater) was founded by Konstantin Stanislavsky and Vladimir Nemirovich-Danchenko in 1897. It soon became famous for its innovative productions of Anton Chekov's plays. During the Soviet period, Stanislavsky's method became "embalmed" as the officially prescribed method for theater productions.

68. "Nash trud i talent—na sluzhbu narodu," *Za sovetskoe iskusstvo*, 27 March 1963, 2.

69. Iu. Prokhorov, "Kak vypolniaiutsia partiinye resheniia" and "Bol'she trebovatel'nosti. S otchetno-vybornogo partiinogo sobraniia baleta," *Za sovetskoe iskusstvo*, 16 April 1963, 1, 2; "Dela i zadachi partiinoi organizatsii. S otchetno-vybornogo partiinogo sobraniia teatra im. S. M. Kirova," *Za sovetskoe iskusstvo*, 29 April 1963, 2–3; A. Klimov, "Vdokhnovliaiushchii prizyv" and "Nedostatki ustraniaiutsia," *Za sovetskoe iskusstvo*, 6 July 1963, 1, 2.

70. TsGALI, f. 337, op. 1, d. 897, ll. 19–24.

71. Makarova, *Dance Autobiography*, 60.

72. TsGALI, f. 337, op. 1, d. 937, l. 27.

73. TsGALI, f. 87, op. 1, d. 54, ll. 34, 59, 80.

74. "Dela i zadachi partiinoi organizatsii," *Za sovetskoe iskusstvo*, 29 April 1963, 2–3.

75. A. Klimov, "Vdokhnovliaiushchii prisyv," *Za sovetskoe iskusstvo*, 5 July 1963, 1.

76. "Nedostatki ustraniaiutsia," *Za sovetskoe iskusstvo*, 5 July 1963, 2.

7. Choreography as Resistance: Yuri Grigorovich's *Spartacus*, 1968

Epigraph: Ekaterina Maksimova, *Madam "Net"* (Moscow: AST-Press Kniga, 2003), 203.

1. RGALI, f. 2329, op. 3, d. 1928, l. 42.

2. Premiered in St. Petersburg in 1862, *The Pharaoh's Daughter* (music by Cesare Pugni) was Marius Petipa's first major success. A sumptuous spectacle lasting four hours, its cast of around four hundred spun an unlikely, exotic tale.

3. N. Volkov, "Tragediia o Spartake," in Bolshoi Theater, *Spartak* (program, Moscow, 1958), 9–12. Appianos was a Greek historian of the second century, also known as Appianus, Appian, and Appiani.

4. N. Volkov, "Tragediia o Spartake," 13; A. Khachaturian, "Balet Spartak," in Bolshoi Theater, *Spartak* (program, Moscow, 1958), 8.

5. Leonid Iakobson, *Pis'ma Noverru* (Tenafly: Hermitage Publishers, 2001), 102.

6. Fedor Lopukhov, *Shest' desiat let v balete. Vospominaniia i zapiski baletmeistera* (Moscow: Iskusstvo, 1966), 319.

7. Iakobson, *Pis'ma Noverru*, 102–3. For a detailed discussion of Iakobson's criticisms of both the libretto and the music, consult 102–18.

8. Ibid., 118, 113.

9. Lopukhov, *Shest' desiat let v balete*, 324.

10. Iakobson, *Pis'ma Noverru*, 119, 121.

11. Lopukhov, *Shest' desiat let v balete*, 325. Lopukhov describes several occasions where Volkov and Khachaturian—at least initially—refused to accept justified, or even necessary, changes proposed by Iakobson (326–27, 329).

12. Irina Iakobson and Vladimir Zeidel'son, *Besedy o Leonide Iakobsone ili neobkhodimyi razgovor i pis'mo, poslannoe vsled* (St. Petersburg: Maksima, 1993), 31.

13. For a detailed description and discussion, see Iakobson, *Pis'ma Noverru*, 101–37; Lopukhov, *Shest' desiat let v balete*, 319–34; Galina Dobrovol'skaia, *Baletmeister Leonid Iakobson* (Leningrad: Iskusstvo, 1968), 76–103.

14. A. Degen and I. Stupnikov, *Leningradskii balet, 1917–1987. Slovar'-spravochnik* (Leningrad: Sovetskii Kompozitor, 1988), 254.

15. TsGALI, f. 337, op. 1, d. 858, l. 17.

16. This statistic is given in the entry for *Spartacus* in Debra Craine and Judith Mackrell, *The Oxford Dictionary of Dance* (Oxford: Oxford University Press, 2000), 446.

17. RGALI, f. 648, op. 7, d. 277, ll. 132–37, 133.

18. Iakobson, *Pis'ma Noverru*, 140.

19. RGALI, f. 648, op. 7, d. 7, l. 132.

20. RGALI, f. 648, op. 7, d. 723, l. 22.

21. Ibid., ll. 22–23.

22. Iakobson, *Pis'ma Noverru*, 141.

23. RGALI, f. 648, op. 11, d. 22, l. 5.

24. RGALI, f. 648, op. 7, d. 277, l. 133.

25. RGALI, f. 648, op. 11, d. 9, ll. 4-5.

26. Ibid., ll. 6, 17–18, 7, 8–10.

27. Ibid., ll. 14–33.

28. Ibid., ll. 35–36.

29. RGALI, f. 648, op. 11, d. 22 and 23.

30. RGALI, f. 648, op. 11, d. 23, l. 30.

31. RGALI, f. 648, op. 11, d., l. 39.

32. RGALI, f. 648, op. 11, d. 23, ll. 29, 23–25.

33. Ibid., ll. 34, 28.

34. Ibid., ll. 24, 25.

35. Iakobson, *Pis'ma Noverru*, 151–66.

36. For example, RGALI, f. 2329, op. 3, d. 1928, ll. 5, 16.

37. Rostislav Zakharov mentioned on 6 June 1963 that "Aleksandr Nikolaevich" had said this the previous day. Given the nature of this appeal, and as the meeting was chaired by A. N. Kuznetsov, deputy minister of culture, it is likely that "Aleksandr Nikolaevich" refers to Kuznetsov (RGALI, f. 2329, op. 3, d. 1928, l. 5). For the notes of the session held on 5 June, see RGALI, f. 2329, op. 3, d. 1927.

38. RGALI, f. 2329, op. 3, d. 1928, l. 43.

39. RGALI, f. 648, op. 11, d. 103, ll. 1–49, 8–9.

40. Ibid., ll. 28, 33, 40.

41. Ibid., ll. 48–49, 38–39, 42, 45–46.

42. The KDS was opened with the Twenty-Second Congress of the CPSU in October 1961. The Bolshoi started performing at the KDS in 1962 ("O rabote Bol'shogo teatra i Kremlevskogo dvortsa s"ezdov i merakh po ee uluchsheniiu," *Sovetskii artist*, 25 November 1966, 3).

43. "O rabote Bol'shogo teatra i Kremlevskogo dvortsa s"ezdov i merakh po ee uluchsheniiu," *Sovetskii artist*, 25 November 1966, 2–3; 2 December 1966, 2–3.

44. "O rabote Bol'shogo teatra i Kremlevskogo dvortsa s"ezdov i merakh po ee uluchsheniiu," *Sovetskii artist*, 25 November 1966, 3.

45. "O rabote Bol'shogo teatra i Kremlevskogo dvortsa s"ezdov i merakh po ee uluchsheniiu," *Sovetskii artist*, 25 November 1966, 2.

46. "Uluchshat' planirovanie. Iz vystupleniia V. Preobrazhenskogo," *Sovetskii artist*, 4 May 1962, 4.

47. "Uluchshat' planirovanie. Iz vystupleniia V. Preobrazhenskogo," *Sovetskii artist*, 4 May 1962, 4, 2.

48. "O rabote Bol'shogo teatra i Kremlevskogo dvortsa s"ezdov i merakh po ee uluchsheniiu," *Sovetskii artist*, 2 December 1966, 3; 25 November 1966, 2.

49. "O rabote Bol'shogo teatra i Kremlevskogo dvortsa s"ezdov i merakh po ee uluchsheniiu," *Sovetskii artist*, 2 December 1966, 3.

50. RGALI, f. 648, op. 11, d. 103, l. 8.

51. "Na sbore truppy," *Sovetskii artist*, 23 September 1966, 1. *An Optimistic Tragedy* was based on the play of the same name by Vs. Vishnevskii. Its plot was set during the days of the civil war on the Baltic Fleet and at the front. The opera's premiere took place on 20 November 1965 in Frunze. *The Fortress* had its premiere under the name *The Fortress of Brest* in Voronezh on 23 March 1967 and is also known under the name *The Unknown Soldier*. The opera's libretto was based on S. Smirnov's book *The Fortress of Brest* and materials from the Museum of the Defence of the Fortress of Brest and the book *Heroic Defence*. Its action was set in 1941, during the German siege of the Fortress of Brest.

52. "Na sbore truppy," *Sovetskii artist*, 23 September 1966, 1.

53. Grigorovich became the Bolshoi Ballet's chief choreographer in 1964, a position he held until 1995.

54. Maksimova, *Madam "Net,"* 203.

55. RGALI, f. 648, op. 12, d. 39, ll. 5–6.

56. RGALI, f. 648, op. 12, d. 41, ll. 4, 5, 6.

57. Ibid., l. 5. For a description of the use of the canopy, consult Grigorovich's exposition (ll. 6–14).

58. Ibid., ll. 16–17.

59. Liepa's and Vasil'ev's performance can be seen in a filmed version of Grigorovich's *Spartacus* from 1975. The film is of the original cast (Spartacus: Vasil'ev, Crassus: Liepa, Aegina: Nina Timofeeva), with the exception of Phrygia, who is danced not by Ekaterina Maksimova but Nataliia Bessmertnova (*Spartak* [Kinostudiia "Mosfil'm"; Moscow: Kinovideoob"edinenie "Krupnyi plan," 2000], DVD).

60. RGALI, f. 648, op. 12, d. 41, ll. 12–13, 14, 18.

61. Ibid., l. 16, 17.

62. Ibid., ll. 18–19, 19.

63. Maksimova, *Madam "Net,"* 203.

64. Maris Liepa, *Vchera i segodnia v balete* (Moscow: Molodaia gvardiia, 1986), 101–2.

65. Liepa, *Vchera i segodnia v balete*, 102–3.

66. Ibid., 100–101.

67. Maksimova, *Madam "Net,"* 203–4.

68. Vladimir Vasil'ev quoted in Maris Liepa, *Ia khochu tantsevat' sto let* (Moscow: Vagrius, 1996), 177.

69. Ekaterina Maksimova quoted in Liepa, *Ia khochu tantsevat' sto let*, 205; Maksimova, *Madam "Net,"* 204.

70. Liepa, *Ia khochu tantsevat' sto let*, 80, 81. Liepa's book was originally published in Riga in 1981, this statistic is therefore likely to refer to 1980.

71. Ibid., 82.

72. Ibid., 82–83, 86. For a detailed description of Liepa's view of his part and his preparations before a performance, consult 84–90.

73. Erik Tivuts, "Kratkoe predislovie," in Liepa, *Ia khochu tantsevat' sto let*, 9. Liepa died in 1989 at the age of fifty-two.

74. Liepa, *Ia khochu tantsevat' sto let*, 89–90.

75. BolshoiTalk, Bolshoi Ballet Discussion Forum, topic ID: 73, posting #12, posted on 9 May 2006, http://ballet.co.uk/cgu-bin/dcforum/dcboard/cgi. Ballet.co.uk was the major British website for ballet enthusiasts, offering reviews, a magazine, and discussion forums until its closure in 2011.

76. John Percival, "Vivid imagery of Bolshoi Spartacus," *Times*, 18 July 1969, 11.

77. John Percival, "MacMillan's intentions for Covent Garden," *Times*, 6 September 1969, 3.

78. "Siianie 'Spartaka,'" in *Spartak. K 25-letiiu postanovki* (program, Bolshoi Theater, Moscow, 1993), 2.

79. Balletco closed and went into archive in January 2012. All materials accumulated remain available online.

80. BolshoiTalk, Bolshoi Ballet Discussion Forum, topic ID: 73, posting #7, posted on 4 May 2006, http://ballet.co.uk/cgu-bin/dcforum/dcboard/cgi.

81. BolshoiTalk, Bolshoi Ballet Discussion Forum, topic ID: 73, posting #1, posted on 6 May 2006, http://ballet.co.uk/cgu-bin/dcforum/dcboard/cgi.

Conclusion

1. Michel Foucault, "The Subject and Power," afterword to *Michel Foucault: Beyond Structuralism and Hermeneutics* by Hubert L. Dreyfus and Paul Rabinow (New York: Harvester Press, 1982), 225.

2. The cultural historian Peter Burke has warned that a cultural history of revolutions should not assume that these events make everything new: apparent innovation may mask the persistence of tradition, and the story of revolutions should include a place for cultural survivals (Peter Burke, *What Is Cultural History?* [Cambridge: Polity Press, 2004], 124).

3. Viktorina Kriger, "Balerina zagovorila," *Zhizn' iskusstva*, 6 March 1928, 6–7.

4. Kriger, "Balerina zagovorila," 6.

5. Ibid., 6–7.

6. Stephen Lovell introduced the concept of a Soviet "middlebrow culture" in his book *The Russian Reading Revolution: Print Culture in the Soviet and Post-Soviet Eras* (London: Palgrave MacMillan, 2000).

7. I am indebted to Professor Yaron Ezrahi for this distinction between monarchic and democratic culture.

8. *Alla Osipenko: Ispoved' baleriny* (Russkoe video, 1989), VHS.

9. Iurii Slonimskii, *Sovetskii balet. Materialy k istorii sovetskogo baletnogo teatra* (Moscow-Leningrad: Iskusstvo, 1950), 310.

10. Sotheby's, London, *Catalogue for Modern and Contemporary Russian Art*, 15 February 2007, 172.

11. Ol'ga Gerdt, "Vse, o chem mechtalos'," *Ogonek*, no. 4, January 1996, 77. The article was dedicated to Igor' Moiseev's ninetieth birthday.

Appendix 1. A Who's Who

1. The Mariinsky/Kirov Ballet's ballet school underwent several name changes during the period under investigation. From approximately 1780 until 1917, it was known as the Imperial Petersburg Theatrical Institute (Imperatorskoe peterburgskoe teatral'noe uchilishche); after the revolution it was renamed the Petrograd (Petrogradskoe) and then Leningrad Choreographic Institute

(Leningradskoe khoreograficheskoe uchilishche; LKhU, also LGKhU); since 1957, LKhU named after A. Ia. Vaganova, from 1961 the word *academic* was added; since 1991, it has been known as the Akademiia russkogo baleta imeni A. Ia. Vaganova. The school of the Bolshoi Ballet was known as the Moscow Theatrical Institute (Moskovskoe tealtral'noe uchilishche) before the revolution and as the Moscow Choreographic Institute (Moskovskoe khoreographicheskoe uchilishche; MKhU) for most of the Soviet period; from 1961, the word *academic* was added; since 1995, it has been known as the Moscow State Academy of Choreography (Moskovskaia gosudarstvennaia akademiia khoreografii).

2. Galina Dobrovol'skaia, *Baletmeister Leonid Iakobson* (Leningrad: Iskusstvo, 1968), 8. The ballet was staged by three choreographers: Vasilii Vainonen, Iakobson (second act), and individual dances by V. Chesnokov. While the ballet was created for dancers of the former Mariinsky, the premiere took place at the Maly Theater in Leningrad (entry for "Zolotoi vek," *Russkii balet entsiklopediia*).

3. "Kandidaty v deputaty gorodskogo soveta," *Za sovetskoe iskusstvo*, 28 February 1961, 2.

4. Biographical entry for Fedor Lopukhov in Arsen Degen and Igor' Stupnikov, *Peterburgskii balet, 1903–2003. Spravochnoe izdanie* (St. Petersburg: Baltiiskie Sezoni, 2003).

5. Igor' Moiseev, *Ia vspominaiu . . . Gastrol' dlinoiu v zhizn'* (Moscow: Soglasie, 1996), 33–34.

6. *Za sovetskoe iskusstvo*, 23 February 1955, 2–3.

7. Solomon Volkov, *St. Petersburg: A Cultural History*, trans. Antonina W. Bouis (New York: Free Press, 1997), 487.

8. "Kirov i Malii Teatri: Deviat' kandidatov dlia organov Sovetskoi vlasti," *Za sovetskoe iskusstvo*, 20 February 1963, 1.

9. Natalia Makarova, *A Dance Autobiography*, ed. Gennady Smakov (London: Adam and Charles Black, 1980), 80.

10. Degen and Stupnikov, *Peterburgskii balet*, 70.

11. Natalia Roslavleva, *Era of the Russian Ballet* (London: Victor Gollancz, 1966), 230–31.

Appendix 2: Ballets

1. Iurii Slonimskii, *Sovetskii balet. Materialy k istorii sovetskogo baletnogo teatra* (Moscow-Leningrad: Iskusstvo, 1950), 160.

2. Mary Clarke and Clement Crisp, *Ballet: An Illustrated History* (London: Hamish Hamilton, 1992), 37.

Bibliography

Archival Materials

Tsentral'nyi gosudarstvennyi arkhiv literatury i iskusstva (TsGALI),
St. Petersburg

Fond 337 (Gosudarstevennyi akademicheskii teatr opery i baleta im. S. M.
Kirova)

Fond 87 (Leonid Iakobson)

Rossiiskii gosudarstvennyi arkhiv literatury i iskusstva (RGALI), Moscow

Fond 648 (Gosudarstvennyi akademicheskii Bol'shoi teatr)

Fond 2329 (Ministerstvo kul'tury SSSR)

opis' 3 (otdel muzykal'nykh uchrezhdenii, 1953–1963)

opis' 8 (otdel vneshnykh snoshenii, 1953–1963)

opis' 9 (upravlenie vneshnykh snoshenii, 1953–1968)

Fond 2930 (Tsentral'nyi dom aktera VTO im. A. A. Iablochkinoi)

Books and Articles

Abyzova, Larisa. *Igor' Bel'skii. Simfoniia zhizni.* St. Petersburg: Akademiia
Russkogo Baleta imeni A. Ia. Vaganova, 2000.

Afanas'eva, E. S., V. Iu. Afiani, Z. K. Vodop'ianova, et al. *Apparat TsK KPSS i
Kul'tura, 1953–1957. Dokumenty.* Moscow: Rosspen, 2001.

Akhmatova, Anna. *Sobranie Sochinenii v shesti tomakh. Tom 3: Poemy. Pro Domo
Mea. Teatr.* Moscow: Ellis Lak, 1998.

Aliakrinskaia, M. A., ed. *Alla Osipenko.* St. Petersburg: Terpsichore, 2007.

Artizov, Andrei, and Oleg Naumov, ed. *Vlast' i khudozhestvennaia intelligentsiia:
Dokumenty TsK RKP (b)-VKP (b), VChK-OGPU-NKVD o kul'turnoi politike
1917–1953gg.* Moscow: Mezhdunarodnii fond "Demokratiia," 1999.

Billington, James. *The Icon and the Axe: An Interpretive History of Russian Culture.*
New York: Vintage Books, 1970.

Bourdieu, Pierre. *The Field of Cultural Production: Essays on Art and Literature.*
Edited by Randal Johnson. Cambridge: Polity Press, 1993.

Brinson, Peter, ed. *Ulanova, Moiseyev, and Zakharov on Soviet Ballet.* Translated
by E. Fox and D. Fry. London: SCR, 1954.

Burke, Peter. *What Is Cultural History?* Cambridge: Polity Press, 2004.

Caute, David. *The Dancer Defects: The Struggle for Cultural Supremacy during the
Cold War.* Oxford: Oxford University Press, 2003.

Chernova, Natalia, and G. D. Andreevska, eds. *Kasian Goleizovskii. Zhizn' i
tvorchestvo. Stat'i. Vospominaniia. Dokumenty.* Moscow: Vserosiiskoe teatral'noe
obshchechstvo, 1984.

Chwidkowskij, Dmitrij. *Sankt Petersburg.* Cologne: Könemann, 1996.

Clark, Katerina. *Petersburg: Crucible of Cultural Revolution.* Cambridge: Harvard
University Press, 1995.

———. *The Soviet Novel: History as Ritual.* 3rd edition. Bloomington: Indiana
University Press, 2000.

Clarke, Mary, and Clement Crisp. *Ballet: An Illustrated History.* London: Hamish
Hamilton, 1992.

Cohen, Stephen. *Bukharin and the Bolshevik Revolution: A Political Biography,
1888–1938.* Oxford: Oxford University Press, 1980.

Craine, Debra, and Judith Mackrell. *The Oxford Dictionary of Dance.* Oxford:
Oxford University Press, 2000.

Cunxin, Li. *Mao's Last Dancer.* London: Fusion Press, 2003.

de Certeau, Michel. *The Practice of Everyday Life.* Translated by Steven Rendall.
Berkeley: University of California Press, 1984.

Degen, Arsen, and Igor' Stupnikov. *Leningradskii balet. 1917–1987. Slovar'-
Spravochnik.* Leningrad: Sovetskii kompositor, 1988.

———. *Peterburgskii balet, 1903–2003. Spravochnoe izdanie.* St. Petersburg:
Baltiiskie Sezoni, 2003.

Dobrovol'skaia, Galina. *Baletmeister Leonid Iakobson.* Leningrad: Iskusstvo, 1968.

Dunham, Vera. *In Stalin's Time: Middleclass Values in Soviet Fiction.* Cambridge:
Cambridge University Press, 1976.

Faier, Iurii. *O sebe, o muzyke, o balete.* Moscow: Sovetskii Kompozitor, 1974.

Figes, Orlando. *Natasha's Dance.* London: Penguin Books, 2003.

Fitzpatrick, Sheila. *The Commissariat of Enlightenment: Soviet Organization of
Education and the Arts under Lunacharsky, October 1917–1921.* Cambridge:
Cambridge University Press, 1970.

———. *The Cultural Front: Power and Culture in Revolutionary Russia.* Ithaca:
Cornell University Press, 1992.

————, ed. *Cultural Revolution in Russia, 1928–1931.* Bloomington: Indiana University Press, 1978.

————. "The Emergence of Glaviskusstvo: Class War on the Cultural Front, Moscow, 1928–29." *Soviet Studies* 23, no. 2 (1971): 236–53.

————. *Everyday Stalinism. Ordinary Life in Extraordinary Times: Soviet Russia in the 1930s.* Oxford: Oxford University Press, 1999.

————. *The Russian Revolution.* Oxford: Oxford University Press, 1994.

Fonteyn, Margot. *Autobiography.* London: W. H. Allen, 1975.

Foucault, Michel. "The Subject and Power," afterword to Hubert L. Dreyfus and Paul Rabinow, *Michel Foucault: Beyond Structuralism and Hermeneutics.* New York: Harvester Press, 1982.

Gaevskii, Vadim. *Divertisment. Sud'by klassicheskogo baleta.* Moscow: Iskusstvo, 1981.

————. *Dom Petipa.* Moscow: Artist. Rezhisser. Teatr, 2000.

————. "The Phenomenon of the St. Petersburg Ballet." In *The Mariinsky Theatre 1783–2003: Theme with Variations,* edited by the Mariinsky Theatre and St. Petersburg State Museum of Theatre and Music. St. Petersburg: JSC "Art Deco," 2003.

Gottlieb, Robert. *George Balanchine: The Ballet Maker.* New York: Harper Collins Publishers, 2004.

Günther, Hans, ed. *The Culture of the Stalin Period.* London: Macmillan, 1990.

Haskell, Arnold. *The Ballet in Britain: Eight Oxford Lectures.* Edited by Peter Brinson. London: Oxford University Press, 1962.

Hosking, Geoffrey. *The First Socialist Society: A History of the Soviet Union from Within.* 2nd enlarged ed. Cambridge: Harvard University Press, 1992.

————. *Rulers and Victims: The Russians in the Soviet Union.* Cambridge: Harvard University Press, 2006.

Iakobson, Irina, and Vladimir Zeidel'son. *Besedy o Leonide Iakobsone ili neobkhodimyi razgovor i pis'mo, poslannoe vsled.* St. Petersburg: Maksima, 1993.

Iakobson, Leonid. *Pis'ma Noverru.* Tenafly: Hermitage Publishers, 2001.

Iakovleva, Iuliia. *Mariinskii Teatr. Balet. XX vek.* Moscow: Novoe Literaturnoe Obozrenie, 2005.

Johnson, Priscilla. *Khrushchev and the Arts: The Politics of Soviet Culture, 1962–1964.* Cambridge: MIT Press, 1965.

Jones, Polly, ed. *The Dilemmas of De-Stalinization: Negotiating Cultural and Social Change in the Khrushchev Era.* London: Routledge, 2006.

Karp, Poel', and S. Levin. "*Kamennyi tsvetok*" *S. S. Prokof'eva.* Leningrad: Gosudarstvennoe Muzykal'noe Izdatel'stvo, 1963.

Karsavina, Tamara. *Theatre Street.* London: Readers Union Constable, 1950.

Kavanagh, Julie. *Secret Muses: The Life of Frederick Ashton.* London: Faber and Faber, 1996.

Kelly, Catriona, and David Shepherd, eds. *Constructing Russian Culture in the Age of Revolution, 1881–1940.* Oxford: Oxford University Press, 1998.

Kemp-Welch, A. "'New Economic Policy in Culture' and Its Enemies." *Journal of Contemporary History* 13, no. 3 (1978): 449–65.

Kirstein, Lincoln. *Thirty Years: The New York City Ballet.* London: Adam and Charles Black, 1979.

Komleva, Gavriela. *Tanets–schast'e i bol'* . . . *Zapiski peterburgskoi baleriny.* Moscow: Rosspen, 2000.

Kotkin, Stephen. *Magnetic Mountain: Stalinism as a Civilization.* Berkeley: University of California Press, 1995.

Krasovskaia [Krasovskaya], Vera. *Stat'i o balete.* Leningrad: *Iskusstvo,* 1967.

Krasovskaya, Vera. *Vaganova: A Dance Journey from Petersburg to Leningrad.* Translated by Vera M. Siegel. Gainesville: University Press of Florida, 2005.

Kshesinskaia, Matil'da. *Vospominaniia.* Moscow: ART, 1992.

Ledeneva, Alena. *Russia's Economy of Favours: Blat, Networking, and Informal Exchange.* Cambridge: Cambridge University Press, 1998.

Liepa, Maris. *Ia khochu tantsevat' sto let.* Moscow: Vagrius, 1996.

———. *Vchera i segodnia v balete.* Moscow: Molodaia gvardiia, 1986.

Lopukhov, Fedor. *Shest' desiat let v balete. Vospominaniia i zapiski baletmeistera.* Moscow: Iskusstvo, 1966.

———. *Writings on Ballet and Music.* Edited by Stephanie Jordan. Madison: University of Wisconsin Press, 2002.

Lovell, Stephen. *The Russian Reading Revolution: Print Culture in the Soviet and Post-Soviet Eras.* London: Palgrave Macmillan, 2000.

Lunacharskii, Anatolii. *V mire muzyki: stat'i i rechi.* Moscow: Sovietskii Kompositor, 1971.

Makarova, Natalia. *A Dance Autobiography.* Edited by Gennady Smakov. London: Adam and Charles Black, 1980.

Maksimova, Ekaterina. *Madam "Net."* Moscow: AST-Press Kniga, 2003.

Mayakovsky, Vladimir. *The Bedbug and Selected Poetry.* Translated by Max Hayward and George Reavey. Edited by Patricia Blake. Bloomington: Indiana University Press, 1975.

Massie, Robert K. *Nicholas and Alexandra: The Tragic, Compelling Story of the Last Tsar and His Family.* London: Indigo, 2002.

Meilakh, Mikhail. *Evterpa, ty? Khudozhestvennye zametki. Besedy s artistami russkoi emigratsii. Tom I Balet.* Moscow: Novoe literaturnoe obozrenie, 2008.

Messerer, Asaf. *Tanets. Mysl'. Vremia.* Moscow: Iskusstvo, 1990.

Messerer, Sulamif'. *Sulamif'. Fragmenty vospominanii.* Moscow: Olimpiia Press, 2005.

Moiseev, Igor'. *Ia vspominaiu . . . Gastrol' dlinoiu v zhizn'.* Moscow: Soglasie, 1996.

Muzykal'nyi teatr i sovremennost'. Voprosy razvitiia sovetskogo baleta. Moscow: Vserossiiskoe teatral'noe obshchestvo, 1962.

Newman, Barbara. *Antoinette Sibley: Reflections of a Ballerina.* London: Hutchinson, 1968.

———. *Grace under Pressure: Passing Dance through Times.* New York: Limelight Editions, 2003.

O'Connor, Timothy. *The Politics of Soviet Culture: Anatolii Lunacharskii.* Ann Arbor: University of Michigan Research Press, 1983.

Paperny, Vladimir. *Architecture in the Age of Stalin: Culture Two.* Translated by John Hill and Roann Barris. Cambridge: Cambridge University Press, 2002.

Percival, John. *Theatre in My Blood: A Biography of John Cranko.* London: Herbert Press, 1983.

Petrov, Oleg, and Tim Scholl. "Russian Ballet and Its Place in Russian Artistic Culture of the Second Half of the Nineteenth Century: The Age of Petipa." *Dance Chronicle* 15, no. 1 (1992): 40–58.

Plisetskaia, Maiia. *Ia, Maiia Plisetskaia.* Moscow: Novosti, 1997.

Prevots, Naima. *Dance for Export: Cultural Diplomacy and the Cold War.* Hanover: Wesleyan University Press, published by the University Press of New England, 1998.

Pushkin, Aleksandr. *Evgenii Onegin. Proza.* Moscow: Eksmo-Press, 1998.

Reynolds, Nancy, and Malcolm McCormick. *No Fixed Points: Dance in the Twentieth Century.* New Haven: Yale University Press, 2003.

Roslavleva, Natalia. *Era of the Russian Ballet.* London: Victor Gollancz, 1966.

Russkii balet entsiklopediia. Moscow: Bol'shaia rosiiskaia entsiklopediia, "Soglasie," 1997.

Scholl, Tim. *"Sleeping Beauty," a Legend in Progress.* New Haven: Yale University Press, 2004.

Schwarz, Boris. *Music and Musical Life in Soviet Russia, 1917–1970.* London: Barrie and Jenkins, 1972.

Scott, James C. *Weapons of the Weak: Everyday Forms of Peasant Resistance.* New Haven: Yale University Press, 1985.

Shklovsky, Viktor. *Mayakovsky and His Circle.* Edited and translated by Lily Feier. New York: Dodd, Mead and Company, 1972.

Slonim, Marc. *Russian Theater: From the Empire to the Soviets.* New York: Collier Books, 1962.

Slonimskii, Iurii. *Chudesnoe bylo riadom s nami.* Leningrad: Sovetskii Kompozitor, 1984.

———. *Sovetskii balet. Materialy k istorii sovetskogo baletnogo teatra.* Moscow and Leningrad: Iskusstvo, 1950.

Sollertinskii, Ivan. "Muzykal'nyi teatr na poroge otkiabria i problema operno-baletnogo naslediia v epokhu voennogo kommunizma." In *Istoriia Sovetskogo*

Teatra. Tom pervyi: Petrogradskie teatry na poroge oktiabria i v epokhu voennogo kommunizma, 1917–1921. Leningrad: Leningradskoe otdelenie gosudarstvennogo izdatel'stva khudozhestvennoi literatury, 1933.

Souritz, Elizabeth. *Soviet Choreographers in the 1920s.* Translated by Lynn Visson. Durham: Duke University Press, 1990.

Stites, Richard. *Revolutionary Dreams: Utopian Vision and Experimental Life in the Russian Revolution.* Oxford: Oxford University Press, 1989.

Surits [Souritz], Elizaveta. *Baletmeister A. A. Gorskii: Materialy. Vospominaniia. Stat'i.* St. Petersburg: Dmitrii Bulanin, 2000.

———. *Khoreograficheskoe iskusstvo dvadtsatykh godov. Tendentsii razvitiia.* Moscow: Iskusstvo, 1979.

———, ed. *Russkii balet i ego zveszdy.* Moscow: Bol'shaia Rosiikaia Entsiklopediia, 1998.

Swift, Mary Grace. *The Art of the Dance in the U.S.S.R.* South Bend: University of Notre Dame Press, 1968.

Taper, Bernard. *Balanchine: A Biography.* 3rd ed. Berkeley: University of California Press, 1996.

Tassie, Gregor. *Yevgeny Mravinsky: The Noble Conductor.* Lanham: Scarecrow Press, 2005.

Taubman, William. *Khrushchev: The Man and His Era.* London: Free Press, 2003.

Teider, Viktor. *Kasian Goleizovskii. "Iosif Prekrasnyi."* Moscow: Flinta and Nauka, 2001.

Thorpe, Edward. *Kenneth MacMillan: The Man and the Ballets.* Foreword by Dame Ninette de Valois. London: Hamish Hamilton, 1985.

Thorpe, Richard. "The Academic Theaters and the Fate of Soviet Artistic Pluralism, 1919–1928." *Slavic Review* 51, no. 3 (1992): 389–410.

Timasheff, Nicholas S. *The Great Retreat: The Growth and Decline of Communism in Russia.* New York: E. P. Dutton, 1946.

Volkogonov, Dmitri. *Stalin: Triumph and Tragedy.* London: Weidenfeld and Nicolson, 1991.

Volkov, Solomon. *St. Petersburg. A Cultural History.* Translated by Antonina W. Bouis. New York: Free Press Paperbacks, 1997.

Wiley, Roland John. *Tchaikovsky's Ballets: Swan Lake, Sleeping Beauty, Nutcracker.* Oxford: Oxford University Press, 1985.

Wilson, Elizabeth. *Shostakovich: A Life Remembered.* New ed. London: Faber and Faber, 2006.

Zakharov, Rostislav. *Iskusstvo baletmeistera.* Moscow: Iskusstvo, 1954.

Zolotbitsky, David. *Sergei Radlov: The Shakespearian Fate of a Soviet Director.* Amsterdam: Harwood Academic Publishers, 1995.

DVDs and Videocassettes

Alla Osipenko: Ispoved' baleriny. Russkoe video, n.d. [1989]. Videocassette (VHS).

Backstage at the Kirov. Kultur, 1983. Videocassette (VHS).

Balet Mariinskogo Teatra. Kinokompaniia Miris, 1995. Lenfil'm-Video, 2001. Videocassette (VHS).

The Children of Theatre Street. Produced by Earle Mack. Kultur, 1978. Videocassette (VHS).

The Glory of the Bolshoi. NVC Arts, 1995. DVD.

The Glory of the Kirov. NVC Arts, 1995. DVD.

Istoriia russkogo baleta. Bol'shoi Teatr (*The Story of the Bolshoi Ballet*). Krupnyi Plan and Castle Communications, 1994. Videocassette (VHS).

Istoriia russkogo baleta. Mariinskii Teatr (*The Story of the Kirov Ballet*). Krupnyi Plan and Castle Communications, 1994. Videocassette (VHS).

Kamennyi Tsvetok. Bolshoi balet. Videofil'm Ten-Video, 1990. Videocassette (VHS).

Katia et Volodia. Les Films du Prieuré/La Sept and Videofilm Goskino, 1989. Videofil'm Servis, 2003. Videocassette (VHS).

Kirov Ballet: Classic Ballet Night. Magnum Video 088. Videocassette (VHS).

Legenda o liubvi. Bol'shoi balet. Videofil'm Ten-Video, 1990. Videocassette (VHS).

The Leningrad Legend. Kultur, 1989. Videocassette (VHS).

Maris Liepa. A dol'she vsego proderzhalas' dusha . . . Ten-Video, 1997. Videocassette (VHS).

Maya Plisetskaya: Diva of Dance. EuroArts, 2006. DVD.

Nataliia Dudinskaia: Dialog so stsenoi. Lentelefil'm, 1988. Kinotsentr "Ochakovo," 2003. Videocassette (VHS).

Prima-baleriny XX-go veka. Galina Ulanova. Raisa Struchkova. Maiia Plisetskaia. Ten-Video, n.d. [video version of documentaries made in 1963, 1998, 1982, 1981]. Videocassette (VHS).

Romeo i Dzhul'etta. Sergei Prokofiev and Leonid Lavrovsky. Mosfil'm, 1954. Krupnyi Plan, 1999. Videocassette (VHS).

Spartacus: Bolshoi Ballet. NVC Arts, 1984. DVD.

Spartak. Kinostudiia Mosfil'm, 1975. Krupnyi plan, 2000. Videocassette (VHS).

Stars of the Russian Ballet. Video Artists International, 2003. DVD.

The Stone Flower: Bolshoi Ballet. Recorded 1990, Arthaus Musik/EuroArts. DVD.

Swan Lake. Maya Plisetskaya and Nikolai Fadeyechev. Sovexportfilm, 1957. Video Artists International, 2003. DVD.

Index

state restrictions on, 100, 114, 187–89, 195, 198–99; during the Thaw, 187–89, 195, 198–99

artistic councils, 74–75

artistic repossession: defined, 7, 103, 273n2, 285n2; in Grigorovich's *Spartacus*, 226–27; ideology used for, 129–35; Kirov Artistic Council and, 78–84; success of, 9; during the Thaw, 103, 118, 126, 128

Asafiev, Boris, 52, 54, 64, 158, 249

Asel' (ballet), 213, 216, 258

Ashton, Frederick, 151, 160, 229; *La Fille mal gardée*, 160, 214

audience, *17*, *99*; composition of, 13, 15; for Grigorovich's *Spartacus*, 228–29; responses of, to ballets, 15–16, 86, 88, 98, 192; Western, 139–40, 148–52, 154, 163. *See also* proletariat and peasants: cultural preferences of autonomy. *See* artistic autonomy

avant-garde: on art's role, 22; ballet and, 11, 18, 37, 63, 175; and socialist realism, 51–52; during the Thaw, 193. *See also* modernism

Avrora, the Piper from Strakonshch (ballet), 92

Bakst, Léon, 244

Balanchine, George, 13, 38, 66, 133, 134, 149, 151, 158, 165–67, 203, 214, 234, 241–42, 275n11

"Baletnaia fal'sh" (*Pravda* article), 31–32, 37, 60–61, 64, 105, 187

baletoman, 13

ballet: advocacy for, 28–29, 40–41; aristocratic support for, 3, 15–16, 31, 33, 232, 235, 274n3; audience for, 15–18, *17*, 20; Cold War impact on, 234; creative processes of, 5–6, 224; criticisms of, 24–25, 29, 35–37, 41,

42, 44, 61–62, 65, 163, 187; cultural legitimacy gained with, 68, 72, 139; dramatization of, 32–33, 41–57; dual nature of, 33–37, 41–45; economic concerns affecting, 22–26; foreign, 3; history of, 11, 33–35, 115; ideological pressures on, 45, 50, 81, 85–86, 113–14, 133, 192–96, 203, 209–10, 224, 226; imperial support for, 2–3, 11–13; music in relation to, 38–40, 43; nonnarrative, 37–40, 44; political context for, 44–45, 60, 72; popular dance and, 274n3; popularization of, 71; postrevolutionary, 2–5, 10–11, 13–21, 26; practical difficulties faced by, 20–21; prerevolutionary, 2–3, 11–13, 70; as propaganda, 28–29, 69, 70; and realism, 161; realism and, 58–62, 70, 155; socialist realism and, 31–32, 48, 58; in Soviet cultural project, 3, 15, 25–29, 69–72, 136, 171; in Soviet Union, 1–9; Soviet-themed, 45, 65, 73, 84, 86–101, 130, 170, 182–84, 188, 191, 200, 201–3, 208–9, 212–14, 236; staging of, 91–101, 122, 124, 140, 182; state support of, 69, 170–71, 239; threats to, 22–25, 37; tradition of, 81–83, 86, 112–13, 237–38; types of, 32, 33–35; verbalization of, 31, 33, 42, 50–51, 65, 114, 234–35; Western perceptions of Soviet, 148–51, 154–55, 161–63. *See also* classical ballet

ballet d'action, 34

ballet de cour, 33

Balletco, 230

Ballets Russes, 10, 35, 148–50

Balzac, Honoré de, *Lost Illusions*, 63

Baryshnikov, Mikhail, 4, 19, 239

The Bathhouse (ballet), 175, 192

batterie, 151, 158, 159

La Bayadère (ballet), 79, 81, 83–84, *84*,
  87, 88, 101, 115, 116, 238, 258, 283n25,
  283n27
Bazhov, Pavel, 88
Beauchamp, Pierre, 33
The Bedbug (ballet), 90, 169–92, *173*,
  174, *190*, 194–95, 197–200, *198*,
  258–59
Beethoven, Ludwig van, *Fourth
  Symphony*, 40
Begak, Dmitry, *207*
Béjart, Maurice, 252
Bel'sky, Igor', 73, 86, 90, 94, 112, 118,
  129, 132–34, 184, 212, 242, 246, 251
Belyutin, Eli, 193
Berezkina, Zoya, 187
Berggol'ts, Olga, 192
Bessmertnova, Nataliia, 298n59
Bialik, M., 188
*Biriuch petrogradskikh gosudarstvennikh
  teatrov* (magazine), 21
Bland, Molly, 147
Blok, Aleksandr, 199
Bogdanov, Aleksandr, 26
Bolshoi Ballet: creative processes of,
  64; diversion of talent to, 72, 79;
  imperial support for, 2–3; in London,
  138–68; in 1970s and 1980s, 239;
  reaction of, to revolution, 14; rep-
  ertoire of, 58, 64, 203, 215, 283n25;
  Spartacus productions, 206–29;
  during the Thaw, 138–68; in United
  States, 141
Bolshoi Theater, Moscow: advocacy for,
  26–27; closure as danger for, 23–25;
  criticisms of, 105; as imperial theater,
  3; postrevolutionary, 18; Russian
  Revolution and, 13–14; state support
  of, 22–24, 69, 72–73, 79
Boris Godunov (opera), 158, 215
Bourdieu, Pierre, 112, 273n2

Bournonville, August, 164
Brezhnev, Leonid, 8–9, 239
The Bright Stream (ballet), 32, 57–63, 156,
  163, 199, 259–60, 277n1
Britain, Bolshoi Ballet in, 138–68,
  228–29
Brodsky, Joseph, 174
The Bronze Horseman (ballet), 87, 88, 89,
  90, 104, 260
Bukharin, Nikolai, 20
Bulganin, Nikolai, 138, 146
Burke, Peter, 299n2

cabarets, 3
Cardin, Pierre, 236
Carneval (ballet), 260
Caucasus, 64
Caute, David, 137–38
Cecchetti, Enrico, 254
censorship and bans, 45, 200, 227
Central Committee of the Communist
  Party of the Soviet Union, 24,
  139–40
Central Intelligence Agency (CIA), 138
Chabukiani, Vakhtang, 78, *84*, 204,
  242–43, 255; *Heart of the Mountain*,
  64; *Laurencia*, 64
Chapaev (ballet), 191
Chapaev, Vasily, 191
character dance, 38, 42, 43, 52, 54, 59,
  62, 63, 163–64
Chenchikova, Olga, 6
Chernyshevsky, Nikolai, 36
China, 85–86
Chistiakova, Valeria, 135
Chopiniana (or *Les Sylphides*) (ballet), 35,
  66, 87, 88, 215, 260
choreographers, 282n9
Choreographic Miniatures, 170, 180,
  200

raphy and, 220–29; classification according to, 45; culture and, 11, 22; "great retreat" from, 46, 48; limited effectiveness of, 50, 86; pressures of, 23–26, 30–66, 81, 85–86, 113–14, 133, 192–96, 203, 209–10, 224, 226; in Soviet system, 4–8. *See also* propaganda

Ilyichev, Leonid, 193

imperial theaters, 2–3

innovation, in choreography, 118–28

intelligentsia: critical of ballet, 63; educational/social orientation of, 28, 36; Khrushchev vs., 135, 170, 192–99; old, 26, 41, 44–45; reconciliation with, 44, 46; and revolutionary debates, 22

International Youth Festival, 91, 118, 125–26, 128

Iordan, Olga, *19, 56*

Iskusstvo (journal), 71

Istoriia sovetskogo teatra (A history of Soviet theater), 49

Ivan Susanin (opera), 215

Ivanov, Lev, 66, 112

Ivanovsky, A. V., 46

Ivanovsky, Nikolai Pavlovich, 82, 284n31

Izvestiia (newspaper), 23–24, 134, 145

Johnson, Priscilla, 193

Jones, Polly, 102

Jordan, Stephanie, 38

jumps, 159

Kabarova (Kirov Artistic Council member), 97

Kaganovich, Lazar, 59

Kandelaki, V. A., 162

Karavaichuk, Oleg, 181

Karsavina, Tamara, 10, 13, 15, 149

Katanova, S., 186

KDS. *See* Kremlin Palace of Congresses

Kelgyn, Iu. V, 74

Kemenov (deputy minister of culture), 108–11

KGB. *See* Committee for State Security

Khachaturian, Aram: *Gayané*, 208; *Spartacus*, 8–9, 112, 178, 183, 201–16, 213, 220, 228, 296n11

Kholminov, A., *An Optimistic Tragedy*, 215–16, 297n51

Khorumii, 220

Khrushchev, Nikita, 8, 67–68, 105, 135, 138, 142, 170, 192–99. *See also* the Thaw

Kirillova, Galina, 85

Kirov Artistic Council, 73–84, 77; and artistic repossession, 78–84; elections for, 75–76; membership of, 74–76, 78; outside participation in, 76; repertoire decisions by, 79–84, 91–101; role of, 76–78; state concern over, 108–10

Kirov Ballet, *89*; artistic board of, 111; artistic policy of, 78–79; conservatism of, 180–81; Iakobson and, 169–200; members of, 106; names of, 275n16; in 1970s and 1980s, 239; post-Soviet, 240; repertoire of, 63, 73–74, 79, 81, 83–101, 107–10, 130, 191, 199; Sergeev's dismissal from, 106–11; *Spartacus* productions, 204–6; state support of, 69, 72–73; during the Thaw, 102–36. *See also* Mariinsky Ballet

Kirov Theater, Leningrad, *75, 99*; Artistic Council of, 73–84, 91–101; during the Thaw, 193–94. *See also* Mariinsky Theater of Opera and Ballet, St. Petersburg

Kirstein, Lincoln, 241

propaganda: art as, 27–31, 105 (*see also* socialist realism); ballet and opera as, 28–29, 69, 70; cultural exchange and, 139. *See also* ideology

prosmotr (viewing; examination), 76, 192

Pugni, Cesare, 295n2

pure art, 36

pure dance, 35, 39, 42, 44, 48–49, 115

Pushkin, Aleksandr, *19*, 36, 46, 64, 87, 116, 256; *The Bronze Horseman*, 87, 104; *Eugene Onegin*, 161; "The Fountain of Bakhchisarai," 54; *The Prisoner of the Caucusus*, 64

Rabochii i teatr (newspaper), 176

Rachinsky, Petr, 77, 252

Radlov, Sergei, 51–52, 54, 156, 256, 280n46, 280n47

Ragozina, Galina, 239

Rambert, Marie, 149

Rampa i zhizn' (newspaper), 14

Rassadin, Konstantin, *174*, *190*, 191, *198*

Ratmansky, Aleksei, 203, 277n1, 280n50

Raymonda (ballet), 18, 87, 88, 267

realism: ballet and, 31, 37, 48, 58–62, 70, 155, 161; debates involving, 60–61, 132–35; modernism vs., 161. *See also* socialist realism

Red Army, 21

The Red Detachment of Women (ballet), 86

The Red Poppy (ballet), 71, 88, 90, 175, 267–68, 293n12

religion, 27

repertoire: of Bolshoi Ballet, 58, 64, 203, 215, 283n25; cultural exchange and, 140; of Kirov Ballet, 63, 73–74, 79, 81, 83–101, 107–10, 130, 191, 199; of Mariinsky Ballet, 18, 45; renewal of, 107; state influence on, 45, 58,

63–64, 68, 70–71, 73, 79, 81, 83–101, 109

resistance: choreography as, 201–31; conservatism as, 83, 85–90; defined, 8; power in relation to, 8; to Soviet regime, 7–9; subconscious, 124–25

Rimsky-Korsakov, Nikolai, 46

Romanov dynasty, 11

Romeo and Juliet (ballet), 54, 64, 71, 73, 87, 88, 90, 140, 143–44, 151–52, *153*, 155–56, *157*, 160, 168, 229, 233, 268

Ross, D. M., 146

Rossi Street (Theater Street), St. Petersburg, 11

Royal Ballet, 160

Ruslan and Ludmilla (opera), 215

Russia, after Soviet Union's collapse, 202–3, 229–30, 239–40

"Russia" Has Come into Port, 92–98, *93*, 100–101, 268–69

Russian Revolution: ballet after, 2–5, 10–11, 13–21; beginning of, 1, 10; goals of, 3–4

Russian Seasons (ballet), 203

Ryndin, Vadim, 165

Sadler's Wells Royal Ballet, 139, 149, 152, 164

Saltykov-Shchedrin, Mikhail, 36–37

Savadov, Arsen, 239–40

Scott, James C., 8

Sekh, Ia., 163

Semenova, Marina, 72, 208

Serenade (ballet), 203

Sergeev, Konstantin, 6, *49*, *55*, 74, *77*, 78–79, *80*, 83, 88, 90–91, 94–96, 98, 100, 106–11, 118–19, 125, 133–34, 180–81, 183, 185, 195, 197, 199, 243, 252–53, 283n22, 286n14

Sevast'ianov, I., 77

Vaganova, Agrippina, 43, 48, 66, 81, 242, 243, 246, 247, 250, 253, 254, 280n47, 284n42

Vaganova School, 82, 83, 239

Vainonen, Vasily, 46, 54, 87; *Nutcracker*, 88; *Partisan Days*, 63–64

Varlamov, A., 163, 213

Vartanian, Z., 191

Vasil'ev, Vladimir, 211, *217*, 218–19, *221*, 221, 223, *225*, 239, 249–50, 254–55, 298n59

Vaziev, Makharbek, 6

Vecheslova, Tatiana, *47*, *56*, 74, 111, 196, 255, 286n14

Veniaminovich, Leonid, 205

verbalization of art/dance, 31, 33, 42, 50–51, 65, 114, 234–35

The Vestal Virgin (ballet), 45

Vestris, August, 251

Viltsin', Velita, 143

Vinogradov, Oleg, 213, 239

Virsaladze, Simon, 119, 122, 255

virtuosity, 32, 34, 41, 54, 133

Vishnevskii, Vs., *An Optimistic Tragedy*, 297n51

Vladimirov (dancer), 21

Vlasov, Vladimir, 213

Volkov, Nikolai, 52, 204–6, 209, 211, 255, 296n11

Volynsky, Akim, 254

VTO. *See* All-Russian Theatrical Society

Wagner, Richard, 28, 32

Webster, David, 138–39

Western audiences, 139–40, 148–52, 154, 163

Westernism, 129, 132, 133, 136, 189

white ballet, 35, 39

workers. *See* proletariat and peasants

youth, as concern during the Thaw, 107–10, 118, 125–26, 128

Za sovetskoe iskusstvo (newspaper), 125–26, 128, 135, 185, 195, 198

Zagursky, B., 181–82

Zaidel'son, Vladimir, 178, 184

Zakharov, Rostislav, 54, *55*, 63, 64, 73, 93–95, 100–101, 104, 134, 158, 255–56, 280n52, 287n33; *Iskusstvo baletmeistera*, 114–15

Zhdanov, Yuri, *153*

Zhizn' iskusstva (magazine), 41–45, 176

Zubkovsky, Nikolai, 107, 286n15